EXISTENTIAL PHENOMENOLOGY AND POLITICAL THEORY: A Reader

EXISTENTIAL PHENOMENOLOGY AND POLITICAL THEORY: A Reader

Hwa Yol Jung, editor
Foreword by John Wild

HENRY REGNERY COMPANY • Chicago

Copyright © 1972 by Hwa Yol Jung
All rights reserved
Published by Henry Regnery Company
114 West Illinois Street, Chicago, Illinois 60610
Manufactured in the United States of America
Library of Congress Catalog Card Number: 76–183819

For Petee, Michael, and Eric, who together embody
a microcosm of true humanity

Contents

Foreword

Political philosophy must begin with some understanding of the being of man, for its many problems develop
from an inclusive grasp of man as he is. Since Husserl's discovery of the *Lebenswelt* and his writing of the Crisis of
European Sciences in the early 1930's, many supposedly
pure descriptive studies have been made. But it has turned
out that such pure description, with its suppression of all
extraneous interpretation, is by no means a simple or easy
task. Many difficulties stand in the way. Many factors not
readily noticed need to be brought into the light. Many obsti-
nate prejudices must be suppressed. Many discoveries of this
sort have been made in the last forty or fifty years, during
what we may call the early ascendancy of phenomenology in
Western Europe. Hence the real need for a book of this kind,
in which many great phenomenologists from Husserl to Merleau-Ponty not only talk about the importance of their descriptions but actually make them.

One whole field of experience that has been opened up for investigation in this way is what we may call knowing by living through. It is not knowledge in the exact and scientific sense, for clearly marked and well-defined concepts are absent from it. And yet vague and indefinite concepts of some kind are certainly present. So it is knowledge or awareness of some kind, as when, in speaking of anger or elation of some sort, we ask a person if he has not lived through or experienced it in any way. When we receive an affirmative reply to this question we feel that the battle is at least half won, and we begin arguments to arrive at more exact concepts, to give us a greater distance from the phenomenon, and a clearer vision. Since such knowledge is direct and close to the phenomenon, I think we are correct in referring to it as unmediated or immediate. Our first view of many phenomena comes to us in this way, and it lacks the mediation of any well-formed and rounded conceptual system. Phenomenology itself originates in this way. It represents a necessary first step in the conceptual organization of experience. Yet it is sufficiently well marked to be given a special name, as a form of knowledge that is closer to experience as immediate and direct.

It has now been shown that my meeting with the other person, the stranger, is a direct experience of this kind, and its many shades and nuances offer a rich field for descriptive analysis already begun by Ortega y Gasset and others. This encounter with the other person may proceed in different ways, which vary all the way from a harmonious sharing of one and the same world to mutual criticism and final conflict. It is important to distinguish the two latter attitudes, for criticism may be motivated in a friendly manner. At the present time, there is little doubt that the most basic revealing criticism I receive comes from the human other who is the object of even the most lengthy discourses, even though he may not be physically present. It is important not to confuse the human other with the negative or the opposite of the self, which is one of the chief ways in which we are led, following Hegel, into a total system, following an ever-present inclination of the self. No other human attitude so totally and exclusively drowns out the freedom and pluralism of original experience.

Other theories, easily turning into attitudes, rest on the confusion of motive with necessary cause, and of obligation with a single, overarching social purpose. This is often correlated with application of the vague term "subjective" to the human individual, and the condemnation of all subjectivity as quixotic and irresponsible. This leads to a universal criticism of the inner life of the individual by a hypostatized social consciousness, and generates tyranny in all its forms. It is radically opposed by the slowly developing individualism of our own time. In this growing richness and variety of the human person, the individual inner life becomes master of itself and subject to nothing, judging not only other individuals, but all forms of group totality. This is condemned by social totalitarianism as unlimited anarchy. But, depending on the weight placed on human rationality, it can lead to a lack of suppression and to social democracy.

The reader will find these matters discussed in the following pages, which constitute for our time, a real introduction to the phenomenology of politics.

John Wild

Preface

This anthology is intended for students of either existential political thought or of contemporary social and political philosophy. Its purpose is twofold: first, it introduces existentialist views to the students of politics; second, it hopes to open up a new perspective for the theory of politics. Students of politics can no longer ignore the significant contributions of existential and phenomenological thought to social and political philosophy and to what is now known as the philosophy of social sciences. There is indeed an urgent need, I believe, for a philosophy of politics and particularly for a rethinking of the old problems of democratic polity in the West. Existential political thought sheds certain new light on these perennial problems of man and his polity. Unfortunately, in the past the intent of existential philosophy and phenomenology has been too often misunderstood by political theorists. I hope that our attitude of negligence and indifference gives way to one of vigilance and serious attention.

The purpose of this anthology will be served well if it arouses a more serious, active, and wide interest in existential political thought than there has been in the past.

However introductory and synoptic an anthology such as this may be in the light of a plethora of existential and phenomenological literature, it is certainly overdue in this country. Even a decade ago it would have been impossible to edit it. It was only in 1962, after many years of neglect, that the seminal and influential work of Martin Heidegger's *Sein und Zeit* (1927) appeared in English translation. Now, in a short span of time, numerous English translations of European existential and phenomenological literature have been appearing. For example, in 1963 the Northwestern University Studies in Phenomenology and Existential Philosophy, under the general editorship of Professor John Wild, began the task of making available to the English-speaking audience the major works of French and German existential philosophers and phenomenologists. Its first publication was Maurice Merleau-Ponty's *In Praise of Philosophy*, and its most recent was the translation of the last posthumous work of Edmund Husserl, *The Crisis of European Sciences and Transcendental Phenomenology* (1970). Formation of the Society for Phenomenology and Existential Philosophy (whose first meeting was held in 1962) is clearly indicative of the growing interest in existential and phenomenological thought in this country. American philosophers themselves —notably young scholars as exemplified in the recent collection of essays, *Patterns of the Life-World: Essays in Honor of John Wild* (1970)—have been making distinctively original and independent contributions to the growing literature of existential philosophy and phenomenology. We may fairly conclude that the existential and phenomenological mode of philosophizing is not just a passing phenomenon but is taking a firm hold in this country and is here to stay.

This anthology is divided into four parts: (I) The Life-World, Phenomenology, and the Social Sciences; (II) Individual Action and Sociality; (III) Freedom, Responsibility, and Human Dignity; and (IV) The Existential Conditions of Politics. I have begun with "An Introductory Essay: The Political Relevance of Existential Phenomenology." The aim of this essay is to set the tone of what follows and to touch on certain issues that from lack of space are covered insufficiently or not at all.

My choice of readings and the organization of the anthology reflect an underlying emphasis on existential phenomenology. I made selections according to what I consider not only the central themes of existential phenomenology but also of direct relevance to the theory of politics and society. I have chosen to present full-length passages rather than a series of snippets in order to preserve fully the logic of a thinker's arguments and the train of his thought within the inevitable bounds of an anthology. A selected bibliography is provided for further readings.

I am grateful to Moravian College for having granted me a sabbatical leave to spend the academic year 1970–71 in the Department of Philosophy at Yale University. To the Department of Philosophy at Yale University I am greatly indebted for a congenial and intellectually stimulating atmosphere. To my friends William McBridge, George Schrader, Edward Casey, and David Carr I am thankful for their engaging suggestions about this anthology. Especially, the critical scrutiny of Bill and George has been invaluable to its final form. At the book's inception Professor Paul Ricoeur and my friend Kuang-ming Wu at Wisconsin State University at Oshkosh also rendered their guidance. For writing a foreword to this anthology I am especially grateful to Professor John Wild. He has been generous in providing his time and wise counsel since he introduced me to existential philosophy and phenomenology in his seminars on Heidegger's *Being and Time* and on responsibility at Northwestern University during the academic year 1961–62. Finally, I thank my brother- and sister-in-law George and Alice Benston, an economist and a humanist, for their intellectual, moral, and material support in this enterprise. Whatever shortcomings this anthology may have, responsibility is entirely mine. I am indebted to my wife Petee, a mathematician who sustains a keen interest in nonmathematical philosophy, for making my work exciting and rewarding.

An Introductory Essay:
The Political Relevance of
Existential Phenomenology

Introduction

For some of its severe critics existentialism represents a temporary outburst of the dark side of man that is
indicative of a passing phenomenon of our age and particularly of the postwar angry generation living on the morbid
edges of death, anxiety, and the absurdity of human existence. They contend that existentialism is not a philosophy,
or at least not a serious and disciplined philosophy. Professor
Henry S. Kariel characterized existential psychology as
"negativism," and its counterpart behavioral psychology as
"positivism." Similarly, Professor Eugene J. Meehan describes the phenomenology of Edmund Husserl as having
sought to find philosophical certainty "in feeling rather than
in thought," an assessment of which indicts phenomenology
falsely as an irrationalism.[1] I have chosen these two political

A shorter version of this essay appeared in *The Review of Politics* 33, no.
4 (October 1971): 538–63. Reprinted by permission.

xvii

theorists as representatives of a widespread misconception of
existential philosophy and phenomenology held as well, I
suspect, by many American political theorists. This essay is
not designed as a direct rebuttal to these misunderstandings
and criticisms; it is, rather, an attempt to show what I consider the significant and positive contributions of existential
philosophy and phenomenology to the foundation of political
theory.

The terms *existential philosophy, phenomenology,* and
radical empiricism have been used more and more synony-
mously in recent literature, although they have separate historical origins in Kierkegaard, Husserl, and William James,
respectively. Not only is there a close affinity between Husserl's phenomenology and James' radical empiricism but
James also has actually been called the first American existential philosopher. Indeed, phenomenology as it has developed
in Europe and in the United States now represents a far
broader movement than when Husserl first initiated it. In
this essay I rely heavily on the second school of phenomenology, called existential phenomenology, which attempts to
synthesize and go beyond the existential thought initiated by
Kierkegaard and the phenomenological thought initiated by
Husserl.

Martin Heidegger in Germany, Jean-Paul Sartre, Maurice
Merleau-Ponty, and Paul Ricoeur in France and John Wild
in the United States are among the outstanding representatives of existential phenomenology.[2] For existential
phenomenologists, phenomenology is essentially a descriptive method by which to explore the different regions of
human existence. These thinkers do not aim at description
for its own sake, however, but rather for the sake of elucidat-
ing the meaning of man's being in the world. Ricoeur says
that "existential phenomenology makes the transition between transcendental phenomenology, born of the reduction of everything to its appearing to me, and ontology,
which restores the question of the sense of being for all that
is said to 'exist.' "[3]

In setting forth the implications of existential phenomenology for political theory, I have divided the balance of this discussion into five sections: (I) the *Lebenswelt* (life-world); (II) phenomenology as radical empiricism; (III) phenomenology and philosophy of political science; (IV) the meaning of human action; and (V) the meaning of sociality. These issues are what I consider the central themes of existential phenomenology; their ramifications are directly relevant to the theory of politics and society.

In Section I, I shall discuss the idea of the life-world as the all-encompassing horizon of meaning in which the rituals of our action and interaction take place in the midst of other people, cultural objects, and natural things. Since the life-world refers to human culture, it has a political dimension as well as historical and social dimensions. Section II deals with phenomenology as a philosophy of lived experience. Phenomenology, first, attempts to examine and justify its own activity as a philosophy; second, it acknowledges the dependence of the conceptual on the preconceptual. Section III is concerned with the phenomenological insistence that the study of human behavior—political science in particular— must adopt methods radically different from those of the natural sciences because there is a qualitative difference between the human (or behavioral) and the natural. Section IV is devoted to the structure of human action, since political science, in common with the other behavioral sciences, is concerned with the meaning structure of individual action in relation to the political system. Section V discusses the concept of sociality as the structure of man's relationships to man, the elucidation of which is most elemental to social and political theory.

I. The *Lebenswelt* (Life-World)

The phenomenology of the everyday life-world has a direct relevance and significance to the theory of politics because *how can we reconcile the life-world with class (& goes on to talk about work)*

it is a philosophy that attempts to describe rigorously the meaning of man's concrete experience, political or otherwise, in his everyday life. The task of describing this human life-world, however, has been neglected in Western philosophy since the time of Plato, who considered it the cave world of impermanent shadows and images. Now phenomenology pays serious attention to the exploration of the everyday life-world.

The relevance of the phenomenology of the life-world to the theory of politics is twofold. First, the life-world is the basic matrix of all theoretical endeavors, including political theorizing. It has a privileged status in the sense that all conceptual activity is founded on the preconceptual world called the life-world. Husserl himself regarded this everyday life-world as the most universal problem of philosophy and as the foundation of all theoretical enterprises. Second, the life-world is a historical, social, and cultural world that encompasses the whole of political reality as the object of political theorizing. The phenomenology of the life-world is a philosophy of social reality in the broadest sense of the term *social.*

The totality of the world consists of subuniverses or subworlds. The world is the comprehensive and inclusive horizon of all possible and actual experiences. This world contains in it innumerable realities—that is, as many as there are orders of experience. These include the world of individual opinion, the world of dreams, the play world of the child, the world of the insane, and others.[4] What is experienced is real and, conversely, what is real is experienceable. Because reality is constituted by the meaning of our experiences, we can speak of "finite provinces of meaning," each of which has in its own way "a specific accent of reality." Each province of meaning is called finite because it has within boundaries of its own a particular cognitive style that appears fictitious, inconsistent, and incompatible with another (finite) province of meaning. The world of the insane, for instance, appears

[handwritten top margin: — what is the place of ideologies in the formation of the natural attitude? Or is it by def'n an attitude which cannot be ideological from the standpt of phenomenology?]

"unreal" to the world of the sane, and vice versa.

Among these multiple realities, the reality of everyday existence is of direct and immediate importance to political and social theory. It is the archetype of reality, and other realities may be considered as its modifications: it is the "home base" of all other realities. This paramount reality of everyday existence is characterized by working—that is, by overt action requiring bodily movement. In contrast to the world of dreams, the world of working is characterized by a state of wide-awake consciousness that attends to the requirements of our activities. As working is most vital for the constitution of the reality of everyday existence, political actions and interactions are necessarily founded on acts of working. *[handwritten: links reality of everyday existence to working]*

[handwritten right margin: but is such a conceptualization unhistorical?]

Husserl's famous urging to go back "to the things themselves" means to return to the primordial and original world of everyday existence that is prior to the derivative and secondary expression of theorizing activity in philosophy and science. This life-world is an ultimate horizon in which natural things, cultural objects, and individual persons are understood in the *natural attitude*. By the natural attitude is meant a prereflective and naïve point of view toward the world where all objects originally appear to us in our perception and where our doings have practical meanings. In the natural attitude the typical contents of the world are accepted as a matter of course or are taken for granted as familiar. Husserl says that the life-world is "pregiven to us all quite naturally, as persons within the horizon of our fellow men, i.e., in every actual connection with others, as 'the' world common to us all. Thus it is . . . the constant ground of validity, an ever available source of what is taken for granted, to which we, whether as practical men or as scientists, lay claim as a matter of course."[5]

[handwritten right margin: preconceptual level of Mannheim & the natural attitude]

For the purpose of relating phenomenology to the theory of politics, the following characteristics of the life-world deserve special attention. First, the life-world is preconceptual.

characteristics of the life-world:
- *pre-conceptual (pregiven to the world of conceptualization)*
- *prephilosophical, prelogical + prescientific world* ← *where language connection*
- *world of "I live through" (on unselfconscious + self-conscious attitude - subject + object are different)*

It is pregiven to the world of conceptualization. Because it precedes conceptual knowledge, the life-world is a prephilosophical, prelogical, and prescientific world. It is the world not of what "I think" but of what "I live through." In this mundane, lived world we experience things and other people immediately rather than mediately. It is foremost the theater of action—for example, the world of political actors in contrast to the conceptual world of political theorists. The theorist *as* theorist does not participate in this life-world as an actor.

Hence, the second and real importance of the life-world lies in its status as the meaningful basis of human action. As an active doer, man is always in the making or on the way: he is *homo viator*. He is what he makes of himself, and he molds his future by his action. Thus man has neither permanently fixed properties nor a predetermined future. The idea that man is always an open possibility constitutes his radical historicity. As Merleau-Ponty succinctly states, "It is true neither that my existence is in full possession of itself, nor that it is entirely estranged from itself, because it is action or doing, and because action is, by definition, the violent transition from what I have to what I aim to have, from what I am to what I intend to be."[6]

Man is capable of refusing what he is, or his *status quo*. Further, value occupies the center of action. As value is not an accidental appendage but, rather, is endemic to a human culture, the structure of action *is* a structure of approvals and disapprovals.[7] Specific values, meanings, concerns, and interests determine our action in the social world as they enter into our motivational field. Precisely because they enter into the plans and projects of our action, José Ortega y Gasset calls the human world of interaction "a field of *pragmata*."[8] As such it represents "an immense ambit" capable of dynamic relations. Because the world is a pragmatic field, nothing in it is purely material. Even things in nature are molded to serve human purposes. They are defined in terms of their

2) life-world: basis of human action (could be beginnings of a theory of why oppressed classes do not overturn their oppression) have false consciousness + ideology in mind).

(actions seem to be value judgements)

serviceability, usability, and manipulability. Thus, for man "nature" is discovered by its use, and by their use things in it become instruments.

③ Third, the world is not the private world of an individual but is from the outset an intersubjective or socialized world. Accordingly, our knowledge of it, whether conceptual or commonsense, is not private but is socialized. Thus social reality is an original datum of the life-world from which the theorist's conceptual knowledge is constructed. The investigation of social reality constitutes the primary object of social and political theory. As with all human activity in society, the stuff of politics *is* other people. Politics is inevitably a mingling with other people. In the meeting of the past and present we inherit from our predecessors a certain political system with its traditions, beliefs, and fixed values, which we ordinarily accept as normal. These given patterns of a political culture, however, are in principle questionable; that is, they become problematical to us. They may be called into question, for example, in a time of crisis, and a new pattern of meanings and values may emerge. To put it differently, when the traditional patterns of behavior are no longer applicable to resolving new problems, the situation is called a crisis.

The life-world as the theater of action, then, is dynamic and changing, which means that it is historical. As there are different cultures in history, moreover, there are different versions of the life-world. To summarize, the life-world is *active, social,* and *historical.* Although they are conceptually distinguishable, these characteristics of the life-world are in reality inseparable.

II. Phenomenology as Radical Empiricism

Phenomenology is a radical empiricism. To be rightly called radical, an empiricism must meet two requirements. First, the ① radicality of an empirical philosophy demands a self-

*radical :
empiricism
a critical theory*

examination and self-clarification of its own theorizing activity. To be radical, then, phenomenology must attempt to
question its own presuppositions. Second, to be radical an
empirical philosophy should include in its theory no more
and no less than what is directly experienced. Therefore,
radical empiricism recognizes the dependence of reflection
on directly lived experience; that is, it accepts the idea that
reflection is founded on lived experience. What is experiential is the primary material of reflection: immediate experience provides the material for later conceptual activity.

Above all, phenomenology examines the nature of theorizing as an activity. It clarifies the nature not only of theorizing
in general but also of political theorizing in particular, for no
other reason than that political theorizing is a form of theorizing. As the *logos* of the phenomenon, phenomenology
deals with the object as it appears to consciousness. The
object or the world that appears to consciousness is not a
thing but the object-as-meant or the world-as-meant. As
phenomena are nothing but meanings, therefore, phenomenology is concerned with meanings. Meaning is made possible by the intentional structure of consciousness. Intentionality is the essence of consciousness, and by intentionality is
understood the active directionality of consciousness towards
an object. Because consciousness is intentional, it is always
consciousness *of* something, whether it be real or ideal, existent or imaginary (for example, thinking is thinking *of* something). To use the language of phenomenology, the act of
intending is called *noesis*; its correlate, the object as intended, is called *noema*. Intentionality suggests an inseparable noetic–noematic bond. In the act of reflection there is a
unity of the thinker *(ego)*, his thinking *(cogito)*, and the object he thinks about *(cogitatum)*. Though these three aspects
are distinguishable, they are existentially inseparable in the
concrete act of thinking. Existentially speaking, intentionality is at the heart of consciousness. It is the source that gives
meaning to human experience.

The idea that conceptual knowledge is derived from and founded on preconceptual knowledge is a prerequisite to the method of radical empiricism as a philosophy of experience. William James speaks of the dependence of "knowledge-about" on "knowledge by acquaintance." According to him, knowledge by acquaintance is knowing things by seeing their colors and by tasting them, and knowing other people in their presence. As pure experience is feeling, knowledge by acquaintance is "felt knowledge," whereas "knowledge-about" is "thought knowledge": "Through feelings we become acquainted with things, but only by our thoughts do we know about them. Feelings are the germ and starting point of cognition, thoughts the developed tree."[9] To say that the conceptual is dependent on the preconceptual simply means that any explicit act of conceptualization, political theorizing notwithstanding, presupposes something that is directly experienced prior to conceptualization.

The felt dimension of our experience has an important function in what we think, observe, and perceive, and in how we behave. Meaning involves experiencing that is preconceptual, presymbolic, and preverbal (that is, something felt). Although it is yet to be articulated, this felt "mass" of our experience is richer and broader than our thought, observation, speech, and action. It makes sense to say that "we know more than we can tell" or "we mean more than we can say." We often grope for words to express the meaning we experience, and we feel dissatisfied with our verbal or written expressions of it. Meaning is not limited to symbolically expressive meaning; that is, it is not concerned merely with the logical, syntactical, and semantic structures of symbols. If it were, our thought process would be like the working programmed computers, and our speech would be like the mechanical voice of a record.

Certainly felt meaning can be symbolized. As feeling and symbolizing go hand in hand we are capable of symbolizing our felt meaning or expressing it in words. Our thought is the

mediation between felt meaning and symbols, and symbols
have a direct reference to felt meaning. Let us illustrate this
from the way we define such a political concept as democracy. In order to define (or conceptualize about) democracy
we first refer directly to the implicit or tacit meaning we
associate with it. Before we articulate the conceptual meaning of democracy we have some positive but inarticulate
understanding of it. We do not conceptualize in a vacuum or
without any basic reference to something we already know
tacitly. A definition of democracy begins from our felt or tacit
meaning of it. Our felt meaning of democracy, therefore, is
not logically but only experientially prior to our conceptual
definition of it.

The dependence of reflection on lived experience, or of
the *objective* meaning of symbolization on *subjective* felt
meaning, leads us to the heart of the controversial issue between subjectivity and objectivity. Phenomenology not only
is criticized as a subjectivism, but we also treat subjectivity
as if it were an anathema to all scientific inquiry. On the
contrary, though, as the notion of intentionality suggests,
subjectivity and objectivity are only two moments of the
same phenomenon. Subjectivity refers to the *intrinsic relatedness* of our experiences and actions to our awareness of
them, and objectivity refers to what is observable from outside. The affirmation of objectivism to the exclusion of subjectivism is misleading because it ignores the place of subjectivity in thought and observation. What is observable (a
datum), for example, is always related to the awareness of an
observer. A datum of observation is not yet a fact, and a fact
is meaningful only in relation to the observer for whom it is
a fact. Thus a fact is nothing but meaning given to a datum
(or data) by the observer in the process of observation. Further, the truth of a fact or thought for one observer is sanctioned intersubjectively—that is, by a scientific or intellectual community. As consciousness is intentional, reflective
thought, whether philosophical or scientific, is neither entirely subjective nor entirely objective.

The existential revolt of Kierkegaard was directed against the intellectualist objectivism of Hegel, against Hegel's "abstract thought," as Kierkegaard called it, which has no reference to the concrete existence of the thinker himself, and in which he becomes merely a thinking substance or thing. Intellectualism defines man's existence in terms of thought, and converts the certainty of existence and the world into the certainty of thought about them or into the *ideas* of them. In other words, it recognizes reality only in the process of thought, in which man is reduced to "a little abstract effigy." A philosophy whose starting point is cognitive experience tends to exalt thought over action, theory over practice.

The rejection of intellectualism does not mean, however, that the philosophy of existence is the tyranny of practice over theory—that is, a kind of utilitarian pragmatism or instrumentalism that discredits the value of disinterested intellectual pursuit. Rather, existential philosophy makes a serious attempt to achieve unity of theory and practice by defining man in terms of how he acts and ought to act. Man is not just a thinking subject, he is active and affective as well as intellectual.

Existentialism is a philosophy not of the "I think" but of the "we are" *(our being in the world)*, which includes theoretical activity as its essential component. To say that man is an active doer means that he is capable of entering relationships with others. Action and sociality imply each other, for the field of action calls for the reciprocity of the existing self with the other. For this reason, the structure of action is always relational. As John Macmurray puts it: "The Self must be conceived, not theoretically as subject, but practically, as agent. . . . [H]uman behaviour is comprehensible only in terms of a dynamic social reference; the isolated, purely individual self is a fiction."[10] Because existential philosophy unites thought with action it is particularly relevant to the theory of politics. Political theory aims at reflection with a view to action as well as with a view to knowledge. It is an attempt to link the self as thinker with the self as actor. This also is the central question of existential philosophy.[11]

When man is viewed as an active, social, and historical being, the way is open for a dialogue between existential philosophy and Marxist humanism. First, both are a philosophy of *praxis* as against that of *theoria*. For them philosophy is not purely an academic game played by intellectuals to construct an abstract system of thought but, on the contrary, is an activity that relates itself to the concrete, living issues of man and society. Second, therefore, the chief concern for both philosophies is a philosophy of man or humanism. It is an effort to restore what is authentically human and to put an end to the dehumanization of man and the deformation of his true sociality, dignity, and integrity. Both Kierkegaard and Marx, each in his own way, revolted against the depersonalization of man in the nineteenth-century European setting.

Particularly, existentialism is a philosophy of revolt against mass man who lost his authentic selfhood in modern technological and industrial culture. Kierkegaard's condemnation of the "present age" was precisely that of the leveling process of individuality. Similarly, Heidegger's existential analysis of the "anonymous public" or "they" (*das Man*) depicts, if it is not a moral condemnation, the pervasive tendency of twentieth-century man, society, and culture; and Jaspers, Marcel, Berdyaev, Buber, and Ortega y Gasset all express their deep concern about this inauthentic mode of human existence. In the same vein Marx, too, showed a humane interest in man's alienation from himself, his labor, nature, and fellow men. To humanize man, Marx focused his attention on the problem of human alienation and the dematerialization of labor (that is, the elimination of human labor as a thing or a commodity).

It is true that to remedy the anonymity of modern man

Kierkegaard and his followers resort primarily to free and responsible individuality, whereas Marx suggested political, social, and economic remedies. However, it would be a gross oversimplification to say, as do many critics, that "By seeing only the individual Existentialism lost society, and by seeing only society Marxism lost the individual."[12] Many contemporary Marxian humanists and existential thinkers alike have now come to the conclusion that *praxis* is essentially a social and historical event that is the product of, and is subject to purposive control by, conscious and free individuals. Thus the events of history are the making of human consciousness and intervention rather than blind, impersonal forces beyond human control. Nothing is "historically inevitable." If history is just the accumulation of impersonal forces, man's conscious effort to make and remake the world would be totally meaningless. To have a dialogue between existential philosophy and Marxist humanism, in the end the deterministic theory of man, society, and history must give way to a philosophy of human freedom and responsibility.

III. Phenomenology and Philosophy of Political Science

Philosophy can no more pass over facts than the empirical sciences can leave out broad epistemological questions raised in philosophy. There must be alliance between philosophy and the social sciences, or between the philosopher who *reflects* and the social scientist who *observes.* As the philosopher and the social scientist are the bearers of reflection on the same life-world from which their knowledge is constructed, there can be neither segregation nor cold war between philosophy and the social sciences. Like the social scientist, the philosopher speaks about man's action, history, and social world. Conversely, the social scientist is already a philosopher at the very moment of the interpretation of social facts.[13]

The contribution of phenomenological investigation to the theory of politics, society, and culture lies especially in its concentration on the meaning of human action. The most basic thesis of phenomenology in the social sciences is set forth by Alfred Schutz.

> The thought objects constructed by the social scientist, in order to grasp this social reality, have to be founded upon the thought objects constructed by the common-sense thinking of men, living their daily life within their social world. Thus, the constructs of the social sciences are, so to speak, constructs of the second degree, that is, constructs of the constructs made by the actors on the social scene, whose behavior the social scientist has to observe and to explain in accordance with the procedural rules of his science.[14]

It follows, then, that all conceptual framework in political science must presuppose and ought to be consonant with man's preconceptual understanding of political things. The ordinary language of political man precedes the objectified language of political science, and the second must be consistent with the first.[15] The language of political science can refine, improve, and supplement but cannot ignore the ordinary discourse of political man. The usefulness of the language of political science is justified by the extent to which it elucidates the reality of the political system.

The recent methodology of political science, however, is far from being immune to abstract conceptualization. One example of the tendency to abstract and reify concepts is found in the *analytic* conception of "philosophy of political science." According to this view, political science is a descriptive discipline that seeks to increase factual knowledge about the political world, whereas political ethics (or political philosophy) is purely normative in that it attends to the substantive issues of what makes a good political society. In contrast,

analytic

the philosophy of political science is a strictly formalistic undertaking, for it deals with the logical and linguistic analysis of concepts and statements about political phenomena. Unlike the first two, it is neither factual nor normative. Viewed in this way, first, values are *scientifically* meaningless; that is, they are unrelated to political science as a factual discipline because they express personal beliefs and preferences rather than report the state of affairs. Second, both facts and values are *philosophically* irrelevant because the function of philosophy is logical and linguistic rather than empirical and normative.[16] As factual and normative inquiries are relegated to political science and political ethics, respectively, the analytic philosophy of political science emphasizes the linguistic aspect of political analysis.

Another example of abstract theorizing that follows the *positive* logical positivist criterion of science is Anthony Downs's "positive" conception of political science.[17] To be "positive," according to him, the model is constructed for the purpose of accurate prediction rather than of accurately describing political reality or understanding the meaning of political phenomena under observation. It is constructed by selecting a few crucial variables as relevant while ignoring others which may have a vital influence on the real world of politics. Since for Downs the utility of theoretical constructs is dependent on "the accuracy of their prediction rather than the reality of their assumptions," the preconceptual reality of how *real* men behave in the *real* world of politics is materially impertinent to his conceptual framework.

Obviously, language is an indispensable instrument in political theorizing and in political life, and the clarification of linguistic uses or misuses helps to settle the issues in question, although the idea that all philosophical problems arise from linguistic confusions is highly presumptuous. Be that as it may, it would be a mistake to treat language as if it were independent of the reality it purports to describe, just as it would be a mistake to think that preconceptual reality can be ignored as materially impertinent to theoretical constructs in political science. The language of politics itself is a part of the complex reality of the political world that the political theorist is to elucidate. [As preconceptual language is the landscape of conceptual thought, the language of political theory is inseparably linked to the political reality it objectifies.]

By the same token, the question of how far political reality is intelligible cannot be answered without at the same time stating how political reality and theoretical concepts are interdependent. Such political *concepts* as power, freedom, justice, democracy (that is, those concepts used in the literature of political theory) have a point of reference somewhere in political life itself. This thesis, of course, does not destroy or diminish the importance of conceptual language but, instead, only recognizes the primacy of the ordinary language of political man. Whether or not a political theorist is willing to admit it, preconceptual political reality serves as the background of his political theorizing, for he is first and foremost a member of that political society he objectifies. Precisely because the ordinary discourse of political life is the primary word, though not the last word, how ordinary language functions in political life and how it is related to political theorizing are two basic but long-neglected issues that political theory can no longer afford to overlook.

Warning must be given that phenomenology's stress on the meaning of human action is not a call for a new kind of knowledge in the social sciences but is, rather, an insistence on the qualitative difference between the orders of reality investigated by natural scientists and by social scientists. The difference between the natural sciences and the social sciences is not that they seek different kinds of knowledge but that they have radically different objects to investigate. Only human beings are, while things in nature are not, capable of endowing with meaning what they do, feel, and perceive. This radical difference between the human and the merely natural is taken into account in the phenomenological method of the social sciences. Like the sociological method of Max Weber, phenomenology accommodates its methodological rigor to this basic fact. Schutz writes:

> The concept of Nature, for instance, with which the natural sciences have to deal is, as Husserl has shown, an idealizing abstraction from the *Lebenswelt*, an abstraction which, on principle and of course legitimately, excludes persons with their personal life and all objects of culture which originate as such in practical human activity. Exactly this layer of the *Lebenswelt*, however, from which the natural sciences have to abstract, is the social reality which the social sciences have to investigate.[18]

Phenomenology is thus opposed to the scientific doctrine that defines the truth of the social sciences essentially according to the procedural rules of the physical sciences because in methodology the physical sciences take for granted the meaning structure of human phenomena that is absent in natural phenomena. This does not mean that phenomenology resorts to the method of introspection. Nor does it reject *in toto* the behavioristic interpretation of human behavior. The phenomenological approach only pinpoints the limits and blind spots of behaviorism. The behavioristic interpretation of human action is correct and valid as long as it refers to the external indications of movement, but it goes wrong when it identifies what is external with the intended meaning the actor imputes to his action. The intended meaning of action cannot be inferred merely from its external indications. Only by combining what is external and what is intended is it possible to understand fully the meaning of human behavior.

In order to see more clearly the implications of phenomenology for political science, it may be well to compare phenomenology with Heinz Eulau's views of the behavioral approach to politics.[19] The following exposition of the similarities and ultimate divergences of these approaches illustrates the value of phenomenology to the theory of politics.

Eulau maintains that the radical goal of political science is man, and that the function of political science is to understand and interpret the political world rather than to change it. Not unlike the phenomenologist, Eulau defines the basic stuff of politics in terms of the conditions and consequences of individual action and the roles that the political actor performs in the social, cultural, and personal milieu. Most significantly, he emphasizes the importance of the *meaning* the actor attaches to his action. The presence of meaning makes the study of human behavior different from the study of natural objects and events. For this very reason, according to Eulau, the distinct merit of the behavioral persuasion lies in its focus on the meaning of human behavior. Moreover, he holds that the observation of political behavior must meet the test of intersubjective agreement between observer and observed. There must be an agreement between the meanings that the observer and the actor himself give to behavior. This does not require, however, that the observational language of political science should be the same as the language of the political actor, but rather that their meanings must be consonant with each other.

In sum, according to both Eulau's behavioral persuasion and phenomenology's basic view, the meaning world of the political observer must be consistent with the meaning world of the political actor. The critical difference that separates these two approaches lies in their differing assessments of objective methods in handling political data. The phenomenologist insists that because a qualitative difference exists between things human and things merely natural, the behavioral sciences' method must be radically different from natural science techniques. Although he recognizes this difference, Eulau insists that nothing in political behavior is "intrinsically immune to scientific analysis," and there are no "natural limits" to the use of scientific methods and techniques in political science. To be sure, the catch phrase is "scientific analysis." By scientific analysis, however, Eulau does not mean any and every objective and rigorous analysis but scientific analysis in a positivistic sense—that is, political analysis taken according to the positivist conception of science.

Eulau, I think, fails to demonstrate in what way the qualitative difference between human and natural phenomena can be reconciled with his vision of scientific technology, however perfect it may become in the future for the analysis of political data.[20] In the final analysis Eulau chooses to opt for what is external, rather than what is intended, as the only legitimate universe of scientific discourse and observation. To put it more bluntly, Eulau has yet to show how a John Watson can be reconciled with a Max Weber.

The phenomenological approach, though, is consistent with its own basic recognition of the radical differences between what is human and what is merely natural. Because political events have meanings for political actors, the observation of political scientists must be founded on the meanings of political events interpreted by political actors themselves. Phenomenology, therefore, centers on the intentional dimensions of human action and the social world. Because it is intentional, human action strictly speaking is neither exclusively external nor exclusively internal; it is both. Phenomenology insists that scientific methods and techniques that are appropriate only for the investigation of natural phenomena are inadequate for the investigation of the intentional structure of human action. Since political science, in common with the other behavioral sciences, presupposes the theory of action, I shall relate the essentials of the phenomenological exposition of human action.

IV. The Meaning of Human Action

Action is human conduct as an ongoing process based on a preconceived project. Action has temporal, intentional, motivational, and bodily dimensions.[21] Man is a responsible agent who knows that he is the author of his acts. He is aware of what is to be done. The presence of the project (in action) makes our action meaningful, rational, and purposive. In that we have internal time-consciousness or the inner flow of duration, we have our lived experience *(Erlebnis)*. However, our lived experience acquires meaning only when it is grasped by the act of attention (that is, reflectively), which is called meaningful experience *(Erfahrung)*. The meaningfulness of our experience refers thus to "having experienced" and never to the ongoing process of experiencing.

The project is the purposive basis of performing an action. It is the practical determination of what is to be done and is geared to achieving a practical goal. It is not a mere fancying, precisely because it is formulated in terms of what I *can* do within my power to reach a desired goal. Since it is only a blueprint for action, the project is independent of the actual execution of action. It refers to the action not yet executed. Because the project is the rehearsing of the course of action yet to take place, it can be modified or canceled at will. But whereas the project is reversible and revocable, the executed action is not. The project has no practical consequences unless it is fulfilled by the act of working. For instance, a man decides to run for a public office to bring about some desirable change in government. Presumably he reaches this decision after a careful consideration of such factors as his availability and his physical and financial capabilities. In order to win an election, which is his immediate goal, he must plan ahead the course of action he will take in his campaign. But the nature of a project being what it is, this does not mean that his plans are fixed once and for all. On the contrary, he may change his plans as the occasion demands.

In essence the project is a deliberation—a thought in the process of making a decision. Since thought always relates itself to an object, the project is what I decide (that is, the object of my decision). By decision I commit and bind myself to my project. Decision thus involves my personal action: it is always *I* who decide what is to be done. "I involve myself in the project," Paul Ricoeur declares, "I impute to myself the action which is to be done. This is what distinguishes decision from a wish or a command in which the thing to be done is not my personal action but the course of things or the action of another, more often expressed by the conditional or the imperative."[22]

Action is motivated behavior. For instance, I decide to close the window because I have a chill. In action the project and the motive are correlative, since to understand a project is to understand it in terms of reasons for it. Behind deliberation of a project is a basic dimension called motivation, which provides an impetus for or sets a motion to action. The motive implies the idea of both a meaning and a force. It is a meaning in that it is a reason for doing something and a force to the extent that it starts a bodily movement.

The phenomenological analysis of motivation endeavors to integrate the psychology and ethics of action. As actors are neither agnostics nor disbelievers of value, in action there is no separation between what is and what ought to be. Indeed, fact and value are cooperative in action. As actors we encounter values in motivating a project. Motives for our action include not only such material values as needs and desires but also such formal values as duty, loyalty, or obligation. The motive in running for a public office may be a search for deference, an addiction to playing the game of politics, a sense of duty, or any combination of these. Even our needs and desires, it must be stressed, cannot be treated simply as physical magnitudes, for they are also meanings and valuations that enter into our motivational field in interaction with other meanings and valuations.

✓ Every theory of politics contains certain explicit or implicit assumptions about human nature, and some theorists tend to oversimplify the nature of political man and the motivational factors of his action. They introduce a one-sided, hence false image of man and reality. Anthony Downs, for example, contends that the people who involve themselves in party politics are motivated by "their personal desire for the income, prestige, and power which come from holding office."[23] He defines man as the consumer who maximizes his own utilities. Man seeks to maximize his self-interest, and his behavior is "rational" to the degree that it is directed primarily toward selfish ends. Thus Downs reduces the image of political man to that of economic man and, for allegedly analytical reasons, all political motivation to the economic motivation of pecuniary gains in market relations.[24]

Downs is guilty of unduly simplifying the image of man by assuming that every motive, or at least every significant motive, in human conduct is reducible to the maximization of individual utilities. A corollary of this is the reduction of the notion of rationality (or political rationality) to the categories of economic rationality in the study of human behavior in society. By so doing, Downs obliterates the distinction between the political and the economic, and narrows the vision of what is distinctively political. Downs's economic reductionism, as has already been indicated, is certainly prompted by his methodological consideration in constructing a deductive model that necessitates a conceptual simplification of "real" man and his motives for the sake of purportedly exact measurement and accurate prediction.

Human action also has a bodily dimension. In fact, the body is a necessary medium for all human activity, whether doing or thinking.[25] The body is an active mode of human existence in the world. We perceive, feel, act, and think *with* our bodies. Thinking is no more the function of mind alone, as the rationalist has it, than acting is merely a physical event, as the behaviorist has it. As John Wild stresses:

Human behavior is neither a series of blind reactions to external "stimuli," nor the projection of acts which are motivated by the pure ideas of disembodied, worldless mind. It is neither exclusively subjective nor exclusively objective, but a dialectical interchange between man and the world, which cannot be adequately expressed in traditional causal terms. It is a circular dialectic in which the independent beings of the life-field, already selected by the structure of the human body, exert a further selective operation on this body's acts. It is out of this dialectical interchange that human meanings emerge.[26]

In short, I *am* my body, and the body is the existing I. The body, as I live it, is not constituted in an objective sense. It is an active subject rather than a passive object. Were the body only an object, man would be nothing but a pure spectator and thus would be deprived of his status as an active doer.

In social relationships, moreover, the body is the apparatus of contact *(con-tact)* with others. All interpersonal contacts require a working act of the body, whether the contact is a politician shaking hands with a voter, a gathering of legislators debating in a legislative chamber to enact a law, or a group of political campaigners working out an election strategy. By reason of his position in the world through the apparatus of the body, a person has direct access to others. The self is incapable of having a direct relationship with real people when there is a deranged perception between the ego and his body in relation to other people and the external world.[27] The body, then, is a crucial locus not only for the self-interpretation of a person's own lived experience but also for the perception and understanding of others and, ultimately, for a man's social and political relationships.

V. The Meaning of Sociality

For man the actor, to be is to be social. He is nothing but a nexus of relationships, and he is not human unless he is a social being. Thus all social philosophy must begin with a clarification of this elemental problem of sociality as the relationship between the self and the other. Existential philosophy is often accused, with some justification, of being a philosophy of rugged individualism. Existential philosophers are to be blamed for in the past having neglected to explore the social and political dimensions of human existence. The founder of existentialism, Kierkegaard, himself took a rather negative and conservative attitude toward politics; for him the truth was the inward subjectivity of an existing individual, and to exist meant to be as "impolitic" as possible. Yet it must not be forgotten that his insight into the ever-present danger of man's anonymity and alienation is prophetic. The individualism of Kierkegaard, eccentric though it may be, is a constant reminder of the importance of an individual who cannot be reduced simply to one of the faceless crowd or to the law of the statistical average. Kierkegaard decisively rejected the phenomenon of the apathetic, indolent, and formless crowd that deprives the moral character of the individual.[28]

Today the existential and phenomenological philosophers attempt in earnest to seek the roots of man's social existence and clarify them. In post-Husserlian phenomenology, the human life-world and intersubjectivity constitute two important areas of investigation. They are interrelated because the life-world is an intersubjective world commonly given to all men. Maurice Merleau-Ponty epitomizes the existentialist idea that human existence *is* social existence.

> [Our] political task is not incompatible with any cultural value or literary task, if literature and culture are defined as the progressive awareness of our multiple relationships

with other people and the world rather than as ex-
tramundane techniques. *If all truths are told, none will
have to be hidden.* In man's co-existence with man, . . .
morals, doctrines, thoughts and customs, laws, works
and words all express each other; everything signifies
everything. And outside this unique fulguration of existence there is nothing.[29]

Sociality is a multiple network of man's relationships with
man. It refers to the relationship between the politician and
the voter, the writer and the reader, husband and wife, and
so on. Politically speaking man as citizen, as voter, as tax-
payer, and as politician implies everywhere certain relationships. Sociality has reference both to the relationship
between one individual and another and to relationships between the individual and a collectivity (for example, to a
nation or to a government). As the self is a responsible agent,
an individual knows not only that he is the author of his acts
but also that by initiating his actions he solicits and invites the
responses of other agents and accepts the consequences of
his actions. Thus intersubjectivity is a natural condition of the
inherence of the self in the world. Because he is intentional,
man is not and cannot be a windowless monad. Rather, the
inner and the outer are a single, indivisible existence. Man
is capable of both internalizing the external and externaliz-
ing the internal; the dialectical process of this capability constitutes the self-making of an individual on the one hand and
the history of a society or a civilization on the other. Individuation and socialization are not expressions of two incompatible opposites but are complementary expressions of
the single process.

Moreover, to say that man is social does not imply only
harmony and cooperation to the exclusion of conflict and
competition. To be social involves also a tension between
harmony and conflict, accord and antagonism, cooperation
and competition. In politics, too, they are two inseparable

faces of Janus. Politics as the process of "conflict resolutions," as it is often called, makes sense only if we take into account these two complementary tendencies of social process. Unfortunately, in contemporary American political theory there is a pervasive tendency that polarizes conflict and cooperation in order to place a one-sided premium on conflict and competition as the essence of politics. For too many the political system is synonymous with a system of conflict. Robert A. Dahl considers politics and conflict as "inseparable twins."[30] For E. E. Schattschneider, similarly, the language of conflict is at the root of all politics. According to him, the socialization of conflict means an expansion of the scope and scale of conflict, and the nature of conflict determines the nature of the public involvement in American polity, whose democratic government is the greatest single instrument for the contagion and nationalization of conflict.[31]

It is important that sociality be described in terms of mutuality between the self and the other (or the world). By mutuality I mean the idea that without the world there is no authentic selfhood, and without selfhood there is no world. The self and the other are reciprocal, and their reciprocity is based on the heterogeneity of the two; that is, they are differentiated, for to exist is to stand out from each other. The idea of mutuality preserves the identity of the self as a unique individual, in which his autonomy is exercised without rejecting or being engulfed by society. In mutuality there is no place for imposition and enslavement, but only the free unfolding and the responsible execution of relationships. The individual is *in* society, but not *of* it as a part in the organic whole. As a balanced view of the self and society, therefore, the idea of mutuality rejects both egocentric and sociocentric interpretations of the individual and society. The absolute sovereignty of the individual over society is as unreal as the affirmation of a collective consciousness independent of and transcending individuals. The extreme views of both atomistic individualism and totalitarian collectivism, in the final analysis, vastly misunderstand the nature of sociality.)

It is as *homo loquens* that man also reveals the social mode of his existence. Speaking is a mode of action. Thus one who says "judge me not by my words but by my deeds" misunderstands speaking as a mode of action and widens the chasm between words and deeds. After all, words, too, are performative. As an actor man is above all the creature capable of speaking and communicating As language is a social phenomenon and serves as the instrument of human communication, so does speaking disclose the sociality of man and the intersubjective structure between the self and the other All communication entails the reciprocity of the self and the other and is necessarily mutual. The ordinary language of politics makes feasible the collective life of man in society. Stimson Bullitt emphasizes:

> Political engagement is essential not only to active citizen contributions to the public good but also to communication, the more essential element of the democratic system. As engagement by citizens can become a satisfying experience only where citizen and politician truly come in touch, the converse also is a fact; successful communication can be established only where citizens can be brought by the offer of satisfying experience into some degree of engagement.[32]

The concept of mutuality also defines the meaning of man's freedom and responsibility in society. As man is an active and social being, freedom and responsibility are two interlocking modalities of action in the social world.[33] Because action is the radical transition from what man *is* to what he *intends to be,* man is a task to be accomplished rather than a set of fixed and predetermined properties. By the exercise of his freedom man is able to refuse to be what he is. To be is in part to be free, and the logic of action requires freedom. Freedom is man's capacity to make himself, transform himself, and to choose his own future. Action, however, is freedom only in reference to the absolute possibility of the self alone, whereas it entails responsibility in the presence of others. Freedom is a necessary quality that human action requires, whereas responsibility is a moral, social, and political relationship in the meeting of the self and the other.

Practical freedom is finite and conditional not only because man exists with other men but also because in the field of action or interaction others, too, assert their own freedom. Absolute and unconditional freedom is an abstraction, as is an isolated individual, because the self exists only in the midst of and in relation to others. Man may be free without being responsible, but he cannot be responsible without first being free. To be responsible is to be free. From the viewpoint of man as a social being, to be is to be responsible. Responsibility is of a higher order than freedom simply because it is the beginning of self-transcendence, whereas freedom is necessary only for self-realization. In the community of active men responsibility is both the capacity and the demand to respond to the call of others. As a demand it is a moral obligation. If sociality is a fact of human existence, responsibility is the moral fulfillment of this social facticity. Only through the fulfillment of responsibility can man hope to establish the linkage between the fact and the value of his existence. In essence, then, responsibility consummates all of what is in man's being in the world with others and hence his humanity. In the end the authenticity of being human must be sought in responsibility—moral, social, and political— which lies at the root of genuine reciprocity.

The social world is a complex network of various kinds of living relationships among people. The social sciences are concerned with various regions of the social world as the objects of their investigation. Social relationship begins with a person's point of view or his attitude toward others. Social meaning emerges then when man holds a certain attitude toward others who, like him, are also capable of having their points of view toward him in the commonly shared world. In this sense, social action presupposes other-orientation among men who are capable of having conscious experiences. One's action may affect others, and they may affect his. Other-orientation can be either reciprocal or one-sided—that is, with or without reciprocation from one's partner. In the framework of Alfred Schutz's phenomenology,[34] the social world is divided into four regions: (1) the world of consociates *(Umwelt);* (2) the world of contemporaries *(Mitwelt);* (3) the world of predecessors *(Vorwelt);* (4) the world of successors *(Folgewelt).* The first two refer to the vivid and active here-and-now, and only in these two worlds can we become both participants and observers, whereas the second two have the temporal character of the past and the future, respectively. The world of predecessors is *history,* or past events, and existed before we were born. As such it is of primary interest for historians. We can take any kind of attitude toward our predecessors, but it is always one-sided and passive; we have no way of influencing them, while they may influence us (that is, our traditional behavior). There is no genuine reciprocation. Nor does the problem of freedom arise here; it already *was,* and what was already done cannot be undone.

The distance of social relationships ranges from "we-relationship" to collective entities such as the state, the government, the political party, the political interest group, and the like, with varying degrees of immediacy, intensity, and intimacy for the nearer entities and of anonymity for those farther away. We-relationship emphasizes the bodily presence of the other in the face-to-face situation, in the temporal and spatial immediacy where the other becomes the *you* or consociate *(Mitmensch).* By contrast the world of contemporaries *(Nebenmenschen)* has they-orientation, which is of immediate and direct significance to typical political relationships and thus to the theory of politics—for that matter to sociology, economics, and jurisprudence. In they-orientation[35] we regard the other as an anonymous individual; we usually take a certain attitude toward the other in terms of the function or role he performs in society. Such terms as politician, voter, president, congressman, and diplomat in political language are functional terms or refer to the special functions individual actors perform. It is always possible that a they-relationship is in principle convertible to a we-relationship. For instance, we meet a politician in the face-to-face situation on his campaign trail, shake hands with him, and exchange a few words with him.

In the world of contemporaries we do not experience others directly, but we know them by inference; that is, we infer their typical characteristics in terms of functions or roles they perform. In short we understand our contemporary as an ideal type. Moreover, in Schutz's words:

> In the world of direct social experience, there is a radical difference between *participation* and *observation*. This difference disappears when we get into the world of contemporaries. The reason is that in the latter we never encounter real living people at all. In that world, whether we are participants or observers, we are dealing only with ideal types. Our whole experience is in the mode of the "They." Nevertheless, the ideal type of an observer in the world of contemporaries necessarily differs from the ideal type of a participant in the same world.[36]

The danger in observing someone indirectly as an ideal type is that the observer can make an error without discovering it, because the observed actor is not a real person. Further, in the phenomenological investigation of human action such as that of Schutz it is important to note that such anonymous collectivities as the state or the government can be concretely analyzed in terms of the ideal types of individual action: "Every 'action' of the state can be reduced to the actions of its functionaries," and "the term 'state' is merely

an abbreviation for a highly complex network of interdependent personal ideal types."[37]

Conclusion

In recent years many have spoken of the decline, if not the
death, of the theory of politics. The chief reasons to which
this alleged decline is attributed are historicism, lack of normative concern resulting from the positivist doctrine of ethical neutrality, excessive preoccupation with methodology
by neglecting the substantive issues of politics, and, not least,
inattention to matters political in philosophical inquiry.
Whatever the reasons for the decline of political theory may
be, the most pressing question is how to revive it if indeed
it is in decline. This essay is written with the conviction that
substantive political theory is worthy of our intellectual en-
deavor and deserves our serious attention. I have attempted
to indicate the direction of substantive political theory based
on the findings of existential phenomenology. To summarize,
the basic contributions of existential phenomenology to the
philosophy of politics are, first, a clarification of the meaning
of theory for human existence and, second, a descriptive
disclosure of the intentional meaning of human action and
sociality.

Phenomenology insists on the relevance of the all-encompassing horizon of meaning called the life-world to theoretical activity in philosophy and science. From beginning to
end phenomenology is a descriptive analysis of the meaning
of what is lived or directly experienced. The life-world refers
to the complex living relationships of man to man in culture,
in society, in history, and in politics. As a philosophy phenomenology is concerned with the meaning of theoretical inquiry
into human existence and thus with the union of theory and
practice, a problem of great importance to the theory of
politics. To insist, as does phenomenology, on the primacy of
lived reality and to insist that the construction of objective

thought is derivative does not downgrade theoretical activity but places it in a proper perspective.

The philosopher, and particularly the political philosopher, ought not to be one who takes delight in the "empty kisses of abstraction" but ought to be one who is ready to speak, for he exists in the world and his thinking is a special way of existing in the world. Nor is the philosopher an acosmic spirit who can transcend in a single breath the vicissitudes of politics and history and indulge in the eternal secrecy of private thought. After all, he exists in the world, and when he thinks, he thinks always of this mundane world, which is pervaded by meaning and value and from which his knowledge originates.

In addition to an elucidation of the meaning of theoretical activity for human existence, phenomenology also contributes in substance and method to the behavioral sciences in that it describes the meaning structure of human action and social reality. By recognizing the qualitative difference between human and natural phenomena, phenomenology attempts to focus on and capture the meaning of action as the actor lives through it, and to avoid conceptual reductionism that encapsulates the lived in a conceptual cocoon and sacrifices it to conceptual neatness and contrivance. It does not deny, however, the importance of what is observable from outside, but instead emphasizes the idea that what is observable from without must also be seen in relation to what is lived from within. In this way phenomenology dissolves the dichotomy between subjectivity and objectivity, because the lived itself precedes all such dichotomies and distinctions. Moreover, when the action of one individual takes into account that of another, there arises the question of social action and, ultimately, of social reality. By virtue of his intentionality man is relational through and through: he is nothing but a nexus of relationships in the atmosphere of humanity. Social reality, indeed, is the total horizon of man's everyday relationships with his fellow men in society. (What would Marx say social reality is?)

In conclusion, it must be stressed that politics and philosophy are intertwined. The underlying basis of political philosophy is the idea that philosophy cannot exclude politics from the legitimate domain of human rationality and thus from its inquiry. Political philosophy is not only a philosophical treatment of politics but is equally a political introduction to philosophy. Although political existence is by no means the whole of human reality, philosophy that abandons politics is unquestionably less than reasonable and complete, for the rationality of politics sustains in part the rationality of philosophy. For this reason existential phenomenology, like every great philosophy, endeavors to understand political rationality in order to understand its own rationality in fullness. Its philosophical insights into political matters in the human life-world help us to gain a sense of direction and open up a new perspective in political theorizing. In seeking the meaning of theory for human existence, Husserl rightly spoke of the philosopher as the "civil servant of humanity." Inspired by this humanist vision, political philosophy hopes to define its true vocation and to integrate the two inseparable realms of theory and practice and values and facts in political life.

Notes

1. Kariel, "The Political Relevance of Behavioral and Existential Psychology," *American Political Science Review* 61 (June 1967): 334–42; and Meehan, *Contemporary Political Thought* (Homewood: The Dorsey Press, 1967), p. 383. Compare Arnold Brecht, *Political Theory* (Princeton: Princeton University Press, 1959), p. 383. For an excellent appraisal and survey of existential phenomenology in relation to the social sciences, see Fred R. Dallmayr, "Existential Phenomenology and Social Science: An Overview and Appraisal," which was presented to the annual meeting of the Midwest Political Science Association in Chicago, April 30–May 2, 1970, and to the annual meeting of the Society for Phenomenology and Existential Philosophy in New York, October 30–November 1, 1970.

2. Heidegger, *Being and Time,* trans. John Macquarrie and Edward Robinson (New York: Harper & Bros., 1962); Sartre, *Being and Nothingness,* trans. Hazel E. Barnes (New York: Philosophical Library, 1956); Merleau-

Ponty, *Phenomenology of Perception*, trans. Colin Smith (New York: The Humanities Press, 1962); Ricoeur, *Fallible Man*, trans. Charles Kelbley (Chicago: Henry Regnery, 1965), and *Freedom and Nature*, trans. Erzim V. Kohák (Evanston: Northwestern University Press, 1966); Wild, *Existence and the World of Freedom* (Englewood Cliffs: Prentice-Hall, 1962). For a comprehensive survey of the development of phenomenology, see Herbert Spiegelberg, *The Phenomenological Movement* (2 vols.; The Hague: Martinus Nijhoff, 1960).

3. *Husserl*, trans. Edward G. Ballard and Lester E. Embree (Evanston: Northwestern University Press, 1967), p. 212. In existential phenomenology, according to Ricoeur, there are three major themes: (1) the idea of "owned body" *(corps propre)*, (2) freedom, and (3) intersubjectivity. See *ibid.*, pp. 208–12.

4. See Alfred Schutz, "On Multiple Realities," in *Collected Papers I: The Problem of Social Reality*, ed. Maurice Natanson (The Hague: Martinus Nijhoff, 1962), pp. 207–59. The process by which the accent of one reality is shifted to another is described as a "shock" or "leap" *(ibid.,* pp. 232 and 343–44). Kierkegaard speaks of the "qualitative leap" as a movement from one psychological state to another; every psychological state is posited by a leap. As every leap is preceded by a state, every state is negated or annulled *(aufgehoben)* in favor of a new state. *The Concept of Dread*, trans. Walter Lowrie (Princeton: Princeton University Press, 1957), pp. 99 ff.

5. *The Crisis of European Sciences and Transcendental Phenomenology*, trans. David Carr (Evanston: Northwestern University Press, 1970), p. 122.

6. *Phenomenology of Perception*, p. 382.

7. See Wild, *op. cit.*, p. 54. Raymond Polin emphasizes that the phenomenological analysis of values is futile unless it contributes to the philosophy of action. *La Création des valeurs* (2nd ed.; Paris: Presses Universitaires de France, 1952), p. 3.

8. *Man and People*, trans. Willard R. Trask (New York: W. W. Norton, 1967), pp. 62–65 and 79–81. Heidegger characterizes human existence as care *(Sorge)* in *Being and Time*, especially, pp. 225ff.

9. William James, *The Principles of Psychology* (2 vols.; New York: Dover Publications, 1950; originally published in 1890), I:222. Also see Eugene T. Gendlin, *The Experiencing and the Creation of Meaning* (Glencoe: The Free Press, 1962), p. 9.

10. *The Self as Agent* (London: Faber and Faber, 1957), p. 38.

11. In his presidential address delivered at the annual meeting of the American Political Science Association in September 1969, David Easton emphasized the idea of unity between political knowledge and action in what he called the "post-behavioral revolution." See "The New Revolution in Political Science," *American Political Science Review* 63 (December 1969): 1051–61. In recent literature the theme of theory and practice is discussed in Nicolas Lobkowicz, *Theory and Practice* (Notre Dame: University of Notre Dame Press, 1967); and Jürgen Habermas, *Theorie und Praxis* (3rd ed.; Neuwied: Luchterhand, 1969).

12. Walter Odajnyk, *Marxism and Existentialism* (New York: Doubleday, 1965), p. 171. Edward A. Tiryakian calls existentialism, in contrast to the "sociologism" of Emile Durkheim, "a philosophy of rugged individualism," and says that the idea that "the authentic selfhood of the person is to be found only through participation in a collectivity, in social reality . . . is antipodal to that of existentialism." *Sociologism and Existentialism* (Englewood Cliffs: Prentice-Hall, 1962), p. 155. However, compare this view with his later one in "Existential Phenomenology and the Sociological Tradition," *American Sociological Review* 30 (October 1965): 674–88. As for the view of Marx on this point, Shlomo Avineri states that "As 'society' does not exist, according to Marx, as an entity distinct from the 'individuals', change in individuals is *ipso facto* also change in society, and change in social circumstances is also change in individuals. For Marx, socialism is about to overcome the traditional gap between individualism and collectivism. For him, the capitalist 'individualists' were as wrong as the socialist 'collectivists'." *The Social and Political Thought of Karl Marx* (Cambridge: The University Press, 1968), p. 92.

13. For a detailed discussion on the interdependence between philosophy and the social sciences, see Maurice Merleau-Ponty, "The Philosopher and Sociology," in *Signs,* trans. Richard C. McCleary (Evanston: Northwestern University Press, 1964), pp. 98–113.

14. *Op. cit.,* p. 59. Compare Merleau-Ponty, *Phenomenology of Perception,* pp. viii and ix: "The whole universe of science is built upon the world as directly experienced, and if we want to subject science itself to rigorous scrutiny and arrive at a precise assessment of its meaning and scope, we must begin by reawakening the basic experience of the world of which science is the second-order expression. . . . To return to things themselves is to return to that world which precedes knowledge, of which knowledge *speaks,* and in relation to which every scientific schematization is an abstract and derivative sign-language, as is geography in relation to the country-side in which we have learnt beforehand what a forest, a prairie or a river is."

15. The "empiricist" Robert A. Dahl criticizes many "trans-empiricists" for using "an unnatural vocabulary far removed from the ordinary language of politics." *Modern Political Analysis* (Englewood Cliffs: Prentice-Hall, 1963), p. 105. In turn, the "trans-empiricist" Leo Strauss charges that while "the language of Aristotelian political science is identical with the language of political man" and "it hardly uses a term that did not originate in the market place and is not in common use there," "the new political science cannot begin to speak without having elaborated an extensive technical vocabulary." "An Epilogue," in *Essays on the Scientific Study of Politics,* ed. Herbert J. Storing (New York: Holt, Rinehart & Winston, 1962), p. 310. It is important to note that both Dahl and Strauss recognize the significance of the ordinary language of political man. Strauss recognizes the dependence of conceptual knowledge on preconceptual understanding. However, I have argued elsewhere that his intellectualism is guilty of self-contradiction, while positivism takes the preconceptual life-world for granted and may be charged with negligence. See my article, "Leo Strauss's Conception

of Political Philosophy: A Critique," *The Review of Politics* 29 (October 1967): 492–517.

16. An example of this approach is T. D. Weldon's *The Vocabulary of Politics* (Baltimore: Penguin Books, 1953). Following the logical positivist criteria of meaning, Weldon views the function of political philosophy as a linguistic therapeutic of political words. According to Felix E. Oppenheim, analytic political philosophy—both philosophy of political science and philosophy of political ethics—is concerned with the logical and linguistic analysis of factual and ethical statements about political phenomena (that is, with what is meta-factual and meta-ethical). *Moral Principles in Political Philosophy* (New York: Random House, 1968), pp. 3–19. Similarly, Richard S. Rudner juxtaposes "substantive" and "methodological" issues in the study of social phenomena. For him "social philosophy" and "philosophy of social science" deal with the substantive and the methodological, respectively: "The philosopher of social science is engaged not with the substance of any social theory nor with a view of what makes a good society but with the logic of any theory construction in social science and with the logic of justification of (any) social-science theory." *Philosophy of Social Science* (Englewood Cliffs: Prentice-Hall, 1966), p. 3.

17. *An Economic Theory of Democracy* (New York: Harper & Row, 1957), particularly pp. 21–35. Downs's conception of positive political science is preceded by Milton Friedman's model of positive economics, which is an application of the positivist conception of science. See Friedman, "The Methodology of Positive Economics," in *Essays in Positive Economics* (Chicago: The University of Chicago Press, 1953), pp. 3–43.

18. *Op. cit.*, p. 59. It is of utmost significance to note that "The foundational analysis and explication of the 'social,' 'behavior,' and the 'human' is necessarily fundamental to the determination of which methods and concepts are appropriate and justifiable. Hence, the 'phenomenology of the social world' is at the same time the 'phenomenology of the social (behavioral, humanistic) sciences'." Richard M. Zaner, "Introduction," in Alfred Schutz, *Reflections on the Problem of Relevance* (New Haven: Yale University Press, 1970), p. xiii. For discussions of phenomenology and the behavioral or humanistic sciences, see particularly Alfred Schutz, *Collected Papers I, The Phenomenology of the Social World*, trans. George Walsh and Frederick Lehnert (Evanston: Northwestern University Press, 1967), and *Reflections on the Problem of Relevance*; Maurice Merleau-Ponty, "Phenomenology and the Sciences of Man," trans. John Wild, in *The Primacy of Perception*, ed. James M. Edie (Evanston: Northwestern University Press, 1964), pp. 43–95; Stephan Strasser, *Phenomenology and the Human Sciences* (Pittsburgh: Duquesne University Press, 1963); Erwin W. Straus, *The Primary World of Senses*, trans. Jacob Needleman (Glencoe: The Free Press, 1963); Eugene T. Gendlin, *Experiencing and the Creation of Meaning;* and Harold Garfinkel, *Studies in Ethnomethodology* (Englewood Cliffs: Prentice-Hall, 1967).

19. *The Behavioral Persuasion in Politics* (New York: Random House, 1963). See further *Micro-Macro Political Analysis* (Chicago: Aldine, 1969),

pp. 148–65 and 370–90. See further my papers: "A Phenomenological Critique of the Behavioral Persuasion in Politics: A Philosophical View," delivered at the 1971 annual meeting of the American Political Science Association, Chicago, September 7–11; and "The Place of Valuation in the Theory of Politics: A Phenomenological Critique of Political Behavioralism;" *The Journal of Value Inquiry*, forthcoming.

20. Compare Eulau's views of scientific technology with those of the phenomenologist Hubert L. Dreyfus in *Alchemy and Artificial Intelligence* (RAND Paper, P-3244; Santa Monica: The RAND Corporation, December 1965); "Phenomenology and Artificial Intelligence," in *Phenomenology in America*, ed. James M. Edie (Chicago: Quadrangle Books, 1967), pp. 31–47; and "Why Computers Must Have Bodies in Order to Be Intelligent," *The Review of Metaphysics* 21 (September 1967): 13–32.

21. For a phenomenology of human action, see Maurice Merleau-Ponty, *The Structure of Behavior*, trans. Alden L. Fisher (Boston: Beacon Press, 1963); Jean-Paul Sartre, *Critique de la Raison Dialectique* (Paris: Gallimard, 1960); Alexander Pfänder, *Phenomenology of Willing and Motivation*, trans. Herbert Spiegelberg (Evanston: Northwestern University Press, 1967); Schutz, *Collected Papers I*, pp. 67–96, and *The Phenomenology of the Social World;* Ricoeur, *Freedom and Nature*, and "Philosophy of Will and Action," in *Phenomenology of Will and Action*, ed. Erwin W. Straus and Richard M. Griffith (Pittsburgh: Duquesne University Press, 1966), pp. 7–33; and Rollo May, *Love and Will* (New York: W. W. Norton, 1969).

22. *Freedom and Nature*, p. 46.

23. *Op. cit.*, p. 34.

24. Compare James M. Buchanan and Gordon Tullock, *The Calculus of Consent* (Ann Arbor: The University of Michigan Press, 1965), p. 27. Although William H. Riker is "eager to create specifically *political* theories of behavior to serve as a base for a future *political* science," there is nonetheless an economic overtone in his game theory. For him "most of the decisions in economics and political life are made by persons acting in a fiduciary relation"; and "rational" behavior is "winning" behavior when he says that "politically rational man is the man who would rather win than lose, regardless of the particular stakes." *The Theory of Political Coalitions* (New Haven: Yale University Press, 1962), p. ix. Yet, as William T. Bluhm points out, " 'winning' as the political value par excellence is not for Riker an entirely selfish object, as the political object is for Downs." *Theories of the Political System* (Englewood Cliffs: Prentice-Hall, 1965), p. 292.

25. For a phenomenological theory of the human body, see Richard M. Zaner, *The Problem of Embodiment* (The Hague: Martinus Nijhoff, 1964).

26. "Foreword," in Merleau-Ponty, *The Structure of Behavior*, pp. xiv–xv.

27. R. D. Laing, *The Divided Self* (Baltimore: Penguin Books, 1965), p. 82.

28. *The Present Age*, trans. Alexander Dru (New York: Harper & Row, 1962). See also my article, "Confucianism and Existentialism: Intersubjectivity as the Way of Man," *Philosophy and Phenomenological Research* 30 (December 1969): 195–98. Among prolific existentialist writings on the subject of mass man in modern society, see particularly Karl Jaspers, *Man in the*

Modern Age, trans. Eden and Cedar Paul (New York: Doubleday, 1957); Gabriel Marcel, *Man Against Mass Society,* trans. G. S. Fraser (Chicago: Henry Regnery, 1952); Nicolas Berdyaev, *The Fate of Man in the Modern World,* trans. Donald A. Lowrie (Ann Arbor: The University of Michigan Press, 1935); and José Ortega y Gasset, *The Revolt of the Masses* (New York: W. W. Norton, 1932).

29. *Sense and Non-Sense,* trans. Hubert L. Dreyfus and Patricia Allen Dreyfus (Evanston: Northwestern University Press, 1964), p. 152. For existential and phenomenological expositions of intersubjectivity, see Emmanuel Levinas, *Totality and Infinity,* trans. Alphonso Lingis (Pittsburgh: Duquesne University Press, 1969); Edmund Husserl, *Cartesian Meditations,* trans. Dorion Cairns (The Hague: Martinus Nijhoff, 1960); Georges Gusdorf, *Speaking,* trans. Paul T. Brockelman (Evanston: Northwestern University Press, 1962); Gabriel Marcel, *The Existential Background of Human Dignity* (Cambridge: Harvard University Press, 1963); Karl Jaspers, *Reason and Existenz,* trans. William Earle (New York: The Noonday Press, 1955); Martin Buber, *Between Man and Man,* trans. Ronald Gregor Smith (New York: Macmillan, 1965); Max Scheler, *The Nature of Sympathy,* trans. Peter Heath (New Haven: Yale University Press, 1954); José Ortega y Gasset, *Man and People;* Nicolas Berdyaev, *Solitude and Society,* trans. George Reavey (London: Geoffrey Bles, 1938); John Macmurray, *Persons in Relation* (London: Faber & Faber, 1961); Remy C. Kwant, *Phenomenology of Social Existence* (Pittsburgh: Duquesne University Press, 1965); Peter L. Berger and Thomas Luckmann, *The Social Construction of Reality* (New York: Doubleday, 1967); and Stephan Strasser, *The Idea of Dialogal Phenomenology* (Pittsburgh: Duquesne University Press, 1970).

30. *Op. cit.,* p. 73. David B. Truman also says that "the activities of political interest groups imply controversy and conflict, the essence of politics. For those who abhor conflict in any form, who long for some past or future golden age of perfect harmony, these consequences of group activity are alone sufficient to provoke denunciation." *The Governmental Process* (New York: Alfred A. Knopf, 1958), pp. 502–3. A balanced view of the political system as the concomitant processes of conflict and integration is found in Maurice Duverger, *The Idea of Politics,* trans. Robert North and Ruth Murphy (Indianapolis: Bobbs-Merrill, 1966).

31. *The Semi-Sovereign People* (New York: Holt, Rinehart & Winston, 1960).

32. *To Be a Politician* (rev. ed.; New York: Doubleday, 1961), p. 197.

33. Concerning the issues of freedom and responsibility, see Jean-Paul Sartre, *Being and Nothingness;* John Wild, *Existence and the World of Freedom,* pp. 101–55; William James, "The Dilemma of Determinism," in *Essays on Faith and Morals* (New York: The World Publishing Co., 1962), pp. 145–83; Nicolas Berdyaev, *Slavery and Freedom,* trans. R. M. French (New York: Charles Scribner's Sons, 1944); Simone de Beauvoir, *The Ethics of Ambiguity,* trans. Bernard Frechtman (New York: The Citadel Press, 1962); Frederick A. Olafson, *Principles and Persons* (Baltimore: The Johns Hopkins Press, 1967); Hazel E. Barnes, *An Existentialist Ethics* (New York:

Alfred A. Knopf, 1967); George A. Schrader, "Responsibility and Existence," in *Responsibility*, ed. Carl J. Friedrich (New York: The Liberal Arts Press, 1960), pp. 43–70; and William Leon McBride, "Voluntary Association: The Basis of an Ideal Model, and the 'Democratic' Failure," in *Voluntary Associations*, ed. Roland Pennock and John W. Chapman (New York: Atherton Press, 1969), pp. 202–32.

34. The following discussion is found in Schutz's *The Phenomenology of the Social World*, pp. 139–214. The uniquely original and dynamic quality of this typology of Schutz lies, I believe, in his singular emphasis on the temporal element in the structure of meaningful action and the social world. Schutz's typology of the social world takes account of the following: (1) the complementarity of individual experience and social action or of the personal and impersonal modes of action; (2) social and political changes (that is, what is known in the profession of political science as "developmental models"); (3) the historical continuity, from the past to the future, of the social world; (4) a mixture or exchangeability of one sub-world to another.

35. It must not automatically be assumed that man's attitude toward another person is always "personal," whereas his attitude toward a collectivity is necessarily "impersonal." Man feels homesick for his native "country" and loyal to the "nation" in which he is a citizen. However, the distinction must be made between devotion (or loyalty) and fanaticism in an individual's relationship to a collectivity such as nation. Dissent is no more a sign of disloyalty than the paranoiac style of chauvinistic "patriotism" is devotion. For a phenomenological discussion of devotion and fanaticism that is applicable to an analysis of the politics of extremism, see Marcel, *Man Against Mass Society*, pp. 133–52; and Wild, *Existence and the World of Freedom*, pp. 167–77.

36. *The Phenomenology of the Social World*, pp. 204–5.

37. *Ibid.*, p. 187.

I

The Life-World, Phenomenology, and the Social Sciences

1

The Life-World and Theoretical *Praxis*

EDMUND HUSSERL

1. The Problem of the "Life-World" as a Partial Problem within the General Problem of Objective Science

Briefly reminding ourselves of our earlier discussions, let us recall the fact we have emphasized, namely, that science is a human spiritual accomplishment which presupposes as its point of departure, both historically and for each new student, the intuitive surrounding world of life, pregiven as existing for all in common. Furthermore, it is an accomplishment which, in being practiced and carried forward, continues to presuppose this surrounding world as it is given in its particularity to the scientist. For example, for the physicist it is the world in which he sees his measuring instruments, hears time beats, estimates visible magnitudes, etc.—

Reprinted from *The Crisis of European Sciences and Transcendental Phenomenology*, trans. David Carr (1970), pp. 121–147, by permission of Northwestern University Press, Evanston, Ill.

the world in which, furthermore, he knows himself to be included with all his activity and all his theoretical ideas.

When science poses and answers questions, these are from the start, and hence from then on, questions resting upon the ground of, and addressed to, the elements of this pregiven world in which science and every other life-praxis is engaged. In this life-praxis, knowledge, as prescientific knowledge, plays a constant role, together with its goals, which are in general satisfactorily achieved in the sense which is intended and in each case usually in order to make practical life possible. But a new civilization (philosophical, scientific civilization), rising up in Greece, saw fit to recast the idea of "knowledge" and "truth" in natural existence and to ascribe to the newly formed idea of "objective truth" a higher dignity, that of a norm for all knowledge. In relation to this, finally, arises the idea of a universal science encompassing all possible knowledge in its infinity, the bold guiding idea of the modern period. If we have made this clear to ourselves, then obviously an explicit elucidation of the objective validity and of the whole task of science requires that we first inquire back into the pregiven world. It is pregiven to us all quite naturally, as persons within the horizon of our fellow men, i.e., in every actual connection with others, as "the" world common to us all. Thus it is, as we have explained in detail, the constant ground of validity, an ever available source of what is taken for granted, to which we, whether as practical men or as scientists, lay claim as a matter of course.

Now if this pregiven world is to become a subject of investigation in its own right, so that we can arrive, of course, at scientifically defensible assertions, this requires special care in preparatory reflections. It is not easy to achieve clarity about what kind of peculiar scientific and hence universal tasks are to be posed under the title "life-world" and about whether something philosophically significant will arise here. Even the first attempt to understand the peculiar ontic sense of the life-world, which can be taken now as a narrower, now as a broader one, causes difficulties.

The manner in which we here come to the life-world as a subject for scientific investigation makes this subject appear an ancillary and partial one within the full subject of objective science in general. The latter has become generally, that is, in all its particular forms (the particular positive sciences), incomprehensible as regards the possibility of its objective accomplishment. If science becomes a problem in this way, then we must withdraw from the operation of it and take up a standpoint above it, surveying in generality its theories and results in the systematic context of predicative thoughts and statements, and on the other side we must also survey the life of acts practiced by working scientists, working with one another—their setting of goals, their termination in a given goal, and the terminating self-evidence. And what also comes under consideration here is precisely the scientists' repeated recourse, in different general manners, to the life-world with its ever available intuited data; to this we can immediately add the scientists' statements, in each case simply adapted to this world, statements made purely descriptively in the same prescientific manner of judging which is proper to the "occasional"[1] statements of practical, everyday life. Thus the problem of the life-world, or rather of the manner in which it functions and must function for scientists, is only a partial subject within the above-designated whole of objective science (namely, in the service of its full grounding).

It is clear, however, that prior to the general question of its function for a self-evident grounding of the objective sciences there is good reason to ask about the life-world's own and constant ontic meaning for the human beings who live in it. These human beings do not always have scientific interests, and even scientists are not always involved in scientific work; also, as history teaches us, there was not always in the world a civilization that lived habitually with long-established scientific interests. The life-world was always there for mankind before science, then, just as it continues its manner of being in the epoch of science. Thus one can put forward by itself the problem of the manner of being of the life-world; one can place oneself completely upon the ground of this straightforwardly intuited world, putting out of play all objective-scientific opinions and cognitions, in order to consider generally what kind of "scientific" tasks, i.e., tasks to be resolved with universal validity, arise in respect to this world's own manner of being. Might this not yield a vast theme for study? Is it not the case that, in the end, through what first appears as a special subject in the theory of science, that "third dimension" is opening up, immediately destined in advance to engulf the whole subject matter of objective science (as well as all other subject matters on the "plane")? At first this must appear peculiar and unbelievable. Many paradoxes will arise; yet they will be resolved. What imposes itself here and must be considered before everything else is the correct comprehension of the essence of the life-world and the method of a "scientific" treatment appropriate to it, from which "objective" scientific treatment, however, is excluded.

2. Exposition of the Problem of a Science of the Life-World

a. The Difference Between Objective Science and Science in General

Is not the life-world as such what we know best, what is always taken for granted in all human life, always familiar to us in its typology through experience? Are not all its horizons of the unknown simply horizons of what is just incompletely known, i.e., known in advance in respect of its most general typology? For prescientific life, of course, this type of acquaintance suffices, as does its manner of converting the unknown into the known, gaining "occasional" knowledge on the basis of experience (verifying itself internally and thereby excluding illusion) and induction. This suffices for everyday praxis. If, now, something more can be and is to be accomplished, if a "scientific" knowledge is supposed to come about, what can be meant other than what objective science has in view and does anyway? Is scientific knowledge as such not "objective" knowledge, aimed at a knowledge substratum which is valid for everyone with unconditioned generality? And yet, paradoxically, we uphold our assertion and require that one not let the handed-down concept of objective science be substituted, because of the century-old tradition in which we have all been raised, for the concept of science in general.

The[2] title "life-world" makes possible and demands perhaps various different, though essentially interrelated, scientific undertakings; and perhaps it is part of genuine and full scientific discipline that we must treat these all together, though following their essential order of founding, rather than treating, say, just the one, the objective-logical one (this particular accomplishment within the life-world) by itself, leaving the others completely out of scientific consideration. There has never been a scientific inquiry into the way in which the life-world constantly functions as subsoil, into how its manifold prelogical validities act as grounds for the logical ones, for theoretical truths.[3] And perhaps the scientific discipline which this life-world as such, in its universality, requires is a peculiar one, one which is precisely not objective and logical but which, as the ultimately grounding one, is not inferior but superior in value. But how is this completely different sort of scientific discipline, for which the objective sort has always been substituted up to now, to be realized? The idea of objective truth is predetermined in its whole meaning by the contrast with the idea of the truth in pre- and extra-scientific life. This latter truth has its ultimate and deepest source of verification in experience which is "pure" in the sense designated above, in all its modes of perception, memory, etc. These words, however, must be understood

actually as prescientific life understands them; thus one must
not inject into them, from current objective science, any
psychophysical, psychological interpretation. And above all
—to dispose of an important point right away—one must not
go straight back to the supposedly immediately given "sense-
data," as if *they* were immediately characteristic of the
purely intuitive data of the life-world. (What is actually first
is the "merely subjective-relative" intuition of prescientific
world-life.) For us, to be sure, this "merely" has, as an old
inheritance, the disdainful coloring of the δόξα. In prescientific life itself, of course, it has nothing of this; there it is a
realm of good verification and, based on this, of well-verified
predicative cognitions and of truths which are just as secure
as is necessary for the practical projects of life that determine
their sense. The disdain with which everything "merely subjective and relative" is treated by those scientists who pursue
the modern ideal of objectivity changes nothing of its own
manner of being, just as it does not change the fact that the
scientist himself must be satisfied with this realm whenever
he has recourse, as he unavoidably must have recourse, to it.

b. The Use of Subjective-Relative Experiences for the Objective Sciences, and the Science of Them

The sciences build upon the life-world as taken for granted
in that they make use of whatever in it happens to be necessary for their particular ends. But to use the life-world in this
way is not to know it scientifically in its own manner of being.
For example, Einstein uses the Michelson experiments and
the corroboration of them by other researchers, with apparatus copied from Michelson's, with everything required
in the way of scales of measurement, coincidences established, etc. There is no doubt that everything that enters in
here—the persons, the apparatus, the room in the institute,
etc.—can itself become a subject of investigation in the usual
sense of objective inquiry, that of the positive sciences. But

Einstein could make no use whatever of a theoretical psycho-logical-psychophysical construction of the objective being of Mr. Michelson; rather, he made use of the human being who was accessible to him, as to everyone else in the prescientific world, as an object of straightforward experience, the human being whose existence, with this vitality, in these activities and creations within the common life-world, is always the presupposition for all of Einstein's objective-scientific lines of inquiry, projects, and accomplishments pertaining to Michel-son's experiments. It is, of course, the one world of experi-ence, common to all, that Einstein and every other re-searcher knows he is in as a human being, even throughout all his activity of research. [But] precisely this world and everything that happens in it, used as needed for scientific and other ends, bears, on the other hand, for every natural scientist in his thematic orientation toward its "objective truth," the stamp "merely subjective and relative." The con-trast to this determines, as we said, the sense of the "objec-tive" task. This "subjective-relative" is supposed to be "over-come"; one can and should correlate with it a hypothetical being-in-itself, a substrate for logical-mathematical "truths-in-themselves" that one can approximate through ever newer and better hypothetical approaches, always justifying them through experiential verification. This is the one side. But while the natural scientist is thus interested in the objec-tive and is involved in his activity, the subjective-relative is on the other hand still functioning for him, not as something irrelevant that must be passed through but as that which ultimately grounds the theoretical-logical ontic validity for all objective verification, i.e., as the source of self-evidence, the source of verification. The visible measuring scales, scale-markings, etc., are used as actually existing things, not as illusions; thus that which actually exists in the life-world, as something valid, is a premise.

c. Is the Subjective-Relative an Object for Psychology?

Now the question of the manner of being of this subjective sphere, or the question of the science which is to deal with it in its own universe of being, is normally disposed of by the natural scientist by referring to psychology. But again one must not allow the intrusion of what exists in the sense of objective science when it is a question of what exists in the life-world. For (what has always gone under the name of psychology, at any rate since the founding of modern objectivism regarding knowledge of the world, naturally has the meaning of an "objective" science of the subjective, no matter which of the attempted historical psychologies we may choose. Now in our subsequent reflections the problem of making possible an objective psychology will have to become the object of more detailed discussions. But first we must grasp clearly the contrast between objectivity and the subjectivity of the life-world as a contrast which determines the fundamental sense of objective-scientific discipline itself, and we must secure this contrast against the great temptations to misconstrue it.

Reread-

d. The Life-World as Universe of What Is Intuitable in Principle; the "Objective-True" World as in Principle Nonintuitable "Logical" Substruction

Whatever may be the chances for realizing, or the capacity for realizing, the idea of objective science in respect to the mental world (i.e., not only in respect to nature), this idea of objectivity dominates the whole *universitas* of the positive sciences in the modern period, and in the general usage it dominates the meaning of the word "science." This already involves a naturalism insofar as this concept is taken from Galilean natural science, such that the scientifically "true,"

the objective, world is always thought of in advance as nature, in an expanded sense of the word. The contrast between the subjectivity of the life-world and the "objective,"
the "true" world, lies in the fact that the latter is a theoretical-logical substruction, the substruction of something that is
in principle not perceivable, in principle not experienceable
in its own proper being, whereas the subjective, in the life-
world, is distinguished in all respects precisely by its being
actually experienceable.*

The life-world is a realm of original self-evidences.[4] That
which is self-evidently given is, in perception, experienced as
"the thing itself,"[5] in immediate presence, or, in memory,
remembered as the thing itself; and every other manner of
intuition is a presentification of the thing itself. Every mediate cognition belonging in this sphere—broadly speaking,
every manner of induction—has the sense of an induction of
something intuitable, something possibly perceivable as the
thing itself or rememberable as having-been-perceived, etc.
All conceivable verification leads back to these modes of
self-evidence because the "thing itself" (in the particular
mode) lies in these intuitions themselves as that which is
actually, intersubjectively experienceable and verifiable and
is not a substruction of thought; whereas such a substruction,
insofar as it makes a claim to truth, can have actual truth only
by being related back to such self-evidences.

It is of course itself a highly important task, for the scientific opening-up of the life-world, to bring to recognition the
primal validity of these self-evidences and indeed their
higher dignity in the grounding of knowledge compared to

*In life the verification of being, terminating in experience, yields a full
conviction. Even when it is inductive, the inductive anticipation is of a
possible experienceability which is ultimately decisive. Inductions can be
verified by other inductions, working together. Because of their anticipa-
tions of experienceability, and because every direct perception itself includes inductive moments (anticipation of the sides of the object which are
not yet experienced), everything is contained in the broader concept of
"experience" or "induction."

that of the objective-logical self-evidences. One must fully clarify, i.e., bring to ultimate self-evidence, how all the self-evidence of objective-logical accomplishments, through which objective theory (thus mathematical and natural-scientific theory) is grounded in respect of form and content, has its hidden sources of grounding in the ultimately accomplishing life, the life in which the self-evident givenness of the life-world forever has, has attained, and attains anew its prescientific ontic meaning. From objective-logical self-evidence (mathematical "insight," natural-scientific, positive-scientific "insight," as it is being accomplished by the inquiring and grounding mathematician, etc.), the path leads back, here, to the primal self-evidence in which the life-world is ever pregiven.

One may at first find strange and even questionable what has been simply asserted here, but the general features of the contrast among levels of self-evidence are unmistakable. The empiricist talk of natural scientists often, if not for the most part, gives the impression that the natural sciences are based on the experience of objective nature. But it is not in this sense true that these sciences are experiential sciences, that they follow experience in principle, that they all begin with experiences, that all their inductions must finally be verified through experiences; rather, this is true only in that other sense whereby experience [yields] a self-evidence taking place purely in the life-world and as such is the source of self-evidence for what is objectively established in the sciences, the latter never themselves being experiences of the objective. The objective is precisely never experienceable as itself; and scientists themselves, by the way, consider it in this way whenever they interpret it as something metaphysically transcendent, in contrast to their confusing empiricist talk. The experienceability of something objective is no different from that of an infinitely distant geometrical construct and in general no different from that of all infinite "ideas," including, for example, the infinity of the number series. Naturally, "rendering ideas intuitive" in the manner of mathematical or natural-scientific "models" is hardly intuition of the objective itself but rather a matter of life-world intuitions which are suited to make easier the conception of the objective ideals in question. Many [such] conceptual intermediaries are often involved, [especially since] the conception itself does not always occur so immediately, cannot always be made so self-evident in its way, as is the case in conceiving of geometrical straight lines on the basis of the life-world self-evidence of straight table-edges and the like.

As can be seen, a great deal of effort is involved here in order to secure even the presuppositions for a proper inquiry, i.e., in order first to free ourselves from the constant misconstructions which mislead us all because of the scholastic dominance of objective-scientific ways of thinking.

e. The Objective Sciences as Subjective Constructs— Those of a Particular Praxis, namely, the Theoretical-Logical, which Itself Belongs to the Full Concreteness of the Life-World

If the contrast [under discussion] has been purified, we must now do justice to the essential interrelatedness [of the elements contrasted]: objective theory in its logical sense (taken universally: science as the totality of predicative theory, of the system of statements meant "logically" as "propositions in themselves," "truths in themselves," and in this sense logically joined) is rooted, grounded in the life-world, in the original self-evidences belonging to it. Thanks to this rooted- *rac. of* *rooted-* ness objective science has a constant reference of meaning to *ness* the world in which we always live, even as scientists and also *of* in the total community of scientists—a reference, that is, to *obj.* the general life-world. But at the same time, as an accom- *theory* plishment of scientific[6] persons, as individuals and as joined in the community of scientific activity, [objective science itself belongs to the life-world.] Its theories, the logical con-

because it is the accomplishment
of persons.

structs, are of course not things in the life-world like
stones, houses, or trees. They are logical wholes and logical
parts made up of ultimate logical elements. To speak with
Bolzano, they are "representations-in-themselves" [*"Vor-
stellungen an sich"*] "propositions in themselves," inferences and proofs "in themselves," ideal unities of signification whose logical ideality is determined by their *telos,*
"truth in itself."

But this or any other ideality does not change in the least
the fact that these are human formations, essentially related
to human actualities and potentialities, and thus belong to
this concrete unity of the life-world, whose concreteness thus
extends farther than that of "things." Exactly the same thing
is true, correlative to this, of scientific activities—those of
experiencing, those of arriving at logical formations "on the
basis of" experience—activities through which these formations appear in original form and original modes of variation
in the individual scientists and in the community of scientists:
the original status of the proposition or demonstration dealt
with by all.

But here we enter an uncomfortable situation. If we have
made our contrast with all necessary care, then we have two
different things: life-world and objective-scientific world,
though of course [they are] related to each other. The knowledge of the objective-scientific world is "grounded" in the
self-evidence of the life-world. The latter is pregiven to the
scientific worker, or the working community, as ground; yet,
as they build upon this, what is built is something new, something different. If we cease being immersed in our scientific
thinking, we become aware that we scientists are, after all,
human beings and as such are among the components of the
life-world which always exists for us, ever pregiven; and thus
all of science is pulled, along with us, into the—merely "subjective-relative"—life-world. And what becomes of the objective world itself? What happens to the hypothesis of being-
in-itself, related first to the "things" of the life-world, the

"objects," the "real" bodies, real animals, plants, and also human beings within the "space-time" of the life-world—all these concepts being understood, now, not from the point of view of the objective sciences but as they are in prescientific life?)

Is it not the case that this hypothesis, which in spite of the ideality of scientific theories has direct validity for the scientific subjects (the scientists as human beings), is but *one* among the many practical hypotheses and projects which make up the life of human beings in this life-world—which is at all times consciously pregiven to them as available? Do not all goals, whether they are "practical" in some other, extrascientific sense or are practical under the title of "theory," belong *eo ipso* to the unity of the life-world, if only we take the latter in its complete and full concreteness?

On the other hand, we have seen also that the propositions, the theories, the whole edifice of doctrine in the objective sciences are structures attained through certain activities of scientists bound together in their collaborative work—or, to speak more exactly, attained through a continued building-up of activities, the later of which always presuppose the results of the earlier. And we see further that all these theoretical results have the character of validities for the life-world, adding themselves as such to its own composition and belonging to it even before that as a horizon of possible accomplishments for developing science. The concrete life-world, then, is the grounding soil [*der gründende Boden*] of the "scientifically true" world and at the same time encompasses it in its own universal concreteness. How is this to be understood? How are we to do justice systematically—that is, with appropriate scientific discipline—to the all-encompassing, so paradoxically demanding, manner of being of the life-world?

We are posing questions whose clarifying answers are by no means obvious. The contrast and the inseparable union [we have been exploring] draw us into a reflection which entangles us in more and more troublesome difficulties. The paradoxical interrelationships of the "objectively true world" and the "life-world" make enigmatic the manner of being of both. Thus [the idea of a] true world in any sense, and within it our own being, becomes an enigma in respect to the sense of this being. In our attempts to attain clarity we shall suddenly become aware, in the face of emerging paradoxes, that all of our philosophizing up to now has been without a ground. How can we now truly become philosophers?

We cannot escape the force of this motivation. It is impossible for us to evade the issue here through a preoccupation with aporia and argumentation nourished by Kant or Hegel, Aristotle or Thomas.

f. The Problem of the Life-World not as a Partial Problem but Rather as a Universal Problem for Philosophy

Of course, it is a new sort of scientific discipline that is required for the solution of the enigmas which now disquiet us: it is not mathematical, nor logical at all in the historical sense; it cannot already have before it, as an available norm, a finished mathematics, logic, or logistic, since these are themselves objective sciences in the sense which is presently problematical and, as included in the problem, cannot be presuppositions used as premises. At first, as long as one only makes contrasts, is only concerned with oppositions, it could appear that nothing more than or different from objective science is needed, just as everyday practical life undertakes its rational reflections, both particular and general, without needing a science for them. It just *is* this way, a fact familiar to all, unthinkingly accepted rather than being formulated as a fundamental fact and thought through as a subject for thinking in its own right—namely, that there are two sorts of truth: on the one side, everyday practical situational truths, relative, to be sure, but, as we have already emphasized, exactly what praxis, in its particular projects, seeks and needs; on the other side there are scientific truths, and their grounding leads back precisely to the situational truths, but in such a way that scientific method does not suffer thereby in respect to its own meaning, since it wants to use and must use precisely these truths.

Thus it could appear—if one allows oneself to be carried along by the thoughtless naïveté of life even in the transition from the extralogical to the logical, to the objective-scientific praxis of thinking—that a separate investigation under the title "life-world" is an intellectualistic enterprise born of a mania, peculiar to modern life, to theorize everything. But, on the other hand, it has at least become apparent that we cannot let the matter end with this naïveté, that paradoxical enigmas announce themselves here: merely subjective relativity is supposedly overcome by objective-logical theory, yet the latter belongs, as the theoretical praxis of human beings, to the merely subjective and relative and at the same time must have its premises, its sources of self-evidence, in the subjective and relative. From here on this much is certain: that all problems of truth and of being, all methods, hypotheses, and results conceivable for these problems— whether for worlds of experience or for metaphysical higher worlds—can attain their ultimate clarity, their evident sense or the evidence of their nonsense, only through this supposed intellectualistic hypertrophy. This will then include, certainly, all ultimate questions of legitimate sense and of nonsense in the busy routine of the "resurrected metaphysics" that has become so vocal and so bewitching of late.

Through this last series of considerations the magnitude, the universal and independent significance, of the problem of the life-world has become intelligible to us in an anticipatory insight. In comparison with this the problem of the "objectively true" world or that of objective-logical science—no matter how pressing it may repeatedly become, and properly so—appears now as a problem of secondary and more specialized interest. (Though the peculiar accomplishment of our modern objective science may still not be understood, nothing changes the fact that it is a validity for the life-world, arising out of particular activities, and that it belongs itself to the concreteness of the life-world.) Thus in any case, for the sake of clarifying this and all other acquisitions of human activity, the concrete life-world must first be taken into consideration; and it must be considered in terms of the truly concrete universality whereby it embraces, both directly and in the manner of horizons, all the built-up levels of validity acquired by men for the world of their common life and whereby it has the totality of these levels related in the end to a world-nucleus to be distilled by abstraction, namely, the world of straightforward intersubjective experiences. To be sure, we do not yet know how the life-world is to become an independent, totally self-sufficient subject of investigation, how it is supposed to make possible scientific statements— which as such, after all, must have their own "objectivity," even if it is in a manner different from that of our sciences, i.e., a necessary validity to be appropriated purely methodically, which we and everyone can verify precisely through this method. We are absolute beginners, here, and have nothing in the way of a logic designed to provide norms; we can do nothing but reflect, engross ourselves in the still not unfolded sense of our task, and thus secure, with the utmost care, freedom from prejudice, keeping our undertaking free of alien interferences (and we have already made several important contributions to this); and this, as in the case of every new undertaking, must supply us with our method. The clarification of the sense of the task is, indeed, the self-evidence of the goal *qua* goal; and to this self-evidence belongs essentially the self-evidence of the possible "ways" to it. The intricacy and difficulty of the preliminary reflections which are still before us will justify themselves, not only because of the magnitude of the goal, but also because of the essential strangeness and precariousness of the ideas which will necessarily become involved.

Thus what appeared to be merely a problem of the fundamental basis of the objective sciences or a partial problem within the universal problem of objective science has indeed (just as we announced in advance that it would) proven to be the genuine and most universal problem. It can also be put this way: the problem first appears as the question of the relation between objective-scientific thinking and intuition; it concerns, on the one hand, then, logical thinking as the thinking of logical thoughts, e.g., the physicist's thinking of physical theory, or purely mathematical thinking, in which mathematics has its place as a system of doctrine, as a theory. And, on the other hand, we have intuiting and the intuited, in the life-world prior to theory. Here arises the ineradicable illusion of a pure thinking which, unconcerned in its purity about intuition, already has its self-evident truth, even truth about the world—the illusion which makes the sense and the possibility, the "scope," of objective science questionable. Here one concentrates on the separateness of intuiting and thinking and generally interprets the nature of the "theory of knowledge" as theory of science, carried out in respect to two correlative sides[7] (whereby science is always understood in terms of the only concept of science available, that of objective science). But as soon as the empty and vague notion of intuition—instead of being something negligible and insignificant compared to the supremely significant logical sphere in which one supposedly already has genuine truth—has become the problem of the life-world, as soon as the magnitude and difficulty of this investigation take on enormous proportions as one seriously penetrates it, there occurs the great transformation of the "theory of knowledge" and the theory of science whereby, in the end, science as a problem and as an accomplishment loses its self-sufficiency and becomes a mere partial problem.

What we have said also naturally applies to logic, as the a

priori theory of norms for everything "logical"—in the overarching sense of what is logical, according to which logic is
a logic of strict objectivity, of objective-logical truths. No one
ever thinks about the predications and truths which precede
science, about the "logic" which provides norms within this
sphere of relativity, or about the possibility, even in the case
of these logical structures conforming purely descriptively to
the life-world, of inquiring into the system of principles that
give them their norms a priori. As a matter of course, traditional objective logic is substituted as the a priori norm even
for this subjective-relative sphere of truth.

3. Analysis of the Transcendental Epochē. First Step: The Epochē of Objective Science

Because of the peculiar nature of the task which has arisen
for us, the method of access to the new science's field of work
—which must be attained before the working problems of
the science are given—is articulated into a multiplicity of
steps, each of which has, in a new way, the character of an
epochē, a withholding of natural, naïve validities and in general of validities already in effect. The first necessary epochē,
i.e., the first methodical step, has already come into view
through the preliminary reflections hitherto carried out. But
an explicit, universal formulation is needed. Clearly required
before everything else is the epochē in respect to all objective sciences. This means not merely an abstraction from
them, such as an imaginary transformation, in thought, of
present human existence, such that no science appeared in
the picture. What is meant is rather an epochē of all participation in the cognitions of the objective sciences, an epochē
of any critical position-taking which is interested in their
truth or falsity, even any position on their guiding idea of an
objective knowledge of the world. In short, we carry out an
epochē in regard to all objective theoretical interests, all
aims and activities belonging to us as objective scientists or

even simply as [ordinary] people desirous of [this kind of] knowledge.

Within this epochē, however, neither the sciences nor the scientists have disappeared for us who practice the epochē. They continue to be what they were before, in any case: facts in the unified context of the pregiven life-world; except that, because of the epochē, we do not function as sharing these interests, as coworkers, etc. We establish in ourselves just one particular habitual direction of interest, with a certain vocational attitude, to which there belongs a particular "vocational time."[8] We find the same thing here as elsewhere: when we actualize one of our habitual interests and are thus involved in our vocational activity (in the accomplishment of our work), we assume a posture of epochē toward our other life-interests, even though these still exist and are still ours. Everything has "its proper time," and in shifting [activities] we say something like: "Now it is time to go to the meeting, to the election," and the like.

In a special sense, of course, we call science, art, military service, etc., our "vocation," but as normal human beings we are constantly (in a broadened sense) involved in many "vocations" (interested attitudes) at the same time: we are at once fathers, citizens, etc. Every such vocation has its time of actualizing activities. Accordingly, this newly established vocational interest, whose universal subject matter is called the "life-world," finds its place among the other life-interests or vocations and it has "its proper time" within the one personal time, the form of the various exercised vocational times.

Of course, to equate the new science in this way with all "bourgeois" [*bürgerliche*] vocations, or even with the objective sciences, is a sort of trivialization, a disregard for the greatest value-distinction there can be between sciences. Understood in this way, it was so happily criticized by the modern irrationalistic philosophers. This way of looking at it makes it appear as if, once again, a new, purely theoretical interest, a new "science" with a new vocational technique, is to be established, carried on either as an intellectualistic game with very ideal pretensions or as a higher-level intellectual technique in the service of the positive sciences, useful for them, while they themselves, in turn, have their only real value in their usefulness for life. One is powerless against the misrepresentations of hurried readers and listeners who in the end hear only what they want to hear; but in any case they are part of the indifferent mass audience of the philosopher. The few, for whom one [really] speaks, will know how to restrain such a suspicion, especially after what we have said in earlier lectures. They will at least wait to see where our path leads them.

(There are good reasons for my stressing so sharply the vocational character of even the "phenomenologist's" attitude) One of the first things to be described about the epochē in question is that it is a habitual epochē of accomplishment, one with periods of time in which it results in work, while other times are devoted to other interests of work or play; furthermore, and most importantly the suspension of its accomplishment in no way changes the interest which continues and remains valid within personal subjectivity—i.e., its habitual directedness toward goals which persist as its validities—and it is for this very reason that it can be actualized again and again, at different times, in this identical sense. This by no means implies, however, that the life-world epochē —to which further significant moments belong, as we shall show—means no more for human existence, practically and "existentially," than the vocational epochē of the cobbler, or that it is basically a matter of indifference whether one is a cobbler or a phenomenologist, or, also, whether one is a phenomenologist or a positive scientist. Perhaps it will even become manifest that the total phenomenological attitude and the epochē belonging to it are destined in essence to effect, at first, a complete personal transformation, comparable in the beginning to a religious conversion, which then, however, over and above this, bears within itself the significance of the greatest existential transformation which is assigned as a task to mankind as such.

4. How Can the Life-World, after the Epochē of the Objective Sciences, Become the Subject Matter of a Science? The Distinction in Principle between the Objective-Logical a priori and the a priori of the Life-World

If our interest is exclusively in the "life-world," we must ask: Has the life-world, through the epochē in respect to objective science, already been laid open as a universal scientific subject matter?*

Do we already have thereby, the subject matter for statements that are generally valid scientifically, statements about

---

*First let us recall that what we call science is, within the constantly valid world, as life-world, a particular type of purposeful activities and purposeful accomplishments like all human vocations in the usual sense of the word; to this sphere also belong those practical intentions of a higher level which do not involve types of vocation or goal-oriented interrelations and accomplishments at all, the more or less isolated, incidental, more or less fleeting interests. All these are, from the human point of view, peculiarities of human life and of human habitualities, and they all lie within the universal framework of the life-world into which all accomplishments flow and to which all human beings and all accomplishing activities and capacities always belong. Of course, the new theoretical interest in the universal life-world itself, in its own manner of being, requires a certain epochē in regard to all these interests, i.e., in regard to the pursuit of our ends, in regard to all the criticism, always belonging to the purposeful life, of the means and the goals or ends themselves, e.g., whether we should factually persist in them, whether certain paths should be taken as general directives, etc. Living toward our ends, which are valid for us habitually, we do, of course, live in the horizon of the life-world, no matter which ends are "having their turn"; everything that happens and develops here exists in the life-world and in the manner of the life-world; but being oriented toward what exists within the life-world is not the same as focusing on the [life-world] as the universal horizon, not the same as making thematic the end in view *as* a being within this horizon, the newly thematic life-world. Thus the first thing we must do is refrain from the pursuit of all scientific and other interests. But the epochē alone is not enough: even all setting of ends, all projecting, presupposes something worldly; the *wherewith*, i.e., the life-world, is given prior to all ends. [This last sentence is only a rough guess at the sense of this somewhat garbled stenographic note.–TRANS.]

facts that are to be established scientifically? How do we have the life-world as a universal field, fixed in advance, of such establishable facts? It is the spatiotemporal world of things as we experience them in our pre- and extrascientific life and as we know them to be experienceable beyond what is [actually] experienced. We have a world-horizon as a horizon of possible thing-experience [*Dingerfahrung*]. Things: that is, stones, animals, plants, even human beings and human products; but everything here is subjective and relative, even though normally, in our experience and in the social group united with us in the community of life, we arrive at "secure" facts; within a certain range this occurs of its own accord, that is, undisturbed by any noticeable disagreement; sometimes, on the other hand, when it is of practical importance, it occurs in a purposive knowing process, i.e., with the goal of [finding] a truth which is secure for our purposes. But when we are thrown into an alien social sphere, that of the Negroes in the Congo, Chinese peasants, etc., we discover that their truths, the facts that for them are fixed, generally verified or verifiable, are by no means the same as ours. But if we set up the goal of a truth about the objects which is unconditionally valid for all subjects, beginning with that on which normal Europeans, normal Hindus, Chinese, etc., agree in spite of all relativity—beginning, that is, with what makes objects of the life-world, common to all, identifiable for them and for us (even though conceptions of them may differ), such as spatial shape, motion, sense-quality, and the like—then we are on the way to objective science. When we set up this objectivity as a goal (the goal of a "truth in itself") we make a set of hypotheses through which the pure life-world is surpassed. We have precluded *this* [type of] "surpassing" through the first epochē (that which concerns the objective sciences), and now we have the embarrassment of wondering what else can be undertaken scientifically, as something that can be established once and for all and for everyone.

But this embarrassment disappears as soon as we consider that the life-world does have, in all its relative features, a *general structure.* This general structure, to which everything that exists relatively is bound, is not itself relative. We can attend to it in its generality and, with sufficient care, fix it once and for all in a way equally accessible to all. As life-world the world has, even prior to science, the "same" structures that the objective sciences presuppose in their substruction of a world which exists "in itself" and is determined through "truths in themselves" (this substruction being taken for granted due to the tradition of centuries); these are the same structures that they presuppose as a priori structures and systematically unfold in a priori sciences, sciences of the *logos,* the universal methodical norms by which any knowledge of the world existing "in itself, objectively" must be bound. Prescientifically, the world is already a spatiotemporal world; to be sure, in regard to this spatiotemporality there is no question of ideal mathematical points, of "pure" straight lines or planes, no question at all of mathematically infinitesimal continuity or of the "exactness" belonging to the sense of the geometrical a priori. The bodies familiar to us in the life-world are actual bodies, but not bodies in the sense of physics. The same thing is true of causality and of spatiotemporal infinity. [These] categorical features of the life-world have the same names but are not concerned, so to speak, with the theoretical idealizations and the hypothetical substructions of the geometrician and the physicist. As we already know, physicists, who are men like other men, who know themselves as living in the life-world, the world of their human interests, have, under the title of physics, a particular sort of questions and (in a broader sense) practical projects directed toward the things of the life-world, and their "theories" are the practical results. Just as other projects, practical interests, and their realizations belong to the life-world, presuppose it as ground, and enrich it with their activity, so it is with science, too, as a human project and praxis. And this includes, as we have said, everything objectively a priori, with its necessary reference back to a corresponding a priori of the life-world. This reference-back is one of a founding of validity [*Geltungsfundierung*]. A certain idealizing accomplishment is what brings about the higher-level meaning-formation and ontic validity of the mathematical and every other objective a priori on the basis of the life-world a priori. Thus the latter ought first to become a subject of scientific investigation in its peculiarity and purity, and then one ought to set the systematic task of understanding how, on this basis and in what manners of new meaning-formation, the objective a priori comes about as a mediated theoretical accomplishment. What is needed, then, would be a systematic division of the universal structures—universal life-world a priori and universal "objective" a priori—and then also a division among the universal inquiries according to the way in which the "objective" a priori is grounded in the "subjective-relative" a priori of the life-world or how, for example, mathematical self-evidence has its source of meaning and source of legitimacy in the self-evidence of the life-world.

This consideration has a particular interest for us even though we have already detached our problem of a science of the life-world from the problem of objective science in that we, caught up through our schooling in the traditional objectivistic metaphysics, at first have no means of access whatever to the idea of a universal a priori belonging purely to the life-world. What we need first is a separation in principle of the latter from the objective a priori which is [always] immediately substituted for it. It is this very separation that is effected by the first epochē of all objective sciences, if we understand it also as the epochē of all objective a priori sciences and make it complete through the considerations we have just carried out. The latter provide us, in addition, with the fundamental insight that the universal a priori of the objective-logical level—that of the mathematical sciences and all others which are a priori in the usual sense—is grounded in a universal a priori which is in itself prior, precisely that of the pure life-world. Only through recourse to this a priori, to be unfolded in an a priori science of its own, can our a priori sciences, the objective-logical ones, achieve a truly radical, a seriously scientific, grounding, which under the circumstances they absolutely require.

Here we can also say: The supposedly completely self-sufficient logic which modern mathematical logicians [*Logistiker*] think they are able to develop, even calling it a truly scientific philosophy, namely, as the universal, a priori, fundamental science for all objective sciences, is nothing but naïveté. Its self-evidence lacks scientific grounding in the universal life-world a priori, which it always presupposes in the form of things taken for granted, which are never scientifically, universally formulated, never put in the general form proper to a science of essence. Only when this radical, fundamental science exists can such a logic itself become a science. Before this it hangs in mid-air, without support, and is, as it has been up to now, so very naïve that it is not even aware of the task which attaches to every objective logic, every a priori science in the usual sense, namely, that of discovering how this logic itself is to be grounded, hence no longer "logically" but by being traced back to the universal prelogical a priori through which everything logical, the total edifice of objective theory in all its methodological forms, demonstrates its legitimate sense and from which, then, all logic itself must receive its norms.

Yet this insight surpasses the interest in the life-world which governs us now; for this, as we have said, all that counts is the distinction in principle between the objective-logical and the life-world a priori; and the purpose of this is to be able to set in motion a radical reflection upon the great task of a pure theory of essence of the life-world.

5. The Formal and most General Structures of the Life-World: Thing and World on the One Side, Thing-Consciousness on the Other

If we seek out, simply looking around us, what is formal and general, what remains invariant in the life-world throughout all alternations of the relative, we involuntarily stop at what alone determines for us in life the sense of talking about the world: the world is the universe of things, which are distributed within the world-form of space-time and are "positional" in two senses (according to spatial position and temporal position)—the spatiotemporal *onta*. Here would thus be found the task of a life-world ontology, understood as a concretely general doctrine of essence for these *onta*. For our interest in the present context it suffices to have indicated this. Rather than spend our time here, we prefer to move on to a task which is much greater, as will soon be seen —one which in fact encompasses such a doctrine. In order to prepare the way for this new subject of investigation, which also essentially concerns the life-world but is not ontological, we shall undertake a general reflection—we, that is, as waking, living human beings in the life-world (and thus naturally within the epochē regarding all interference of positive scientific discipline).

This general reflection will at the same time have the function of making evident an essential distinction among the possible ways in which the pregiven world, the ontic universe [*das ontische Universum*], can become thematic for us. Calling to mind what has repeatedly been said: the life-world, for us who wakingly live in it, is always already there, existing in advance for us, the "ground" of all praxis whether theoretical or extratheoretical. The world is pregiven to us, the waking, always somehow practically interested subjects, not occasionally but always and necessarily as the universal field of all actual and possible praxis, as horizon. To live is always to live-in-certainty-of-the-world. Waking life is being awake to the world, being constantly and directly "conscious" of the world and of oneself as living *in* the world, actually experiencing [*erleben*] and actually effecting the ontic certainty of the world. The world is pregiven thereby, in every case, in such a way that individual things are given. But there exists a fundamental difference between the way we are conscious of the world and the way we are conscious of things or objects (taken in the broadest sense, but still purely in the sense of the life-world), though together the two make up an inseparable unity. Things, objects (always understood purely in the sense of the life-world), are "given" as being valid for us in each case (in some mode or other of ontic certainty) but in principle only in such a way that we are conscious of them as things or objects *within the world-horizon*. Each one is something, "something of" the world of which we are constantly conscious as a horizon. On the other hand, we are conscious of this horizon only as a horizon for existing objects; without particular objects of consciousness it cannot be actual [*aktuell*]. Every object has its possible varying modes of being valid, the modalizations of ontic certainty. The world, on the other hand, does not exist as *an* entity, as an object, but exists with such uniqueness that the plural makes no sense when applied to it. Every plural, and every singular drawn from it, presupposes the world-horizon. This difference between the manner of being of an object in the world and that of the world itself obviously prescribes fundamentally different correlative types of consciousness for them.

6. The Two Possible Fundamental Ways of Making the Life-World Thematic: the Naïve and Natural Straightforward Attitude and the Idea of a Consistently Reflective Attitude toward the "How" of the Subjective Manner of Givenness of Life-World and Life-World Objects

These most general features of waking life make up the formal framework within which it now becomes possible to distinguish the different ways this life is carried on, though in all cases the world is pregiven and, within this horizon, objects are given. These ways result in the different manners, we could also say, in which we are awake to the world and to the objects in the world. The first, the naturally normal

one which absolutely must precede the others not for accidental but for essential reasons, is that of straightforwardly
living toward whatever objects are given, thus toward the
world-horizon, in normal, unbroken constancy, in a synthetic
coherence running through all acts. This normal, straightforward living, toward whatever objects are given, indicates
that all our interests have their goals in objects. The pregiven
world is the horizon which includes all our goals, all our ends,
whether fleeting or lasting, in a flowing but constant manner,
just as an intentional horizon-consciousness implicitly "encompasses" [everything] in advance. We, the subjects, in our
normal, unbroken, coherent life, know no goals which extend beyond this; indeed we have no idea that there could
be others. All our theoretical and practical themes, we can
also say, lie always within the normal coherence of the life-
horizon "world." World is the universal field into which all
our acts, whether of experiencing, of knowing, or of outward
action, are directed. From this field, or from objects in each
case already given, come all affections, transforming themselves in each case into actions.

Yet there can be a completely different sort of waking life
involved in the conscious having of the world. It would consist in a transformation of the thematic consciousness of the
world which breaks through the normality of straightforward
living. Let us direct our attention to the fact that in general
the world or, rather, objects are not merely pregiven to us
all in such a way that we simply have them as the substrates
of their properties but that we become conscious of them
(and of everything ontically meant) through subjective manners of appearance, or manners of givenness, without notic-
ing it in particular; in fact we are for the most part not even
aware of it at all. Let us now shape this into a new universal
direction of interest; let us establish a consistent universal
interest in the "how" of the manners of givenness and in the
onta themselves, not straightforwardly but rather as objects
in respect to their "how"—that is, with our interest exclu-

manner of givenness.

sively and constantly directed toward *how,* throughout the alteration of relative validities, subjective appearances, and opinions, the coherent, universal validity *world—the* world —comes into being for us; how, that is, there arises in us the constant consciousness of the universal existence, of the universal horizon, of real, actually existing objects, each of which we are conscious of only through the alterations of our relative conceptions [*Auffassungen*] of it, of its manners of appearing, its modes of validity, even when we are conscious of it in particularity as something simply being there.

In this total change of interest, carried out with a new consistency founded on a particular resolve of the will, we notice that we acquire a number of never thematically investigated types, not only of individual things but also of syntheses, in an inseparable synthetic totality which *a new.* is constantly produced by intentionally overlapping *organi-* horizon-validities; and the latter influence each other recip- *of* rocally in the form of corroborating verifications of existence, *perception* or refuting cancelings-out, or other modalizations. This is the essential character of the synthetic totality in which we can take possession of something previously completely unknown, something never envisioned or grasped as a task for knowledge; this is the universal accomplishing life in which the world comes to be as existing for us constantly in flowing particularity, constantly "pregiven" to us. We can also say: this is the synthetic totality in which we now discover, for the first time, that and how the world, as correlate of a discoverable universe of synthetically connected accomplishments, acquires its ontic meaning and its ontic validity in the totality of its ontic [*ontische*] structures.

But here we do not need to go into more detailed expositions, into everything that can become thematic. What is essential for us here is the distinction between the two types of investigation,[9] each regarded as a universal investigation.

The natural life, whether it is prescientifically or scientifically, theoretically or practically interested, is life within a universal unthematic horizon. This horizon is, in the natural attitude, precisely the world always pregiven as that which exists. Simply living on in this manner, one does not need the word "pregiven"; there is no need to point out that the world is constantly actuality for us. All natural questions, all theoretical and practical goals taken as themes—as existing, as perhaps existing, as probable, as questionable, as valuable, as project, as action and result of action—have to do with something or other within the world-horizon. This is true even of illusions, nonactualities, since everything characterized through some modality of being is, after all, related to actual being. For, in advance, "world" has the meaning "the universe of the 'actually' existing actualities": not the merely supposed, doubtful, or questionable actualities but the actual ones, which as such have actuality for us only in the constant movement of corrections and revisions of validities [*Umgeltungen von Geltungen*]—all this considered as the anticipation of an ideal unity.

Instead of persisting in this manner of "straightforwardly living into the world," let us attempt a universal change of interest in which the new expression "pregivenness of the world" becomes necessary because it is the title for this differently directed and yet again universal theme of the manners of pregivenness. In other words, nothing shall interest us but precisely that subjective alteration of manners of givenness, of manners of appearing and of the modes of validity in them, which, in its constant process, synthetically connected as it incessantly flows on, brings about the coherent consciousness of the straightforward "being" of the world.

Among the objects of the life-world we also find human beings, with all their human action and concern, works and suffering, living in common in the world-horizon in their particular social interrelations and knowing themselves to be such. All this, too, then, shall be included as we carry out our new universal direction of interest. A coherent theoretical interest shall now be directed exclusively toward the universe of the subjective, in which the world, in virtue of the universality of synthetically bound accomplishments in this universe, comes to have its straightforward existence for us. In the natural and normal world-life this subjective manifold constantly goes on, but there it remains constantly and necessarily concealed. How, by what method, is it to be revealed? Can it be shown to be a self-enclosed universe with its own theoretical and consistently maintained inquiry, revealing itself as the all-encompassing unity of ultimately functioning and accomplishing subjectivity which is to account for the existence of the world—the world for us, our natural life-horizon? If this is a legitimate and a necessary task, its execution implies the creation of a new science of a peculiar sort. In opposition to all previously designed objective sciences, which are sciences on the ground of the world, this would be a science of the universal *how* of the pregivenness of the world, i.e., of what makes it a universal ground for any sort of objectivity. And included in this is the creation of a science of the ultimate grounds [*Gründe*] which supply the true force of all objective grounding, the force arising from its ultimate bestowal of meaning.

Our historically motivated path, moving from the interpretation of the interplay of problems between Hume and Kant, has now led us to the postulate of clarifying the pregiven world's character of universally "being the ground" for all objective sciences and—what followed of itself—for all objective praxis; it has led us, then, to the postulate of that novel universal science of subjectivity as pregiving the world. We shall now have to see how we can fulfill this postulate. We notice thereby that the first step which seemed to help at the beginning, that epochē through which we freed ourselves from all objective sciences as grounds of validity, by no means suffices. In carrying out this epochē, we obviously continue to stand on the ground of the world; it is now reduced to the life-world which is valid for us prescientifically; it is just that we may use no sort of knowledge arising from the sciences as premises, and we may take the sciences into consideration only as historical facts, taking no position of our own on their truth.

But nothing about this affects our interested looking-around in the prescientifically intuited world or our paying attention to its relative features. In a certain way, concern with this sort of thing belongs continually even to [one type of] objective investigation, namely, that of the historians, who must, after all, reconstruct the changing, surrounding life-worlds of the peoples and periods with which they deal. In spite of this, the pregiven world is still valid as a ground [for them] and has not been transposed into the universe of the purely subjective, a universal framework in its own right, which is our concern now.

The same thing holds [even] if we take as our subject of investigation, in the unity of a systematic survey, all [historical] periods and peoples and finally the entire spatiotemporal world, paying constant attention to the relativity of the surrounding life-worlds of particular human beings, peoples, and periods as mere matters of fact. It is clear that the same thing is true of this world survey, in the form of an iterated synthesis of relative, spatiotemporal life-worlds, that is true of a survey of one such life-world individually. It is taken one part at a time and then, at a higher level, one surrounding world, one temporal period, at a time; each particular intuition [yields] an ontic validity, whether in the mode of actuality or possibility. As each intuition occurs, it presupposes others having objective validity—presupposes for us, the observers, the general ground of the validity of the world.

NOTES

1. *okkasionelle.* A term from the second of the *Logische Untersuchungen,* § 26 (1913 ed., Vol. II, p. 81): an expression is "essentially subjective and occasional" if its actual meaning depends "on the occasion [*Gelegenheit*], the person speaking, and his situation."

2. This whole paragraph is crossed out in the MS.

3. This sentence was added by Fink. It does not seem to fit in, and it breaks the continuity between the preceding and following sentences.

4. Husserl's use of *Evidenz* does not permit of its always being translated in the same way. But when used in its most special or technical sense, as it is here, "self-evidence" is better than simply "evidence." As can be seen from the context here, it means "self-givenness"; whereas the English word "evidence" usually has a very different meaning, that of something testifying to the existence of something else (e.g., evidence in a trial).

5. *"es selbst."* The use of the word "thing" in this expression is not out of place as long as Husserl is talking about perception. But in another context that which is "itself" given might not be a "thing"; it could be an ideal state of affairs, for example in mathematical or logical intuition.

6. The text reads "prescientific persons," which must be a mistake.

7. I.e., the subjective and the objective.

8. *Berufszeit,* colloq., "working hours." But I have translated it literally as "vocational time" in order to preserve the notion of *Beruf,* a "calling."

9. This could refer either to the "two ways of making the life-world thematic" (cf. section heading) or to the investigation of the "how" of the objects *vs.* the investigation of the subjective syntheses.

2

Work and the Word

PAUL RICOEUR

The nexus in our life between speech and work testifies in the most manifest way as to what tensions are maintained by the dynamics of personal existence and the distressing ups and downs of civilizations. This nexus is at once a very primitive and fundamental articulation of our condition and a very rarefied product of the cultures and techniques which history displays. Consequently, one may catch sight of it in a nascent state within a very elementary phenomenological analysis of *saying* and *doing*, as well as capture it at a very high level of complexity in terms of the problems raised in our time by the situation of literature in a technical civilization, by the uneasy feeling in the universities, by the orientation of technical education, by the human problems posed by industrial mechanization, etc. We shall therefore attempt to place ourselves at the two extremities

Reprinted from *History and Truth*, trans. Charles A. Kelbley (1965), pp. 197–219, by permission of Northwestern University Press, Evanston, Ill.

of this reflection: the side of the radical and the side of the present; the side of the roots of work and of speech, and the side of the contemporary tasks of a civilization of work and speech. A meditative interlude on the power of speech will separate the two versants.

But why this theme? For me it is the means of approaching the problem of the unity of civilization from a new angle, a problem which I approach elsewhere by the question of truth and the multiple orders of truth. It had already occurred to me that a civilization advances as much by pluralization and complication of tasks as by the progress of this organic unity which is witnessed in great periods. The primordial dialectic of speech and work leads us to the scene of the same debate. In point of fact, this essay results from deception and anxiety: deception before the contemporary philosophies of work (Marxist, Existentialist, Christian); anxiety in face of the notion of the civilization of work.

The discovery or rediscovery of man as worker is one of the great events of contemporary thought. Our aspiration to establish a civilization of work is in complete accord with the presuppositions of this philosophy of work, and I fully adhere to these philosophical presuppositions and to this socio-economic aspiration. My whole analysis tends to reply to the deception and anxiety which arise within and which are fostered by this adhesion.

My deception is in seeing this rehabilitation of work triumph in a void. Such a reflection starts with a determined form of work: work as a struggle with physical nature in the traditional crafts and in industrial machinery; then, by degrees, the notion of work swells until it encompasses all scientific, moral, and even speculative activities, tending toward the very indeterminate notion of a militant and non-contemplative form of human existence. From this standpoint, work designates the entire human condition of man, since there is nothing that man effects but by a toilsome act; there is nothing human which is not *praxis*. Moreover, if one considers that man's being is identical with his activity, then one must say that man *is* work. And this leads one to ask whether the philosophy of work should not extend itself so as to include the contemplation which is available to man, if it is true that a new realm of becoming and militant activity is yet opened within the core of an eternal life of man. Let it be said, therefore, that human contemplation is work also.

Lastly, by situating work within the continuation of divine creation, can we not see how a theology of work would thus reinforce the foundations and broaden the perspectives of a philosophy of work?

It is precisely this glorification of work which troubles me. A notion which signifies everything no longer signifies anything. Reflection pretends to retain the benefit of the analyses in-which the notion of work has a determined meaning —it was expressed extremely well as the rugged virtue of the manual trades "in which one does not play with matter as with words or with a culture based upon words." But at the same time, the notion of work is broadened to the extreme so as to cumulate also the advantages which may be drawn from the indetermination of this notion. One is still thinking of manual work when one bestows upon man the general maxim: make and by making, make oneself [*faire et en faisant se faire*].

And yet there is no deceit in this mode of reflection which gradually changes the meaning of *doing* from the most material to the most intellectual activity. Resistances become more refined and rebellious nature, with which man the worker battles, takes shelter successively in the obscurity of a world to be understood and, ultimately, in ourselves, in the resistance of a defiant body and in the opacity of our passions. Herein there is no fraud but a dissimulated partiality and, it may be said, a sort of overzealousness.

The problem does not lie in somewhere interrupting this progress of reflection which gradually relates all the sectors of man's activity to his militant condition. The question is rather one of combining with this interpretation of the human condition another interpretation which penetrates it through and through. For step by step, the spoken word also annexes to itself everything human; there is not a kingdom of work and an empire of the spoken word which would set bounds to each other from without, but there is a power of the spoken word which traverses and penetrates everything human, including the machine, the utensil, and the hand.

My deception suddenly takes on meaning: does not this sort of relaxation in the void of the admirable notion of work result from the absence of a contrary which would be proportioned to it and which, by limiting it, would determine it? It is to be noted that amid this glorification of work, one selects for it a contrary which is too remote, too vague, and, in short, one which is visionary and foreign to the human condition: contemplation. This does not mean a human contemplation which is pragmatic, but *pure* contemplation, the gaze which would make itself present to everything in the instant, vision without effort because it is without resistance, possession without duration because it is without effort. To identify existence with work amounts to excluding pure contemplation from the properly human condition. All of which is vain, and in any case scarcely instructive, for such a limiting idea is not a valid counter-pole for reflection. It is a chimera which withdraws from us, it fails to consider the full scope of the human. Is it not more fruitful to discriminate meaningful contrasts within the very core of human finitude, within the heart of man's militant life? Is it not more enlightening to find in work a counter-pole of proper proportions, which heightens the meaning of it while calling into question its sufficiency? For example: should I say that I am working when I go home and rest? Am I working when I read, when I am at the theatre, when I am taking a walk? Am I working in friendship and in love? And am I working when I am tinkering around the house? The splendor of work lies in being in debate with other manners of existing and of thereby limiting them and being limited by them. For us, the spoken word will be this *other*—this other among others which justifies and challenges the glory of work.

I. Doing and Saying

Let it be said that the spoken word is also human; it too is a mode of finitude. It is not, as is pure contemplation, the transcending of the human condition; it is not the Word of God, the creative word, but the word of man, one aspect of his militant existence; it brings about and makes something within the world. Or to be more precise, speaking man makes something and makes himself, but otherwise than by working.

Let us watch the birth of the word on the brink of the gesture. Let us give the most favorable interpretation to the pragmatist conception of language: let us assume with Pierre Janet that the simplest word was a sort of imperative cry which, at first, accompanied and emotionally facilitated action (the experience called forth has no need of taking place in reality: it stands for an imaginative reconstruction which throws light on the present structure of language). The cry of the leader is detached from action as the initial phase which launches it; and thus the cry is word as soon as it incites to action instead of acting. The imperative cry therefore belongs to the cycle of the gesture: in a certain way it brings about the gesture. The cry is as a first, initiating fragment, then regulative of action. Step by step, every word may thus be brought back to *praxis:* in the simplest case it is only a moment of *praxis;* this moment becomes a stage of *praxis* as soon as the brief imperative cry takes on the proportions of an anticipating scheme, a Plan, this plan being only the verbal anticipation of *praxis.* Lastly, the whole structure of culture may be considered as the long detour which starts with action and returns to action.

Moment, stage, detour: the spoken word is, in a sense and

an authentic sense, an annex of the enterprises of transforming the human milieu by the human agent. This fundamental
possibility justifies a Marxist interpretation of culture in
which work is seen as the power which reorganizes the full
scope of the human.

And yet, from the outset, the spoken word transgresses the
bounds of the gesture and bolts forward. For the imperative
is now no longer an emotional portion of action in process;
in a certain way it already stands for the whole of action. It
"means" the whole of the gesture; it has an overview of it,
it supervises it. (We shall presently find that among the psy-
cho-technicians of industrial work this function of supervi-
sion—*Übersichtlichkeit*—contains in an embryonic way the
intellectuality capable of redeeming repetitious piecework;
thus we are not straying onto the fringes of the concrete
problems of civilization, but situating ourselves in advance
within the very core of the problems raised, for example, by
technical humanism.)

The imperative which presently arose on the confines of
the gesture in the act of being performed, allows for the
fulfillment of a first level of aloofness, a first reflective withdrawal, which, thanks to the interval, the gap hollowed into
the plenum of the gesture in the act of being performed,
allows for the projective design of the total gesture.

Taken at the level of the gesture, the spoken word outruns
every gesture by *signifying* it. It is the understood meaning
of what is to be done. On this basis, it is always possible to look
upon the history of work as saturated and carried forward by
a history of the spoken word. Garrulous man transforms his
utensils by anticipating in language new ways of relating the
body to matter. The tool prolongs the body to such an extent
that it cannot contain the principles of its own revolution
within itself. If the tool is left, so to speak, to itself, then it is
of the order of custom and dormancy, as is shown by the
permanence and resistance to change of small craft and farm
equipment. It is the spoken word which upsets the estab-

lished form of the gesture and the tool; failure and suffering plunge man into reflection and questioning. At this moment, the interior word takes form: what other way is there? The tool held in suspense, the spoken tool is suddenly penetrated by other forms of action; a disruption of the form, a restructuration of the uses of the body is effected by language; language anticipates, signifies, and assays all transformations within the imagination, within this inventive void opened by failure and interrogation on failure.

But above all, it is the spoken word which effects the passage from the tool to the machine. As Emmanuel Mounier said in *La Petite Peur du XXe siècle*, "the machine is not, as is the tool, a mere material prolongation of our limbs. It is of another order: an annex of our language, an auxiliary language of mathematics to penetrate, stamp out, and reveal the secret of things, their implicit intentions, their untapped possibilities."

It is because man has expressed space in geometry, instead of living and experiencing it in actual measurements, that mathematics has been possible and, through it, mathematical physics and the techniques resulting from successive industrial revolutions. It is striking that Plato contributed to the construction of Euclidian geometry through his work of denominating such concepts as line, surface, equality, and the similarity of figures, etc., which strictly forbade all recourse and all allusion to manipulations, to physical transformations of figures. This asceticism of mathematical language, to which we owe, in the last analysis, all our machines since the dawn of the mechanical age, would have been impossible without the logical heroism of a Parmenides denying the entirety of the world of becoming and of *praxis* in the name of the self-identity of significations. It is to this denial of movement and work that we owe the achievements of Euclid, of Galileo, modern mechanism, and all our devices and apparatus. For within these, all our knowledge is contracted, all the words which at first did not attempt to transform the world. Thanks to this conversion of language into pure thought, the technical world may today appear to us in its entirety as the invasion of the verbal world into the muscular world. This absorption of pragmatic behaviors by the comprehensive behavior is very illuminating: within the very core of productive activity it reveals to us the initial composition of, but also the nascent debate between the spoken word and work. This mutual encroachment is already original contestation: *praxis* annexes the spoken word to itself as a language of planning; but the spoken word is originally reflective aloofness, "consideration of meaning," *theoria* in the nascent state. This primitive and ever-recurring dialectic invites us to reject once and for all every behaviorist and, *a fortiori*, epiphenomenalist interpretation of the so-called cultural superstructures of society. Language is just as much infrastructure as superstructure. The schema of the infrastructure and the superstructure must be rejected resolutely, for here we encounter a strictly circular phenomenon in which the two terms, in turn, implicate each other and transcend each other.

2. Power of the Spoken Word

The word which is closest to work, the imperative word, is in its nascent state already a *critique* of work in the double sense of a judgment and an imposition of limits. It is a critique of work because it suspends from the outset the concern with living which is the soul of work. It assumes an aloof attitude, it *reflects*. But if it suspends this concern, it returns to it differently; it substitutes a new way of approach which still belongs to the militant condition of man, to human finitude: it returns to this concern on the level of *signs*. Let us linger for a while within the narrow framework of the imperative word which provided us with the means for opening a first breach in the closed preoccupation of action. What new *operation* does the word bring into play within the confines of work?

First, it initiates a specific action upon others, and this

pertains to *influence* and not to *production*. Production bears upon nature, be it material or not—upon an "it" in the third person. The influence, in the same imperative form of exigency, already presupposes another, a second person: whether it be urgent or refined, brutal or disguised, the exigency stirs up in others a "sequel" which is no longer an "effect." The relation of exigency-sequel[1] transcends the production-product relationship. The interhuman relationship, born of the word, endows work with both a contrast and a component. A contrast: for influence is something other than this action of non-reciprocal transformation characteristic of production. A component: for the influence at the same time enriches work with the whole gamut of interhuman relations: all labor is collaboration, that is, work which is not only shared but communicated to others. Psycho-sociology is constantly referring to this social and verbal stratum—social *because* verbal—of work. Thus low efficiency and fatigue are influenced by the deterioration of human relations which result not only from the division of work as such, but also from the social organization of work: relations of camaraderie within work-centers, relations of execution between research departments and workshops, relations of social subordination between management and labor, without excluding all the social relations which weave their way into the vast enterprise of business and labor. All these relations which order work (in all the senses of the word order) are found within the universe of the spoken word.

But the imperative word does not only work with respect to others, but also with regard to man who, through the word, becomes a signifying being. Whoever speaks pronounces also upon himself, decides himself; he thus passes judgment upon himself and this elucidates him and breaks up the previous affective confusion. The interior word, which every decision involves, is a striking manifestation of the promotion of mankind represented by the word: if I say nothing to myself, I do not emerge from the inhuman confusion of the beast. Without the word I am no more ordered than my work.

We shall have to distinguish, behind this work upon others and upon the self—behind the word which influences, behind the word by which I pass judgment upon myself and decide myself—the most dissimulated operation of the word: the operation of the sign itself on meaning, the promotion of meaning achieved by the word. The word, we said, does not "make" anything, at most it incites to action (whether this be by another or by myself treated as another); but if it incites to action this is because it *signifies* what is to be done and because the exigency signified to another is "understood" by him and "followed" by him.

To signify a meaning is, in a very complex way, to operate. It is not possible within the limitations of this essay to give more than a few allusive ideas on this operation which is nevertheless the true counterpart of work, even within work.

To begin with, there is no word without an activity of discrimination by which the verb of action and its agent (and eventually its term, its effect, its means) are distinguished. To this activity of discrimination is connected the great work of denomination, for the two activities are linked together: to distinguish and name objects, the aspects of objects, actions, qualities, etc. To discriminate is the first work, to articulate is the second. The word articulates in phrases, verbs and nouns, adjectives, complements, plurals, etc., and because of this we are able to master our action by a sort of "phrasing" of our gestures. All of our action is thus based upon distinctions and relations. Without this "phrasing" man remains inarticulate and in a state of confusion. The meaning of this phrasing is not a transformation of things or of ourselves, is not a production in the literal sense, but a signification, and every signification designates emptily what work will fulfill in the sense in which one fulfills a plan, a wish, a purpose.

This void of significations is undoubtedly the source of the misery of language and the misery of philosophy; but it is primarily responsible for the splendor of language, for it is through this void of significations, which designate without making something, that the word connects and structures action.

Now this "powerlessness" of the word, compared with the "power" of work, is certainly an operation, an achievement, without the word being, however, a work in the literal sense of the word. To express the same thing more concretely, what we called the "phrasing" of action is a "proposition" (in the sense in which we speak in grammar of a relative proposition or clause). Now, every proposition manifests an act of *setting forth*. The man who speaks *sets forth* a meaning; this is his verbal way of working.

This positional activity is dissimulated within the ordinary word, overworked as it is by use. It comes to the fore in mathematical language in which denomination is always fresh. "We call volume a portion of space limited in every direction. We call surface . . . we call line . . . lastly we call point. . . ." A short time ago, Brice Parain was amazed over this power of setting forth, of *forming* a meaning by naming: "Denomination is the first judgment . . . Our words create beings and . . . are not content to manifest sensations . . . Language is by its nature an abstraction in this sense that it does not manifest reality but signifies it in truth."[2] The responsibility of speaking correctly is surely overwhelming.

1. The Dubitative Word

The word is not only imperative; it is time to remove the restrictions which were imposed on our analysis by an entirely pedagogical fiction. Besides, a reflection on the positional work of language already transcended the framework of the imperative.

The word which wishes to express, the word which tries to understand and which aspires to be understood, is also the word as dubitative, as optative, and as poetic.

The imperative incites to action. The dubitative word

questions: What? What does that mean? There is questioning only because there is doubt; calling into question and putting into doubt. Just as the tool is characterized by custom and dormancy, the word in its first movement is custom and dormancy: one says that . . . The "one does it thus" is sustained by the "one says." Stagnant civilizations lie dormant upon their treasure of tools and phrases.

Belief, as a spontaneous movement of pre-critical existence, stamps with its everydayness all manners of working and speaking, and preserves gestures and locutions in dead tradition. The word is the awakening of the tool, as we said earlier, only because the word is the awakening of the word: "You think so?"

The dubitative word is directed toward the other, toward me, toward meaning. The dubitative word is *par excellence* the word addressed to another. The other is the man with a response. And in the response he is wholly second person; he is no longer the "it" characteristic of the factory-produced product but the "thou" who answers. Yet the word does imitate industrial work when it tries to produce a psychological effect after the fashion in which work obtains its effect, that is to say without reciprocity between the product and the producer. Such is the word of propaganda which achieves its psychological effects in the manner in which the machine draws an efficacious form from a wrought material. This word is quite removed from the cycle of question and answer. It produces; it does not call forth. Only doubt converts the word into question and questioning into dialogue, that is to say into a question *in view* of an answer and into an answer *to* a question.

The world of dialogue penetrates and outruns the world of work: it penetrates it because there is no work without a division of work and no division of work without a verbal exchange which portions out tasks and brings out the social meaning of human work. But the world of dialogue also transcends the world of work: the psycho-sociology of repetitious piecework informs us that, oddly enough, workers who are capable of freeing themselves mentally from a work which is the more effectual as it is the more automatic have a better output when they can "talk" while working. Here the word is an aid to work because it compensates it, because it *distracts* it. What shall we say, then, of dialogue as *leisure*, this leisure in which so many men are increasingly seeking their true self-expression, work becoming the necessary social sacrifice for its conquest?

But we shall prolong these diverse bearings of the word on work with respect to the civilization of work.

This appeal to another, turned toward myself, is the essential calling into question which creates the space of reflection and the space of freedom: "I wonder if. . . ." Interior dialogue is reflection itself. I make myself the man of *irony*. Henceforth, the indisputable worm is in the fruit of my own customs, in the tree of work, in the stump of belief. The word is critical and makes every position critical. The end of "naïveté" begins. Naïveté is of the order of the "there is": there are things, there is nature, there is history, there is the law of work, there is the power of those who command. The thing, the act of making and inciting to action is virtually brought into question by the dubitative word: world, work, and tyrants are globally contested by the corrosive power of the word. The great philosophers of the question—and of the "calling into question"—Socrates, Descartes, Hume, Kant, Husserl have elucidated and carried to its extreme point this dubitative genius of the word. In this they are the soul of every culture which rebels against the always premature syntheses proposed and imposed by the civilizations of collective belief, whether the unifying theme of these civilizations be the robe, the sword, or the tool.

Still more radically, the dubitative word effects the decisive revolution within the order of significations: it introduces the dimension of the *possible* into the undivided fabric of the brute fact (in the double sense of being a fact and the reporting of a fact). By creating the realm of the free play

of possibility, the word recaptures the meaning of the real—
of doing and of the fact—in terms of possible meaning; this
is what is done by scientific law, juridical law. It is also this
"disengagement" of thought by means of the question which
makes possible all "engagement," as a movement subsequent upon reflection, as a responsible act.

If we examine the matter closely, we find that dubitative
thought is the true founder of all thought which denies and
which affirms, and ultimately of the most simple statements.
For the decisive response, the first response, is the one which
says *no*, the one which introduces negativity into significations: all that is, is; but the word can express what is not; and
in this way what is done may be undone. To deny is to cancel
out a possible meaning. It is the unproductive gesture *par
excellence;* a gesture which does not work; but a gesture
which introduces into spontaneous belief, into the naïve positing of meaning, the decisive feature which cancels and
deposes the positing, much as a prince is deposed. Hereafter
the world of the word is one in which one *denies.* This is why
this world is also one in which one affirms: affirmation under-
scores what negation may cancel or has already cancelled; it
validates what negation invalidates. It is in the world of the
dubitative word that there are contestations. It is in the
world of contestation that there are affirmations.

Consequently, one may say that even statements which on
the surface only record facts are conquests of dubitative
thought; for a statement is like an answer whose question is
left out. There is no narrative which does not answer virtually the question: what happened? How did that take place?
And all science is like an answer to the quandaries of perception, erected by philosophy into doubt over the meaning of
sensible qualities and into denial of the prestige of appearances.

This doubt and this denial alone have been able to open
this realm of possibility in which we have seen appear a law
as abstract and as unreal as, for example, the principle of
inertia, to which no submissiveness to appearances had been

able to lead and from which we have nevertheless derived all thought on mechanism.

2. Invocation

It would not be just, however, to enclose the whole of the power of the word within the alternative between the imperative and the critical functions, even when broadening the empire of the dubitative word to affirmation and expression.

Protagoras maintained that the four roots of the word were the command, the wish or request, the question, and the answer. This title—*eukhôlé:* wish, request—opens a vast arena of the word which protects speaking man from the alternative between the imperative, which would ultimately become identified with work, and doubt which, in the last analysis, would destroy man as worker.

Strictly speaking, another empire opens up here: the request which expects everything from another, which offers man to the benevolence of another, is no longer concerned with the self as worker, nor with the ironic self, but, if you will, with the "beseeching" [*orant*] self. It is a human word which is not altogether disenchanted: turned toward God, it *invokes Him* in the language of the chorus of Greek tragedy, in that of the Hebraic psalm, in that of Christian liturgies, in that of the spontaneous prayer of the believer which borders on the everyday modality. Turned toward the world, it attempts to be the *veritable chant* expressing the uncommon meaning, the freshness, the strangeness, the horror, the sweetness, the first upheaval, peace: Hölderlin and Rilke, Ramuz and Claudel demonstrate that the word is not confined to the verbal function of daily living, to techniques and sciences, to codes, politics, politeness, and ordinary conversations.

Turned toward abstract significations, the word which requests is the *optative* of value, the fundamental act of evaluation. It is not by chance that Socrates fought the battle of language over the meaning of the word "virtue," that is to say, the good in man. In opening the field of the possible, the word opens also that of the better. Henceforth the question is posed: what does my work mean, that is to say, what is its value? Work is human work beginning with this question concerning the personal and communal value of work; and this question is a matter for the word.

Turned toward men and toward myself, the word which "entreats" is *par excellence* the language of *exclamation*. If the human condition may be discovered and expressed in its fundamental affective dispositions, it is because the cry has been replaced by the chant, a language similar to that of invocation which has seized the daily expressions of sadness and joy, of anger and fear so as to elevate them to the lyrical level of purified expression. Greek tragedy, the tragedy of Aeschylus, chanted the bitter knowledge which the human heart forges in the rugged school of sorrow, transfigured by the chant and placed under the sign of invocation:

> Zeus, whatever his true name be,
> If this be a name acceptable,
> By this name will I call him.
> When I have reckoned all, only
> Zeus I recognize as capable of
> Removing the burden which weighs
> Me down with Anguish. . . .
> He has shown man the way of
> Wisdom in giving him this maxim:
> 'That man must learn by suffering.'
> In the fullness of sleep, like dropping
> Rain, descend the many memories of pain
> Before the vision of the Spirit.
> —Wisdom thus acquired against the will.
> And this, I believe, is the grace of the
> Gods forced upon us from above.
> (Agamemnon)

Thus the word develops self-awareness and self-expression in multiple directions which we have only outlined in passing: the imperative word by which I come to a decision, bringing judgment upon my affective confusion; the dubitative word by which I question myself and bring myself into question; the indicative word by which I consider, deem, and declare myself to be such; but also the lyrical word by which I chant the fundamental feelings of mankind and of solitude.

At the end of this interlude on the power of the word, the mutual permeation of work and the word becomes evident as well as their latent dissociation.

Perhaps it may be said that there is work whenever man produces a useful effect which answers his needs and that this is done by means of a more or less toilsome effort working against the resistant qualities of nature, whether this latter be outside of us or within us.

In a sense, work encompasses the word, since speaking requires also a more or less laborious effort or even a profession which produces useful effects responding to the demands of a group, even if this were only a stage in the production of things. But the essence of language falls outside of the scope of work: *the word signifies and does not produce.* The end of production is a real effect, that of the word an understood meaning. Moreover, the word is always in some degree *gratuitous;* it is never certain that a word will be useful. Because it searches, it arouses needs, transforms tools; but it may also be sufficient unto itself in axioms; it witnesses, it questions, it invokes. It may also be used so as to say nothing, to gossip, to lie, to deceive and, lastly, to lead to delirium. Consequently, work may easily put to shame the word which, it seems, does not make anything. Hamlet *speaks* of the vanity of speech: *words! words! words!*

But what would the civilization of work be without the splendor and vanity of the word?

3. Toward a Civilization of Work and the Spoken Word

How does this dialectic of work and the word help us to become oriented in the present problems of civilization? Essentially in this: that it puts us on guard against a sham resolution of the tensions which support the movement of our civilization.

The present form of this dialectic will pass away, and this is as it should be. But other forms will rise up and pose new problems.

1. "Alienation" and "Objectification" in Work

The present historical form of the dialectic of work and the word is dominated by two factors which may not be reduced to each other:

1. Human work is *alienated in the wage-earning classes*, it is contracted for as work detached from the person; it is treated as a thing which is subject to the laws of the market. This *socio-economic* degradation of work is a function of the socio-economic regime of capitalism. One may hope that it disappears along with the conditions of the wage-earner. To this socio-economic degradation of work corresponds the usurped dignity of the word which is all the more arrogant as it does not seem to realize that it too is negotiated on a market of services: there is an arrogance in culture which is precisely symmetrical with the humiliation in work, both of which must disappear. The roots of this arrogance are deep-seated; they are immersed in Antiquity (Greek, and not Jewish, it should be noted); work being the act of the slave— being *servile*—culture was the deed of the free man, it was *liberal*. The opposition between the servile arts and the liberal arts is therefore greatly dependent upon the social condition assigned to the worker himself within historical societies; and culture evaluates itself, or rather over-evalu-

ates itself, in the measure that it solidifies the regime which devaluates work.

Furthermore, there is a culpability which clings to culture to the extent that it is directly or indirectly a means of exploiting work: those who possess knowledge, the articulate, are the ones who command, who undertake, who run the risks (since a capitalistic economy is one which is based upon calculations and risks). "Intellectuals" are needed to construct the theory of the system, to teach it and justify it in the very eyes of its victims. In short, capitalism has been able to perpetuate itself as an economy only because it has also been a culture, or even an ethic and a religion. Thus the word is culpable for the degradation of work. This is why revolutionary thought kindles an understandable resentment against the whole of classical culture, that is, when this culture is viewed as a bourgeois culture which has paved the way for and kept in power an exploiting class. Every man who thinks and writes, without being hindered in his study or his research by a regime in which his work is negotiated as a merchandise, must perceive that his freedom and joy are corrupt, for they are the counterpart and, whether closely or remotely, the condition and means of work which elsewhere is without freedom and without joy, because he knows himself and feels himself being treated as a thing.

2. But the modern condition of work is not merely defined by the socio-economic conditions of capitalism, but also by the *technological form* given to it by successive industrial revolutions. This form is relatively independent of the regime of capital and work and raises problems which are not solved by revolutions at the level of the social and economic regime of work, even if these revolutions should permit a clearer presentation of the problems and lead to an easier solution of them. The fragmentation of ancient crafts into partial and repetitious tasks which demand less and less professional qualification raises a disturbing problem. The philosopher's and theologian's eulogy of work must not lose

itself in the clouds, not at the very moment when an ever-increasing mass of workers tends to consider its work as a mere social sacrifice which no longer has meaning and joy in itself, but outside of itself: in the enjoyment of the consumer and the pleasures of leisure time won through the shortening of the workday. Today this fragmentation into partial and repetitious tasks reaches not only industrial work, but also office work and is found in different forms in scientific specialization, in medical specialization, and in varying degrees, in all forms of intellectual work.

It is true that this fragmentation and specialization are counterbalanced at all levels by the appearance of new crafts: constructors, regulators, machine repairers; likewise, we are witnessing reorganizations of scientific disciplines, thanks to new theories which encompass and systematize disciplines which up to now have been separate. Later on, we shall have to come back to the measure in which this *polyvalence*, which counterbalances *specialization*, is not the fruit of a theoretical and disinterested culture, a culture with a remote efficacity, which constantly returns to and corrects the technical training of the specialized worker and the specialized scientific researcher.

I am wondering, then, whether the technological condition of modern work does not manifest, over and above social "alienations," a misery of work which pertains to its "objectifying" function. This "objectification," by which man realizes himself, fulfills himself, and reaches his perfection, has certainly been extolled. It has even been looked upon as the philosophical solution of the debates between realism and idealism, subjectivism and materialism, etc., and, in short, the solution to the ancient problems arising from the theory of knowledge and from ontology. The essence of work lies in linking me to a precise and finite task; herein I show what I am by demonstrating what I can do; and I show what I am capable of by doing something limited; it is the "finiteness" of my task which reveals me to others and to myself. This is certainly true; but this same movement which reveals me also dissimulates me; what realizes me depersonalizes me. One can easily see in the evolution of crafts—including that of the intellectual—that there is a limit toward which this movement of objectification is tending: this limit constitutes my destruction in the gesture devoid of meaning, in activity which is literally meaningless because it is without horizon. But to be a man is not only to concern oneself with the finite, but it is also to comprehend the whole and thus to direct oneself toward this other limit, the inverse of the gesture devoid of meaning, toward the horizon of the totality of human existence which I call world or being. By means of this breakthrough proposed to us by modern work, we are suddenly brought back to our remarks on the word as signifying the whole, as a will to understand by the whole.

Perhaps the modern evolution of work therefore only serves to reveal a profound tendency of work which is to absorb us into the finite while fulfilling us. This imperceptible loss of self is betrayed by a sort of *ennui* which gradually replaces the *suffering* connected to the execution of work, as if the labor of objectification became reincarnated more subtly in a sort of psychic illness inherent in the fragmentation and the repetition of modern work.

This tendency is irreducible to "alienation," which in the literal sense is the swallowing up of man not only into another, but also to the profit of another man who exploits him. Alienation raises a social and ultimately *political* problem; objectification raises a *cultural* problem.

Let us ask, therefore, if there is not, in the present-day unrest of culture, something which answers correlatively to the fundamental unrest in contemporary work. Over and above the bourgeois perversion of culture, we find that the arts, literature, and university teaching express man's muffled resistance to adapt himself to the modern world.

This resistance is certainly not unadulterated. It betrays the panic of adolescent man in face of the abrupt mutations of the technical world. It expresses the rupture of an ancient relation of man to a "natural" environment; it attests to the anxiety over a disrupted temporal rhythm. This confusion is also found in a bad conscience, that of Valéry's Socrates who, encountering the architect Eupalinos in Hell, regrets having constructed nothing with his hands and having merely thought, that is, *talked*. And the bad conscience, as always, turns to resentment: for if Socrates finds that he has not left the shadows of the cave for the reality of Ideas, but that he has merely left the reality of machines for the shadows of discourse, then Socrates will hate machines and reality.

Nothing in all of the above is pure or absolutely authentic. Over and above this confusion and this bad conscience, which, oddly enough, come together, culture expresses a legitimate refusal toward adaptation. Culture is also that which unadapts man, keeps him ready for the open, for the remote, for the other, for the all. It is the function of the humanities, of history, and especially of philosophy to offset "objectification" by "reflection," to compensate for the adaptation of man as worker to finite tasks by the interrogation of critical man upon his human condition in its entirety and by the chant of poetic man. *Education*, in the strong sense of the word, is perhaps only the just but difficult equilibrium between the exigency for objectification—that is, adaptation— and the exigency for reflection and unadaptation. It is this taut equilibrium which keeps man standing.[3]

2. Civilization of Work

I can now express the scope and limitations of my adhesion to the notion of civilization of work. I wholly subscribe to the definition proposed by Bartoli: "A civilization in which work is the dominant social and economic category." There is no problem with this definition once one has accepted the critique, which all of us make in other respects, of capitalism in its economic, social, political, and cultural form. This definition is all the more valid as the point of it is not directed against the phantom of contemplation but against the fetish of money. This is what constitutes the superiority of the economist's reflection over that of the philosopher with respect to the question of work.

In the spirit of Bartoli, I shall therefore maintain the following points:

1. A civilization of work is primarily an *economy of work* in which the rational direction of the general plan replaces the laws of the market. From this standpoint, money and price are stripped of their function as the so-called spontaneous regulators of economy; the distribution of goods is carried out at least provisionally in accordance with work and even in accordance with the productivity of work: wages are no longer the cost of work-merchandise, they are the means of dividing the net social product. In this sense, an economy of work is already realized in countries which practice socialist principles; it is only a trend in the modern capitalistic economy, particularly in the form of an organizing law of work, of a transformation of the structure of wages and a politics of full employment.

2. An economy of work does not constitute a civilization of work if it is not an *economy of workers themselves*, that is, if the workers do not actually manage the factories and industries themselves, or if they have not acquired the capacity and the responsibility of management so as to escape a new form of domination, that of administrators and technocrats.

3. An economy of work is false if it is not also a *democracy of work*, that is, if on the constitutional plane, workers do not share in the structuring of the State.

Hence, does not a civilization of work imply more than the incorporation of unions into the apparatus of the State, but rather a whole network of decentralizations, of divisions, of oppositions of powers, something very different from the structure of the centralizing State which the phase of industrialization imposes upon socialist economies? In this sense, no civilization of work as yet exists, even if an economy of work is already in operation in a part of the world or even present in some degree everywhere in the world.

4. Lastly, let us note that a civilization of work is a civilization in which a *new culture takes form on the basis of work.* The social mixing of professions and functions, which the division into classes considerably checks although without impeding it altogether, cannot fail to have a tremendous *repercussion* in the culture of a nation. When workers have ready access not only to the direction of the economy and of the State, but also to scientific and liberal careers and especially to literary and artistic expression, there necessarily results a profound renewal of culture *independently of an ideological direction of culture.* Modern culture has need of being cured of the unwholesome, of the artificial, of narcissism, by a confrontation and mixing of thinkers and artists in the world of work; it can in this way reachieve fraternal feelings, themes which are at once more vigorous and fresher and thereby free us from Byzantinism. A civilization of work therefore also involves the correction of the miseries of the word by means of the virtues of work.

The theme of the civilization of work mounts up to this repercussion of the world of work in the world of culture by the social mixing of professions and of functions. It mounts legitimately up to this point, but it goes no further. Beyond this point, two serious "mystifications" are to be feared. The first consists in making the whole of culture the celebration of the technician enterprise and, to speak plainly, a factor of industrialization. If the civilization of work consists in propagating a type of man who is efficient, pragmatic, fascinated by the success of techniques, by the collective enterprise of production, and consumed by the daily usage of the products of social work, then this new fetish which is offered for our admiration under the lofty label of civilization of work must be challenged.

The second mystification consists of confusing a culture

inspired by work and nourished by workers with a culture directed by *ideology*. This danger is the extreme form of the preceding one; in the phase of instituting a socialist economy, which normally corresponds to a phase of rapid industrialization, the apparatus of the State tries to orient the whole of culture toward the enterprise of collectivization and to impose upon the community the conception of the world which presides over this enterprise.

Hence, the civilization of work is no longer merely the one in which work has a *repercussion* on the word, but one in which the word no longer has but two objects: work itself and the ideology of the State which constructs socialism. Our whole analysis of the dialectics of work and the spoken word warns us that a civilization which fails to maintain this sort of intangible communications between the critical and poetic function of the word and the efficacious function of work is condemned in the end to stagnation. A civilization retains momentum only if it assumes all the risks of the word and establishes a right to error as an indispensable political function. This risk of the word is the price that a civilization of work must pay for the service which the word renders to work.

3. The Service Rendered to Work by the Word

This service of the word will outlive the social "alienations" of work in the wage-earner. For this service responds to the more enduring problems posed by the "objectification" of man in a finite work which is increasingly fragmented and monotonous. Nothing could be more baleful than to deny these problems in the name of the more urgent tasks of the "de-alienation" of work: all action and all reflection ought to be staggered in depth in function of urgent dangers but also in function of abiding dangers.

1. A first service of the word within the realm of work may be looked upon as a *corrective* of the division of work. Here

we enter upon a whole network of concerns which are being investigated by the social psychology of industrial work. At its lowest degree, this corrective function of the word corresponds to the role of distraction, of chattering in workshops in which jobs are so fragmented and so monotonous that it would be better to carry automation to its logical extreme and openly surrender work to a sort of medullary vigilance so as to occupy the mind of the worker with something else: chatter, informal talks, music, and—why not?—instructive lectures, etc.[4] At a higher degree, this corrective function takes the form of a general perception of the various situations in a factory, of a general apprehension of the sequence of operations which take place in an enterprise, even in terms of the various markets scattered throughout the world. This perception and this apprehension of the whole of production are comparable to an "interior word" which situates piecework and endows it with meaning. At a still higher degree, this corrective function becomes identified with a polyvalent professional training which allows for job-interchange and combats against the depersonalization provoked by automation. It may be seen that our dialectic of work and the spoken word leads us also to the very core of the problems raised by technical education which necessarily has two faces, one turned toward specialized professional training and the other toward general culture. It must be said that the most utilitarian training already has a cultural value as soon as it subordinates manual dexterity to theoretical knowledge of a physico-mathematical type. Literature and history conclude the "opening" of professional training upon the world and confirm that technical education is truly a *culture*.

At the highest degree, the *corrective* function of the word consists in endowing work with a social meaning. It is not by chance that books, a book like *Das Kapital*, are at the source of modern revolutions. Ultimately, to speak one's work is to approach the word of the political man. For when he is not in power, the politician, like the preacher, is only armed with the deadly efficacity of the word. This is the element of truth in the profound maxim of Georges Navel which Friedmann gives an account of: "There exists a sadness among the working classes which may be cured only by political participation."

2. The second service of the word is to *compensate* for the division of work by leisure. Leisure will be more and more the great problem of civilization, for the same reason as work.

It is by means of the word—but also by sports, camping, hobbies, etc.—that we may restore and renew the lost contact with nature, with life, with the raw elements. And thereby perhaps one may find a more extensive temporal rhythm, one which is more spontaneous, more relaxed than the exhausting tempo of modern living.

Now, the modern world is a world in which leisures, in the measure that they multiply, become degraded by the invasion of the very techniques which revolutionized production, transportation, and all human relationships. The very meaning of our leisures—won with difficulty through the shortening of the workday—will depend in large measure upon the quality of the human word, upon respect for the human word in politics and in the novel, in the theater and in conversation. For what will a man gain if he earns his living by work only to lose his soul through leisure? Thus, the construction of the socialist state must not degrade the word with the glib rhetoric of propaganda and ideological parlance. In the last analysis, this is why the socialist state must bear the risks of free speech if it wishes to avoid the spiritual destruction of the man it materially constructs.

3. The word has, moreover, a function of *foundation* with respect to all the pragmatic activities of man. It conveys the "theoretical" function in its entirety. There is no technique which is not an applied knowledge, and there is no applied knowledge which is not dependent upon a knowledge which at first repudiated all application. *Praxis* does not give us the

whole of man. *Theoria* is its *raison d'être*. This founding *theoria* goes from mathematics to ethics, from physical theory to history, from science to ontology. All radical problems are posed in an attitude which suspends the utilitarian concern and vital impatience. This is why there is no civilization which can survive without some sphere of free play left to disinterested speculation, to research without immediate or apparent applications. Earlier, we called *education* the interplay between adaptation and disadaptation in the formation of man. The university should be *par excellence* the seat of this pulsation. Thus it is legitimate to ask it to answer better than it does to the needs of modern society and also to continue without disgrace the time-honored tradition of the *universitas,* which more than ever will appear as a privileged means of dominating the tasks of modern work, under the condition that all workers may have access to it.

4. Lastly, in addition to this function of foundation, the word borders upon a function of *creation:* through literature and the arts is pursued the invention and the discovery of a sense of man which no state can systematically plan or arrange, which is the supreme risk for the artist and for the society which produces him. The true creator is not the one who *expresses* the already known needs of his times, the needs which the politician has already enunciated, but the artist whose work is an innovation in relation to the already catalogued and recognized knowledge of human reality. We find here the poetic function of the word with which our meditation on the power of the word ended. We now understand that the word is at the roots of a project of a civilization, even the project of a civilization of work.

Is it possible that the word here touches upon a fundamental creation? Is it possible that a theology of the word coincides in the end with a theology of work? Perhaps. But this means primarily that in human finitude we have need both of work and of the word in order to situate ourselves in the direction of a creative word which we are not.

Hence, every human civilization will be both a civilization of work *and* a civilization of the word.

NOTES

1. With respect to this point and certain others in the following pages, I am indebted to the recent book by Walter Porzer, *das Wunder der Sprache*, chap. ix: "Die Leistung der Sprache" (The Achievement of the Word).

2. Brice Parain, *Recherches sur la nature et les fonctions du langage* (Paris, 1946).

3. *"La Parole est mon royaume,"* *Esprit* (February 1955).

4. Georges Friedmann, *"Des écouteurs aux oreilles?"* in *Où va le travail humain?* (Paris: Gallimard, 1950), pp. 207ff.

3

The Philosopher and Sociology

Maurice Merleau-Ponty

[handwritten: ways phil + soc. have been treated has obscured their rel"ship, and interfered with our understanding of culture.]

Philosophy and sociology have long lived under a segregated system which has succeeded in concealing their rivalry only by refusing them any meeting-ground, impeding their growth, making them incomprehensible to one another, and thus placing culture in a situation of permanent crisis. As always, the spirit of inquiry has gotten around these interdicts; it seems to us that both philosophy and sociology have now progressed far enough to warrant a reexamination of their relationships.

We would also like to call attention to the thought Husserl gave to these problems. Husserl seems to us to be exemplary in that he may have realized better than anyone else that all forms of thought are in a certain sense interdependent. We need neither tear down the behavioral sciences to lay the foundations of philosophy, nor tear down philosophy to lay

Reprinted from *Signs*, trans. Richard C. McCleary (1964), pp. 98–113, by permission of Northwestern University Press, Evanston, Ill.

65

the foundations of the behavioral sciences. Every science secretes an ontology; every ontology anticipates a body of knowledge. It is up to us to come to terms with this situation and see to it that both philosophy and science are possible.

The segregation of philosophy and sociology has perhaps nowhere been described in the terms in which we are going to state it. Fortunately, the practices of philosophers and sociologists are often less exclusive than their principles. Yet this segregation nevertheless constitutes a part of a certain common sense of philosophers and sociologists which, by reducing philosophy and the behavioral sciences to what it believes is their ideal type, ultimately endangers scientific knowledge just as much as philosophical reflection.

Even though all the great philosophies are recognizable by their attempt to think about the mind *and its dependency*— ideas and their movement, understanding and sensibility— there is a myth about philosophy which presents it as an authoritarian affirmation of the mind's absolute autonomy. Philosophy so conceived is no longer an inquiry. It is a certain body of doctrines, made to assure an absolutely *unfettered* spirit full possession of itself and its ideas. In another connection, there is a myth about scientific knowledge which expects to attain from the mere recording of facts not only the science of the things of the world but also the science of that science—a sociology of knowledge (conceived of itself in an empiricist fashion) which should make the universe of facts self-contained by including even the ideas we invent to interpret the facts, and thus rid us, so to speak, of ourselves. These two myths sustain one another in their very antagonism. For even though the philosopher and the sociologist are opposed to one another, they at least agree upon a delimitation of boundaries which assures them of never meeting. But if the *cordon sanitaire* were removed, philosophy and sociology would destroy one another. Even now, they battle for our minds. Segregation is cold war.

In this atmosphere, any investigation which seeks to take

(M-P does not say yet what interests would divide the two so thoroughly)

both ideas and facts into account is immediately bifurcated. Facts, instead of being taken as the spur and warrant for a constructive effort to reach their inner dynamics, are worshipped as a sort of peremptory grace which reveals all truth. And ideas are exempted as a matter of principle from all confrontation with our experience of the world, others, and ourselves. The movement back and forth from facts to ideas and from ideas to facts is discredited as a bastard process— neither science nor philosophy—which denies scientists the final interpretation of the very facts that they have taken the pains to assemble, and which compromises philosophy with the always provisional results of scientific research.

We must be fully aware of the *obscurantist* consequences of this rigid segregation. If "mixed" investigations really have the inconveniences we have just mentioned, then we shall have to admit that a simultaneously philosophical and scientific view of experience is impossible, and that philosophy and sociology can attain certain knowledge only if they ignore one another. We shall have to hide from the scientist that "idealization" of brute fact which is nevertheless the essence of his work. He will have to ignore the deciphering of meanings which is his reason for being, the construction of intellectual models of reality without which there would no more be any sociology today than there would formerly have been Galilean physics. We shall have to put the blinders of Baconian or "Millian" induction back on the scientist, even though his own investigations obviously do not follow these canonical recipes. Consequently, he will pretend to approach social fact as if it were alien to him, as if his study owed nothing to the experience which, as social subject, he has of intersubjectivity.

Under the pretext that as a matter of fact sociology is not yet constructed with this lived experience but is instead an analysis, an explicit formulation and objectification of it which reverses our initial consciousness of social relationships (and ultimately shows that these experienced social

(source of false c.?)

relationships are very special variants of a dynamics we are originally unaware of and can learn about only in contact with other cultural formations), objectivism forgets another evident fact. We can expand our experience of social relationships and get a proper view of them only by analogy or contrast with those we have lived. We can do so, in short, only by subjecting the social relationships we have experienced to an *imaginary variation.* [These lived relationships will no doubt take on a new meaning in comparison with this imaginary variation (as the fall of a body on an inclined plane is put in a new light by the ideal concept of free fall), but they will provide it with all the sociological meaning it can have.]

Anthropology teaches us that in such and such cultures children treat certain cousins as their "kin," and facts of this sort allow us ultimately to draw up a diagram of the kinship structure in the civilization under consideration. But the correlations thus noted give only the silhouette or contour of kinship in that civilization, a cross-section of behavior patterns which are nominally defined as those of "kinship" at certain significant but still anonymous points X . . . , Y . . . , Z. . . . In short, these correlations do not yet have a sociological meaning. As long as we have not succeeded in installing ourselves in the institution which they delimit, in understanding the style of kinship which all these facts allude to and *the sense in which* certain subjects in that culture perceive other subjects of their generation as their "kin," and finally, in grasping the basic personal and interpersonal structure and the institutional relationships with nature and others which make the established correlations possible, the formulas which sum up these correlations could just as well represent a given physical or chemical process of the same form. Let us make it perfectly clear that the underlying dynamics of the social whole is certainly not *given* with our narrow experience of living among others, yet it is only by throwing this experience in and out of focus that we succeed in representing it to ourselves, just as the generalized number remains number for us only through the link which binds it to the whole number of elementary arithmetic.

On the basis of Freudian conceptions of pre-genital sexuality, we can make up a list of all the possible modes of accentuation of the orifices of the child's body, and the ones which are realized by our cultural system and have been described by the Freudians appear on the list as singular variants among a great number of possible ones which are perhaps current in civilizations as yet unknown to us. But this list tells us *nothing* about the relationships with others and with nature which define these cultural types, as long as we do not refer to the psychological meaning of the mouth, the anus, or the genital equipment in our own experience, so as to see in the different uses which are made of them by different cultures, different crystallizations of an initial polymorphism of the body as vehicle of being-in-the-world. The list we are shown is only an invitation to imagine, on the basis of our experience of the body, other techniques of the body. The technique which happens to be actualized in us can never be reduced to simply one among all possible techniques; for it is against the background of this privileged experience, where we learn to know the body as a "structuring" principle, that we glimpse the other "possibles," no matter how different from it they may be.

It is essential never to cut sociological inquiry off from our experience of social subjects (which of course includes not only what we have experienced ourselves but also the behavior we perceive through the gestures, tales, or writings of our fellow men). For the sociologist's equations begin to represent something social only at the moment when the correlations they express are connected to one another and enveloped in a certain unique *view* of the social and of nature which is characteristic of the society under consideration and has come to be institutionalized in it as the hidden principle of all its overt functioning—even though this view may be rather different than the official conceptions which are current in that society. If objectivism or scientism were ever to succeed in depriving sociology of all recourse to significations, it would save it from "philosophy" only by shutting it off from knowledge of its object. Then we might do mathematics in the social, but we would not have the mathematics of the society being considered. The sociologist philosophizes every time he is required to not only record but comprehend the facts. At the moment of interpretation, he is himself already a philosopher. This means that the professional philosopher is not disqualified to reinterpret facts he has not observed himself, if these facts say something more and different than what the scientist has seen in them. As Husserl says, eidetic analysis of the physical thing did not begin with phenomenology but with Galileo. And reciprocally, the philosopher has the right to read and interpret Galileo.

The segregation we are fighting against is no less harmful to philosophy than to the development of scientific knowledge. How could any philosopher aware of the philosophical tradition seriously propose to forbid philosophy to have anything to do with science? For after all the philosopher always thinks *about something:* about the square traced in the sand, about the ass, the horse, and the mule, about the cubic foot of size, about cinnabar, the Roman State, and the hand burying itself in the iron filings. The philosopher thinks about his experience and his world. Except by decree, how could he be given the right to forget what science says about this same experience and world? Under the collective noun "science" there is nothing other than a systematic handling and a methodical use—narrower and broader, more and less discerning—of this same experience which begins with our first perception. Science is a set of means of perceiving, imagining, and, in short, living which are oriented toward the same truth that our first experiences establish an urgent inner need for. Science may indeed purchase its exactness at the price of schematization. But the remedy in this case is to confront it with an integral experience, not to oppose it to philosophical knowledge come from who knows where.

Husserl's great merit is that from the time he reached philosophical maturity, and increasingly so as he pursued his efforts, he made use of his "intuition of essences," "morphological essences," and "phenomenological experience" to mark out a realm and an attitude of inquiry where philosophy and effective knowledge could meet. We know that he began by affirming, and continued to maintain, a rigorous distinction between the two. Nevertheless, it seems to us that his idea of a psycho-phenomenological parallelism (or as we may say in generalizing, his thesis of a parallelism between positive knowledge and philosophy such that there is for each affirmation of one a corresponding affirmation of the other) leads him in truth to the idea of *reciprocal envelopment*. As far as the social is concerned then, the problem is to know how it can be both a "thing" to be acquainted with without prejudices, and a "signification" which the societies we acquaint ourselves with only provide an occasion for— how, that is, the social can exist both in itself and in us. Having entered this labyrinth, let us follow the stages by which Husserl makes his way towards his last conceptions, in which, moreover, these stages will be as much retained as gone beyond.

At the outset, he asserts philosophy's rights in terms which seem to abolish those of actual knowledge. Speaking of that eminently social relation, language, he states as a principle[1] that we could not possibly understand the functioning of our own language, or break away from the pseudo-certainties which result from the fact that it is ours and gain a true acquaintance with other languages, unless we had first constituted a schema of the "ideal form" *of* language and of the modes of expression which must in strict necessity pertain to it if it is to be language. Only then will we be able to understand how German, Latin, and Chinese participate (each in its own way) in this universal structure of essential meanings, and to define each of these languages as a mixture in original proportions of universal "forms of signification"—a "confused" and incomplete realization of the "general and rational grammar." The actually existing language was thus to be reconstructed by a synthetic operation which began with the essential structures of any possible language and enveloped it in their ideal clarity. Philosophical thought took on an air of absolute autonomy, it and only it being capable of attaining true understanding through recourse to essences which provided the key to things.

Generally speaking, this stage of Husserl's thought calls our whole historical experience of social relationships into question in the interest of determining essences. Historical experience does present us with many "social processes" and "cultural formations" such as forms of law, art, and religion. But as long as we stick to such empirical realizations, we do not even know the meaning of these headings we class them under. And, consequently, we know even less whether the historical changes in a given religion or a given form of law or art are really essential and provide a true standard of their value; or whether on the contrary this law, this art, this religion contain yet other possibilities. History, Husserl used to say at this point, cannot judge an idea; and when it does, this "evaluating" *(wertende)* history borrows surreptitiously from the "ideal sphere" the necessary connections which it pretends to bring forth from the facts.[2]

As for the "world-views" which submit to being no more than the balance of what the knowledge available at any given moment allows us to think, Husserl grants that the problem they raise is a real one, but he objects that it is raised in such a way as to block any serious solution. The real problem stems from the fact that philosophy would lose its meaning if it refused to judge the present. Just as a morality which was "as a matter of principle transfinite and endless" would no longer be a morality, a philosophy which as a matter of principle gave up taking any position in the present would no longer be a philosophy.[3] But the fact is that in wanting to face up to present problems, "to have their system, and in time enough to be able to live afterwards,"[4] the *Weltanschauung* philosophers miss everything. They can bring no more rigor to the solution of these problems than other men, because like them they are within the *Weltanschauung* and have no *Weltwissenschaft*. And in devoting themselves entirely to thinking about the present, they rob true philosophy of the unconditional devotion she demands. Now once constituted, true philosophy would allow us to think about the present as well as the past and the eternal. To go straight to the present is thus to relinquish the solid for the illusory.

When in the second part of his career Husserl returns to the problems of history, and especially to the problem of language, we no longer find the idea of a philosopher-subject, master of all that is possible, who must first put *his own* language at a distance in order to find the ideal forms of a universal language this side of all actuality. Philosophy's first task in respect to language now appears to be to reveal to us anew our inherence in a certain system of speech of which we make fully efficacious use precisely because it is present to us just as immediately as our body. Philosophy of language is no longer contrasted to empirical linguistics as an attempt at total objectification of language to a science which is always threatened by the preconceptions of the native language. On the contrary, it has become the rediscovery of the subject in the act of speaking, as contrasted to a science of language which inevitably treats this subject as a thing. Pos[5] has shown quite clearly how the phenomenological attitude is contrasted to the scientific or observational attitude. The latter, since it is directed toward an already established language, takes that language in the past and breaks it down into a sum of linguistic facts in which its unity disappears. The former has become the attitude that permits direct access to the living language present in a linguistic community which uses it not only to preserve but to establish, and to envisage and define a future. So here a language is no longer broken down into elements which can be added up piece by piece; it is like an organ whose tissues all contribute to its unified functioning, irrespective of the diversity of their origins and the fortuitousness of their original insertion into the whole.

Now if it is really the peculiar office of phenomenology to approach language in this way, phenomenology is no longer the synthetic determination of all possible languages. Reflection is no longer the return to a pre-empirical subject which holds the keys to the world; it no longer circumambulates its present object and possesses its constitutive parts. Reflection must become aware of its object in a contact or frequenting which at the outset exceeds its power of comprehension. The philosopher is first and foremost the one who realizes that he is situated in language, that he *is speaking;* and phenomenological reflection can no longer be limited to a completely lucid enumeration of the "conditions without which" there would be no language. It must show why there is speech—that paradox of a subject turned toward the future who speaks and understands—in spite of all we know about the accidents and shifts of meaning which have created the language. Present speech casts a light which is not found in any merely "possible" expression. It is an operation in our linguistic "field of presence" which, far from being a particular case of other possible systems of expression, serves as our model for conceiving of them. Reflection is no longer the passage to a different order which reabsorbs the order of present things; it is first and foremost a more acute awareness of the way in which we are rooted in them. From now on, the absolute condition of a valid philosophy is that it pass by way of the present.

To tell the truth, we do not have to wait until Husserl recognizes that the *Lebenswelt* is phenomenology's principal theme to note the repudiation of formal reflection in his thought. The reader of the *Ideen I* will have already noticed that eidetic intuition has always been a "confirmation," and

phenomenology an "experience" (a phenomenology of seeing, Husserl said, should be constructed on the basis of a
Sichtigkeit which we have actually experienced to begin
with; and he generally rejected the possibility of a "mathematics of phenomena" or a "geometry of what is lived"). It
is just that the ascending movement was not stressed.
Thought barely supported itself on its actually existing structures in order to sift out its possible ones: a wholly imaginary
variation extracted a treasure of eidetic assertions from the
lowest-grade experience. When the recognition of the life-
world, and thus too of language as we live it, becomes characteristic of phenomenology (as it does in the last writings), this
is only a more resolute way of saying that philosophy does not
possess the truth about language and the world from the
start, but is rather the recuperation and first formulation of
a Logos scattered out in our world and our life and bound to
their concrete structures—that "Logos of the aesthetic
world" already spoken of in the *Formal and Transcendental
Logic*. Husserl will only be bringing the movement of all his
previous thought to completion when he writes in a posthumous fragment that transitory inner phenomena are brought
to ideal existences by becoming incarnate in language.[6] Ideal
existence, which at the beginning of Husserl's thought was to
have been the foundation for the possibility of language, is
now the most characteristic possibility *of* language.

But if philosophy no longer consists in passing to the infinity of possibles or leaping into absolute objectivity, then it
is understandable that certain linguistic investigations should
anticipate Husserl's own, and that certain linguists should
without knowing it tread upon the ground of phenomenology. Husserl does not say it, nor does Pos, but it is hard not
to think of Saussure when Husserl insists that we return from
language as object to the spoken word.

In reality, philosophy's whole relationship to history
changes in the very movement of reflection which was trying
to free philosophy from history. In proportion as he reflects

further upon the relation between eternal and factual truths, Husserl finds it necessary to replace his initial delimitations with a far less simple relation. His meditations on transcendental reflection and its possibility, which he pursued for at least twenty years, show clearly enough that in his view this term did not designate some sort of distinct faculty which could be circumscribed, pointed out, and actually isolated side by side with other modalities of experience. In spite of all his trenchant formulations constantly reaffirming the radical distinction between the natural and the transcendental attitude, Husserl is well aware from the start that they do in fact encroach upon one another, and that every *fact of consciousness* bears the transcendental within it. As far as the relation of fact and essence is concerned, in any case, a text as old as *Philosophy as a Rigorous Science* (after having distinguished, as we have been recalling, the "ideal sphere" and historical facts) expressly foresaw the overlapping of the two orders. For it pointed out that the reason why historical criticism really shows that a given order of institutions has no substantial reality, and is actually only a common noun to designate a mass of facts with no internal relation, is that empirical history includes confused intuitions of essences, and criticism is always the reverse side or emergence of a positive assertion which is already there.

In the same article, Husserl was already admitting that history is precious to the philosopher *because it reveals the Gemeingeist to him.* It is not so hard to go from these first formulations to the later ones. To say that history teaches the philosopher what the *Gemeingeist* is, is to say that it gives him the problem of intersubjective communication to think about. It makes it necessary for him to understand how there are not only individual minds (each incumbent in a perspective on the world) which the philosopher can inspect by turns without being allowed (and even less required) to think of them *together,* but also a community of minds coexisting for one another and as a consequence invested individually with an exterior through which they become visible. As a result, the philosopher may no longer speak of mind in general, deal with each and every mind under a single name, or flatter himself that he constitutes them. Instead he must see himself within the dialogue of minds, situated as they all are, and grant them the dignity of self-constituting beings at the very moment that he claims that dignity for himself. We are on the verge of the enigmatic formulation Husserl will arrive at in the texts of the *Krisis der europäischen Wissenschaften*, when he writes that "transcendental subjectivity is intersubjectivity."

Now if the transcendental is intersubjectivity, how can the borders of the transcendental and the empirical help becoming indistinct? For along with the other person, all the other person sees of me—all my facticity—is reintegrated into subjectivity, or at least posited as an indispensable element of its definition. Thus the transcendental descends into history. Or as we might put it, the historical is no longer an external relation between two or more absolutely autonomous subjects but has an interior and is an inherent aspect of their very definition. They no longer know themselves to be subjects simply in relation to their individual selves, but in relation to one another as well.

In the unpublished manuscripts of the final period, the contrast between fact and essence will be explicitly mediated by the idea that the purest reflection discloses a "genesis of meaning" *(Sinngenesis)* immanent in its objects—the need for each manifestation of its objects to have a "before" and "after" and develop through a series of steps or stages in which each step anticipates and is taken up in a subsequent one that could not possibly exist "at the same time" as the preceding one yet presupposes it as its past horizon. Of course this intentional history is not simply the sum of all manifestations taken one by one. It takes them up again and puts them in order; in the actuality of a present, it reanimates and rectifies a genesis which could miscarry without it. But it can do so only in contact with what is given, by seeking its motives within it. It is no longer just through an unfortunate accident that the study of significations and the study of facts encroach upon one another. If it did not condense a certain development of *truth,* a signification would be empty.

It is to be hoped that we shall soon be able to read, in the complete works of Husserl,[7] the letter that he wrote to Lévy-Bruhl on March 11, 1935, after having read *La mythologie primitive.* Here he seems to admit that the philosopher could not possibly have immediate access to the universal by reflection alone—that he is in no position to do without anthropological experience or to construct what constitutes the meaning of other experiences and civilizations by a purely imaginary variation of his own experiences. "It is a possible and highly important task," he writes, "it is a great task to project ourselves into *(einzufühlen)* a human community enclosed in its living and traditional sociality, and to understand it insofar as, in and on the basis of its total social life, that human community possesses the world, which is not for it a 'representation of the world' but the real world." Now our access to archaic worlds is barred by our own world. Lévy-Bruhl's primitives "have no history" *(geschichtlos);* for them "life is only a passing present" *(ein Leben, das nur stromende Gegenwart ist).* We on the contrary live in an historical world; a world, that is, which "has a partly realized future (the national 'past') and a partly to be realized future." No intentional analysis seeking to recover and reconstitute the structures of the archaic world could possibly limit itself to making those of our own explicit; for what gives meaning to these structures is the milieu or *Umwelt* of which they are the typical style, and thus we cannot understand them without understanding how time passes and being is constituted in these cultures. Husserl goes so far as to write that "on the path of that already largely developed intentional analysis, historical relativism is incontestably justified as an anthropological fact."

To bring things to a close, how does Husserl now conceive of philosophy? The last lines of the letter give us an idea: philosophy must accept all the acquisitions of science (which have the first word concerning knowledge), and thus historical relativism along with them. But as philosophy, it cannot be content to simply make note of the variety of anthropological facts. "Although anthropology, like every positive science and all these sciences as a whole, may have the first word concerning knowledge, it does not have the last." Judging by Husserl's later views, philosophy would gain autonomy after, not before, positive knowledge. This autonomy would not exempt the philosopher from gathering in everything anthropology has to offer us, which means, basically, testing our effective communication with other cultures. Nor could it withhold anything from the scientist's jurisdiction which was accessible to his methods of research. It would simply set itself up in a dimension where no scientific knowledge can dispute it. Let us try to show which one.

Suppose the philosopher no longer lays claim to the unconditional power to think his own thought through and through. He agrees that his "ideas" and his "certainties" are always to some extent naïve, and that caught up as they are in the fabric of the culture he belongs to, they cannot be truly known by just being scrutinized and varied in thought, but must be confronted with other cultural formations and viewed against the background of other preconceptions. Then has he not from this moment on abdicated his office and handed his rights over to empirical investigation and the positive disciplines? No, he has not; that is just the point. The same dependence upon history which prohibits the philosopher from arrogating to himself an immediate access to the universal or the eternal prohibits the sociologist from taking the philosopher's place in this function and giving ontological value to the scientific objectification of the social. The concept of history in its most profound sense does not shut the thinking subject up in a point of space and time; he can seem to be thus contained only to a way of thinking which is itself capable of going outside all time and place in order to see him in his time and place.

Now it is precisely this presumption to absolute thought which is discredited by the historical sense. There can be no question of simply transferring to science the grand-mastery denied to systematic philosophy, as historicism does. "You believe you think for all times and all men," the sociologist says to the philosopher, "and by that very belief you only express the preconceptions or pretentions of your culture." That is true, but it is no less true of the dogmatic sociologist than it is of the philosopher. *Where does he speak from*, the sociologist who speaks in this way? The sociologist can only form this idea of an historical time which allegedly contains philosophers as a box contains an object by placing himself outside history in turn and claiming the privileged position of absolute spectator.

In reality, it is the very concept of the relationships of mind to its object that historical consciousness invites us to reshape. The point is that my thought's inherence in a certain historical situation of its own and, through that situation, in other historical situations which interest it—since it is the fundamental origin and original foundation of the objective relations which science speaks to us about—makes knowledge of the social self-knowledge, and calls forth and authorizes a *view of intersubjectivity as my own* which science forgets even as it utilizes it, and which is proper to philosophy. Since we are all hemmed in by history, it is up to us to understand that whatever truth we may have is to be gotten not in spite of but through our historical inherence. Superficially considered, our inherence destroys all truth; considered radically, it founds a new idea of truth. As long as I cling to the ideal of an absolute spectator, of knowledge with no point of view, I can see my situation as nothing but a source of error. But if I have once recognized that through it I am grafted onto every action and all knowledge which can have a meaning for me, and that step by step it contains everything which can *exist* for me, then my contact with the social in the finitude of my situation is revealed to me as the point of origin of all truth, including scientific truth. And since we have an idea of truth, since we are in truth and cannot escape it, the only thing left for me to do is to define a truth in the situation.

Knowledge will then be based upon the unimpeachable fact that we are not in a situation like an object in objective space. Our situation is for us the source of our curiosity, our investigations, and our interest in first other situations as variants of our own and then in our own life, illuminated by (and this time considered as a variant of) the lives of others. Ultimately, our situation is what links us to the whole of human experience, no less than what separates us from it. "Science" and "sociology" will designate the effort to construct ideal variables which objectify and schematize the functioning of this effective communication. We shall call "philosophy" the consciousness we must maintain—as our consciousness of the ultimate reality whose functioning our theoretical constructions retrace but could not possibly replace—of the open and successive community of *alter egos* living, speaking, and thinking in one another's presence and in relation to nature as we sense its presence behind, around, and before us at the limits of our historical field.

Thus philosophy is not defined by a peculiar domain of its own. Like sociology, it only speaks about the world, men, and mind. It is distinguished by a certain *mode* of consciousness we have of others, of nature, or of ourselves. It is nature and man in the present, not "flattened out" (Hegel) in a derivative objectivity but such as they are presented in our present cognitive and active commerce with them. Philosophy is nature in us, the others in us, and we in them. Accordingly, we must not simply say that philosophy is compatible with sociology, but that it is necessary to it as a constant reminder of its tasks; and that each time the sociologist returns to the living sources of his knowledge, to what operates within him as a means of understanding the forms of culture most remote from him, he practices philosophy spontaneously. Philosophy is not a particular body of knowledge; it is the vigilance which does not let us forget the source of all knowledge.

We are not claiming that Husserl would ever have agreed to some definition of this sort, since up until the end he always thought of the return to living history and the spoken word—the return to the *Lebenswelt*—as a preparatory step which should be followed by the properly philosophical task of universal constitution. Yet it is a fact that in his last published work, rationality is no longer more than one of two possible alternatives we face, the other being chaos. And it is precisely with an awareness of a sort of nameless adversity threatening rationality that Husserl searches for that which can stimulate knowledge and action. Reason as a summons and a task, the "latent reason" which must be changed into itself and brought to explicit consciousness, becomes the criterion of philosophy. "It is only in this way that it will be decided whether the end *(Telos)* innate in the European conception of man since the birth of Greek philosophy—his will to be human on the basis of philosophical reason (and his inability to be so in any other way), in an unending movement from latent to manifest reason, and in an unending attempt to govern himself through his own human truth and authenticity—whether all this is only the mere historical fact of an illusion, the accidental acquisition of one accidental human community among other wholly different human communities and histories. Or whether, on the contrary, there did not come to light for the first time in the Greek conception of man what is essentially inherent as entelechy in the quality of man as man. Taken in itself, the quality of man consists essentially in being human within human communities bound together generatively and socially. And if man is a rational being, he can be so only to the extent that

the whole human community he belongs to is a rational community, either latently disposed to reason or openly disposed
to an entelechy which has arrived at self-awareness or become evident to itself, and is thus consciously guiding human
development according to its essential necessity. Philosophy
and science would then be the historical movement of revelation of universal reason, 'innate' in the human community
as such.'"[8] Thus the essence of man is not given, nor is his
essential necessity unconditional. His essence will energize
his actions only if the rationality first conceived for us by the
Greeks does not remain accidental but proves to be essential
by the knowledge and the action it makes possible, and gets
itself recognized by irrational human communities. The Husserlian essence is now borne by an "entelechy."

Philosophy's role as consciousness of rationality in contingency is no insignificant residue. In the last analysis, only the
philosophical consciousness of intersubjectivity enables us to
understand scientific knowledge. Without this philosophical
consciousness, scientific knowledge remains indefinitely in
suspense, always deferred until the termination of discussions of causality which, having to do with man, are by their
nature interminable. We wonder for example whether social
relationships are (as psychoanalytic sociology would have it)
only the amplification and generalization of the sexual-
aggressive drama, or whether on the contrary this drama
itself (in the form described by psychoanalysis) is only a particular case of the institutional relationships of Western societies. These discussions have the value of inducing the sociologists to make observations, of revealing facts, and of giving
rise to analyses and insights. But they admit of no conclusion
as long as we remain on the level of causal and "objective"
thought, since we can neither reduce one of the causal chains
to nothing nor think of them together as causal chains. We
can hold that both these views are true (as they are) only on
the condition that we move to an a-causal mode of thought,
which is philosophy. For there are two truths which must be

grasped simultaneously. The individual drama takes place among *roles* which are already inscribed in the total institutional structure, so that from the beginning of his life the child proceeds—simply by perceiving the attentions paid to him and the utensils surrounding him—to a deciphering of meanings which from the outset generalizes his own drama into a drama of his culture. And yet it is the whole symbolic consciousness which in the last analysis elaborates what the child lives or does not live, suffers or does not suffer, feels or does not feel. Consequently, there is not a single detail of his most individual history which does not contribute something to that personal significance he will manifest when (having first thought and lived as he thought best, and perceived according to his culture's imagery) he finally comes to the point of reversing the relationship and slipping into the meanings of his speech and his behavior, converting even the most secret aspects of his experience into culture. From the causal point of view it is unthinkable that this centripetal movement and this centrifugal movement are compossible. These reversals, these "metamorphoses," this proximity and distance of the past and present (of the archaic and the "modern"), this way that cultural time and space roll up on themselves, and this perpetual overdetermination of human events which makes the social fact (no matter how singular the local or temporal conditions) always appear to us as a variant of a single life that ours is also part of, and makes every *other person another ourself* for us—all these things become conceivable or even visible to the philosophical attitude alone.

Philosophy is indeed, and always, a break with objectivism and a return from *constructa* to lived experience, from the world to ourselves. It is just that this indispensable and characteristic step no longer transports it into the rarified atmosphere of introspection or into a realm numerically distinct from that of science. It no longer makes philosophy the rival of scientific knowledge, now that we have recognized that the "interior" it brings us back to is not a "private life" but an intersubjectivity that gradually connects us ever closer to the whole of history. When I discover that the social is not simply an object to begin with my situation, and when I awaken within myself the consciousness of this social-which-is-mine, then my whole synchrony becomes present to me, through that synchrony I become capable of really thinking about the whole past as the synchrony it has been in its time, and all the convergent and discordant action of the historical community is effectively given to me in my living present. Giving up systematic philosophy as an explanatory device does not reduce philosophy to the rank of an auxiliary or a propagandist in the service of objective knowledge; for philosophy has a dimension of its own, the dimension of coexistence—not as a *fait accompli* and an object of contemplation, but as the milieu and perpetual event of the universal *praxis*. Philosophy is irreplaceable because it reveals to us both the movement by which lives become truths, and the circularity of that singular being who in a certain sense already *is* everything he *happens to think*.

NOTES

1. *Logische Untersuchungen*, II, 4te Unters., p. 339.
2. *Philosophie als strenge Wissenschaft*, p. 325.
3. *Ibid.*, p. 332.
4. *Ibid.*, p. 338.
5. H. Pos, *"Phénoménologie et Linguistique,"* Revue Internationale de Philosophie, (January, 1939).
6. "Ursprung der Geometrie," *Revue Internationate de Philosophie* (January, 1939): 210.
7. In the process of being published at The Hague by Martinus Nijhoff, under the direction of H. L. Van Breda. The editors have not granted us any rights to quote the few unpublished excerpts to be found here. Consequently we ask the reader not to expect any more than a foretaste of texts whose only authorized edition is being prepared by the Husserl Archives of Louvain.
8. "Die Krisis der Europäischen Wissenschaften und die transzendentale Phänomenologie," *Philosophia* 1 (1936):92.

4

Concept and Theory Formation in the Social Sciences

Alfred Schutz

The title of my paper[1] refers intentionally to that of a Symposium held in December, 1952, at the annual meeting of the American Philosophical Association.[2] Ernest Nagel and Carl G. Hempel contributed highly stimulating comments on the problem involved, formulated in the careful and lucid way so characteristic of these scholars. Their topic is a controversy which for more than half a century has split not only logicians and methodologists but also social scientists into two schools of thought. One of these holds that the methods of the natural sciences which have brought about such magnificent results are the only scientific ones and that they alone, therefore, have to be applied in their entirety to the study of human affairs. Failure to do so, it has been maintained, prevented the social sciences from developing systems of explanatory theory comparable in precision to those

Reprinted from *The Journal of Philosophy*, Vol. 51, No. 9 (April 29, 1954), pp. 257–73, by permission.

offered by the natural sciences and makes debatable the empirical work of theories developed in restricted domains such as economics.

The other school of thought feels that there is a basic difference in the structure of the social world and the world of nature. This feeling led to the other extreme, namely the conclusion that the methods of the social sciences are *toto coelo* different from those of the natural sciences. In order to support this position a variety of arguments was proffered. It has been maintained that the social sciences are idiographic, characterized by individualizing conceptualization and seeking singular assertory propositions, whereas the natural sciences are nomothetic, characterized by generalizing conceptualization and seeking general apodictic propositions. The latter have to deal with constant relations of magnitude which can be measured and can perform experiments, whereas neither measurement nor experiment is practicable in the social sciences. In general, it is held that the natural sciences have to deal with material objects and processes, the social sciences, however, with psychological and intellectual ones and that, therefore, the method of the former consists in explaining, that of the latter in understanding.

Admittedly, most of these highly generalized statements are untenable under closer examination, and this for several reasons. Some proponents of the characterized arguments had a rather erroneous concept of the methods of the natural sciences. Others were inclined to identify the methodological situation in one particular social science with the method of the social sciences in general. Because history has to deal with unique and nonrecurrent events, it was contended that all social sciences are restricted to singular assertory propositions. Because experiments are hardly possible in cultural anthropology, the fact was ignored that social psychologists can successfully use laboratory experiments at least to a certain extent. Finally, and this is the most important point, these arguments disregard the fact that a set of rules for scientific procedure is equally valid for all empirical sciences whether they deal with objects of nature or with human affairs. Here and there, the principles of controlled inference and verification by fellow-scientists and the theoretical ideals of unity, simplicity, universality, and precision prevail.

This unsatisfactory state of affairs results chiefly from the fact that the development of the modern social sciences occurred during a period in which the science of logic was mostly concerned with the logic of the natural sciences. In a kind of monopolistic imperialism the methods of the latter were frequently declared to be the only scientific ones and the particular problems which social scientists encountered in their work were disregarded. Left without help and guidance in their revolt against this dogmatism, the students of human affairs had to develop their own conceptions of what they believed to be the methodology of the social sciences. They did it without sufficient philosophical knowledge and stopped their effort when they reached a level of generalization which seemed to justify their deeply felt conviction that the goal of their inquiry could not be reached by adopting the methods of the natural sciences without modification or implementation. No wonder that their arguments are frequently ill-founded, their formulations insufficient, and that many misunderstandings obfuscate the controversy. Not what social scientists *said* but what they *meant* is therefore our main concern in the following.

The writings of the late Felix Kaufmann[3] and the more recent contributions by Nagel[4] and Hempel[5] have criticized many fallacies in the arguments proposed by social scientists and prepared the ground for another approach to the problem. I shall here concentrate on Professor Nagel's criticism of the claim made by Max Weber and his school that the social sciences seek to "understand" social phenomena in terms of "meaningful" categories of human experience and that, therefore, the "causal functional" approach of the natural sciences is not applicable in social inquiry. This school, as

Dr. Nagel sees it, maintains that all socially significant human behavior is an expression of motivated psychic states, that in consequence the social scientist cannot be satisfied with viewing social processes simply as concatenations of "externally related" events, and that the establishment of correlations or even of universal relations of concomitance cannot be his ultimate goal. On the contrary, he must construct "ideal types" or "models of motivations" in terms of which he seeks to "understand" overt social behavior by imputing springs of action to the actors involved in it. If I understand Professor Nagel's criticism correctly, he maintains:

1. That these springs of action are not accessible to sensory observation. It follows and has frequently been stated that the social scientist must imaginatively identify himself with the participants and view the situation which they face as the actors themselves view it. Surely, however, we need not undergo other men's psychic experiences in order to know that they have them or in order to predict their overt behavior.

2. That the imputation of emotions, attitudes, and purposes as an explanation of overt behavior is a twofold hypothesis: it assumes that the agents participating in some social phenomenon are in certain psychological states; and it assumes also definite relations of concomitance between such states, and between such states and overt behavior. Yet none of the psychological states which we imagine the subjects of our study to possess may in reality be theirs, and even if our imputations should be correct none of the overt actions which allegedly issue from those states may appear to us understandable or reasonable.

3. That we do not "understand" the nature and operations of human motives and their issuance in overt behavior more adequately than the "external" causal relations. If by meaningful explanation we assert merely that a particular action is an instance of a pattern of behavior which human beings exhibit under a variety of circumstances and that, since some

of the relevant circumstances are realized in the given situation, a person can be expected to manifest a certain form of that pattern, then there is no sharp gulf separating such explanations from those involving merely "external" knowledge of causal connections. It is possible to gain knowledge of the actions of men on the evidence supplied by their overt behavior just as it is possible to discover and know the atomic constitution of water on the evidence supplied by the physical and chemical behavior of that substance. Hence the rejection of a purely "objective" or "behavioristic" social science by the proponents of "meaningful connections" as the goal of social sciences is unwarranted.

Since I shall have to disagree with Nagel's and Hempel's findings in several questions of a fundamental nature, I might be permitted to start with a brief summary of the no less important points in which I find myself happily in full agreement with them. I agree with Professor Nagel that all empirical knowledge involves discovery through processes of controlled inference, and that it must be statable in propositional form and capable of being verified by anyone who is prepared to make the effort to do so through observation[6]— although I do not believe, as Professor Nagel does, that this observation has to be sensory in the precise meaning of this term. Moreover, I agree with him that "theory" means in all empirical sciences the explicit formulation of determinate relations between a set of variables in terms of which a fairly extensive class of empirically ascertainable regularities can be explained.[7] Furthermore, I agree wholeheartedly with his statement that neither the fact that these regularities have in the social sciences a rather narrowly restricted universality, nor the fact that they permit prediction only to a rather limited extent, constitutes a basic difference between the social and the natural sciences, since many branches of the latter show the same features.[8] As I shall try to show later on, it seems to me that Professor Nagel misunderstands Max

Weber's postulate of subjective interpretation. Nevertheless, he is right in stating that a method which would require that the individual scientific observer identify himself with the social agent observed in order to understand the motives of the latter, or a method which would refer the selection of the facts observed and their interpretation to the private value system of the particular observer, would merely lead to an uncontrollable private and subjective image in the mind of this particular student of human affairs, but never to a scientific theory.[9] I merely submit that I do not know of any social scientist of stature who ever advocated such a concept of subjectivity as that criticized by Professor Nagel. Most certainly this was not the position of Max Weber.

Yet I submit also that our authors are prevented from grasping the point of vital concern to social scientists by their basic philosophy of sensationalistic empiricism or logical positivism, which identifies experience with sensory observation and which assumes that the only alternative to controllable and, therefore, objective sensory observation is that of subjective and, therefore, uncontrollable and unverifiable introspection. This is certainly not the place to renew the age-old controversy relating to the hidden presuppositions and implied metaphysical assumptions of this basic philosophy. On the other hand, in order to account for my own position, I should have to treat at length certain principles of phenomenology. Instead of doing so, I propose to defend a few rather simple propositions:

1. The primary goal of the social sciences is to obtain organized knowledge of social reality. By the term "social reality" I wish to be understood the sum total of objects and occurrences within the social cultural world as experienced by the common-sense thinking of men living their daily lives among their fellow-men, connected with them in manifold relations of interaction. It is the world of cultural objects and social institutions into which we all are born, within which we have

to find our bearings, and with which we have to come to terms. From the outset, we, the actors on the social scene, experience the world we live in as a world both of nature and of culture, not as a private but as an intersubjective one, that is, as a world common to all of us, either actually given or potentially accessible to everyone; and this involves inter-communication and language.

2. All forms of naturalism and logical empiricism simply take for granted this social reality, which is the proper object of the social sciences. Intersubjectivity, interaction, inter-communication, and language are simply presupposed as the unclarified foundation of these theories. They assume, as it were, that the social scientist has already solved his funda-mental problem, before scientific inquiry starts. To be sure, Dewey emphasized, with a clarity worthy of this eminent philosopher, that all inquiry starts and ends within the social cultural matrix; to be sure, Professor Nagel is fully aware of the fact that science and its self-correcting process is a social enterprise.[10] But the postulate to describe and explain hu-man behavior in terms of controllable sensory observation stops short before the description and explanation of the process by which scientist B controls and verifies the observa-tional findings of scientist A and the conclusions drawn by him. In order to do so, B has to know what A has observed, what the goal of his inquiry is, why he thought the observed fact worthy of being observed, i.e., relevant to the scientific problem at hand, etc. This knowledge is commonly called understanding. The explanation of how such a mutual under-standing of human beings might occur is apparently left to the social scientist. But whatever his explanation might be, one thing is sure, namely, that such an intersubjective under-standing between scientist B and scientist A occurs neither by scientist B's observations of scientist A's overt behavior, nor by introspection performed by B, nor by identification of B with A. To translate this argument into the language dear to logical positivism, this means, as Felix Kaufmann[11] has

shown, that so-called protocol propositions about the physical world are of an entirely different kind than protocol propositions about the psycho-physical world.

3. The identification of experience with sensory observation in general and of the experience of overt action in particular (and that is what Nagel proposes) excludes several dimensions of social reality from all possible inquiry.

(a) Even an ideally refined behaviorism can, as has been pointed out for instance by George H. Mead,[12] merely explain the behavior of the observed, not of the observing behaviorist.

(b) The same overt behavior (say a tribal pageant as it can be captured by the movie-camera) may have an entirely different meaning to the performers. What interests the social scientist is merely whether it is a war dance, a barter trade, the reception of a friendly ambassador, or something else of this sort.

(c) Moreover, the concept of human action in terms of common-sense thinking and of the social sciences includes what may be called "negative actions," *i.e.*, intentional refraining from acting,[13] which, of course, escapes sensory observation. Not to sell certain merchandise at a given price is doubtless as economic an action as to sell it.

(d) Furthermore, as W. I. Thomas has shown,[14] social reality contains elements of beliefs and convictions which are real because so defined by the participants and which escape sensory observation. To the inhabitants of Salem in the seventeenth century, witchcraft was not a delusion but an element of their social reality and is as such open to investigation by the social scientist.

(e) Finally, and this is the most important point, the postulate of sensory observation of overt human behavior takes as a model a particular and relatively small sector of the social world, namely, situations in which the acting individual is given to the observer in what is commonly called a face-to-face relationship. But there are many other dimensions of the social world in which situations of this kind do not prevail. If we put a letter in the mailbox we assume that anonymous fellow-men, called postmen, will perform a series of manipulations, unknown and unobservable to us, with the effect that the addressee, possibly also unknown to us, will receive the message and react in a way which also escapes our sensory observation; and the result of all this is that we receive the book we have ordered. Or if I read an editorial stating that France fears the re-armament of Germany, I know perfectly well what this statement means without knowing the editorialist and even without knowing a Frenchman or a German, let alone without observing their overt behavior.

In terms of common-sense thinking in everyday life men have knowledge of these various dimensions of the social world in which they live. To be sure, this knowledge is not only fragmentary since it is restricted principally to certain sectors of this world, it is also frequently inconsistent in itself and shows all degrees of clarity and distinctness from full insight or "knowledge-about," as James[15] called it, through "knowledge of acquaintance" or mere familiarity, to blind belief in things just taken for granted. In this respect there are considerable differences from individual to individual and from social group to social group. Yet, in spite of all these inadequacies, common-sense knowledge of everyday life is sufficient for coming to terms with fellow-men, cultural objects, social institutions—in brief, with social reality. This is so, because the world (the natural and the social one) is from the outset an intersubjective world and because, as shall be pointed out later on, our knowledge of it is in various ways socialized. Moreover, the social world is experienced from the outset as a meaningful one. The other's body is not experienced as an organism but as a fellow-man, its overt behavior not as an occurrence in the space-time of the outer world, but as our fellow-man's action. We normally "know" what the other does, wherefore he does it, why he does it at this particular time and in these particular circumstances. That means that we experience our fellow-man's action in terms of his motives and goals. And in the same way we experience cultural objects in terms of the human action of which they are the result. A tool, for example, is not experienced as a thing in the outer world (which of course it is also) but in terms of the purpose for which it was designed by more or less anonymous fellow-men and its possible use by others.

The fact that in common-sense thinking we take for granted our actual or potential knowledge of the meaning of human actions and their products, is, so I submit, precisely what social scientists want to express if they speak of understanding or *Verstehen* as a technique of dealing with human affairs. *Verstehen* is, thus, primarily not a method used by the social scientist, but the particular experiential form in which common-sense thinking takes cognizance of the social cultural world. It has nothing to do with introspection, it is a result of processes of learning or acculturation in the same way as the common-sense experience of the so-called natural world. *Verstehen* is, moreover, by no means a private affair of the observer which cannot be controlled by the experiences of other observers. It is controllable at least to the same extent to which the private sensory perceptions of an individual are controllable by any other individual under certain conditions. You have just to think of the discussion by a trial-jury whether the defendant has shown "pre-meditated malice" or "intent" in killing a person, whether he was capable of knowing the consequences of his deed, etc. Here we even have certain "rules of procedure" furnished by the "rules of evidence" in the juridical sense and a kind of verification of the findings resulting from processes of *Verstehen* by the Appellate Court, etc. Moreover, predictions based on *Verstehen* are continuously and with high success made in common-sense thinking. There is more than a fair chance that a duly stamped and addressed letter put in a New York mail-box will reach the addressee in Chicago.

Nevertheless, both defenders and critics of the process of *Verstehen* maintain, and with good reason, that *Verstehen* is "subjective." Unfortunately, however, this term is used by each party in a different sense. The critics of understanding call it subjective, because they hold that understanding the motives of another man's action depends upon the private, uncontrollable, and unverifiable intuition of the observer or refers to his private value system. The social scientists, such as Max Weber, however, call *Verstehen* subjective because its goal is to find out what the actor "means" in his action, in contrast to the meaning which this action has for the actor's partner or a neutral observer. This is the origin of Max Weber's famous postulate of subjective interpretation, of which more will have to be said in what follows. The whole discussion suffers from the failure to distinguish clearly between *Verstehen* (1) as the experiential form of common-sense knowledge of human affairs, (2) as an epistemological problem, and (3) as a method peculiar to the social sciences.

So far we have concentrated on *Verstehen* as the way in which common-sense thinking finds its bearing within the social world and comes to terms with·it. As to the epistemological question: "How is such understanding or *Verstehen* possible?" I have to answer, alluding to a statement Kant made in another context, that it is a "scandal of philosophy" that so far the problem of our knowledge of other minds and, in connection therewith, of the intersubjectivity of our experience of the natural as well as the socio-cultural world, has not found a satisfactory solution and that, until rather recent times, this problem has even escaped the attention of philosophers. But the solution of this most difficult problem of philosophical interpretation is one of the first things taken for granted in our common-sense thinking and practically solved without any difficulty in each of our everyday actions. And since human beings are born of mothers and not concocted in retorts, the experience of the existence of other human beings and of the meaning of their actions is certainly the first and most original empirical observation man makes.

On the other hand, philosophers as different as James, Bergson, Dewey, Husserl, and Whitehead agree that the common-sense knowledge of everyday life is the unquestioned but always questionable background within which inquiry starts and within which alone it can be carried out. It is this *Lebenswelt,* as Husserl calls it, within which, according to him, all scientific and even logical concepts originate; it is the social matrix within which, according to Dewey, unclarified situations emerge, which have to be transformed by the process of inquiry into warranted assertibility; and Whitehead has pointed out that it is the aim of science to produce a theory which agrees with experience by explaining the thought-objects constructed by common sense through the mental constructs or thought objects of science. For all these thinkers agree that any knowledge of the world, in common-sense thinking as well as in science, involves mental constructs, syntheses, generalizations, formalizations, idealizations specific to the respective level of thought organization. The concept of Nature, for instance, with which the natural sciences have to deal is, as Husserl has shown, an idealizing abstraction from the *Lebenswelt,* an abstraction which, on principle and of course legitimately, excludes persons with their personal life and all objects of culture which originate as such in practical human activity. Exactly this layer of the *Lebenswelt,* however, from which the natural sciences have to abstract, is the social reality which the social sciences have to investigate.

This insight sheds a light on certain methodological problems peculiar to the social sciences. To begin with, it appears that the assumption that the strict adoption of the principles of concept and theory formation prevailing in the natural sciences will lead to reliable knowledge of the social reality, is inconsistent in itself. If a theory can be developed on such principles, say in the form of an ideally refined behaviorism —and it is certainly possible to imagine this—, then it will not tell us anything about social reality as experienced by men in everyday life. As Professor Nagel himself admits,[16] it will be highly abstract, and its concepts will apparently be remote from the obvious and familiar traits found in any society. On the other hand, a theory which aims at explaining social reality has to develop particular devices foreign to the natural sciences in order to agree with the common-sense experience of the social world. This is indeed what all theoretical sciences of human affairs—economics, sociology, the sciences of law, linguistics, cultural anthropology, etc.—have done.

This state of affairs is founded on the fact that there is an essential difference in the structure of the thought objects or mental constructs formed by the social sciences and those formed by the natural sciences.[17] It is up to the natural scientist and to him alone to define, in accordance with the procedural rules of his science, his observational field, and to determine the facts, data, and events within it which are relevant for his problem or scientific purpose at hand. Neither are those facts and events pre-selected, nor is the observational field pre-interpreted. The world of nature, as explored by the natural scientist, does not "mean" anything to the molecules, atoms, and electrons therein. The observational field of the social scientist, however, namely the social reality, has a specific meaning and relevance structure for the human beings living, acting, and thinking therein. By a series of common-sense constructs they have pre-selected and pre-interpreted this world which they experience as the reality of their daily lives. It is these thought objects of theirs which determine their behavior by motivating it. The thought objects constructed by the social scientist, in order to grasp this social reality, have to be founded upon the thought objects constructed by the common-sense thinking of men, living their daily life within their social world. Thus, the constructs of the social sciences are, so to speak, constructs of the second degree, namely constructs of the constructs made by the actors on the social scene, whose behavior the social scientist has to observe and to explain in accordance with the procedural rules of his science.

Thus, the exploration of the general principles according to which man in daily life organizes his experiences, and especially those of the social world, is the first task of the methodology of the social sciences. This is not the place to outline the procedures of phenomenological analysis of the so-called natural attitude by which this can be done. We shall briefly mention only a few problems involved.

The world, as has been shown by Husserl, is from the outset experienced in the pre-scientific thinking of everyday life in the mode of typicality. The unique objects and events given to us in a unique aspect are unique within a horizon of typical familiarity and pre-acquaintanceship. There are mountains, trees, animals, dogs—in particular Irish setters and among them my Irish setter, Rover. Now I may look at Rover either as this unique individual, my irreplaceable friend and comrade, or just as a typical example of "Irish setter," "dog," "mammal," "animal," "organism," or "object of the outer world." Starting from here, it can be shown that whether I do one or the other, and also which traits or qualities of a given object or event I consider as individually unique and which as typical, depends upon my actual interest and the system of relevances involved therein—briefly, upon my practical or theoretical "problem at hand." This "problem at hand," in turn, originates in the circumstances within which I find myself at any moment of my daily life and which I propose to call my biographically determined situation. Thus, typification depends upon my problem at hand for the definition and solution of which the type has been formed. It can be further shown that at least one aspect of the biographically and situationally determined systems of interests and relevances is subjectively experienced in the thinking of everyday life as systems of motives for action, of choices to be made, of projects to be carried out, of goals to be reached. It is, so I submit, this insight of the actor into the dependencies of the motives and goals of his actions upon his biographically determined situation which social scientists have in view when speaking of the subjective meaning which the actor "bestows upon" or "connects with" his action. This implies that, strictly speaking, the actor and he alone knows what he does, wherefore and why he does it, and when and where his action starts and ends.

But the world of everyday life is from the outset also a social cultural world in which I am interrelated in manifold ways of interaction with fellow-men known to me in varying degrees of intimacy and anonymity. To a certain extent, sufficient for many practical purposes, I understand their behavior, if I understand their motives, goals, choices, and plans originating in *their* biographically determined circumstances. Yet only in particular situations, and then only fragmentarily, can I experience the others' motives, goals etc.— briefly, the subjective meanings they bestow upon their actions, in their uniqueness. I can, however, experience them in their typicality. In order to do so I construct typical patterns of the actors' motives and ends, even of their attitudes and personalities, of which their actual conduct is just an instance or example. These typified patterns of the others' behavior become in turn motives of my own actions, and this leads to the phenomenon of self-typification well known to social scientists under various names.

Here, I submit, in the common-sense thinking of everyday life, is the origin of the so-called constructive or ideal types, a concept which as a tool of the social sciences has been analyzed by Professor Hempel in such a lucid way. But at least at the common-sense level the formation of these types involves neither intuition nor a theory, if we understand these terms in the sense of Hempel's statements.[18] As we shall see, there are also other kinds of ideal or constructive types, those formed by the social scientist, which are of a quite different structure and indeed involve theory. But Hempel has not distinguished between these two kinds.

Next we have to consider that the common-sense knowledge of everyday life is from the outset socialized in many respects.

It is, first, structurally socialized, since it is based on the fundamental idealization that if I were to change places with my fellow-man I would experience the same sector of the world in substantially the same perspectives as he does, our particular biographical circumstances becoming for all practical purposes at hand irrelevant. I propose to call this idealization that of the reciprocity of perspectives.

It is, second, genetically socialized, because the greater part of our knowledge, as to its content and the particular forms of typification under which it is organized, is socially derived, and this in socially approved terms.

It is, third, socialized in the sense of social distribution of knowledge, each individual knowing merely a sector of the world and common knowledge of the same sector varying individually as to its degree of distinctness, clarity, acquaintanceship, or mere belief.

These principles of socialization of common-sense knowledge, and especially that of the social distribution of knowledge, explain at least partially what the social scientist has in mind in speaking of the functional structural approach to studies of human affairs. The concept of functionalism—at least in the modern social sciences—is not derived from the biological concept of the functioning of an organism, as Nagel holds. It refers to the socially distributed constructs of patterns of typical motives, goals, attitudes, personalities, which are supposed to be invariant and are then interpreted as the function or structure of the social system itself. The more these interlocked behavior-patterns are standardized and institutionalized, that is, the more their typicality is socially approved by laws, folkways, mores, and habits, the greater is their usefulness in common-sense and scientific thinking as a scheme of interpretation of human behavior.

These are, very roughly, the outlines of a few major features of the constructs involved in common-sense experience of the intersubjective world in daily life, which is called *Verstehen*. As explained before, they are the first-level constructs upon which the second-level constructs of the social sciences have to be erected. But here a major problem emerges. On the one hand, it has been shown that the constructs on the first level, the common-sense constructs, refer to subjective elements, namely the *Verstehen* of the actor's action from his, the actor's, point of view. Consequently, if the social sciences aim indeed at explaining social reality, then the scientific constructs on the second level, too, must include a reference to the subjective meaning an action has for the actor. This is, I think, what Max Weber understood by his famous postulate of subjective interpretation, which has, indeed, been observed so far in the theory-formation of all social sciences. The postulate of subjective interpretation has to be understood in the sense that all scientific explanations of the social world *can*, and for certain purposes *must*, refer to the subjective meaning of the actions of human beings from which the social reality originates.

On the other hand, I agreed with Professor Nagel's statement that the social sciences, like all empirical sciences, have to be objective in the sense that their propositions are subjected to controlled verification and must not refer to private uncontrollable experience.

How is it possible to reconcile these seemingly contradictory principles? Indeed, the most serious question which the methodology of the social sciences has to answer is: How is it possible to form objective concepts and an objectively verifiable theory of subjective meaning-structures? The basic insight that the concepts formed by the social scientist are constructs of the constructs formed in common-sense thinking by the actors on the social scene offers an answer. The scientific constructs formed on the second level, in accordance with the procedural rules valid for all empirical sciences, are objective ideal typical constructs and, as such, of a different kind from those developed on the first level of common-sense thinking which they have to supersede. They are theoretical systems embodying testable general hypotheses in the sense of Professor Hempel's definition.[19] This device has been used by social scientists concerned with theory long before this concept was formulated by Max Weber and developed by his school.

Before describing a few features of these scientific constructs, let us briefly consider the particular attitude of the theoretical social scientist to the social world, in contradistinction to that of the actor on the social scene. The theoretical scientist—qua scientist, not qua human being (which he is, too)—is not involved in the observed situation, which is to him not of a practical but merely of a cognitive interest. The system of relevances governing common-sense interpretation in daily life originates in the biographical situation of the observer. By making up his mind to become a scientist, the social scientist has replaced his personal biographical situation by what I shall call, following Felix Kaufmann,[20] a scientific situation. The problems with which he has to deal might be quite unproblematic for the human being within the world and vice versa. Any scientific problem is determined by the actual state of the respective science, and its solution has to be achieved in accordance with the procedural rules governing this science, which among other things warrant the control and verification of the solution offered. The scientific problem, once established, alone determines what is relevant for the scientist and therewith the conceptual frame of reference to be used by him. This and nothing else, so it seems to me, is what Max Weber means when he postulates the objectivity of the social sciences, namely their detachment from value patterns which govern or might govern the behavior of the actors on the social scene.

How does the social scientist proceed? He observes certain

facts and events within social reality which refer to human action and he constructs typical behavior or course-of-action patterns from what he has observed. Thereupon he co-ordinates to these typical course-of-action patterns models of an ideal actor or actors, whom he imagines as being gifted with consciousness. Yet it is a consciousness restricted so as to contain nothing but the elements relevant to the performing of the course-of-action patterns observed. He thus ascribes to this fictitious consciousness a set of typical notions, purposes, goals, which are assumed to be invariant in the specious consciousness of the imaginary actor-model. This homunculus or puppet is supposed to be interrelated in interaction patterns to other homunculi or puppets constructed in a similar way. Among these homunculi with which the social scientist populates his model of the social world of everyday life, sets of motives, goals, roles—in general, systems of relevances—are distributed in such a way as the scientific problems under scrutiny require. Yet—and this is the main point —these constructs are by no means arbitrary. They are subject to the postulate of logical consistency and to the postulate of adequacy. The latter means that each term in such a scientific model of human action must be constructed in such a way that a human act performed within the real world by an individual actor as indicated by the typical construct would be understandable to the actor himself as well as to his fellow-men in terms of common-sense interpretation of everyday life. Compliance with the postulate of logical consistency warrants the objective validity of the thought objects constructed by the social scientist; compliance with the postulate of adequacy warrants their compatibility with the constructs of everyday life.

As the next step, the circumstances within which such a model operates may be varied, that is, the situation which the homunculi have to meet may be imagined as changed, but not the set of motives and relevances assumed to be the sole content of their consciousness. I may, for example, construct a model of a producer acting under conditions of un-regulated competition, and another of a producer acting under cartel restrictions, and then compare the output of the same commodity of the same firm in the two models.[21] In this way, it is possible to predict how such a puppet or system of puppets might behave under certain conditions and to discover certain "determinate relations between a set of variables, in terms of which . . . empirically ascertainable regularities . . . can be explained." This, however, is Professor Nagel's definition of a theory.[22] It can easily be seen that each step involved in the construction and use of the scientific model can be verified by empirical observation, provided that we do not restrict this term to sensory perceptions of objects and events in the outer world but include the experiential form, by which common-sense thinking in everyday life understands human actions and their outcome in terms of their underlying motives and goals.

Two brief concluding remarks may be permitted. First a key concept of the basic philosophic position of naturalism is the so-called principle of continuity, although it is under discussion whether this principle means continuity of existence, or of analysis, or of an intellectual criterion of pertinent checks upon the methods employed.[23] It seems to me that this principle of continuity in each of these various interpretations is fulfilled by the characterized device of the social sciences, which even establishes continuity between the practice of everyday life and the conceptualization of the social sciences.

Second, a word on the problem of the methodological unity of the empirical sciences. It seems to me that the social scientist can agree with the statement that the principal differences between the social and the natural sciences have not to be looked for in a different logic governing each branch of knowledge. But this does not involve the admittance that the social sciences have to abandon the particular devices they use for exploring social reality for the sake of an

ideal unity of methods which is founded on the entirely unwarranted assumption that only methods used by the natural
sciences, and especially by physics, are scientific ones. So far
as I know no serious attempt has ever been made by the
proponents of the "unity of science" movement to answer or
even to ask the question whether the methodological problem of the natural sciences in their present state is not merely
a special case of the more general, still unexplored, problem
how scientific knowledge is possible at all and what its logical
and methodological presuppositions are. It is my personal
conviction that phenomenological philosophy has prepared
the ground for such an investigation. Its outcome might quite
possibly show that the particular methodological devices developed by the social sciences in order to grasp social reality,
are better suited than those of the natural sciences to lead to
the discovery of the general principles which govern all human knowledge.

NOTES

1. Paper presented at the 33rd Semi-Annual Meeting of the Conference
on Methods in Philosophy and the Sciences, New York, May 3, 1953.

2. Published in the volume *Science, Language and Human Rights* (American Philosophical Association, Eastern Division, Vol. 1) (Philadelphia: University of Pennsylvania Press, 1952), pp. 43–86 (referred to as *SLH*).

3. Especially his *Methodology of the Social Sciences* (New York: Oxford
University Press, 1941).

4. *SLH*, pp. 43–64.

5. *SLH*, pp. 65–86.

6. *SLH*, p. 56.

7. *SLH*, p. 46.

8. *SLH*, pp. 60 ff.

9. *SLH*, pp. 55–57.

10. *SLH*, p. 53.

11. *Op. cit.*, p. 126.

12. *Mind, Self and Society* (Chicago: The University of Chicago Press,
1937).

13. See Max Weber, *The Theory of Social and Economic Organization*,
trans. A. M. Henderson and Talcott Parsons (New York, 1947), p. 88.

14. See W. J. Thomas, *Social Behavior and Personality*, ed. E. H. Volkart (New York: Social Science Research Council, 1951), p. 81.

15. *Principles of Psychology*, 1: 221 f.

16. *SLH*, p. 63.

17. Some of the points dealt with in the following are presented more elaborately in my paper, "Common-Sense and Scientific Interpretation of Human Action," in *Philosophy and Phenomenological Research* 14 (September 1953): 1–37.

18. *SLH*, pp. 76ff. and 81.

19. *SLH*, pp. 77ff.

20. *Op. cit.*, pp. 52 and 251.

21. See Fritz Machlup, *The Economics of Seller's Competition; Model Analysis of Seller's Conduct* (Baltimore: The Johns Hopkins Press, 1952), pp. 9ff.

22. *SLH*, p. 46; see also p. 90 above.

23. See Thelma Z. Lavine, "Note to Naturalists on the Human Spirit," *The Journal of Philosophy* 50 (1953): 145–54, and Ernest Nagel's answer, *ibid*, pp. 154–57.

II

Individual Action and Sociality

5

Existential Psychoanalysis

JEAN-PAUL SARTRE

If it is true that human reality—as we have attempted to establish—identifies and defines itself by the ends which it pursues, then a study and classification of these ends becomes indispensable. In the preceding chapter we have considered the For-itself only from the point of view of its free project, which is the impulse by which it thrusts itself toward its end. We should now question this end itself, for it *forms a part* of absolute subjectivity and is, in fact, its transcendent, objective limit. This is what empirical psychology has hinted at by admitting that a particular man is defined by his desires. Here, however, we must be on our guard against two errors. First, the empirical psychologist, while defining man by his desires, remains the victim of the illusion of substance. He views desire as being *in* man by virtue of

Used by permission of Philosophical Library, Inc. from *Being and Nothingness* by Jean-Paul Sartre, © copyright, 1956, by Philosophical Library, Inc., New York.

being "contained" by his consciousness, and he believes that the meaning of the desire is inherent in the desire itself. Thus he avoids everything which could evoke the idea of transcendence. But if I desire a house or a glass of water or a woman's body, how could this body, this glass, this piece of property reside in my desire, and how can my desire be anything but the consciousness of these objects as desirable? Let us beware then of considering these desires as little psychic entities dwelling in consciousness; they are consciousness itself in its original projective, transcendent structure, for consciousness is on principle consciousness *of* something.

The other error, which fundamentally is closely connected with the first, consists in considering psychological research as terminated as soon as the investigator has reached the concrete ensemble of empirical desires. Thus a man would be defined by the bundle of drives or tendencies which empirical observation could establish. Naturally the psychologist will not always limit himself to making up the *sum* of these tendencies; he will want to bring to light their relationships, their agreements and harmonies; he will try to present the ensemble of desires as a synthetic organization in which each desire acts on the others and influences them. A critic, for example, wishing to explain the "psychology" of Flaubert, will write that he "appeared in his early youth to know as his normal state, a continual exaltation resulting from the twofold feeling of his grandiose ambition and his invincible power. . . . The effervescence of his young blood was *then* turned into literary passion as happens about the eighteenth year in precocious souls who find in the energy of style or the intensities of fiction some way of escaping from the need of violent action or of intense feeling, which torments them."[1]

In this passage there is an effort to reduce the complex personality of an adolescent to a few basic desires, as the chemist reduces compound bodies to merely a combination of simple bodies. The primitive givens will be grandiose ambition, the need of violent action and of intense feeling; these elements when they enter into combination, produce a permanent exaltation. Then—as Bourget remarks in a few words which we have not quoted—this exaltation nourished by numerous well chosen readings, is going to seek to delude itself by self-expression in fictions which will appease it symbolically and channel it. There in outline is the genesis of a literary "temperament."

Now in the first place such a psychological *analysis* proceeds from the postulate that an individual fact is produced by the intersection of abstract, universal laws. The fact to be explained—which is here the literary disposition of the young Flaubert—is resolved into a combination of *typical,* abstract desires such as we meet in "the average adolescent." What is concrete here is only their combination; in themselves they are only possible patterns. The abstract then is by hypothesis prior to the concrete, and the concrete is only an organization of abstract qualities; the individual is only the intersection of universal schemata. But—aside from the logical absurdity of such a postulate—we see clearly in the example chosen, that it simply fails to explain what makes the individuality of the project under consideration. The fact that "the need to feel intensely," a universal pattern, is disguised and channeled into becoming the need to write—this is not the *explanation* of the "calling" of Flaubert; on the contrary, it is what must be explained. Doubtless one could invoke a thousand circumstances, known to us and unknown, which have shaped this need to feel into the need to act. But this is to give up at the start all attempt to explain and refers the question to the undiscoverable.[2] In addition this method rejects the pure individual who has been banished from the pure subjectivity of Flaubert into the external circumstances of his life. Finally, Flaubert's correspondence proves that long before the "crisis of adolescence," from his earliest childhood, he was tormented by the need to write.

At each stage in the description just quoted, we meet with an hiatus. Why did ambition and the feeling of his power produce in Flaubert *exaltation* rather than tranquil waiting or gloomy impatience? Why did this exaltation express itself specifically in the need to act violently and feel intensely? Or rather why does this need make a sudden appearance by spontaneous generation at the end of the paragraph? And why does this need instead of seeking to appease itself in acts of violence, by amorous adventures, or in debauch, choose precisely to satisfy itself symbolically? And why does Flaubert turn to writing rather than to painting or music for this symbolic satisfaction; he could just as well not resort to the artistic field at all (there is also mysticism, for example). "I could have been a great actor," wrote Flaubert somewhere. Why did he not try to be one? In a word, we have understood nothing; we have seen a succession of accidental happenings, of desire springing forth fully armed, one from the other, with no possibility for us to grasp their genesis. The *transitions*, the becomings, the transformations, have been carefully veiled from us, and we have been limited to putting order into the succession by invoking empirically established but literally unintelligible sequences (the need to act preceding in the adolescent the need to write).

Yet this is called psychology! Open any biography at random, and this is the kind of description which you will find more or less interspersed with accounts of external events and allusions to the great explanatory idols of our epoch— heredity, education, environment, physiological constitution. Occasionally, in the better works the connection established between antecedent and consequent or between two concomitant desires and their reciprocal action is not conceived merely as a type of regular sequence; sometimes it is "comprehensible" in the sense which Jaspers understands in his general treatise on psychopathology. But this comprehension remains a grasp of general connections. For example we will realize the link between chastity and mysticism, between fainting and hypocrisy. But we are ignorant always of the concrete relation between *this* chastity (this abstinence in relation to a particular woman, *this* struggle against a definite temptation) and the individual content of the mysticism; in the same way psychiatry is too quickly satisfied when it throws light on the general structures of delusions and does not seek to comprehend the individual, concrete content of the psychoses (why this man believes himself to be that particular historical personality rather than some other; why his compensatory delusion is satisfied with specifically these ideas of grandeur instead of others, *etc.*).

But most important of all, these "psychological" explanations refer us ultimately to inexplicable original givens. These are the simple bodies of psychology. We are told, for example, that Flaubert had a "grandiose ambition" and all of the previously quoted description depends on this original ambition. So far so good. But this ambition is an irreducible fact which by no means satisfies the mind. The irreducibility here has no justification other than refusal to push the analysis further. There where the psychologist stops, the fact confronted is given as primary. This is why we experience a troubled feeling of mingled resignation and dissatisfaction when we read these psychological treatises. "See," we say to ourselves, "Flaubert was ambitious. He was that kind of man." It would be as futile to ask why he was such as to seek to know why he was tall and blond. Of course we have to stop somewhere; it is the very contingency of all real existence. This rock is covered with moss, the rock next to it is not. Gustave Flaubert had literary ambition, and his brother Achille lacked it. That's the way it is. In the same way we want to know the properties of phosphorus, and we attempt to reduce them to the structure of the chemical molecules which compose it. But why are there molecules of this type? That's the way it is, that's all. The explanation of Flaubert's psychology will consist, if it is possible, in referring the complexity of his behavior patterns, his feelings, and his tastes back to certain *properties,* comparable to those of chemical bodies, beyond which it would be foolish to attempt to proceed. Yet we feel obscurely that Flaubert had not "received" his ambition. It is meaningful; therefore it is free. Neither heredity, nor bourgeois background nor education can account for it, still less those physiological considerations regarding the "nervous temperament," which have been the vogue for some time now. The nerve is not *meaningful;* it is a colloidal substance which can be described in itself and which does not have the quality of transcendence; that is, it does not transcend itself in order to make known to itself by means of other realities what it is. Under no circumstances could the nerve furnish the basis for meaning. In one sense Flaubert's ambition is a fact with all a fact's contingency— and it is true that it is impossible to advance beyond that fact —but in another sense *it makes itself,* and our satisfaction is a guarantee to us that we may be able to grasp beyond this ambition something more, something like a radical decision which, without ceasing to be contingent, would be the veritable psychic irreducible.

What we are demanding then—and what nobody ever attempts to give us—is a *veritable* irreducible; that is, an irreducible of which the irreducibility would be self-evident, which would not be presented as the postulate of the psychologist and the result of his refusal or his incapacity to go further, but which when established would produce in us an accompanying feeling of satisfaction. This demand on our part does not come from that ceaseless pursuit of a cause, that infinite regress which has often been described as constitutive of rational research and which consequently—far from being exclusively associated with psychological investigation —may be found in all disciplines in all problems. This is not the childish quest of a "because," which allows no further "why?" It is on the contrary a demand based on a pre-ontological comprehension of human reality and on the related refusal to consider man as capable of being analyzed and reduced to original givens, to determined desires (or "drives"), supported by the subject as properties by an object. Even if we were to consider him as such, it would be necessary to choose: either *Flaubert*, the man, whom we can love or detest, blame or praise, who represents for us *the Other*, who directly attacks our being by the very fact that he has existed, would be originally a substratum unqualified by these desires; that is, a sort of indeterminate clay which would have to receive them passively or he would be reduced to the simple bundle of these irreducible drives or tendencies. In either case the *man* disappears; we can no longer find "the one" to *whom* this or that experience has *happened*; either in looking for the *person*, we encounter a useless, contradictory metaphysical substance—or else the being whom we seek vanishes in a dust of phenomena bound together by external connections. But what each one of us requires in his very effort to comprehend another is that he should never have to resort to this idea of substance which is inhuman because it is well this side of the human. Finally the fact is that the being considered does not crumble into dust, and one can discover in him that unity—for which substance was only a caricature—which must be a unity of responsibility, a unity agreeable or hateful, blamable and praiseworthy, in short *personal*. This unity, which is the being of the man under consideration, is a *free unification*, and this unification can not come *after* a diversity which it unifies.

But *to be*, for Flaubert, as for every subject of "biography," means to be unified in the world. The irreducible unification which we ought to find, which is Flaubert, and which we require biographers to reveal to us—this is the unification of an *original project*, a unification which should reveal itself to us as a *non-substantial absolute*. Therefore we should forego these so-called irreducible details and, taking the very evidence of them for a criterion, not stop in our investigation before it is evident that we neither can nor ought to go any further. In particular we must avoid trying to reconstruct a person by means of his inclinations, just as Spinoza warns us not to attempt to reconstruct a substance or its attributes by the summation of its modes. Every desire if presented as an irreducible is an absurd contingency and involves in absurdity human reality taken as a whole. For example, if I declare of one of my friends that he "likes to go rowing," I deliberately intend to stop my investigation there. But on the other hand, I thus establish a contingent *fact*, which nothing can explain and which, though it has the gratuity of free decision, by no means has its autonomy. I can not in fact consider this fondness for rowing as the fundamental project of Pierre; it contains something secondary and derived. Those who portray a character in this way by successive strokes come close to holding that each of these strokes—each one of the desires confronted—is bound to the others by connections which are purely contingent and simply external. Those who, on the other hand, try to explain this liking will fall into the view of what Comte called *materialism;* that is, of explaining the higher by the lower. Someone will say, for example, that the subject considered is a sportsman who likes violent exercise and is in addition a man of the outdoors who especially likes open air sports. By more general and less differentiated tendencies he will try to explain *this* desire, which stands in exactly the same relation to them as the zoological species does to the genus. Thus the psychological explanation when it does not suddenly decide to stop, is sometimes the mere putting into relief relations of pure concomitance or of constant succession, and it is at other times a simple classification. To explain Pierre's fondness for rowing is to make it a member of the family of fondness for open air sports and to attach this family to that of fondness for sport in general. Moreover we will be able to find still more general and barren rubrics if we classify the taste for sports as one aspect of the love of chance, which will itself be given as a specific instance of the fundamental fondness for play. It is obvious that this so-called explanatory classification has no more value or interest than the classifications in ancient botany; like the latter it amounts

to assuming the priority of the abstract over the concrete—
as if the fondness for play existed first in general to be subsequently made specific by the action of these circumstances
in the love of sport, the latter in the fondness for rowing, and
finally the rowing in the desire to row on a particular stream,
under certain circumstances in a particular season—and like
the ancient classifications it fails to explain the concrete en-
richment which at each stage is undergone by the abstract
inclination considered.

Furthermore how are we to believe that a desire to row is
only a desire to row. Can we truthfully admit that it can be
reduced so simply to what it is? The most discerning ethicists
have shown how a desire reaches beyond itself. Pascal believed that he could discover in hunting, for example, or
tennis, or in a hundred other occupations, the need of being
diverted. He revealed that in an activity which would be
absurd if reduced to itself, there was a meaning which transcended it; that is, an indication which referred to the reality
of man in general and to his condition. Similarly Stendhal in
spite of his attachment to ideologists, and Proust in spite of
his intellectualistic and analytical tendencies, have shown
that love and jealousy can not be reduced to the strict desire
of possessing a *particular* woman, but that these emotions
aim at laying hold of the world in its entirety through the
woman. This is the meaning of Stendhal's crystallization, and
it is precisely for this reason that love as Stendhal describes
it appears as a mode of being in the world. Love is a fundamental relation of the for-itself to the world and to itself
(selfness) through a particular woman; the woman represents
only a conducting body which is placed in the circuit. These
analyses may be inexact or only partially true; nevertheless
they make us suspect a method other than pure analytical
description. In the same way Catholic novelists immediately
see in carnal love its surpassing toward God—in Don Juan,
"the eternally unsatisfied," in sin, "the place empty of God."
There is no question here of finding again an abstract behind

the concrete; the impulse toward God is no *less concrete* than the impulse toward a particular woman. On the contrary, it is a matter of rediscovering under the partial and incomplete aspects of the subject the veritable concreteness which can be only the totality of his impulse toward being, his original relation to himself, to the world, and to the Other, in the unity of internal relations and of a fundamental project. This impulse can be only purely individual and unique. Far from estranging us from the person, as Bourget's analysis, for example, does in constituting the individual by means of a summation of general maxims, this impulse will not lead us to find in the need of writing—and of writing particular books—the need of activity in general. On the contrary, rejecting equally the theory of malleable clay and that of the bundle of drives, we will discover the individual person in the initial project which constitutes him. It is for this reason that the irreducibility of the result attained will be revealed as self-evident, not because it is the poorest and the most abstract but because it is the richest. The intuition here will be accompanied by an individual fullness.

The problem poses itself in approximately these terms: If we admit that the person is a totality, we can not hope to reconstruct him by an addition or by an organization of the diverse tendencies which we have empirically discovered in him. On the contrary, in each inclination, in each tendency the person expresses himself completely, although from a different angle, a little as Spinoza's substance expresses itself completely in each of its attributes. But if this is so, we should discover in each tendency, in each attitude of the subject, a meaning which transcends it. A jealousy of a particular date in which a subject historicizes himself in relation to a certain woman, signifies for the one who knows how to interpret it, the total relation to the world by which the subject constitutes himself as a self. In other words this *empirical* attitude is by itself the expression of the "choice of an intelligible character." There is no mystery about this. We no longer have to do with an intelligible pattern which can be present in our thought only, while we apprehend and conceptualize the unique pattern of the subject's empirical existence. If the empirical attitude signifies the choice of the intelligible character, it is because it is itself this choice. Indeed the distinguishing characteristic of the intelligible choice, as we shall see later, is that it can exist only as the transcendent meaning of each concrete, empirical choice. It is by no means first effected in some unconscious or on the noumenal level to be *subsequently* expressed in a particular observable attitude; there is not even an *ontological* pre-eminence over the empirical choice, but it is on principle that which must always detach itself from the empirical choice as its *beyond* and the infinity of its transcendence. Thus if I am rowing on the river, I am nothing—either here or in any other world—save this concrete project of rowing. But this project itself inasmuch as it is the totality of my being, expresses my original choice in particular circumstances; it is nothing other than the choice of myself as a totality in these circumstances. That is why a special method must aim at detaching the fundamental meaning which the project admits and which can be only the individual secret of the subject's being-in-the-world. It is then rather by a *comparison* of the various empirical drives of a subject that we try to discover and disengage the fundamental project which is common to them all—and not by a simple summation or reconstruction of these tendencies; each drive or tendency is the entire person.

There is naturally an infinity of possible projects as there is an infinity of possible human beings. Nevertheless, if we are to recognize certain common characteristics among them and if we are going to attempt to classify them in larger categories, it is best first to undertake individual investigations in the cases which we can study more easily. In our research, we will be guided by this principle: to stop only in the presence of evident irreducibility; that is, never to believe that we have reached the initial project until the projected end appears as *the very being* of the subject under consideration. This is why we can not stop at those classifications of "authentic project" and "unauthentic project of the self" which Heidegger wishes to establish. In addition to the fact that such a classification, in spite of its author's intent, is tainted with an ethical concern shown by its very terminology, it is based on the attitude of the subject toward his own death. Now if death causes anguish, and if consequently we can either flee the anguish or throw ourselves resolutely into it, it is a truism to say that this is because we wish to hold on to life. Consequently anguish before death and resolute decision or flight into unauthenticity can not be considered as fundamental projects of our being. On the contrary, they can be understood only on the foundation of an original project of *living;* that is, on an original choice of our being. It is right then in each case to pass beyond the results of Heidegger's interpretation toward a still more fundamental project.

This fundamental project must not of course refer to any other and should be conceived by itself. It can be concerned neither with death nor life nor any particular characteristic of the human condition; the original project of a for-itself *can aim only at its being.* The project of being or desire of being or drive toward being does not originate in a physiological differentiation or in an empirical contingency; in fact it is not distinguished from the being of the for-itself. The for-itself is a being such that in its being, its being is in question in the form of a project of being. To the for-itself *being* means to make known to oneself what one is by means of a possibility appearing as a value. Possibility and value belong to the being of the for-itself. The for-itself is defined ontologically as a *lack of being,* and possibility belongs to the for-itself as that which it lacks, in the same way that value haunts the for-itself as the totality of being which is lacking. What we have expressed in Part Two in terms of lack can be just as well expressed in terms of *freedom.* The for-itself chooses because it is lack; freedom is really synonymous with lack. Freedom is the concrete mode of being of the lack of being. Ontologically then it amounts to the same thing to say that value and possibility exist as internal limits of a lack of being which can exist only as a lack of being—or that the upsurge of freedom determines its possibility and thereby circumscribes *its* value.

Thus we can advance no further but have encountered the self-evident irreducible when we have reached the *project of being;* for obviously it is impossible to advance further than *being* and there is no difference between the project of being, possibility, value, on the one hand, and *being,* on the other. Fundamentally man is *the desire to be,* and the existence of this desire is not to be established by an empirical induction; it is the result of an *a priori* description of the being of the for-itself, since desire is a lack and since the for-itself is the being which is to itself its own lack of being. The original project which is expressed in each of our empirically observable tendencies is then the *project of being;* or, if you prefer, each empirical tendency exists with the original project of being in relation of expression and symbolic satisfaction just as conscious drives, with Freud, exist in relation to the complex and to the original libido. Moreover the desire to be by no means exists *first* in order to cause itself to be expressed subsequently by desires *a posteriori.* There is nothing outside of the symbolic expression which it finds in concrete desires. There is not first a single desire of being, then a thousand particular feelings, but the desire to be exists and manifests itself only in and through jealousy, greed, love of art, cowardice, courage, and a thousand contingent, empirical expressions which always cause human reality to appear to us only as *manifested* by *a particular man,* by a specific person.

As for the being which is the object of this desire, we know *a priori* what this is. The for-itself is the being which is to itself its own lack of being. The being which the for-itself lacks is the in-itself. The for-itself arises as the nihilation of the in-itself and this nihilation is defined as the project toward the in-itself. Between the nihilated in-itself and the projected in-itself the for-itself is nothingness. Thus the end and the goal of the nihilation which I am is the in-itself. Thus human reality is the desire of being-in-itself. But the in-itself which it desires can not be pure contingent, absurd in-itself, comparable at every point to that which it encounters and which it nihilates. The nihilation, as we have seen, is in fact like a revolt of the in-itself, which nihilates itself against its contingency. To say that the for-itself lives its facticity, as we have seen in the chapter concerning the body, amounts to saying that the nihilation is the vain effort of a being to found its own being and that it is the withdrawal to found being which provokes the minute displacement by which nothingness enters into being. The being which forms the object of the desire of the for-itself is then an in-itself which would be to itself its own foundation; that is, which would be to its facticity in the same relation as the for-itself is to its motivations. In addition the for-itself, being the negation of the in-itself, could not desire the pure and simple return to the in-itself. Here as with Hegel, the negation of the negation can not bring us back to our point of departure. Quite the contrary, what the for-itself demands of the in-itself is precisely the totality detotalized—"In-itself nihilated in for-itself." In other words the for-itself projects *being as for-itself*, a being which is what it is. It is as being which is what it is not, and which is not what it is, that the for-itself projects being what it is. It is as consciousness that it wishes to have the impermeability and infinite density of the in-itself. It is as the nihilation of the in-itself and a perpetual evasion of contingency and of facticity that it wishes to be its own foundation. This is why the possible is projected in general as what the for-itself lacks in order to become in-itself-for-itself. The fundamental value which presides over this project is exactly the in-itself-for-itself; that is, the ideal of a consciousness which would be the foundation of its own being-in-itself by the pure consciousness which it would have of itself. It is this ideal which can be called God. Thus the best way to conceive of the fundamental project of human reality is to say that man is the being whose project is to be God. Whatever may be the myths and rites of the religion considered, God is first "sensible to the heart" of man as the one who identifies and defines him in his ultimate and fundamental project. If man possesses a pre-ontological comprehension of the being of God, it is not the great wonders of nature nor the power of society which have conferred it upon him. God, value and supreme end of transcendence, represents the permanent limit in terms of which man makes known to himself what he is. To be man means to reach toward being God. Or if you prefer, man fundamentally is the desire to be God.

It may be asked, if man on coming into the world is borne toward God as toward his limit, if he can choose only to be God, what becomes of freedom? For freedom is nothing other than a choice which creates for itself its own possibilities, but it appears here that the initial project of being God, which "defines" man, comes close to being the same as a human "nature" or an "essence." The answer is that while the *meaning* of the desire is ultimately the project of being God, the desire is never *constituted* by this meaning; on the contrary, it always represents a particular discovery of its ends. These ends in fact are pursued in terms of a particular empirical situation, and it is this very pursuit which constitutes the surroundings *as a situation*. The desire of being is always realized as the desire of a mode of being. And this desire of a mode of being expresses itself in turn as the meaning of the myriads of concrete desires which constitute the web of our conscious life. Thus we find ourselves before very complex symbolic structures which have *at least* three stories. In empirical desire I can discern a symbolization of a fundamental concrete desire which is the person himself and which represents the mode in which he has decided that being would be in question in his being. This fundamental desire in turn expresses concretely in the world within the particular situation enveloping the individual, an abstract meaningful structure which is the desire of being in general; it must be considered as human reality in the person, and it brings about his community with others, thus making it possible to state that there is a truth concerning man and not only concerning individuals who cannot be compared. Absolute concreteness, completion, existence as a totality belong then to the free and fundamental desire which is the unique person. Empirical desire is only a symbolization of this; it refers to this and derives its meaning from it while remaining partial and reducible, for the empirical desire can not be conceived in isolation. On the other hand, the desire of being in its abstract purity is the *truth* of the concrete fundamental desire, but it does not exist by virtue of reality. Thus the fundamental project, the person, the free realization of human truth is everywhere in all desires (save for those exceptions treated in the preceding chapter, concerning, for example, "indifferents"). It is never apprehended except through desires—as we can apprehend space only through bodies which shape it for us, though space is a specific reality and not a concept. Or, if you like, it is like the *object* of Husserl, which reveals itself only by *Abschattungen,* and which nevertheless does not allow itself to be absorbed by any one *Abschattung.* We can understand after these remarks that the abstract, ontological "desire to be" is unable to represent the fundamental, *human* structure of the individual; it cannot be an obstacle to his freedom. Freedom in fact, as we have shown in the preceding chapter, is strictly identified with nihilation. The only being which can be called free is the being which nihilates its being. Moreover we know that nihilation is *lack of being* and can not be otherwise. Freedom is precisely the being which makes itself a lack of being. But since desire, as we have established, is identical with lack of being, freedom can arise only as being which makes itself a desire of being; that is, as the project-for-itself of being in-itself-for-itself. Here we have arrived at an abstract structure which can by no means be considered as the nature or essence of freedom. Freedom is existence, and in it existence precedes essence. The upsurge of freedom is immediate and concrete and is not to be distinguished from its choice; that is, from the person himself. But the structure under consideration can be called the *truth* of freedom; that is, it is the human meaning of freedom.

It should be possible to establish the human truth of the person, as we have attempted to do by an ontological phenomenology. The catalogue of empirical desires ought to be made the object of appropriate psychological investigations, observation and induction and, as needed, experience can serve to draw up this list. They will indicate to the philosopher the comprehensible relations which can unite to each other various desires and various patterns of behaviors, and will bring to light certain concrete connections between the subject of experience and "situations" experientially defined (which at bottom originate only from limitations applied in the name of positivity to the fundamental situation of the subject in the world). But in establishing and classifying fundamental desires of *individual persons* neither of these methods is appropriate. Actually there can be no question of determining *a priori* and ontologically what appears in all the unpredictability of a free act. This is why we shall limit ourselves here to indicating very summarily the possibilities of such a quest and its perspectives. The very fact that we can subject any man whatsoever to such an investigation—that is what belongs to human reality in general. Or, if you prefer, this is what can be established by an ontology. But the inquiry itself and its results are on principle wholly outside the possibilities of an ontology.

On the other hand, pure, simple empirical description can only give us catalogues and put us in the presence of pseudo-irreducibles (the desire to write, to swim, a taste for adventure, jealousy, *etc.*). It is not enough in fact to draw up a list of behavior patterns, of drives and inclinations, it is necessary also to *decipher* them; that is, it is necessary to know how to *question* them. This research can be conducted only according to the rules of a specific method. It is this method which we call existential psychoanalysis.

The *principle* of this psychoanalysis is that man is a totality and not a collection. Consequently he expresses himself as a whole in even his most insignificant and his most superficial behavior. In other words there is not a taste, a mannerism, or an human act which is not *revealing*.

The *goal* of psychoanalysis is to *decipher* the empirical behavior patterns of man; that is to bring out in the open the revelations which each one of them contains and to fix them conceptually.

Its *point of departure* is *experience;* its pillar of support is the fundamental, pre-ontological comprehension which man has of the human person. Although the majority of people can well ignore the indications contained in a gesture, a word, a sign and can look with scorn on the revelation which they carry, each human individual nevertheless possesses *a priori* the *meaning* of the revelatory value of these manifestations and is capable of deciphering them, at least if he is aided and guided by a helping hand. Here as elsewhere, truth is not encountered by chance; it does not belong to a domain where one must seek it without ever having any presentiment of its location, as one can go to look for the source of the Nile or of the Niger. It belongs *a priori* to human comprehension and the essential task is an hermeneutic; that is, a deciphering, a determination, and a conceptualization.

Its *method* is comparative. Since each example of human conduct symbolizes in its own manner the fundamental choice which must be brought to light, and since at the same time each one disguises this choice under its occasional character and its historical opportunity, only the comparision of these acts of conduct can effect the emergence of the unique revelation which they all express in a different way. The first outline of this method has been furnished for us by the psychoanalysis of Freud and his disciples. For this reason it will be profitable here to indicate more specifically the points where existential psychoanalysis will be inspired by psychoanalysis proper and those where it will radically differ from it.

Both kinds of psychoanalysis consider all objectively discernible manifestations of "psychic life" as symbols maintaining symbolic relations to the fundamental, total structures which constitute the individual person. Both consider that there are no primary givens such as hereditary dispositions, character, *etc.* Existential psychoanalysis recognizes nothing *before* the original upsurge of human freedom; empirical psychoanalysis holds that the original affectivity of the individual is virgin wax *before* its history. The libido is nothing besides its concrete fixations, save for a permanent possibility of fixing anything whatsoever upon anything whatsoever. Both consider the human being as a perpetual, searching, historization. Rather than uncovering static, constant givens they discover the meaning, orientation, and adventures of this history. Due to this fact both consider man in the world and do not imagine that one can question the being of a man without taking into account all his *situation*. Psychological investigations aim at reconstituting the life of the subject from birth to the moment of the cure; they utilize all the objective documentation which they can find; letters, witnesses, intimate diaries, "social" information of every kind. What they aim at restoring is less a pure psychic event than a twofold structure: the crucial event of infancy and the psychic crystallization around this event. Here again we have to do with a *situation*. Each "historical" fact from this point of view will be considered at once as a *factor* of the psychic evolution and as a *symbol* of that evolution. For it is nothing in itself. It operates only according to the way in which it is taken and this very manner of taking it expresses symbolically the internal disposition of the individual.

Empirical psychoanalysis and existential psychoanalysis both search within an existing situation for a fundamental attitude which can not be expressed by simple, logical definitions because it is prior to all logic, and which requires reconstruction according to the laws of specific syntheses. Empirical psychoanalysis seeks to determine the *complex*, the very name of which indicates the polyvalence of all the meanings which are referred back to it. Existential psychoanalysis seeks to determine the *original choice*. This original choice operating in the face of the world and being a choice of position in the world is total like the complex; it is prior to logic like the complex. It is this which decides the attitude of the person when confronted with logic and principles; therefore there can be no possibility of questioning it in conformance to logic. It brings together in a prelogical synthesis the totality of the existent, and as such it is the center of reference for an infinity of polyvalent meanings.

Both our psychoanalyses refuse to admit that the subject is in a privileged position to proceed in these inquiries concerning himself. They equally insist on a strictly objective method, using as documentary evidence the data of reflection as well as the testimony of others. Of course the subject *can* undertake a psychoanalytic investigation of himself. But in this case he must renounce at the outset all benefit stemming from his peculiar position and must question himself exactly as if he were someone else. Empirical psychoanalysis in fact is based on the hypothesis of the existence of an unconscious psyche, which on principle escapes the intuition of the subject. Existential psychoanalysis rejects the hypothesis of the unconscious; it makes the psychic act coextensive with consciousness. But if the fundamental project is fully experienced by the subject and hence wholly conscious, that certainly does not mean that it must by the same token be *known* by him; quite the contrary. The reader will perhaps recall the care we took in the Introduction to distinguish between consciousness and knowledge. To be sure, as we have seen earlier, reflection can be considered as a quasi-knowledge. But what it grasps at each moment is not the pure project of the for-itself as it is symbolically expressed— often in several ways at once—by the concrete behavior which it apprehends. It grasps the concrete behavior itself; that is, the specific dated desire in all its characteristic network. It grasps at once symbol and symbolization. This apprehension, to be sure, is entirely constituted by a pre-ontological comprehension of the fundamental project; better yet, in so far as reflection is almost a non-thetic consciousness of itself as reflection, it *is* this same project, as well as the non-reflective consciousness. But it does follow that it commands the instruments and techniques necessary to isolate the choice symbolized, to fix it by concepts, and to bring it forth into the full light of day. It is penetrated by a great light without being able to express what this light is illuminating. We are not dealing with an unsolved riddle as the Freudians believe; all is there, luminous; reflection is in full possession of it, apprehends all. But this "mystery in broad daylight" is due to the fact that this possession is deprived of the means which would ordinarily permit *analysis* and *conceptualization*. It grasps everything, all at once, without shading, without relief, without connections of grandeur—not that these shades, these values, these reliefs exist somewhere and are hidden from it, but rather because they must be established by another human attitude and because they can exist only *by means of* and *for* knowledge. Reflection, unable to serve as the basis for existential psychoanalysis, will then simply furnish us with the brute materials toward which the psychoanalyst must take an objective attitude. Thus only will he be able to *know* what he *already understands*. The result is that complexes uprooted from the depths of the unconscious, like projects revealed by existential psychoanalysis, will be apprehended *from the point of view of the Other*. Consequently the *object* thus brought into the light will be articulated according to the structures of the transcended-transcendence; that is, its being will be the being-for-others even if the psychoanalyst and the subject of the psychoanalysis are actually the same person. Thus the project which is brought to light by either kind of psychoanalysis can be only the totality of the individual human being, the irreducible element of the transcendence with the structure of *being-for-others*. What always escapes these methods of investigation is the project as it is for itself, the complex in its own being. This project-for-itself can be experienced only as a living possession; there is an incompatibility between existence for-itself and objective existence. But the object of the two psychoanalyses has in it nonetheless the *reality of a being;* the subject's knowledge of it can in addition contribute to *clarify* reflection, and that reflection can then become a possession which will be a quasi-knowing.

At this point the similarity between the two kinds of psychoanalysis ceases. They differ fundamentally in that empirical psychoanalysis has decided upon its own irreducible instead of allowing this to make itself known in a self-evident intuition. The libido or the will to power in actuality constitutes a psycho-biological residue which is not clear in itself and which does not appear to us as *being beforehand* the irreducible limit of the investigation. Finally it is experience which establishes that the foundation of complexes is this libido or this will to power; and these results of empirical inquiry are perfectly contingent, they are not convincing. Nothing prevents our conceiving *a priori* of a "human reality" which would not be expressed by the will to power, for which the libido would not constitute the original, undifferentiated project.

On the other hand, the choice to which existential psychoanalysis will lead us, precisely because it is a choice, accounts for its original contingency, for the contingency of the choice is the reverse side of its freedom. Furthermore, inasmuch as it is established on the *lack of being,* conceived as a fundamental characteristic of being, it receives its legitimacy *as a choice*, and we know that we do not have to push further. Each result then will be at once fully contingent and legitimately irreducible. Moreover it will always remain *particular;* that is, we will not achieve as the ultimate goal of our investigation and the foundation of all behavior an abstract, general term, libido for example, which would be differentiated and made concrete first in complexes and then in detailed acts of conduct, due to the action of external facts and the history of the subject. On the contrary, it will be a choice which remains unique and which is from the start absolute concreteness. Details of behavior can express or *particularize* this choice, but they can not make it more concrete than it already is. That is because the choice is nothing other than the being of each human reality; this amounts to saying that a particular partial behavior *is* or expresses the original choice of this human reality since for human reality there is no difference between existing and choosing for itself. From this fact we understand that existential psychoanalysis does not have to proceed from the fundamental "complex," which is exactly the choice of being, to an abstraction like the libido which would explain it. The complex is the ultimate choice, it is the choice of being and *makes itself such.* Bringing it into the light will reveal it each time as evidently irreducible. It follows necessarily that the libido and the will to power will appear to existential psychoanalysis neither as general characteristics common to all mankind nor as irreducibles. At most it will be possible after the investigation to establish that they express by virtue of particular ensembles in certain subjects a fundamental choice which can not be reduced to either one of them. We have seen in fact that desire and sexuality in general express an original effort of the for-itself to recover its being which has become estranged through contact with the Other. The will to power also originally supposes being-for-others, the comprehension of the Other, and the choice of winning its own

salvation by means of the Other. The foundation of this attitude must be an original choice which would make us understand the radical identification of being-in-itself-for-itself
with being-for-others.

The fact that the ultimate term of this existential inquiry
must be a *choice*, distinguishes even better the psychoanalysis for which we have outlined the method and principal
features. It thereby abandons the supposition that the environment acts mechanically on the subject under consideration. The environment can act on the subject only to the
exact extent that he comprehends it; that is, transforms it
into a situation. Hence no objective description of this environment could be of any use to us. From the start the environment conceived as a situation refers to the for-itself which
is choosing, just as the for-itself refers to the environment by
the very fact that the for-itself is in the world. By renouncing
all mechanical causation, we renounce at the same time all
general interpretation of the symbolization confronted. Our
goal could not be to establish empirical laws of succession,
nor could we constitute a universal symbolism. Rather the
psychoanalyst will have to rediscover at each step a symbol
functioning in the particular case which he is considering. If
each being is a totality, it is not conceivable that there can
exist elementary symbolic relationships (*e.g.;* the faeces =
gold, or a pincushion = the breast) which preserve a constant
meaning in all cases; that is, which remain unaltered when
they pass from one meaningful ensemble to another ensemble. Furthermore the psychoanalyst will never lose sight of
the fact that the choice is living and consequently can be
revoked by the subject who is being studied. We have shown
in the preceding chapter the importance of the *instant*,
which represents abrupt changes in orientation and the assuming of a new position in the face of an unalterable past.
From this moment on, we must always be ready to consider
that symbols change meaning and to abandon the symbol
used hitherto. Thus existential psychoanalysis will have to be

completely flexible and adapt itself to the slightest observable changes in the subject. Our concern here is to understand what is *individual* and often even instantaneous. The method which has served for one subject will not necessarily be suitable to use for another subject or for the same subject at a later period.

Precisely because the goal of the inquiry must be to discover a *choice* and not a *state*, the investigator must recall on every occasion that his object is not a datum buried in the darkness of the unconscious but a free, conscious determination—which is not even resident in consciousness, but which is one with this consciousness itself. Empirical psychoanalysis, to the extent that its method is better than its principles, is often in sight of an existential discovery, but it always stops part way. When it thus approaches the fundamental choice, the resistance of the subject collapses suddenly and he *recognizes* the image of himself which is presented to him as he were seeing himself in a mirror. This involuntary testimony of the subject is precious for the psychoanalyst; he sees there the sign that he has reached his goal; he can pass on from the investigation proper to the cure. But nothing in his principles or in his initial postulates permits him to understand or to utilize this testimony. Where could he get any such right? If the complex is really unconscious—that is, if there is a barrier separating the sign from the thing signified—how could the subject *recognize* it? Does the unconscious complex recognize itself? But haven't we been told that it lacks *understanding?* And if of necessity we granted to it the faculty of understanding the signs, would this not be to make of it by the same token a conscious unconscious? What is understanding if not to be conscious of what is understood? Shall we say on the other hand that it is the subject as conscious who recognizes the image presented? But how could he compare it with his true state since that is out of reach and since he has never had any knowledge of it? At most he will be able to judge that the psychoanalytic explanation of his case is a *probable* hypothesis, which derives its probability from the number of behavior patterns which it explains. His relation to this interpretation is that of a third party, that of the psychoanalyst himself; he has no privileged position. And if he *believes* in the probability of the psychoanalytic hypothesis, is this simple belief, which lives in the limits of his consciousness, able to effect the breakdown of the barriers which dam up the unconscious tendencies? The psychoanalyst doubtless has some obscure picture of an abrupt coincidence of conscious and unconscious. But he has removed all methods of conceiving of this coincidence in any positive sense.

Still, the enlightenment of the subject is a fact. There is an intuition here which is accompanied by evidence. The subject guided by the psychoanalyst does more and better than to give his agreement to an hypothesis; he touches it, he sees what it is. This is truly understandable only if the subject has never ceased being conscious of his deep tendencies; better yet, only if these drives are not distinguished from his conscious self. In this case as we have seen, the traditional psychoanalytic interpretation does not cause him to attain *consciousness* of what he is; it causes him to attain *knowledge* of what he is. It is existential psychoanalysis then which claims the final intuition of the subject as decisive.

This comparison allows us to understand better what an existential psychoanalysis must be if it is entitled to exist. It is a method destined to bring to light, in a strictly objective form, the subjective choice by which each living person makes himself a person; that is, makes known to himself what he is. Since what the method seeks is a *choice of being* at the same time as a *being,* it must reduce particular behavior patterns to fundamental relations—not of sexuality or of the will to power, but *of being*—which are expressed in this behavior. It is then guided from the start toward a comprehension of being and must not assign itself any other goal than to discover being and the mode of being of the being confronting this being. It is forbidden to stop before attaining this goal. It will utilize the comprehension of being which characterizes the investigator inasmuch as he is himself a human reality; and as it seeks to detach being from its symbolic expressions, it will have to rediscover each time on the basis of a comparative study of acts and attitudes, a symbol destined to decipher them. Its criterion of success will be the number of facts which its hypothesis permits it to explain and to unify as well as the self-evident intuition of the irreducibility of the end attained. To this criterion will be added in all cases where it is possible, the decisive testimony of the subject. The results thus achieved—that is, the ultimate ends of the individual—can then become the object of a classification, and it is by the comparison of these results that we will be able to establish general considerations about human reality as an empirical choice of its own ends. The behavior studied by this psychoanalysis will include not only dreams, failures, obsessions, and neuroses, but also and especially the thoughts of waking life, successfully adjusted acts, style, *etc.* This psychoanalysis has not yet found its Freud. At most we can find the foreshadowing of it in certain particularly successful biographies. We hope to be able to attempt elsewhere two examples in relation to Flaubert and Dostoevsky. But it matters little to us whether it now exists; the important thing is that it is possible.

NOTES

1. Paul Bourget: *Essai de Psychologie contemporaine: G. Flaubert.*
2. Since Flaubert's adolescence, so far as we can know it, offers us nothing specific in this connection, we must suppose the action of imponderable facts which on principle escape the critic.

6

The Subject as Social

Mikel Dufrenne

To personalize the self completely, we must say about society what we have said of the body. For the subject is not only incarnated, but social, that is, living among other subjects and participating with them in a certain style of life. The subject is also natural, living in the environment of a natural world;[1] we have said this implicitly in examining corporeality: naturality is a direct consequence of corporeality. But it is not exactly the same for sociality: for I am not among others as I am among things; this is so not only because the other is not a thing, but also because my relation to things is mediated by my body—whereas society, even though related to me through my body, *is* my body in a certain sense. My relation with the human environment is more immediate than my relation with the natural environment, and is experienced as such: things usually reach me

Reprinted from *The Notion of the A Priori*, trans. Edward S. Casey (1966), pp. 168–84, by permission of Northwestern University Press, Evanston, Ill.

only through men, and men always concern me more passionately than things. Consequently, we must compare the social milieu with my body, rather than with the natural milieu, though we should be prepared to abandon this comparison in the course of our investigation.

Now, reflection of the *a priori* can put us on the right path here, and help to avoid the solipsistic impasse to which a philosophy of the *cogito* is often driven. But we must proceed cautiously: all that we can expect to discover is the sociality of the subject; we cannot deduce society, any more than we were able to deduce the body. Sartre is right: instead of deducing the other, we encounter him; he is found outside ourselves, not within; even my equal or my neighbor is always an other. We can say of society—understood in the largest sense of collectivity: a collection of others—what Sartre says about the body: it attests my contingence because it is an unengenderable fact, but a fact which, like the body, affects me profoundly. Yet if society is a fact known *a posteriori*, reflection on the *a priori* may at least indicate, within the subject understood as the bearer of the *a priori*, the openness to others which is the foundation of intersubjectivity—what we shall call "sociality," corresponding to society—just as we have shown above a certain passivity in consciousness, a certain opacity in the subject, to which the body corresponds.

First of all, when we consider the objective *a priori* in its constitutive role, it seems that the objectivity it manifests in the object appeals to the attention and assent of others: when I experience a meaning as evident, even if I do not know that the evidence for this meaning is different from the subjective feeling of evidence (as Husserl stresses), at least I tend to think that this feeling is an homage offered to the objectivity of the meaning; I appeal to others, having the impression of being in a certain sense humanity's delegate in the experience I have. The objectivity of the meaning compels me to be objective myself, and this second objectivity implies a relation to others: the concern to obtain their assent, or rather the assurance of already having it, since, if the meaning I recognize is not created by me, it cannot be for me alone. In other words, the logical universality of the *a priori* or the judgments in which I make it explicit suggest a concrete universality, a society of subjects. This is why, following another path, we were able to contest this logical universality and reduce it to an empirical generality: this reduction is justifiable only if the second form of universality is at least announced by the first. As long as we deal with logical universality, others are not present, but they are presupposed, even demanded. Moreover, it is noteworthy that this primary relation to possible others is provoked by the experience of objectivity, and poses others as the fellow creatures from whom I expect assent because I assume that they are capable of objectivity, or rather I assume that the objectivity of the *a priori* will impose itself on them. This does not in any way exclude the possibility that my relations with others may be more dramatic, but this possibility is perhaps founded on equality and reciprocity: others are other only because they are also similar, as fellow men whose co-operation is necessary for founding the universality of a judgment or the strength of the evidence for a meaning.

But everything is possible with these possible others: they can betray my expectations and be blind to the evidence that I experience. Must I then be suspicious of this evidence? No; it is not illusory just because others fail to acknowledge it. Their failure to do so does not teach me the precariousness of the evidence, but rather its historicity and fragmentation [*morcellement*]. Certain *a priori* may escape me and others, and the comprehension of the total system of *a priori* requires a total humanity. The totality of the *a priori* implies a totality of the human, a total system of others, an end of history; and it is against such a background that the historicity of the *a priori* appears, the contingency of its revelation resulting from the diversity of subjects. Thus, the *a priori* suggests a reference to intersubjectivity in two ways: on account of its apprehension insofar as it is objective, and because of its systematization insofar as it is subjective. Its objectivity evokes the presence of others, while its historicity calls forth a history: the two dimensions of society, static and dynamic, are thereby indicated—without, of course, any real society being deduced in this way.

Moreover, the *a priori* refers to others, not just in calling them forth, but also in attesting to them: there are certain *a priori* of intersubjectivity—in Husserlian language, categories of the region "others," as distinguished from the region "thing" or even "life." This means that, as soon as we encounter men, we always recognize them as such; we always know already what is human. Once again, this does not exclude the possibility that this recognition may give way to a struggle: the other can appear as a formidable and despicable stranger, suspect because he is different: he is not of my race, and the rules governing my society do not apply to him; he is an outlaw, above or below the law, a god or a monster to be adored or enslaved. Yet we must beware of rationalizations which justify actions performed out of passion. If the other sometimes appears strange, inspiring fear or adoration, and if we have difficulty recognizing him—that is, doing him justice—this is because we have already recognized him, but refused him justice; he is the other on the basis of identity; he is different only as similar. If he were fundamentally different, action would lose this passional ambiguity whose source is perhaps already bad faith. This immediate and certain knowledge [*connaissance*] of the other as *alter ego* is what we attribute to the *a priori* of intersubjectivity. The term is undoubtedly ambiguous: can we speak of *a priori* of intersubjectivity as we speak of *a priori* of the understanding? There are two different principles for classifying the *a priori:* one concerns the faculties of the subject possessing them, the other the object for which they are the constitutive meaning; as we shall see in another book,[2] it is not easy to choose between these two principles. In any case, we mean here that certain *a priori* are ingredient in our relations with others: they do not govern or orient them, but they make them possible, as well as their affective vicissitudes and historical developments, just as the *a priori* of the object make a technique or a science of the object possible. There are categories of intersubjectivity just as much as there are categories of objectivity.

This has two implications; the first is that we possess a certain idea of man. *Homo cogitat,* says one of Spinoza's axioms—an axiom by means of which man abruptly breaks into a meditation which, up to this point, considered only Substance. We recognize this *homo cogitans* at first glance; even if we do not know what his thoughts are, or what thought itself is, we know that he thinks. He may possess a secret aspect: this also defines him; his actions are unforeseeable: we recognize him as free without imputing this unforeseeability to our ignorance. (Occasionally we can foresee his responses because we know their motives, which are not causes: because we have learned to know him rather than the universe surrounding him, or at least this universe insofar as it has meaning for him.) I do not recognize my fellow man by projecting onto him a certain idea that I have of him: I know him before knowing myself, and I learn to know myself through him. Even before saying that he is similar to *me,* I have to realize that I am similar to *him;* this is perhaps the most irritating discovery, one that we are careful to dissimulate and forget; yet it is the primary discovery, even in the order of reasons: I am made in the image of the other.

Consequently, I can speak of man, and in speaking of him say "I" or "we" with equal ease. And this "we" is not an editorial we. Here, at any rate, is one of the reasons why the *cogito* may appear to be impersonal. This impersonality represents a condemnation of solipsism, and introduces others in two ways. First of all, impersonality involves universality because its correlate is a universal: when consciousness is evident to itself—when it is the consciousness of this evidence—it appeals to the concrete universality of others. Yet it is I who think, and what we say about the passage from the impersonal to the person remains valid. Here again, however, the appearance of impersonality can be justified, for the personalization of the "I" is itself universal; the first person is both singular and plural. There are others, and they are also persons. Humanity is not a species; it is an assemblage of persons before whom I am myself a person.[3] Of course, I can subsume humanity under a general idea, but I cannot avoid speaking of man: an indeclinable, yet universal subject. We have already stressed that the dialectic of singular and universal occurs in every man. Now we must add that the *a priori* idea of man is the idea of man as endowed with the *a priori*, hence with a universal; since this endowment has limitations, and since the *a priori* is never made wholly explicit or given as a total system, singularity is a universal human trait. Moreover, just as in terms of intension [*compréhension*] universality is never rigorous because the *a priori* is not purely logical, so, similarly, universality is not rigorous in extension because it includes singularity and because particularity is not totally surpassed in singularity; the universal is still general in a certain sense. This points again to the contingency of the other, and to the empirical particularity of societies or cultures. But the empirical is present here only in filigree form. In the realm of the *a priori*, the universal is the idea of man as universal—an idea I possess before any science and thanks to which I can always recognize man as similar to himself, thus as similar to me [*mon semblable*].[4]

But the categories of intersubjectivity go beyond this idea. For man is man only on the condition of being *a* man, and singularity is universal because it is essential; men also resemble one another in that they are all dissimilar. Now, this difference can be known by the *a priori*. Not only do we recognize man at first glance, but we also recognize him as singular; this does not occur with any object whatsoever that we know as a single object, even as a monad, yet do not know as singular, that is, as having its own personality (personality being the immanence of the universal in the particular).[5] Of course, this personality of the other is made explicit by us only little by little, through the patience involved in dialogue or friendship; it is never perfectly clear to us: the social sciences do not overcome the coefficient of otherness harbored by the personality (they say in a different way what naïve knowledge says, because they attempt to determine causes or motivations; but they do not say more).

It would be absurd to claim that we have an *a priori* idea of every man as we have an idea of man in general: to know that man is always singular is not to know *what* his singularity consists of; this singularity appears to us en bloc, yet as a problem to be solved. We can, nevertheless, attack this problem because we possess other *a priori:* the affective qualities brought into relief by expression have an immediate meaning for us. These qualities are not the projection of our emotion onto an object; instead, they excite emotion, if emotion is indeed present; they are a meaning proposed to us by the object. This object is not necessarily human: a landscape, a work of art, any object will work, if it is expressive. Yet man has priority here, for he is naturally expressive, even if what he expresses is inexpressible. Expression is so much the peculiar property of subjectivity that we can speak of expressive objects as quasi-subjects; they reveal the inner principle that unifies and singularizes a being, a principle elevating this being to the status of a meaningful totality, inhabited by a soul which is its meaning. In man, this meaning is both manifest and hidden: subjectivity, said Hegel, is infinite. Therefore, it is menacing and maddening: the other is the stranger because he is inexhaustible, even if he belongs to our race. But since this meaning is constantly offered, it helps us to identify others: for us, their identity is that of an expression which reveals to us their existential *a priori*, though we cannot at first delineate and master this knowledge [*connaissance*] that is hidden in a feeling.

Empiricism is perfectly justified in believing that experience is necessary for understanding someone, whether it is acquired in everyday relations or in scientific (or pseudoscientific) observation. The existential *a priori* constituting the person is only revealed *a posteriori*. Yet it is itself given *a priori*, though in a very obscure way; it is given in the immediate and global experience which, in the very first glance at a face, provides me with the essence of a person and allows me to identify him from now on. Empiricism can accept this description only if it is gestaltist and if it recognizes certain *Gestalten* as constitutive meanings: in brief, if it is a transcendental empiricism. It is also true that at certain moments expression can particularize itself and make itself explicit: thus we sense fear, anger, or tenderness in someone's action; and we always know already what these signify. We can create an eidetic psychology as a propaedeutic to an empirical psychology because we possess an inherent knowledge [*savoir*] of essences; this knowledge underlies the possibility of understanding the phenomena through which others are manifested and intersubjective relations are formed.

Thus, the *a priori* in its subjective aspect prepares me to encounter others: it attests to and permits sociality.[6] But sociality, like incarnation, is a destiny for the subject. Therefore, we must pass now to the empirical level, although we shall ask ourselves later if the empirical can still be understood as transcendental in certain respects. Thus we arrive at concrete society as it offers itself to the experience of the individual and the sociologist. Does this society have the same relation to the subject as the body does? However far we must push the identification of the subject and society, in comparison with the identification of the subject and his body, we must agree that the subject is his body immediately, while he is his society only at the end of a period of socialization. To be social is both to be one's society and not to be it. The second point is easier to establish first. For to be social is to be in a society. This relation implies a linkage and proximity, but also a difference of the same kind as that between "having" and "had": to belong to a society is to have a society, as we say that we have a body. Society has a definite character of objectivity which forces us to consider it as exterior to the subject; similarly, the body is also a body-as-object. Society is objective spirit realized on the condition of its particularization in history.[7] Society as such is not myself; I no more choose my society than my body, and in oppression or revolt I can experience society's otherness vividly—just as I can feel myself constrained by my body and rebel against it by neglecting or mortifying it. It is a common experience when living abroad not to feel part of the society in which one dwells. The conflict of the individual and society is not a dialectical moment that we can easily surpass, either through the ideality of *logos* or in the reality of history.

Yet we must attempt this surpassing, though without giving the last word to an *Aufhebung* or to a movement towards the absolute.[8] On the contrary, there is no last word: the status of the subject is essentially ambiguous. But we must attempt to oppose a monism to the dualism of the individual and society. The body-as-object is also my body: the penitent flagellates his body with his own hand; he punishes himself for being a body, yet in this very act he *is* his body. Similarly, we say "my society," and the rebel denounces his society with the very language of that society; in fact, the more completely integrated into society he is, the more skillfully and perhaps ardently he will denounce it.[9] Thus it seems that I am my society as I am my body, whether I want to be or not; and this last clause is not immaterial. For my freedom is at stake here, manifesting itself in the attitude I adopt and in the action I take with respect to my body and my society. But the fact that my freedom always exists in a situation signifies that I cannot exercise it without identifying myself with my body and my society.

Moreover, there is a way to make this identification more plausible. Rather than saying that I myself am society, I should say that society is a self [*moi*]: it is a subject, insofar as it is culture.[10] Cultural anthropology, perhaps inspired in America by questions raised by logical positivism, has investigated the being and meaning of culture at great length.[11] Yet the concept itself of culture remains uncertain; this is because culture is the subjective aspect of society. It is subjective in two converging senses. First, it appears to exist only in subjects. Society has a more objective, exterior, and official existence, residing both in impersonal institutions and in statistical, demographic, ecological, and economic realities. Of course, culture also has an objective aspect: there are cultural objects, as well as a collective aspect: it can be represented statistically. But it is above all a way of life—of experiencing social reality—and as such it belongs to the individual. Urbanization and law are social realities, but the way in which people adapt themselves to urban life or respect law is a cultural reality: culture lives in individuals. Naturally, it is hard to determine the exact boundary between society and culture: we can say with Malinowski that every institution is at once a social reality so far as it is institutionalized, and a cultural reality insofar as it is experienced; neither of these two realities can exist without the other. But since the difference between them is irreducible, the subjective character of culture is confirmed: being experienced by subjects, culture is like the soul of society; it is to society what the soul is to the body. Because individuals possess a certain way of living in and experiencing their city, there is a spirit of the city; and there is a spirit of the law because individuals have a certain attitude toward their laws. Now, when we consider culture rather than society, and society-as-subject rather than society-as-object, we can understand the sociality of individuals as an identification of individual and society. Yet how are we to understand *this* identification? Does it not lead to the affirmation of a sociologism ruinous to the concept of the individual?

This question can be clarified by answering one it presupposes: what exactly is the reality of culture? Admitting that

I am coextensive with it, what is its extension? We must agree
that the domain of a culture is difficult to delimit: can we say
where a society ends, except in terms of geography or international law? Can we trace a boundary between the social
and the natural environment, and claim that only the latter
is ontologically different from the subject? Certainly not:
even the stars are part of the cultural milieu, as soon as
telescopes are focused on them and institutions are devoted
to their study. In fact, the boundary between subject and
milieu appears to be blurred as soon as we consider the body;
the body's limits are more apparent than real, and it mingles
with all the objects, far and near, with which it has commerce, whether to endure or master them. Thus the voice of
the Pythic oracle is not so much her voice as that of the waves
and woods, because "the whole universe sways and swirls on
her stem."[12] Similarly, when culture is more closely examined, at one extremity it is seen to merge with the cultures
peculiar to particular groups, and at the other with a culture
belonging to the whole species. This indeterminateness appears in the subject himself: he participates in culture only
partially, usually through the intermediary of subcultures;
and he participates in history only through the edge of the
present expressing his engagement in the world. In the same
way, at the other pole, culture is surpassed [*débordée*] by a
human universal: what Comte called humanity, and Hegel
termed the concrete universal. It is true that humanity is
never realized, but I still *am* it in a certain sense—both
because, insofar as it is a norm, I am able to contribute to its
advent, and because, insofar as it is a given, I possess the
means of justifying this advent. Nevertheless, in the present
state of history (for we are here on the empirical level) culture seems to have a differentiated and independent reality,
precisely to the extent that it can be discovered in the actions
of all the members of a society, that is, to the extent that I
am it. In addition, if it is possible to deny that culture is

delimited between the superculture and the various subcultures, it is again only in reference to myself, to the exact degree that I am *not* it. But this does not signify that, determined by culture, I am also determined in other ways, as if my being were the result of a sum of determinations; it signifies that I am still something else, that I cannot be reduced to any determination, and that in one sense I am coextensive with humanity and in another sense irreducibly singular.

In fact, the *rapprochement* of the individual and society must not be performed to the detriment of the individual and to the benefit of society. This might be quite possible: does not the assertion that I am my society—or better, my culture—simply mean that I am determined by it and that I am reduced to being its effect or its reflection? Does this not represent a return to a purely empiricist conception of the subject, a return achieved with the aid of a social naturalism? No—just as asserting that I am my body is not equivalent to saying that I am only my body or that I am determined by it. Moreover, these last two affirmations are not equivalent and are in fact opposed: the first denies that there is something in me distinct from the body; the second asserts that there is something distinct, but denies its independence. In any case, we disagree with both affirmations: on the one hand, I am not reducible to my body, because I *am* it in the mode of not being it: I express it by saying that *it* is what I am. On the other hand, my body does not determine me (though it remains exterior to me in a sense) because it is too near me to act on me; at the very most I can say that it constitutes me, thus limiting me, because *I* am what it is.

Similarly, culture cannot determine me from without, and the ambiguous relation that I have with it must be expressed by always conjoining these two propositions: first, I am *it*, and to this extent it structures and limits me; secondly, it is I [*moi*], and to this extent I structure and limit it: I live in it and it lives in me. These two propositions justify the procedures of cultural anthropology or social psychology, on the condition that their reciprocity be always respected and that a determinism (if science insists on using this language) be immediately compensated and neutralized by a determinism working in the opposite direction. (In fact, determinism thrives only between a society-as-object and a self-as-object, and the self is never an object.) This limit to sociologism is also a limit to the identification of the subject and society. Insofar as I accentuate subjectivity and affirm it as negativity, or conversely insofar as I emphasize the objectivity of society and affirm it as positivity, I cannot identify myself with it. There is undoubtedly a certain excess involved in pushing the parallelism between body and society too far: after all, society is less close, less adherent to the subject. And the following question could be posed: must society be understood in terms of the body or vice versa? If we interpret the body in terms of society, we are tempted to return to dualism. In any event, when it is a question of the body, the ambiguity is found in the body itself, which is both subject and object, since it is more easily identified with the subject; when it is a question of society, the ambiguity resides in the subject himself, in the way in which he experiences his integration into this society.

We can clarify our discussion of the relation between individual and culture in still another way. For it inspires a new question, which we have already encountered when we were dealing with the body. We have admitted that culture, though difficult to circumscribe between the subcultures which it involves and the superculture in which it participates, has a certain autonomy. Must we then see in it a certain personality? In that case, if I am my culture to a certain extent, we must also say that my culture is a "myself" [*moi*]. This means that it lives in me [*moi*] as inseparable from me; but it also means that it is a self [*moi*], capable of detaching itself from me to claim its prerogatives as a person. The question then becomes: is culture a transcendental? Does it possess certain *a priori?* This question leads to two others: first, is culture itself an *a priori*—that is, does it perform the transcendental function, normally assumed by consciousness, which consists in knowing the constitutive *a priori* of the object? Secondly, does culture have an *a priori*—that is, is it constituted itself by an *a priori* or by a system of various *a priori?* Both questions seem to us to require an affirmative answer. By saying that I am society, we have been led to say that society is a self; we have even had to support the first proposition by the second. Thus we come to admit that society is itself individualized and animated by an existential *a priori.* Hence we rejoin Hegel at this point. He can speak of objective spirit only if this spirit is also, in a people, subjective, defining society as a concrete consciousness and as a universal person.

Through its observation of individual behavior, cultural anthropology also strives to grasp this personality—whether by means of Benedict's comprehensive psychology, or by Kardiner's and Linton's use of psychoanalysis and the various procedures of the psychology of personality. Even a functionalist analysis, inspired by the idea of a necessary correlation of institutions, aims at a synthesis expressing culture as a totality and defining its singular essence. The psychological language of this culturology suggests that society is considered here as a person. Therefore, it is not sufficient to say that, for the person perceiving and studying it, society is constituted by an objective *a priori* like any other object; for we must not confuse the *a priori* of sociality with the existential *a priori* belonging to a particular society.[13] Society itself experiences the *a priori* as objective, and in this way may claim to have an existential *a priori.* Society itself performs the transcendental function, it is itself a certain look cast onto the world, a certain living relation to the world, an aptitude for recognizing and experiencing certain aspects of the world. Having made the *a priori* descend into the body, we must now let it descend into society as well. In fact, this enterprise arouses less opposition than the preceding: sociological reflection has made it natural to think of society as a person.

The difficulty lies elsewhere; it stems from the individual's protest against this bold assimilation. In developing the idea that society is an "I" [*je*], it is tempting to forget that I am society; it becomes easy to overlook the individual subject, or rather to make him the instrument or the effect of society. The collective person begins to seem more authentic than the singular person, and in this way we land back in sociologism. We cannot, however, accept sociologism, even under this new form; although it is more subtle than the sociological determinism which objectifies the subject, it is no less ruinous for the transcendental being of the subject. There is a new reason for our refusal: no longer because the subject is never wholly an object determined by a society-as-object, but now because society is never wholly a subject on the same level with the individual subject and somehow substitutable for him. As subjective or existential (whether mental or physical matters little here), the *a priori* is rooted in a singular subjectivity, a first-person consciousness [*une conscience-je*]; even if this consciousness claims universality for its acts and refers itself to others, it is singular by nature. The *a priori* attributed to a society or a culture must be present and actualized in individuals; even though we may consider it as a subject, society remains an object for a subject. It exists *for* a subject, and it exists only *through* individuals. It is not exactly an object, being more than an object; but it is not a subject: it is a quasi-subject.[14]

This reservation does not in any way condemn the psychologizing approach of cultural anthropology. It simply warns us that, first of all, we must not be the dupes of metaphor, however legitimate it may be: objective spirit is never a merely subjective mind; and that, secondly, this psychologizing research must be compensated for, on the plane of science, by the objectifying research of sociology. Yet the singularity of the subject is irreducible: the transcendental function is a privilege which he possesses by right and which cannot be granted him by society. Once again, this does not deny that society may aid the individual to affirm and manifest his personality. It permits the actualization of the virtual, as does the corporeal schematism on another level. A feudal society does not create the sense of honor, but allows it to be manifested—just as a capitalistic society lets the sense of competition emerge. Yet if an individual in a capitalistic society possesses a compelling sense of honor, he will find, in spite of the institutions, the means of affirming it: witness Bernanos.[15] The transcendental in itself is irreducible to the historical; the existential *a priori* is, like Sartre's notion of original choice, nontemporal. Nevertheless, since the subject is also historical, the historical in its turn participates in the transcendental, and the empirical in the apriorical.[16]

The relation of the transcendental to the social must be understood in the same way—somewhat as Bergson conceived the relation of matter and life, matter being an obstacle to life, yet also life's residue. Society is an object and is first of all opposed to me as is matter to life. Yet I am open to it, experiencing it as my destiny: thus I am it; furthermore, it is at once composed, experienced, and thought by individuals: thus it is a self [*moi*]. For these reasons, it is also more than an object, just as matter, even if it were only life's waste, is more than mere matter. Nevertheless, there is an important difference between the body and society: the body can be more totally identified with the subject. When we contest the identity of the body and the subject, we manifest our fear of an ambiguity; but what is ambiguous is the identity of the body and consciousness, for the body is consciousness and it is not; yet this does not prevent the body from always being a self. Society, however, is never wholly a self: both because as object it surpasses me infinitely and because as subject it is only a quasi-subject. Therefore, we cannot translate "I am social" exactly by "I am my society." Nonetheless, it remains the case that the relation of the subject and society is close and that it exerts an inverse effect on our understanding of these two terms: it obliges us to consider *society* as a quasi-subject; and to consider the *subject* as a quasi-object, extending itself into society and finding its roots and destiny in it: yet without losing its quality as subject, without being determined by society as an effect by a cause, and without its transcendental nature or function being altered. The subject is and is not his society; even as social, he remains transcendental; but if the transcendental is thus social, the social is not truly transcendental—being so only through the mediation of the subject.

In brief, by virtue of his contingency the person must live in a society, just as he must be a body. Through the agency of its culture, this society exerts a considerable influence on him, but one which consists in allowing him to actualize certain of his *a priori* without absolutely forbidding the actualization of others; and we can say neither that the person is reducible to society nor that he is determined by it.

A few final words are perhaps in order. In addition to the quasi-spatial dimension of the intersubjective being of the subject, we should consider his temporal dimension: in addition to social being, historical being. There is little question that the subject's relation to history is quite similar to his relation with society. Above all, it can be shown that access to history is prepared for within the transcendental being of the subject, not only by the various *a priori* of intersubjectivity, but also by the *a priori* of temporality: the subject is open to the past as he is to the present. Before any explicit use of memory, I immediately apprehend that an object present to me has a past, because temporality is a constitutive *a priori* belonging to every object, as well as to the subject himself. But it is not because consciousness is in flux that, as Hume believed, the object appears as temporal, nor is it because there are permanent and nontemporal objects that, as Kant thought, consciousness discovers itself as being in flux. Instead, temporality is universal.

This, however, leads us to conclude that the subject is in history as he is in society—as the soul is in the body—but not that he *is* history. Now, history may be defined as the totality of the past insofar as it ends in my present; this totality is unspecifiable, for there is always a past for each past, and the present of every past is indefinite in its extension. In any case, the exact boundary cannot be drawn between history, properly speaking—i.e., human history—and natural history. Should we claim that natural history is only a pseudo-history? Life has a history linked with the history of matter, and to the extent that we are objects we are tied down to this history; thus it is already ours, just as the natural world is already the human world. This solidarity is one of the signs of our facticity. Admittedly, certain parts of the past can be objectively reconstituted: history as being [*être*] is inseparable from history as science, and the past for me is what I know of it. Nevertheless, even considered as the object of this knowledge and as limited to it, history infinitely surpasses me, as does society: I am not history, and my own history is only one small history within history itself. In what sense could I say that I am history? This statement can have only one meaning: I am the result of history, as it is said that I am the product of my culture. But what about my singularity and freedom? In fact, the above statement may be opposed by another: history is contained in *me*, signifying that in me history takes on its meaning and recapitulates itself. I make history, not only because my acts are immediately inscribed in it in the present, but also because they presuppose that I determine its meaning by joining the past to the future. The historian who writes history, and thus helps to make it, must conjoin these two approaches, paradoxically considering the individual both as the product of an objective history and as the author of a subjective history. This helps us to interpret in another way the idea that I am history: I carry within myself the history of which I am the heir, not the product.

This subjective history is not, however, a subject. It is not a person who would be more authentic than the individual. It *has* a meaning through the subject who relates and relives it; it *is* not a meaning. To conceive it as a subject is possible only if it is conceived as an absolute subject in Hegelian fashion; here "subject" signifies becoming, and temporal becoming is made the illustration of logical becoming, so that history realizes meaning, even if meaning is not historical. For Hegel, history is not only reason, but also reasonable. For us, this would mean that history possesses an existential *a priori* and that it performs the transcendental function. We are certainly tempted to agree; the historicity that we have found in the *a priori* leads us to attribute these *a priori* to history; they are successively revealed in history, and their totality defines a total history: humanity as history. The existential *a priori* of history, the *logos* of becoming, would be the total system of all *a priori*. History would then be the universal consciousness which becomes aware of itself through man by manifesting various *a priori*. Yet, as we have said, such a totality is unspecifiable: humanity is an infinite task.

The historicity of the *a priori* also signifies that they do not form a neat totality: each culture or each era reveals certain *a priori* only by neglecting others. History is not a triumphant reason or a meaning certain of itself because what is surpassed is not necessarily preserved in what surpasses it; the present is not necessarily richer than the past, nor is the past necessarily pregnant with the present, or the beginning with the end. There may be reason in history conceived as a quasi-subject, but history is not itself reasonable, and this reason exists only for and through men. For men, because they alone find history meaningful. Through men, because their activities alone, even when objectified and alienated as in a statistical reality, propose this meaning: migrations of peoples differ from the migrations of schools of fish, and the laws of the market place do not operate like the laws governing scales. It is man who bears and reveals the *a priori*. Historicity signifies not the infinitude of history, but the finitude of man.

Finitude: history is man's destiny. To be finite is to be in history. This is why man is not wholly history: as objectively or quantitatively greater than man, history surpasses him; yet history is not wholly man either, being subjectively or qualitatively less than man. Since history is the trace of man —as matter is the trace left by life—it is more than a blind positivity or a brute facticity. Although man continually denounces history's inhuman character, he discovers himself in it as in a familiar landscape. Thus history is already man. And man is history because he is its heir and the agent responsible for its meaning. Yet he is not its product: history proposes, and man disposes. In brief, as a transcendental subject man is irreducible. The transcendental is historical because it belongs to man, who is in history, and because it is revealed empirically; but the historical is not truly transcendental.

NOTES

1. That is, to the extent that the natural and human environment [*milieu*] can be distinguished; at least the relation to others can be distinguished from the relation to things, even when these things are humanized.

2. Dufrenne refers here to the book on "the inventory of the *a priori*" which will form a sequel to the present essay.—Trans.

3. This is why Heidegger's "they" *(das man)* is not necessarily inauthentic; it may designate the person that I am and that we are.

4. This idea should be made explicit as the *a priori* of a science of man; yet, as in every instance, the *a priori* can be made explicit only historically and apropos of the *a posteriori*. (The social sciences have not found their Thales. Why?) Moreover, this *a priori* is both cognitive and axiological; it is also the content of a formal ethics.

5. The case of the animal could be considered here: the peasant who discovers a personality in each member of his flock; but this occurs only after

the fact, *a posteriori*. Nevertheless, he can comprehend the meaning of expressions—even if the expression conveys incommunicability, as in the case of the sphinx. The combination of men and animals in mythological creatures opens up a whole line of possible speculation.

6. It is another matter to determine whether there are *a priori*—especially objective *a priori*—belonging to society: whether there is a pure sociology like a pure mathematics. We could say that certain social relations (e.g., *rapprochement,* domination, collaboration, competition—structures analyzed by men like Weber, Von Wiese, and Parsons) are immediately apprehensible as necessary structures of every society; we might also consider here the fact that society is a whole, having a culture like a soul, and even an existential *a priori*. Thus society would have an immediately accessible meaning, like life or physical objects. This would be still another proof of the sociality of the subject.

7. This contains an allusion to Hegel's theory of objective spirit.—Trans.

8. This reservation neither intends to disqualify the Marxist idea of the end of a particular history within history itself, nor to question that alienation may be overcome to the extent that it is an economic fact.

9. The case of the Negroes analyzed by Sartre in his article, "Black Orpheus," differs here only in that they have or *are* two societies; they deny one only to affirm the other: to proclaim their race as an honor rather than as an object of shame. But in order to combat white society they must borrow their weapons from it—their only efficacious and available arms; thus, in order not to be this society, they must be it after all.

10. "Culture" here does not refer to taste in fine arts, but to the object studied in cultural anthropology.—Trans.

11. See the author's *La Personnalité de base—un concept sociologique* (Paris, Presses Universitaires de France, 1953).—Trans.

12. This is adapted from a line of Paul Valéry's "La Jeune Parque": "Tout l'univers chancelle et tremble sur ma tige" (*Oeuvres*, Edition de la Pléiade [Paris, Gallimard, 1957], I, 102).—Trans.

13. Moreover, they are not necessarily different: the relation of competition, for example, can be considered as an *a priori* of sociality, just as the relation of finality is an *a priori* of vitality, or spatiality is an *a priori* of corporeality. We can say with Margaret Mead (in all deference to the objections of Claude Levi-Strauss) that a certain society is competitive, or with Ruth Benedict that the Zuñi society is Apollonian, in an attempt to name (though in an admittedly precarious fashion) the existential *a priori* of this society. Yet there remains a difference: in the first case, the social *a priori* define a possible characteristic of society in general and are only partially constitutive for a given society, just as extension constitutes the body only partially; in the second case, the existential *a priori* defines the essential aspect of a given society: its essence, to the extent that it can be defined. The existential *a priori* is more profoundly constitutive because it constitutes a subject and the way in which a subject possesses and experiences a multiplicity of subjective *a priori*.

14. The term "quasi-subject" can also be employed in a more elastic sense

to designate every expressive object: quasi-subject insofar as it addresses itself to me as an equal, not insofar as it performs a quasi-transcendental function. A quasi-subject is usually the work of an individual subject—e.g., the work of art. But such an object is known, not knowing: the pregnancy of the objective *a priori* constituting it does not authorize us to attribute to it, even metaphorically, a subjective, thus an existential, *a priori*.

15. Georges Bernanos (1888–1948) was a French writer who was also an intransigent Catholic. He was the author of novels and various polemical works.—Trans.

16. *L'apriorique*—this adjectival form of *"a priori"* is also a neologism in French.—Trans.

7

The Nature of Social Man

MAURICE NATANSON

The history and philosophy of social man are inseparable, for history encompasses philosophy and philosophy
includes the critique of historical experience. No priorities in
chronology are appropriate here. Nor is it possible to understand the relationship between history and philosophy without recognizing the special sense in which philosophy is
included in the historian's province. The arguments of the
philosophers are part of the subject matter of history only to
the extent that they are deemed relevant to the age, to the
events considered worthy of recollection, and to the transformations of societal structure. The arguments themselves,
strangely enough, are left alone; or, more strictly, they are
left to the puzzlement, the haggling, or the bemusement of
the philosophers. Hegel's thought is certainly important to

Reprinted from *Patterns of the Life-World: Essays in Honor of John Wild,*
ed. James M. Edie, Francis H. Parker, and Calvin O. Schrag (1970), pp.
248–70, by permission of Northwestern University Press, Evanston, Ill.

the understanding of nineteenth- and twentieth-century history, but it would be odd to suggest that it is the historian's responsibility to vindicate or refute Hegel's philosophy. He must know *about* Hegel; he is not professionally committed to philosophize with Hegel. It is possible, then, to learn a great deal about the history of philosophy—what the major thinkers said—without fully encountering the conceptual problems which worried them or turning to the phenomena which occasioned them and to which the arguments are directed. Philosophy stands in a qualitatively different position. Its concern is with the assumptions and presuppositions of historical experience, not with the factual content of what happened or with the orderly narrative reconstruction of the significant past. It is not the leavings of history to which the philosopher turns but to the leaven of the unexamined and the unformulated. The embrace of history is then a selective enclosure of philosophy's formulations but not of its conceptual content. The latter remains untouched by observation and report, almost, one is tempted to say, as a poem transcends print or music a score. On the side of philosophy a corresponding distinction is called for. As a critique of historical experience, philosophy restricts itself to the meaning of our ordering of the past and is not interested in the description or analysis of the events involved. Occasionally we have individuals who are both historians and philosophers—R. G. Collingwood, for example—but the disciplinary difference remains. The inseparability of history and philosophy is far from constituting a unity. Indeed, the inseparables live very distinct though related lives. In the restless ménage of knowledge, the historian and the philosopher live together without sharing either board or bed.

The difference between history and philosophy is directly reflected in their formulations of the nature of social man. A history of social man would face the overwhelming task of ordering materials into a coherent account of much of world civilization, but there would be no problem in the identification of the subject matter—man as a social being. Understanding, interpreting, analyzing, comprehending, and explaining social man are demanding and troublesome ventures, but there is little suggestion in history that man himself is a problematic phenomenon or that the social is inherently elusive. In fine, the recognition of social man is historically taken for granted. The historian's professional enterprise begins—properly and necessarily—where the philosopher's craft ends. The issue, the bond and yet the contention between them, is the nature and status of the public, readily available, common-sense world of everyday life which we all share as mundane beings. For the historian, the real world all of us inhabit is the unchallenged ground and foundation for the events which comprise the story he tries to tell. For the philosopher, it is the very reality of our world which calls for scrutiny. The central terms of discourse, then, must be subjected to inspection: "man," "world," and "sociality" are necessary as well as proper themes for inquiry. It is not a question of definition, at least in the usual sense of offering a few carefully formulated sentences which explain how each term is being used. At best, philosophers end with definitions; they cannot begin with them without endangering their quest. The reason is simply that in trying to define such fundamental concepts as social man the terms of discourse are already inflected with philosophical attitudes and commitments. If we were to start defining man "as a being who . . ."—for example—we would be presupposing a difference between beings and Being, and would be treading on ontological ground. Being is no problem for the historian; it is perhaps the most basic question for the philosopher. If we cannot start by simply defining our terms, we can begin by sketching the large outline of certain thematic issues which may lead to a philosophic understanding of social man.

Amid the variables of human experience, there are certain features of man's existence which are essentially unchanging and, I believe, unchangeable. It is a constant of human being that each of us is born into a world already inhabited by Others, fellow-men like ourselves. It is a constant of mundane reality that each of us is born into a historical and cultural order, that we have language, that we experience the limits of existence in terms of the religious or the magical, that we grow older together, and that we are destined to die. But it is also true that each of us can say "we," that we are able to share selected aspects of reality—appreciate the same poem, respond to the same music—without reducing them to idiosyncratic expressions or private contents of consciousness. And it is a prime fact of daily life that we take communication with fellow-men for granted, that is, we perceive the world and act in it on the unstated, completely immanent assumption that Others see the world essentially as we do, that the one umbrella of reality serves us all. We are not, of course, at the level of individual or socio-cultural differences. Rather, we are trying to grasp the conditions necessary for the very possibility of experience in the social world. In these terms, the individual's knowledge of an experience of his fellow-men emerges as the definitive theme of social reality, and the essential features of intersubjective experience are what provide the basis for understanding social man. The "social," let us say, is located by way of the philosophical problem of intersubjectivity. Once again, it is the privileged responsibility of the philosopher to look after this issue. "And he's welcome to it!" an unfriendly voice may catcall. Before proceeding any further, we should face the not uncommon charge that the philosopher who worries about intersubjectivity is like a man going down in a sinking ship who asks whether Archimedes' principle really holds water.

The charge amounts to this: given the actuality of war, riot, assassination, famine, overpopulation, plague, revolt, oppression, prejudice, and apartheid, how dare the philosopher ask whether there are really other people in the world or how it is possible to have knowledge of them? Isn't that a continuation of the same inconsequentiality philosophers indulged in centuries ago when they asked how many angels could dance on the head of a pin? If I may be permitted one aside, I would like to put in a good word for the angels and suggest that their discussion by St. Thomas Aquinas and Maimonides is well worth study by those who are willing to exchange the jingling for the genuine. But whatever other failings philosophers may have, they are not guilty of triviality in turning to the problem of intersubjectivity. On the contrary, there is hardly a theme in their discipline with more immediate and vital implications for the scene of human action. To set matters straight, it must be said that the philosopher is not an innocent, nor is he isolated from the harshness of the world. The best man in the history of our profession died in jail. Since the fourth century B.C., working conditions for us may have become better but certainly not less complicated. When we ask about fellow-men, then, we are not wondering whether there is anybody else around besides ourselves, nor are we suggesting that social life is somehow unreal. *Of course,* there are Others, and *of course,* we communicate with them. The difficulty is in understanding how the obvious is possible, how the givenness of sociality is to be explained. The choice is not between affirming or denying intersubjectivity but between taking its philosophical structure for granted or trying to account for it. The choice is between assumption and explanation. What we are really asking is what "of course" means when we bank on its certitude. Nor is there any simple option in choosing between common sense and philosophy, for, as I hope to show in quite some detail, common sense is built on philosophical commitments, and the purpose of philosophy is to illuminate its structure.

I have contrasted common sense with philosophy. Whatever account we give of philosophy, we are at least on mutual ground when it comes to common sense, for it is, at first approximation, our natural habitat, the arena of work and love, of everyday performances. It is the world we are all wise to, whatever our station in life. Most simply, common sense is the typical; common sense is the familiar. To avoid one possible misunderstanding, however, it should be understood that in the context I am relying on, common sense refers to the structure of man's action in daily life, not to the quality of his judgment. Interestingly enough, even when we do have judgment in mind when we speak of common sense, there is a quantitative rather than a qualitative ascription made. We say that someone has a "lot" of common sense or else "very little," and we may also say, "He showed good common sense" on that occasion. But the last would seem to translate into "He showed a great deal of common sense," for what would it mean to say—and could we possibly say—"He showed bad common sense"? It would seem that common sense is always good, though often in short supply. In invoking it we are not appealing to a special faculty of mind but to the character of social order, its traditions, its formulas for handling problems, and its recipes for action. Common sense is not so much a personal possession as a mark of sociality, an emblem of man's involvement in the public world. It is this social pull that common sense responds to which leads us to speak of its structural dimension. Rather than common sense, perhaps we should more properly speak of the common-sense world. In any case, what we have before us as a problem can be formulated fairly simply. Each of us lives in a world which is organized along typical and typically taken for granted lines. The content of that world varies from individual to individual, from culture to culture, and from one era to another, but its formal properties, its underlying guidelines, remain universally secure and pertinent. What we called the constants of man's existence hold for common sense: from birth to death we are plunged and immersed in the currents of a meaning-laden sociality, created by Others and sustained by intersubjective resolve and complicity. How are we to understand the forms and forces of social reality? How is a philosophy of the common-sense world possible?

To be clear about our procedure in presenting a philosophy of common-sense reality, it is instructive to note what we are *not* concerned with. No effort will be made here to account for the genesis or causal development of the social world. There are valid and urgent questions of causation related to man's mundane existence, but we are explicitly setting them aside for our purposes. Further, no attempt will be made here to evaluate or promote some judgment of what is right or wrong, good or bad, about social structure. Again, judgments of value are profoundly relevant to some of the topics we are examining, but not in our context. We choose, then, to set them aside, along with many other dispositions and interpretive attitudes men share in their appraisal of life, in order to turn directly to the structure of the common-sense world so that we may describe its terrain and determine its constitution. Positively stated, we are embarked on a descriptive enterprise which seeks to render the world of man's social being an explicit object of scrutiny and which is concerned with uncovering the thick and often hidden meaning of social reality by a radical conception of consciousness. In its distinctively modern form, this philosophical orientation is known as phenomenology. In what follows, as in what has already been said, I am indebted to the work of the founder of phenomenology, Edmund Husserl, and to the phenomenologist who has subsequently done most to develop a theory of the social world, Alfred Schutz. If I have not credited them with particular notions already presented it is because I have done so elsewhere, and because it is tiresome to have to say, "as Husserl showed" or "as Schutz maintained," and, finally, because I am not simply expositing their views but utilizing them in my own way, a more nearly existential way than either man would have cared to be associated with. To get started, though, I will appeal to Schutz for an initial depiction of social man. He writes:

Let us try to characterize the way in which the wide-awake grown-up man looks at the intersubjective world of daily life within which and upon which he acts as a man amidst his fellow-men. This world existed before our birth, experienced and interpreted by others, our predecessors, as an organized world. Now it is given to our experience and interpretation. All interpretation of this world is based on a stock of previous experiences of it, our own or those handed down to us by parents or teachers; these experiences in the form of "knowledge at hand" function as a scheme of reference.

Furthermore:

Man finds himself at any moment of his daily life in a biographically determined situation, that is, in a physical and socio-cultural environment as defined by him, within which he has his position, not merely his position in terms of physical space and outer time or of his status and role within the social system but also his moral and ideological position. To say that this definition of the situation is biographically determined is to say that it has its history; it is the sedimentation of all man's previous experiences, organized in the habitual possessions of his stock of knowledge at hand, and as such his unique possession, given to him and to him alone.[1]

Expressed in first-person terms, I am thrust into a world which is always "already" in process, that is, for me, the actor on the social scene, the participant in daily life, there is no point at which it could be said that the slate is clean, experience is untouched by the past, or everything is just starting. At any moment of reflection, I can look back and locate the ground or source of the present; in fact, reflection by its very nature presupposes a something prior, a something already there to which attention is to be given. A pattern of intention and attitude, merged with memorial notes and sly expectancies, underlies even the most casual elements of experience. Nothing is presented to me which is pristinely stripped of association and implication, nor is anything received by me which enters my perceptual doors without ringing a bell that reverberates throughout my being. I am speaking of the social, not the physical. A light flashed in my eyes during a medical examination produces a characteristic response, a reflex reaction, without presenting a challenge to my being as a person. A light flashed in my eyes during a police investigation provokes a different kind of response. The pupil contracts in the same manner in both instances, but the meaning of the light derives from the situation of authority and privacy, and reaction gives way to response. The moment of reflection, then, is bound to the total reality of my continuity as an individual and cannot be understood apart from the unity of my being as a person. But each time something happens which occasions reflection, the event is appropriated by the categories and schemas of common-sense interpretation. As a social being I am always in the midst of experience and always undergirded by the structure of mundanity. The seemingly and even genuinely novel is irretrievably caught in a matrix of the familiar. William James, speaking as a pragmatist, made essentially the same point in a different way:

Our minds . . . grow in spots; and like grease-spots, the spots spread. But we let them spread as little as possible: we keep unaltered as much of our old knowledge, as many of our old prejudices and beliefs, as we can. We patch and tinker more than we renew. The novelty soaks in; it stains the ancient mass; but it is also tinged by what absorbs it. Our past apperceives and co-operates; and in the new equilibrium in which each step forward in the process of learning terminates, it happens relatively seldom that the new fact is added *raw*. More usually it is embedded cooked, as one might say, or stewed down in the sauce of the old.[2]

If we grant the force of the traditional in the sphere of common sense, it is still necessary to determine the relationship between the general field of social life and the concrete reality of the individual. What is the point of access each of us has as an individual to the typified world of social man? The reply I will give may appear both eccentric and out of keeping with what has been said so far. Explanation will follow swiftly, but the immediate answer is: my body!

As a purely physical phenomenon, my body is measurable and classifiable chemically and biologically. Its physics is that of a remarkable but faulty machine. It may be understood qualitatively in the same way that other animal machines are studied and explained. Apart from incidental differences, my guess is that an autopsy on my cadaver would, were it performed soon, reveal unexciting, rather mediocre results. I'm afraid that my case records would be indistinguishable from hundreds of thousands of others. Since I have no hopes for posthumous medical glory, I am resigned to seeking other fields of conquest. A more positive domain is that of my body as an expressive rather than a sheerly physical reality. By that I mean my body as a primordially experienced means through which I am able to insert myself in the world, through which I am able to achieve both intimacy and distance, and whose immediacy is the agency for my locating objects and persons, events and feelings, as *here* and as *mine*. To be sure, the body is the functioning sensory screen which enables me to contact the world and respond to it. At the same time, however, it may be understood as the active instrument which brings to life, which activates and indeed creates, the resplendent and baffling variety of human involvements: work, love, disease, and death. There is a terrible familiarity about the body which tends to disguise its centrality to the individual's organization of the world. First,

it has always been with us; second, it is always there when
called on; third, it seems as though it invariably manages to
be there when we arrive. In between awareness of it, times
when we inspect it or self-consciously utilize it, it hovers, an
obedient wraith. When it fails, in disease, in trauma, in extreme conditions, we tend to think of the body in beast-of-
burden terms: we speak of having to drive, push, propel
ourselves. Or, if we are seriously incapacitated, it is as though
insurrection had occurred: the body revolts, is crushed, de-
feated. Apart from the more obvious circumstances of pa-
thology or injury, there is the oblique dimension of the body's
relationship to us. Familiar, ally, friend, despot, slacker, trou-
blemaker, it sustains us and betrays us, bears us and abandons
us. The discussion of the existential motility of the body in
Sartre and Merleau-Ponty is extensive and, I think, impres-
sive even to those who might not be persuaded by the larger
philosophical positions advanced by those authors. Rather
than rehearse those theories, I prefer a more direct route to
the point they make, the active and integral relationship
between person and body. Quoting Whitehead's phrase, "the
withness of the body," as a motto for his poem, Delmore
Schwartz says in "The Heavy Bear Who Goes With Me":[3]

> The heavy bear who goes with me,
> A manifold honey to smear his face,
> Clumsy and lumbering here and there,
> The central ton of every place,
> The hungry beating brutish one
> In love with candy, anger, and sleep,
> Crazy factotum, dishevelling all,
> Climbs the building, kicks the football,
> Boxes his brother in the hate-ridden city.
>
> Breathing at my side, that heavy animal,
> That heavy bear who sleeps with me,
> Howls in his sleep for a world of sugar,

A sweetness intimate as the water's clasp,
Howls in his sleep because the tight-rope
Trembles and shows the darkness beneath.
—The strutting show-off is terrified,
Dressed in his dress-suit, bulging his pants,
Trembles to think that his quivering meat
Must finally wince to nothing at all.

That inescapable animal walks with me,
Has followed me since the black womb held,
Moves where I move, distorting my gesture,
A caricature, a swollen shadow,
A stupid clown of the spirit's motive,
Perplexes and affronts with his own darkness,
The secret life of belly and bone,
Opaque, too near, my private, yet unknown,
Stretches to embrace the very dear
With whom I would walk without him near,
Touches her grossly, although a word
Would bare my heart and make me clear,
Stumbles, flounders, and strives to be fed
Dragging me with him in his mouthing care,
Amid the hundred million of his kind,
The scrimmage of appetite everywhere.

The discovery of my body, myself incarnate in the world, mysteriously and paradoxically strapped to something I both am and am not, is achieved or avoided within common-sense existence, for the "here" of my body has no place on any official map. It is, however, the null point, the center zero, of the mundane coordinates which mark my position in everyday life.

At every moment of my life, I occupy some "here," marked by the locus of my body. Obviously, the "here" keeps changing as I move about, yet it is perpetually renewed. From that "here" the shape and organization of the world is discerned or hypothesized by the individual as a mundane being. Right now, the world opens up before me, around me, from *Here,* where I stand; and what I perceive as near or distant, as within or out of reach, as *There,* is defined by the place of my body. That I can move from Here to There, that I can have a new Here, means that a principle of exchangeability tacitly underlies the location of the individual in the world, for not only is it the case that I can move from Here to There but I take it for granted that from the new Here the world will unfold, be structured in essentially the same way it was before, in my old Here. Exchangeability is not a physical directive; it is an axiom of social life. What it posits is the thesis that all transformations of the placement of the body will yield an unchanging and stable world in which the individual will have everything laid out before him essentially as he did before. Certainly, the new vantage point may present a very different, sometimes a surprisingly new, view of some event or situation, but transformation rules are available which take the altered circumstances into account and enable the individual to confront the "same" segment of reality he perceived before. What remains constant in the transformation is the principle of centrality, that in the exchange of places from Here to There the null point remains the same. The most vital implication of that presupposed constancy is that the individual who is Here can change places with his fellow-man who is There and that both of them will find the transposition continuous with the flow of their prior experience. The constancy of the null point is thus not a geographical but a sociological insight. I regard it as decisive for the constitution of intersubjectivity.

A closer examination of the insertion of the body in the world reveals a major difference between the assumption the individual makes about his own transposibility from Here to There and the supposed analogous counterpart he thinks is true for his fellow-man. In first-person terms, I have direct evidence regarding my own transposition but none regarding my alter ego. I simply take it for granted that what is true for me is also true for him. In that act of "animal faith," I take the first, the crucial step in the epistemic journey which leads to intersubjectivity. That act is unsupported by any argumentation, it is not based on inductive procedures, and it cannot be accounted for by a chain of causal reasoning. Rather, it is more modest to say that belief in the sameness of my and the Other's standpoint in the world and faith in the reciprocity of our world-organizing principles are already evidenced in the experience of the social world within whose limits questions about the individual's relationship to his fellow-men arise. It is within the intersubjective world of daily life that our inquiry into its structural possibility emerges. And it is through the body that the outlines of that world are initially glimpsed and gauged. If that is so, then the act of faith which takes for granted the sameness of the Other's placement in the world must take its clue from the appearance of *his* body. How then is the body of the Other perceived? It might appear reasonable to answer, "Why, just as I perceive my own." But that won't do for a number of reasons. First, I don't perceive my body directly. In fact, there are parts I have no direct visual access to without artificial aids: my face and my back. Second, even those parts I can see directly are features of the body which is seeing, that is, they are integral to my presence as a perceiving being; they are *me!* By a special effort I can, of course, observe my hands or my toes or my teeth, but they are then removed from the taken-for-grantedness of my bodily stance and rendered objects for inspection, like soldiers on parade. My body, then, is the vital instrument through which perception takes place; it is not in its mundane being a phenomenon for perception. The Other's body presents itself to me in altogether different circumstances. It *is* an object for my perceptual experience, but it is an object of a special sort. Unlike my seeing and touching sticks and stones, my awareness of the body of the Other is suffused by a recognition that it is *the Other*, a fellow-man, I greet when I catch his eye, touch his hand, hear his voice. All apparent evidence to the contrary, the fishiest handclasp ever offered belongs to a man, not a fish. But just as the movement from the Here of the individual to the There of his fellow-man is based on the assumption of the reciprocity of null points, so we may say that the recognition of the body of the Other as animately *his* is grounded in the perception of the Other as a presence whose cognitive and affective life manifests itself in simultaneity with the presentation of his body. We do not see flesh and infer a human being inside it; we confront a psyche in seeing a man. The Other lives and is recognized at the focus of his glance, in the space he warms, and in the void his language fills. In this bodily presence the sociality of man achieves its primordial expression.

The discussion thus far of the body might tend to give the impression that even if it does offer a valid starting point for the understanding of intersubjectivity, the model it is based on—man confronting fellow-man—is too narrow to serve as a paradigm for all sociality. That is quite true, and I hasten to turn now to an equally important aspect of the problem, that of time. If it is true to say that the body is the clue to social man, that is certainly not the whole truth, for man's being articulates itself in temporal no less than spatial terms. To the Here of bodily presence must be added the Now of social encounter. The immediate liberation that results from introducing this category should be evident, for we can share a temporal reality with fellow-men we do not see and cannot touch, not only those at great distance from us but those who died before we were born and even those who will be born after we die. The social world is made up of predecessors and successors no less than of contemporaries. Not only are we influenced by them and oriented to them, but we share with them the history of sociality, for each of us is destined to be a predecessor and a successor as long as a social world goes on. Moreover, our relationship to contemporaries with whom we have a face-to-face relationship is marked by the temporal roots which anchor our social immediacy. Those seen now may move off and drop out of all perceptual contact. Those once encountered may return. In a sense, the social world is constructed out of interruptions and mortared with expectancies; it is a patchwork of presence and departure. If this were the end of the story, it might well appear that all we could say about intersubjectivity is a bland and unrewarding, "Here today, there tomorrow." I propose an altogether different refrain as a preliminary conclusion to these proceedings: Here means type, Now means form. The analysis of the body brings us to the concept of typification as the form of social existence. It returns us also to social man as a being immersed in as well as generated by the taken for granted and the familiar. Once again we turn to Alfred Schutz as a guide to the phenomenology of typification. He writes:

> The factual world of our experience . . . is experienced from the outset as a typical one. Objects are experienced as trees, animals, and the like, and more specifically as oaks, firs, maples, or rattlesnakes, sparrows, dogs. This table I am now perceiving is characterized as something recognized, as something foreknown and, nevertheless, novel. What is newly experienced is already known in the sense that it recalls similar or equal things formerly perceived. But what has been grasped once in its typicality carries with it a horizon of possible experience with corresponding references to familiarity, that is, a series of typical characteristics still not actually experienced but expected to be potentially experienced.[5]

Applied to the social world, we may say that our experience of each other is typified not only by common-sense attitudes and expectancies but more fundamentally by the very perceptual process through which apprehension and interpretation occur. In seeing the embodied Other, I am presented, strictly speaking, with only an aspect of his being, his face, his intonation, his gesture; but that glimpse is enough for me to perceive him as an individual having a multitude of attributes, all of which are features of a being *like* myself. That "likeness" is the initial typification which permits me to commence the movement from I to we. But the typification of the Other goes far beyond the immediacy of our bodies in face-to-face situations. As I have said, in addition to the Here of immediacy there is also the Now of transcendence. The Other who is *not* present is also typified. Indeed, our knowledge of predecessors is largely limited to knowledge by way of type, and what we surmise of our successors is completely restricted to typified expectancies and fantasies. The insertion of my body in the world is then only the beginning of a long and complex series of performances which account for the construction of a social world. Within the larger present of contemporaries with whom I do not share common space, there is an infinitely complex system of typifications which enable me to understand them and their activities and permit me to translate their demands and offers in appropriate ways. With Joseph K., most of us will never penetrate to the high courts, but we organize our lives in terms of that exclusion. What remains as the field of our social action is similarly typified: whether it is City Hall or the State Department, the local police force or the United States Army, the university, the movies, the stock exchange, or the Library of Congress, most of us know about the workings of these local or national organizations and institutions only in typified ways. Some of us may know one of them intimately, but then the rest are known vaguely, hypothetically, and indirectly. The remainder of contemporary experience, the entire sociocultural world now in process, is known in essentially the same manner. The result of such typification is that the strange and the foreign are accommodated in mundane terms. We may never meet any of the great heroes of our times, but we know about them in common-sense terms, and that *is* the way they enter our lives and become part of our reality. Neither may we ever meet the men who handle the mail, who repair telephone lines, who unload freight, or who grow wheat, but we have typified concepts of them and their jobs. They are no less contemporaries than the pedestrians we pass on streets or the crowds we mingle with on public occasions. If, as I have suggested, the typical is the clue to mundane existence, then it is possible to say that it is also the secret of the familiarity of common sense. Rather than the familiar being defined by the concrete actuality of what each of us has directly experienced, it is more nearly the opposite case: the familiar is what is typically possible, what is potentially experienceable. Common sense is a tissue of possibilities.

If we have stressed our relationship to fellow-men so far, it should not be thought that the existence of the individual has been sacrificed on the altar of sociality. Nor should it be concluded that typification applies only to the Other. Man is a self-typifying no less than an Other-typifying creature. If it is only an aspect of the Other which manifests itself to me, it is also only a fragment of my own being I am aware of or have come to terms with, and only a facet of myself which presents itself to my fellow-man on any occasion. Once again, this fragmentation is taken for granted in common-sense life. We don't ask clerks questions which are appropriate for priests, nor do we go to the corner newsstand in search of rare first editions. Most basically, we know, as common-sense men, that certain forms or types of behavior are called for in certain situations, and we all serve an apprenticeship in the academy of daily life which trains us for taking the roles we must inevitably play in social reality. Roles and role-playing are the forms that typification takes in moving from the beginnings of intersubjectivity in bodily presence to the schemas and constructs of the public world in the regions of distance and absence. Whatever interpretations and explanations social scientists may give to roles, the primal status they enjoy is expressed in mundane life, in the midst of common-sense experience. There man and fellow-man, understood as actors in as well as observers of the social scene, build the reality within whose limits all history is lived. To locate the uniqueness of the individual, the existential sphere of the person, we are obliged to honor common sense rather than to sidetrack it. The whole point of our discussion of typification is that it provides a wedge into the nature of social man. It would be a misreading of my words to conclude that common sense and personal identity are antagonists. Before we can say that there is enmity between them we must first make certain that the relationship is understood in its positive sense. Where, precisely, do we locate the concrete individual in the matrix of societal typifications? Having discussed the body and the dialectic of intersubjectivity, having stressed the familiar structure of mundane existence and the world at distance from us, where at last shall we find the pulse of a single, actual, splendidly or miserably existent human being? Where in the castle of social man can we find our own small bedroom?

Let me turn to an example for help. Years ago I had to pass reading examinations in French and German in order to fulfill requirements for the Ph.D. I remember the German exam especially well because of an incident which disrupted it. A group of doctoral candidates were given the test together in one room. Among them was a graduate student, quite a bit older than the rest of us, a married man with several children, who had come back to the university late in academic life, who was an able and a hard worker but whose nemesis was German. He had failed the examination twice and was given a special dispensation to try a third time. He had passed all other requirements for his degree but would be forced to abandon his career if he failed German a third time. We all knew him, liked him, admired his spirit and fortitude, and were hoping he would make it this time. He had worked with a private tutor, spent a great many hours in preparation, and had, he thought, a decent chance to pass. As soon as the text for translation was distributed, we all set to work. The room was a cube of perfect silence, but seconds after we got started, I heard a small but peculiar noise. One of the examinees had a rather full, laden nose and was snuffling. I wasn't particularly disturbed but I noticed that our last-chance friend, who was sitting next to the sniffler, was upset. He gave him two or three withering looks, tapped his pencil vigorously, rearranged his chair severely— all to no effect. The offender seemed immune to all signals, lost in the complexity of some endless German sentence. And the noises went on. Indeed, by some strange nasal chemistry, the sounds grew not only in volume but in variability. Little bubbles seemed to erupt from time to time with tiny explosiveness, inhalation was accompanied by liquid grunts, and the perilous moment when what was there seemed about to flee its tunneled prison was obviated by a quick save of almost passionate intake. Meanwhile our friend was frantic. Unable to concentrate, at a disadvantage under the best of circumstances, under the added pressure of the time limit of the examination, confronted with the knowledge that it was now or never in his career, undoubtedly aware of the years of work he had already put in and the hardships his family had suffered on his behalf, poised at the linguistic Rubicon, his face screwed into a torment of ire, he slammed his fist on the table and screamed at the villain: "JESUS CHRIST! BLOW YOUR NOSE!"

How does one go about understanding such an outburst? How does one account for an otherwise mild person exploding into paroxysm? And how is it possible to distinguish between *this* individual and the typified class of "men of that type"? It would seem that the most natural way of proceeding to answer these questions is to turn to the background of our friend, to study his past, work up a detailed analysis of the pressures on him, and, having come to terms with the causes and motivational grounds of his personality and behavior, offer an explanation of the examination events consistent with the causal conditions which produced them. My insistence on a phenomenological framework for analysis has ruled out that general line of explanation for the present context. Committed as we are to a structural and descriptive account of social man, we shall have to look to other sources for help in assessing his action. To understand the examination scene—limited as that example may be—it is necessary to locate our friend in the midst of what existential philosophers call a "situation," that is, an ensemble of forces and projects defined by the constants of man's being, the goals he has set himself, and the freedom he displays in choosing the meaning of what limits and liberates him. If we assume that a present action is explained by certain states of affairs in the past, then explosive behavior is the "result" of tension, pressure, and frustration. However, if we allow for present action being defined by present choice, stemming from the continuous decision the individual makes in interpreting his world, then irruption proves to be the point of departure for reconstructing some causal history of a human career rather than the other way around. Nor is it then possible to file away men according to their "type" and say, "Well, after all, what can you expect of him? He's a choleric." There are times when we are surprised by a moderate voice when we expect the Other to be enraged, and there is no assurance that a typified expectation will in fact yield the expected result. Part of the fund of common-sense knowledge is the distinctive recognition that the unexpected is always possible and that fellow-men, ourselves included, are always capable of breaking out of the circuit of the taken for granted and the condoned and of acting in novel and sometimes erratic ways. The prime lesson of common sense is that we must comprehend man in his situation if we are to understand him. The performances of social man are shadow plays apart from the meaning human action has to those who are actors situated in mundane reality.

It is the status of meaning which marks the center of the network of problems we have been examining and which provides the basis for a solution to the puzzle of sociality and the paradox of identity and typicality in common-sense life. Meaning, we suggest, is a function of the interpretation an actor on the social scene gives to his own act. The ground of meaning in the social world, then, is not the observer's explanation of the actor's behavior but the participant's understanding of his own acts. In seeking to grasp the meaning of his alter ego's action, the individual tries to determine what the Other's action means to him, the one who performs that action. Now there is no claim being made at this point that either the actor or his fellow-man has a full comprehension of his own or his alter ego's action. As we have insisted on before, all action is expressed in fragmentary modes, all understanding arises through the typifications the individual makes of his social reality. But within the limits of fragmentation and typicality, the actor constructs a world whose form and content are composed of the interpretation he gives both to his own acts and to the action of Others. To say that such interpretation is *situated* is to suggest that the "same" behavioral act is not at all necessarily the same social act. I understand the meaning of an act when I determine what it signifies to the actor. The Other understands my action when he determines what it means to me. That much determination is partial and faulty is precisely the truth of social existence, for the necessary reliance on typicality—the very construction of common-sense life—is a recognition that we know ourselves, let alone Others, in partial and hidden ways and yet are bound, if not condemned, to find our way in the world within the restrictions of an opaque sociality. At the same time, typicality rewards us with a certain freedom and a measure of consistency. The anonymity of types assures the steady flow of social traffic, the commerce of everyday needs and desires, the business of our surface involvements. I can deal successfully with much of the content of everyday life because its typified form permits *any* individual in a certain societal position to act in a routine way. Identity and typicality need each other.

The location of meaning in the actor's intention, in his interpretation of the meaning of his own act, not only makes his situation the definitively important focus of social life but places a major stress on participation rather than observation as the proper point of departure for understanding social man. By this I mean only that the field of social action is initially that of the actor. To be sure, the actor is also an observer, but, as I have tried to show, his observation is directed in action to the situated reality of his fellow-man. His observation is an effort to interpret the meaning of his alter ego's action. The observer in this context is a participant because he is geared into his fellow-man's reality and shares the social scene with him. His history and that of his fellow-man mesh with a communal order; they share certain sectors of the same situation because they are immersed in the common-sense world. However, if we mean by observation the role of the scientist who takes human beings as objects of inquiry, then the meaning of observation changes, for the scientist is a participant in the scene he observes only in a special and quite restricted way. To the extent that he fulfills the role of scientific observer, the individual scientist relinquishes the Here and Now of mundane reality, gives up the placement of his body in the arena of social action, suspends the history of his biographical situation, renounces the demands of his project at hand, and identifies himself totally with the methodological commitments of his discipline. Two cautions are immediately necessary. First, even if it is agreed that such abstention is the ideal goal of the scientist, it hardly follows that he in fact realizes that goal in his actual work. Second, and more significant, the scientist does not cease to be a human being while he operates professionally. I am not saying that when he "does" science he is transformed into a weightless wonder, a free-floating phantom. The point is that the scientist elects to stand outside of common sense when he commits himself to taking the role of the professional observer. That such a choice involves conflict and compromise, that it is horrifically difficult to succeed in disengaging oneself from the sources of sociality, that the entire realm of value orientation and value commitment presents intense ambivalence, is granted. The qualitative difference in mundane and scientific role-obligations remains. And, of course, it is the social scientist who is caught most cunningly in the crosscurrents of disciplinary commitment and mundane estrangement. He is compelled to face a problem which is not unknown in the natural science but which has its strongest expression in the study of social reality: man's inquiry into himself. With that theme we come to the relationship between the natural and the social sciences and are led in turn to the question of the similarities and differences between human beings and animals.

At this point I must confine the discussion to a table of conclusions and forego the discussion necessary to support them. I hope that the analysis of everyday experience which I have developed will be sufficient to give some ballast to what otherwise might appear to be a scantly burdened vessel. The root difference between natural and social science is in the world that both investigate. The natural order is fundamentally one discovered and explored by man; the social order is paramountly one preinterpreted by its inhabitants. The models and constructs the natural scientist makes are of the first degree, that is, they are schemas of objects and events themselves unschematized; the interpretations of the social scientist are constructs of the second degree, schemas of realities already schematized. The self-interpretation of social man takes place by way of the typifications of common-sense life, and, as I have argued, the locus of everyday existence includes a very powerful temporal dimension: ours is a world of predecessors and successors no less than of contemporaries. The preinterpreted world of common-sense experience is then historically oriented in its very texture, for it is impossible to turn to social reality without finding the sedimentation of meaning, the memorial residue, left by our ancestors and their action. Language is one of the cardinal instruments by which we come to appreciate the history of meaning which grounds our social being, but there are other structures of mundanity to be considered. It is possible for man to move from the world of common sense to the worlds of religion, art, fantasy, and dreams because the immediacy of Here and Now can be transcended by means of a reflective decision. Transcension does not mean permanent abandonment. Quite the opposite: we are able to pray and to imagine because our position in mundane life as common-sense men can always be regained. The movement from life to art presupposes the possibility of interrupting the mundane and then rejoining it. Alternation makes us human. Animals, to the contrary, live in a permanent present; for them it is always Now. To shove the point to a final resting place, it should be said that common sense is a distinctively human achievement because it depends on a subjunctive capacity of consciousness. Let me explain.

Typification as the ground of intersubjectivity, the condition of the social, is an "as-if" mode of cognition. If a voice could be given to consciousness in its perceptual activity it might be heard to say: There is a fellow-man, standing before me, waiting for me to join him. His presence co-presents his world, his action, his interpretation of me and of our shared and unshared situation. Were he to say this, I would reply with that; were he to do this, I would do that. Since it is only a part of his world that shows itself at this moment of our meeting, I assume that a host of typicalities would manifest themselves in his action were I to get to know him over a long period of time and were we in close touch with each other. Even further, the very perceptual acts through which I have experience of the Other are selective and formative, for consciousness is an active partner in the construction of the

social world. In setting aside the detailed specificity of the
Other and seeing him in typified terms, consciousness de-
ploys a hypothetical mode of awareness and revels in the
liberation of the subjunctive. Animal consciousness is dominated by the indicative tense. And it is destined to enter a
world which is perpetually renewed as the same. That non-
historical constancy is the animal substitute for common
sense. The hypothetical is precluded by the mechanisms of
instinct and habit. I do not mean to strip the animal world of
its variety, subtlety, and richness. Nor do I mean to treat its
denizens as automata. The refreshing and remarkable gifts
the animal world offers its human associates and observers
are perhaps possible precisely because the situation of Here
and Now can always be generated in the same way. I'm not
sure we have as much to offer the animals, but, for better or
worse, humanity is enmeshed in a historical order which
utterly transcends the comprehension of our closest and
most intelligent animal companions.

For man, then, mundane reality is historical reality; that is
at once the reassurance and the anguish of his situation. How
does social man stand with respect to himself? It is here that
the convergence of phenomenology and existentialism is
most dramatically evident. Our answer will retrace the
course we have followed and will offer a glance beyond. To
understand ourselves and our fellow-men as social beings it
is necessary to examine the philosophical presuppositions of
mundane existence. In the taken for granted attitude of daily
life, the historicity and intersubjectivity of the public world
are assumed to be both obvious and valid. Whatever special
problems arise for consideration are already taken to be
within the horizon of *our* common world. But to come to
terms with the meaningful structure of social reality it is
necessary to set aside our believing in the obvious and call to
scrutiny and account the basis for our beliefs. When we turn
our critical glance to the social world we inhabit, we find that
its epistemological center is the domain of common sense,

understood as the matrix of typification and familiarity. From
that center arise the constructs which organize our experience of life and toward that center are directed the problems
and crises which disturb or plague our being. We find our
direction in mundane reality by the coordinates of space and
time at whose zero point lies our body, and it is from that
orientation that we discover the bodies of fellow-men and
are able to move from personal to intersubjective interpretation. Both self-understanding and the appreciation of Others
involve a recognition that social action is meaningful initially
to the actor himself and that no human act can be com-
prehended apart from the situation in which it has significance for the human agent. Participation rather than observation is the prime moment of the dialectic of social life.
Accordingly, the task of the social scientist is to honor the
preinterpreted order of common-sense experience by discerning and describing its structure and by trying to illuminate its relevance for the total range of man's historical and
cultural reality. Our being in the social world is above all a
thematic problem for us, concrete men in action in daily life,
not a topic for social science. It is in our reflective potential
that common-sense experience emerges as strikingly human,
for in reflection we are able to transcend the Here and Now
of social immediacy and encounter the full complexity of the
possibility, the subjunctive options, of the immediate and the
actual. Within the orbit of the mundane, then, we find the
freedom of social man. At the same time, we find a definition
of his—our—nature. Man is the being who creates social order out of the typifications of common sense.

With that we reach the end of our phenomenology of social
man and come in sight of those existential questions regarding human identity and choice which our discussion has
pointed to without ever broaching directly. The creature at
the null point of space and time, confronting the social world,
is not a body without a personal core. It is yourself or myself
who awaits the philosopher's rendezvous. Yet the approach

to that self is possible only by the discipline of knowledge. Therein lies the paradox of thought. How is it possible to capture social man without destroying his spontaneity? Isn't the analysis of common sense damaging to its autonomy? At this point we can do no more than raise the question and transpose it to the sphere of valuation we explicitly bracketed out of our discussion at the outset. There is little profit in saying that man is always social man because he cannot be otherwise. There is certainly a sense of the social which is normative and which is a measure of the distance which separates man's accidental birth from the attainment of dignity and justice. The social, in these terms, is as much an ideal as it is an attribute. It is somehow always left to final paragraphs to pay tribute to the spirit of man, his final mystery, and his ultimate transcendence. It is rather like saying, "Don't misunderstand me, I'm for man." Existential philosophy begins with the ambiguity of self-assessment and confronts the strangeness of having to account for ourselves. If I have centered the discussion on the structure of the mundane, it is not because I prefer to avoid existential concerns but because I am convinced that the secret of individual identity is locked in the nature of the social world. If common sense is the region in which our sociality is grounded, it may also be the existential locus of our normative possibilities. And if history is the covenant between man and God, daily life is the record of its fulfillment. There in the unexalted chronicle of the familiar is disclosed the image of what we may still become.

NOTES

1. Alfred Schutz, *Collected Papers* (The Hague: Martinus Nijhoff, 1962), 1: 7–9.

2. *Pragmatism* (London and New York: Longmans, Green, 1940), pp. 168–69.

3. Delmore Schwartz, *Selected Poems: Summer Knowledge*. Copyright

1938 by New Directions. Reprinted by permission of New Directions Publishing Corporation, New York.

4. Alfred Schutz, *Collected Papers*, 1: 281.

8

The World of Contemporaries as a Structure of Ideal Types

ALFRED SCHUTZ

1. The Transition from Direct to Indirect Social Experience. Continuous Social Relationships

We have already noted that the We-relationship can occur with varying degrees of concreteness. We have seen that in the relationship we may experience our fellow men with greater or lesser directness, intimacy, or intensity. However, in the face-to-face situation, directness of experience is essential, regardless of whether our apprehension of the Other is central or peripheral and regardless of how adequate our grasp of him is. I am still "Thou-oriented" even to the man standing next to me in the subway. When we speak of "pure" Thou-orientation or "pure" We-relationship, we are ordinarily using these as limiting concepts referring to the simple givenness of the Other in abstraction from any

Reprinted from *The Phenomenology of the Social World*, trans. George Walsh and Frederick Lehnert (1967), pp. 176–206, by permission of Northwestern University Press, Evanston, Ill.

specification of the degree of concreteness involved. But we can also use these terms for the lower limits of experience obtainable in the face-to-face relationship, in other words, for the most peripheral and fleeting kind of awareness of the other person.

We make the transition from direct to indirect social experience simply by following this spectrum of decreasing vividness. The first steps beyond the realm of immediacy are marked by a decrease in the number of perceptions I have of the other person and a narrowing of the perspectives within which I view him. At one moment I am exchanging smiles with my friend, shaking hands with him, and bidding him farewell. At the next moment he is walking away. Then from the far distance I hear a faint good-by, a moment later I see a vanishing figure give a last wave, and then he is gone. It is quite impossible to fix the exact instant at which my friend left the world of my direct experience and entered the shadowy realm of those who are merely my contemporaries. As another example, imagine a face-to-face conversation, followed by a telephone call, followed by an exchange of letters, and finally messages exchanged through a third party. Here too we have a gradual progression from the world of immediately experienced social reality to the world of contemporaries. In both examples the total number of the other person's reactions open to my observation is progressively diminished until it reaches a minimum point. It is clear, then, that the world of contemporaries is itself a variant function of the face-to-face situation. They may even be spoken of as two poles between which stretches a continuous series of experiences.

It would be the task of a detailed survey of the social world to study these transformations of direct social experience in terms of their specific meaning-content. The studies of "contact situations," especially those lying in the intermediate zone between direct and indirect social experience, and the studies of men's behavior toward and with respect to one

another—in short, Wiese's whole "theory of relationships"—
are now shown to be well founded and justified. They belong
to the special theory of the social world. It was the great
merit of Wiese, and recently also of Sander,[1] to have seen
these problems and to have made valuable contributions toward their solution.

Our purpose in this work, however, is not to set forth such
a special theory of the social world. Nor is it our purpose even
to formulate the basic principles of such a theory. But it is
quite clear that before we describe the situation of being a
contemporary, we must first discover how this is constituted
out of the face-to-face situation.

In everyday life there seems to be no practical problem of
where the one situation breaks off and the other begins. This
is because we interpret both our own behavior and that of
others within contexts of meaning that far transcend the
immediate here and now. For this reason, the question
whether a social relationship we participate in or observe is
direct or indirect seems to be an academic one. But there is
a yet deeper reason for our customary indifference to this
question. Even after the face-to-face situation has receded
into the past and is present only in memory, it still retains its
essential characteristics, modified only by an aura of pastness.
Normally we do not notice that our just-departed friend,
with whom we have a moment ago been interacting, perhaps
affectionately or perhaps in an annoyed way, now appears to
us in a quite different perspective. Far from seeming obvious, it actually seems absurd that someone we are close to has
somehow become "different" now that he is out of sight,
except in the trite sense that our experiences of him bear the
mark of pastness. However, we must still sharply distinguish
between such memories of face-to-face situations, on the one
hand, and an intentional Act directed toward a mere contemporary, on the other. The recollections we have of another bear all the marks of direct experience. When I have
a recollection of you, for instance, I remember you as you

were in the concrete We-relationship with me. I remember you as a unique person in a concrete situation, as one who interacted with me in the mode of "mutual mirroring" described above. I remember you as a person vividly present to me with a maximum of symptoms of inner life, as one whose experiences I witnessed in the actual process of formation. I remember you as one whom I was for a time coming to know better and better. I remember you as one whose conscious life flowed in one stream with my own. I remember you as one whose consciousness was continuously changing in content. However, now that you are out of my direct experience, you are no more than my contemporary, someone who merely inhabits the same planet that I do. I am no longer in contact with the living you, but with the you of yesterday. You, indeed, have not ceased to be a living self, but you have a "new self" now; and, although I am contemporaneous with it, I am cut off from vital contact with it. Since the time we were last together, you have met with new experiences and have looked at them from new points of view. With each change of experience and outlook you have become a slightly different person. But somehow I fail to keep this in mind as I go about my daily round. I carry your image with me, and it remains the same. But then, perhaps, I hear that you have changed. I then begin to look upon you as a contemporary—not any contemporary, to be sure, but one whom I once knew intimately.

Examples of this situation are those social relationships within which, according to Weber, "there is a probability of the repeated occurrence of the behavior which corresponds to its subjective meaning, behavior which is an understandable consequence of the meaning and hence is expected."[2] We tend to picture marriage or friendship as primarily face-to-face relationships, especially intimate ones at that. We do this because of a tendency we have to conceive the actions of the partners as integrated into the larger unity of the relationship and goal-directed toward that unity.

In actual life, however, a marriage or a friendship is made up of many separate events occurring over a long period of time. Some of these events involve face-to-face situations, in others the partners simply exist side by side as contemporaries. To call such social relationships as these "continuous" is erroneous in the extreme,[3] since discontinuity and repeatability are included in their very definition. What, then, do friends mean when they speak of their "friendship"? We can distinguish three different meanings they may have in mind.

1. When *A* speaks of his friendship with *B*, he may be thinking of a series of past face-to-face relationships which he shared with *B*. We say "series," because *A* does remember that during the course of his friendship with *B* he did spend some time alone or with other people.

2. When *A* speaks of his friendship with *B*, he may mean that, over and above such face-to-face situations, his behavior is oriented to *B*'s expected behavior or to the fact that *B* exists—that he is the kind of man he is. In this case, *A* is oriented toward *B* as a contemporary, and their relationship is the kind that exists between contemporaries. This relationship can be either one of orientation or of social interaction.[4] For instance, *A* may perform a certain action because he thinks it will please *B* as soon as the latter finds out about it. Whereas in the face-to-face situation he would literally see *B*'s reaction, here he is confined to merely imagining it. Within the "friendship" such contemporary-oriented acts are inserted between consociate-oriented acts. Face-to-face interaction involves mutual engagement in which the partners can witness the literal coming-to-birth of each other's experiences. Interaction between contemporaries, however, merely involves the expectation on the part of each partner that the other will respond in a relevant way. But this expectation is always a shot in the dark compared to the knowledge one has of one's consociate in the face-to-face situation. Actions between contemporaries are only mutually *related*, whereas actions between consociates are mutually *inter-*

locked.[5] The being related to each other of contemporaries occurs in imagination, whereas the interlocking mutual engagement of the We-relationship is a matter of immediate experience. Between these two situations we find many intermediate degrees. For instance, think of the gradually decreasing immediacy of the following: (a) carrying on an imagined conversation with a friend, (b) wondering what my friend would say if I were to do such and such, (c) doing something "for him."

3. When *A* speaks of his friendship with *B*, he may be referring to the fact that, external obstacles aside, they can always get together again and begin where they have left off. This is parallel to what happens in the sphere of judgment. We showed in our analysis of the concept "knowledge" that the latter refers to a sum of already constituted objectified judgments [or judgment-objectivities—*Urteilsgegenständlichkeiten*]. Knowledge, then, is a storehouse which can be drawn on at any time by the reactivation of the judgments in question. In the same way, when *A* speaks of his friendship with *B*, he is referring to a storehouse of past experiences of *B*. But he is assuming at the same time that these experiences can be reactivated in a revived We-relationship and that, on that basis, both parties can proceed as before. What is here revived, of course, is not so much the specific lived experiences that previously occurred within the We-relationship but the lived experience of the We-relationship itself.

In the last few pages we have been describing the intermediate zone between the face-to-face situation and the situation involving mere contemporaries. Let us continue our journey. As we approach the outlying world of contemporaries, our experience of others becomes more and more remote and anonymous. Entering the world of contemporaries itself, we pass through one region after another: (1) the region of those whom I once encountered face to face and could encounter again (for instance, my absent friend); then (2) comes the region of those once encountered by the person I am now talking to (for instance, your friend, whom you are promising to introduce to me); next (3) the region of those who are as yet *pure* contemporaries but whom I will soon meet (such as the colleague whose books I have read and whom I am now on my way to visit); then (4) those contemporaries of whose existence I know, not as concrete individuals, but as points in social space as defined by a certain function (for instance, the postal employee who will process my letter); then (5) those collective entities whose function and organization I know while not being able to name any of their members, such as the Canadian Parliament; then (6) collective entities which are by their very nature anonymous and of which I could never in principle have direct experience, such as "state" and "nation"; then (7) objective configurations of meaning which have been instituted in the world of my contemporaries and which live a kind of anonymous life of their own, such as the interstate commerce clause and the rules of French grammar; and finally (8) artifacts of any kind which bear witness to the subjective meaning-context of some unknown person. The farther out we get into the world of contemporaries, the more anonymous its inhabitants become, starting with the innermost region, where they can almost be seen, and ending with the region where they are by definition forever inaccessible to experience.

2. The Contemporary as an Ideal Type. The Nature of the They-Relationship

My mere contemporary (or "contemporary"), then, is one whom I know coexists with me in time but whom I do not experience immediately. This kind of knowledge is, accordingly, always indirect and impersonal. I cannot call my contemporary "Thou" in the rich sense that this term has within the We-relationship. Of course, my contemporary may once have been my consociate or may yet become one, but this in no way alters his present status.

Let us now examine the ways in which the world of contemporaries is constituted and the modifications which the concepts "Other-orientation" and "social relationship" undergo in that world. These modifications are necessitated by the fact that the contemporary is only indirectly accessible and that his subjective experiences can only be known in the form of *general types* of subjective experience.

That this should be the case is easy to understand if we consider the difference between the two modes of social experience. When I encounter you face to face I know you as a person in one unique moment of experience. While this We-relationship remains unbroken, we are open and accessible to each other's intentional Acts. For a little while we grow older together, experiencing each other's flow of consciousness in a kind of intimate mutual possession.

It is quite otherwise when I experience you as my contemporary. Here you are not prepredicatively given to me at all. I do not even directly apprehend your existence *(Dasein)*. My whole knowledge of you is mediate and descriptive. In this kind of knowledge your "characteristics" are established for me by inference. From such knowledge results the indirect We-relationship.

To become clear about this concept of "mediacy," let us examine two different ways in which I come to know a contemporary. The first way we have already mentioned: my knowledge is derived from a previous face-to-face encounter with the person in question. But this knowledge has since become mediate[6] or indirect because he has moved outside the range of my direct observation. For I make inferences as to what is going on in his mind under the assumption that he remains much the same[7] since I saw him last, although, in another sense, I know very well that he must have changed through absorbing new experiences or merely by virtue of having grown older. But, as to how he has changed, my knowledge is either indirect or nonexistent.

A second way in which I come to know a contemporary is

to construct a picture of him from the past direct experience
of someone with whom I am now speaking (for example,
when my friend describes his brother, whom I do not know).
This is a variant of the first case. Here too I apprehend the
contemporary by means of a fixed concept, or type, derived
ultimately from direct experience but now held invariant.
But there are differences. First, I have no concrete vivid
picture of my own with which to start: I must depend on
what my friend tells me. Second, I have to depend on my
friend's assumption, not my own, that the contemporary he
is describing has not changed.

These are the modes of constitution of all the knowledge
we have of our contemporaries derived from our own past
experience, direct or indirect, and of all the knowledge we
have acquired from others, whether through conversation or
through reading. It is clear, then, that indirect social experiences derive their original validity from the direct mode of
apprehension. But the instances cited above do not exhaust
all the ways by which I can come to know my contemporaries. There is the whole world of cultural objects, for instance,
including everything from artifacts to institutions and conventional ways of doing things. These, too, contain within
themselves implicit references to my contemporaries. I can
"read" in these cultural objects the subjective experiences of
others whom I do not know. Even here, however, I am making inferences on the basis of my previous direct experience
of others. Let us say that the object before me is a finished
product. Once, perhaps, I stood by the side of a man who was
manufacturing something just like this. As I watched him
work, I knew exactly what was going on in his mind. If it were
not for this experience I would not know what to make of the
finished product of the same kind that I now see. I might
even fail to recognize it as an artifact at all and would treat
it as just another natural object, like a stone or a tree. For
what we have called the general thesis of the alter ego,
namely, that the Thou coexists with me and grows older with

me, can only be discovered in the We-relationship. Even in this instance, therefore, I have only an indirect experience of the other self, based on past direct experiences either of a Thou as such or of a particular Thou. My face-to-face encounters with others have given me a deep prepredicative knowledge of the Thou as a self. But the Thou who is *merely* my contemporary is never experienced personally as a self and never prepredicatively. On the contrary, all experience *(Erfahrung)* of contemporaries is predicative in nature. It is formed by means of interpretive judgments involving all my knowledge of the social world, although with varying degrees of explicitness.

Now this is real Other-orientation, however indirect it may be. And under this indirect Other-orientation we will find the usual forms of simple Other-orientation, social behavior and social interaction. Let us call all such intentional Acts directed toward contemporaries cases of "They-orientation,"[8] in contrast to the "Thou-orientation" of the intentional Acts of direct social experience.

The term "They-orientation" serves to call attention to the peculiar way in which I apprehend the conscious experiences of my contemporaries. For I apprehend them as anonymous processes.[9] Consider the contrast to the Thou-orientation. When I am Thou-oriented, I apprehend the other person's experiences within their setting in his stream of consciousness. I apprehend them as existing within a subjective context of meaning, as being the unique experiences of a particular person. All this is absent in the indirect social experience of the They-orientation. Here I am not aware of the ongoing flow of the Other's consciousness. My orientation is not toward the existence *(Dasein)* of a concrete individual Thou. It is not toward any subjective experiences now being constituted in all their uniqueness in another's mind nor toward the subjective configuration of meaning in which they are taking place. Rather, the object of my They-orientation is my own experience *(Erfahrung)* of social reality in general, of human beings and their conscious processes as such, in abstraction from any individual setting in which they may occur. My knowledge of my contemporaries is, therefore, inferential and discursive. It stands, by its essential nature,[10] in an objective context of meaning and only in such. It has within it no intrinsic reference to persons nor to the subjective matrix within which the experiences in question were constituted. However, it is due to this very abstraction from subjective context of meaning that they exhibit the property which we have called their "again and again" character. They are treated as typical conscious experiences of "someone" and, as such, as basically homogeneous and repeatable. The unity of the contemporary is not constituted originally in his own stream of consciousness. (Indeed, whether the contemporary has any stream of consciousness at all is a difficult question and one which we shall deal with later.) Rather, the contemporary's unity is constituted in my own stream of consciousness, being built up out of a synthesis of my own interpretations of his experiences. This synthesis is a synthesis of recognition in which I monothetically bring within one view my own conscious experiences of someone else. Indeed, these experiences of mine may have been of more than one person. And they may have been of definite individuals or of anonymous "people." It is in this synthesis of recognition that the *personal ideal type* is constituted.

We must be quite clear as to what is happening here. The subjective meaning-context has been abandoned as a tool of interpretation. It has been replaced by a series of highly complex and systematically interrelated objective meaning-contexts. The result is that the contemporary is anonymized in direct proportion to the number and complexity of these meaning-contexts. Furthermore, the synthesis of recognition does not apprehend the unique person as he exists within his living present. Instead it pictures him as always the same and homogeneous, leaving out of account all the changes and rough edges that go along with individuality. Therefore, no matter how many people are subsumed under the ideal type, it corresponds to no one in particular. It is just this fact that justified Weber in calling it "ideal."

Let us give a few examples to clarify this point. When I mail a letter, I assume that certain contemporaries of mine, namely, postal employees, will read the address and speed the letter on its way.[11] I am not thinking of these postal employees as individuals. I do not know them personally and never expect to. Again, as Max Weber pointed out, whenever I accept money I do so without any doubt that others, who remain quite anonymous, will accept it in turn from me. To use yet another Weberian example,[12] if I behave in such a way as to avoid the sudden arrival of certain gentlemen with uniforms and badges, in other words, to the extent that I orient myself to the laws and to the apparatus which enforces them, here, too, I am relating myself socially to my contemporaries conceived under ideal types.

On occasions like these I am always expecting others to behave in a definite way, whether it be postal employees, someone I am paying, or the police. My social relationship to them consists in the fact that I interact with them, or perhaps merely that, in planning my actions, I keep them in mind. But they, on their part, never turn up as real people, merely as anonymous entities defined exhaustively by their functions. Only as bearers of these functions do they have any relevance for my social behavior. How they happen to feel as they cancel my letter, process my check, or examine my income-tax return—these are considerations that never even enter my mind. I just assume that there are "some people" who "do these things." Their behavior in the conduct of their duty is from my point of view defined purely through an objective context of meaning. In other words, when I am They-oriented, I have "types" for partners.

The use of ideal types is not limited to the world of contemporaries. It is to be found in our apprehension of the world of predecessors as well. Moreover, since ideal types are interpretive schemes for the social world in general, they become part of our stock of knowledge about that world. As a result, we are always drawing upon them in our face-to-face dealings with people. This means that ideal types serve as interpretive schemes even for the world of *direct* social experience. However, they are carried along with and modified by the We-relationship as it develops. In the process they cease to be mere types and "return to reality" again. Let us give an example.

Sometimes I am face to face with several people at once. Thus, in a sense, we have here a *direct* They-relationship. But this "They" can always be broken down into a Thou and Thou and Thou, with each of whom I can enter into a We-relationship. Suppose, for instance, that I am watching a group of men playing cards. I can pay special attention to any one of them. As I do so, I am aware of him as a Thou. No longer, now, am I seeing him as "man playing cards," which would merely be an interpretation of my own perceptions. Rather, I am now aware of the way he plays the game. I follow his every move with interest, guessing what is going on in his mind at each particular play. And, as I observe the other partners, I find that they too are playing the game out of their own unique contexts of meaning.

But suppose I suspend for a moment my participation in this vivid We-relationship. Suppose I shift my mode of observation, transporting the players into my world of contemporaries. I can then make a statement like "They are playing a game of poker." This statement will apply to each individual player only to the extent that the course-of-action type "poker game" corresponds to a series of conscious experiences in his mind and stands in a subjective meaning-context for him. In this way the action of each player will be "oriented" to the rules of poker.[13] But what we have here is really a postulate: "If A, B, and C are playing poker, then their behavior is oriented to a certain action-model M." This postulate of course does not apply merely to A, B, and C.

Rather it defines the ideal type "poker player." And the postulate will apply to A, B, and C only insofar as they exemplify individually that ideal type. But insofar as I myself look upon the players as examples of an ideal type, to the same extent must I disregard their individuality. No concrete lived experience of A is ever either identical or commensurable with one of B. For these experiences, belonging as they do to different streams of consciousness, are unique, unrepeatable, and incapable of being juxtaposed. *The typical and only the typical is homogeneous,* and it is always so. In the typifying synthesis of recognition I perform an act of anonymization in which I abstract the lived experience from its setting within the stream of consciousness and thereby render it impersonal.

The opposite process is also possible. The objective meaning-context defining the subjective experiences of an ideal type can be translated back into a subjective meaning whenever I apply it to an individual in a concrete situation. Thus I may say, "Oh, he's one of those!" or "I've seen that type before!" This is the explanation for the fact that I experience my contemporary as an individual with an ongoing conscious life, yet one whose experiences I know by inference rather than by direct confrontation. Therefore, even though I think of him as an individual, still he is for me an individual exhaustively defined by his type, an "anonymous" individual.

3. The Constitution of the Ideal-Typical Interpretive Scheme

In the foregoing section we have described how we understand the behavior of others in terms of ideal types. We saw that the process consisted essentially of taking a cross-section of our experience of another person and, so to speak, "freezing it into a slide." We saw that this is done by means of a synthesis of recognition. However, there is something ambiguous about this concept of an ideal type of human behavior.[14] It denotes at one and the same time ideal types covering (1) pregiven objective meaning-contexts, (2) products, (3) courses of action, and (4) real and ideal objects, whenever any of the above are the result of human behavior. Included also would be interpretations of the products of ideal-typical behavior. The latter are the interpretations to which we resort when we know nothing of the individual experiences of those who created these products. Whenever we come upon any ordering of past experience under interpretive schemes, any act of abstraction, generalization, formalization, or idealization, whatever the object involved, there we shall find this process in which a moment of living experience is lifted out of its setting and then, through a synthesis of recognition, frozen into a hard and fast "ideal type." Insofar as the term "ideal type" can be applied to any interpretive scheme under which experience is subsumed—as in Max Weber's early writings—it raises no special problem for the social scientist. We could speak in exactly the same sense of ideal types of physical objects and processes, of meteorological patterns, of evolutionary series in biology, and so forth. How useful the concept of ideal types would be in these fields is not for us to say, since we are concerned here with a specific group of problems in the social sciences.

The concept "ideal type of human behavior" can be taken in two ways. It can mean first of all the ideal type of another person who is expressing himself or has expressed himself in a certain way. Or it may mean, second, the ideal type of the expressive process itself, or even of the outward results which we interpret as the signs of the expressive process. Let us call the first the "personal ideal type" and the second the "material" or "course-of-action *type.*"[15] Certainly an inner relation exists between these two. I cannot, for instance, define the ideal type of a postal clerk without first having in mind a definition of his job. The latter is a course-of-action type, which is, of course, an objective context of meaning. Once I am clear as to the course-of-action type, I can construct the personal ideal type, that is "the person who performs this job." And, in doing so, I imagine the corresponding subjective meaning-contexts which would be in his mind, the subjective contexts that would have to be adequate to the objective contexts already defined. The personal ideal type is therefore *derivative,* and the course-of-action type can be considered quite independently as a purely objective context of meaning.

By looking at language we can see the personal ideal type in the very process of construction. I am referring to those nouns which are merely verbs erected into substantives. Thus every present participle is the personal typification of an act in progress, and every past participle is the ideal type of a completed act. Acting is that act maybe. Consequently, when I seek to understand another's behavior in ideal-typical fashion, a twofold method is available to me. I can begin with the finished act, then determine the type of action that produced it, and finally settle upon the type of person who must have acted in this way. Or I can reverse the process and, knowing the personal ideal type, deduce the corresponding act. We have, therefore, to deal with two different problems. One problem concerns which aspects of a finished act[16] are selected as typical and how we deduce the personal type from the course-of-action type. The other problem concerns how we deduce specific actions from a given personal ideal type. The first question is a general question about the genesis of the typical. It has to do with the constitution of ideal types—whether course-of-action types or personal types— from given concrete acts. The second question has to do with the deduction of an action from a personal ideal type, and we shall deal with it under the heading "the freedom of the personal ideal type."

Let us first clarify the point that the understanding of personal ideal types is based on the understanding of course-of-action types.

In the process of understanding a given performance via

an ideal type, the interpreter must start with his own perceptions of someone else's manifest act. His goal is to discover the in-order-to or because-motives (whichever is convenient) behind that act. He does this by interpreting the act within an objective context of meaning in the sense that the same motive is assigned to any act that repeatedly achieves the same end through the same means. This motive is postulated as constant for the act regardless of who performs the act or what his subjective experiences are at the time. For a personal ideal type, therefore, there is one and only one typical motive for a typical act. Excluded from consideration when we think of the personal ideal type are such things as the individual's subjective experience of his act within his stream of consciousness, together with all the modifications of attention and all the influences from the background of his consciousness which such experiences may undergo. Ideal-typical understanding, then, characteristically deduces the in-order-to and because-motives of a manifest act by identifying the constantly achieved goal of that act. Since the act is by definition both repeatable and typical, so is the in-order-to motive. The next step is to postulate an agent behind the action, a person who, with a typical modification of attention, typically intends this typical act—in short, a personal ideal type.

The conscious processes of the personal ideal types are, therefore, logical constructions. They are deduced from the manifest act and are pictured as temporally prior to that act, in other words, in the pluperfect tense. The manifest act is then seen as the regular and repeatable result of these inferred conscious processes. It should be noted that the conscious processes themselves are conceived in a simplified and tailored form. They are lacking all the empty protentions and expectations that accompany real conscious experiences. It is not an open question as to whether the typical action will succeed in being a finished act. Such success has been built into it by definition. The ideal-typical actor never has the experience of choosing or of preferring one thing to another. Never does he hesitate or try to make up his mind whether to perform a typical or an atypical action. His motive is always perfectly straightforward and definite: the in-order-to motive of the action is the completed act on whose definition the whole typification is based. This completed act is at the same time the *major* goal of the actor's typical state of mind at that time. For if the act were merely a means to another goal, then it would be necessary for the interpreter to construct for his ideal actor another typical state of mind capable of planning out that wider goal. This would mean that the wider goal would have to become the objective meaning-context of primary importance from the interpreter's point of view. In other words, the wider goal would be the one in terms of which the act would be defined. Finally, all this will hold true for the construction of the genuine because-motive. This must be postulated in some typical experience or passage of experience that could have given rise to the in-order-to motive we have already constructed.

The following, then, is the way in which a personal ideal type is constructed: The existence of a person is postulated whose actual living motive could be the objective context of meaning already chosen to define a typical action. This person must be one in whose consciousness the action in question could have been constructed step by step in polythetic Acts. He must be the person whose own lived experiences provide the subjective context of meaning which corresponds to the objective context, the action which corresponds to the act.

And now we see the basic reason why, in both the social sciences and the everyday understanding of another's behavior, we can ignore the "total action" in the sense that the latter concept includes the ultimate roots of the action in the person's consciousness. The technique of constructing personal ideal types consists in postulating persons who can be motivated by the already defined material ideal type. The manifest act or external course of action which the observer sees as a unity is changed back into a subjective context of meaning and is inserted into the consciousness of the personal ideal type. But the unity of this subjective context derives entirely from the original objective context of meaning, the context of meaning which is the very basis of the personal ideal type. And we cannot too strongly emphasize that this unity of "the other person's action" is only a cross-section which the observer lifts out of its total factual context. What is thus defined in abstraction as the unity of the other person's act will depend on the point of view of the observer, which will vary in turn with his interests and his problems. This point of view will determine both the meaning which the observer gives to his own perceptions of the act and the typical motive which he assigns to it. But for every such typical motive, for every such frozen cross-section of consciousness, there is a corresponding personal ideal type which could be subjectively motivated in the manner in question. Therefore, the personal ideal type is itself always determined by the interpreter's point of view. *It is a function of the very question it seeks to answer.* It is dependent upon the objective context of meaning, which it merely translates into subjective terms and then personifies.

It is precisely this point which the theory of ideal types overlooks. It fails to take into account the fact that the personal ideal type is *by definition* one who acts in such and such a way and has such and such experiences. Rather, it reverses the direction of the inference and, starting out with the personal ideal type as a "free entity," seeks to "discover" what the latter means by acting in such and such a manner. Moreover, it is naïve enough to suppose that the boundaries of the act can be objectively demarcated while the actor is at the same time free to give the act any meaning he chooses! Interpretation of this kind, whether carried on in everyday life or in sociology, has at least the advantage of a neat division of labor. While leaving to the personal ideal type the function of "attaching a meaning" to its action, it reserves to itself the privilege of saying what that meaning is. Contradictions are avoided by making sure that the personal type is so constructed that it must subjectively attach to its act precisely the meaning that the interpreter is looking for. The illusion consists in regarding the personal ideal type as a real person, whereas actually it is only a shadow person. It "lives" in a never-never temporal dimension that no one could ever experience. It lives through just the minimum number of subjective experiences to qualify it as the author of the given act. To be sure, it must be pictured as "free"; otherwise it could hardly bestow "its own" meaning to the course of action in question. However, its freedom is only apparent, because the original act which the social scientist or the common-sense observer takes as his datum already has ready-made and unambiguous in-order-to and because-motives built into it by definition. The ideal type of the actor is, then, that of the person who by definition experiences polythetically the act already conceived monothetically by the social scientist. And so anything the social scientist permits his ideal type to report about its actions is only a prophecy after the event.

The illusion of the "freedom" of the personal ideal type arises from the fact that we do ask what kind of future acts we can expect from a given personal ideal type. How behavior ascribed to a given ideal type will be carried out remains a matter of conjecture and of "wait and see." To all appearances the awaited action, already defined with respect to its in-order-to and because-motives, may or may not occur. Suppose I call A, a man I know, a miser, thereby identifying him with a personal ideal type. Still, it remains an open question whether he will give a donation to charity. However, strictly speaking, the real question here is not whether the ideal type's action is free and less than determinate. Rather, it is whether A is really a miser at all. To be sure, even the determination of the motives of the ideal type must be subjected to the test of indirect, and ultimately of direct, social experience. And even in direct social encounters, as we have seen, the interpretive schemes used in understanding the other person are constantly changing with experience. However, in the face-to-face relationship a real, free, enduring human being is present in person. But the contemporary appears to us in principle in the form of an ideal type with neither freedom nor duration. For, as we have seen, the mere fact that we can make only probable statements about a contemporary conceived under the heading of an ideal type does not imply that the ideal type itself is free. It is important to realize that the person so conceived is behaving *as* a type only insofar as he acts in the stipulated manner. In other situations his behavior need by no means be typical. When Molière involves Harpagon in a love affair, it does not follow that the latter's love behavior, whether individual or typical, can be predicted with accuracy from the fact that he is a tightwad. Rather, his love relationships will be in another category—they will be *type-transcendent*. Even so, once Harpagon is recognized as a typical miser, a number of interpretive schemes become immediately applicable to him. To put it in a more general way, the personal type can be, and usually is, constructed on the basis of other ideal types already known to the interpreter. Should the situation under interpretation change, the interpreter can always fall back on these ready-made ideal types in the background and substitute one of them for the ideal type with which he started. But he usually does this without full awareness; and because he uses the old name for the new ideal type, he tends naïvely to identify the new ideal type with the old. And suddenly it seems as if the ideal type has taken on a kind of freedom and has become a real person rather than an abstract, timeless concept. Suddenly it seems able to choose between alternatives, and the illusion is produced that one hardly knows what to expect of the ideal type. However, this illusion of ideal-typical conduct that is carried out freely cannot stand up under logical analysis. Wherever it turns up, it is a sign that the interpreter has not carried all the way the alteration in logical construct that is called for by his new problem. Of course, the illusion itself, arising as it does from the interpreter's confusion about what he is doing, can cause him to make real mistakes in action. The story of Pygmalion, whose statues came to life, is a parable illustrating the lengths to which such naïve interpretive ventures can go.

But this problem is by no means confined to interpretation of the world of contemporaries. The direct observer, and even more the participant in a social relationship, brings to the situation a whole armory of interpretive schemes for understanding others. Included will be schemes derived from his direct social experience, from his experience of his contemporaries, and from his experience of his predecessors. He will have on hand both personal types and course-of-action types. By constantly scrutinizing, shuffling, and juxtaposing these ideal types, he can keep up with the many changes occurring in the other person and thus grasp him in his living reality. (Of course this kind of personal understanding is usually possible only in the direct We-relationship and as a result of the living intentionality peculiar to that intimate situation.)

There are vast problems here for sociological research, but they are beyond the scope of this treatise. It is our hope to deal with them on a future occasion in a detailed study of the *sociological person.*

We can, however, briefly demonstrate the peculiar way in which the ideal types vary and shift in accordance with the observer's point of view, the questions he is asking, and the total complex of his experience. If I observe, or even hear about, a man tightening a nut, my first interpretive scheme will picture him as joining together two parts of an apparatus with a wrench. The further information that the event is taking place in an automobile factory permits me to place the operation within the total context of "automobile manufacturing." If I know in addition that the man is an auto worker, then I can assume a great deal about him, for instance, that he comes to work every morning and goes home every night, that he picks up his check every payday, and so on. I can then bring him into a wider context of meaning by applying to him the ideal type "urban worker" or, more specifically, "Berlin worker of the year 1931." And once I have established the fact that the man is a German and a Berliner, then all the corresponding interpretive schemes become applicable to him. Obviously I can increase indefinitely the number of the schemes I apply, depending on the questions I choose to ask and the particular kind of interest that lies behind them. Suppose, now, that my interest is in the worker's politics or in his religion. I can hardly extract such information from the purely factual and external interpretive schemes I have so far established. From this point on, lacking additional data, any ideal type I set up will be on shaky grounds. Suppose I say, "Workers of this kind typically vote Social Democratic." My judgment would be based on the statistical information that in the last election the majority of the Berlin workers voted for the party in question. However, what I do not know is that this particular worker belonged to the majority; all I have is a probability. The probability would increase if I knew that the worker was a union member or that he carried a party card. We have already noted that every interpretation based on ideal-typical construction is only probable. It is possible, for instance, that the man turning the nut in front of me is not a worker at all but an engineer or a student on a summer job. In this case, of course, all the deductions I have made about him by using the ideal type "Berlin worker" are false. But this only shows that every ideal-typical construction is determined by the limits of the observer's knowledge at the time. The example we have given shows clearly how meaning-context, interpretive scheme, and ideal type are correlated. They are all expressions of a common problem, *the problem of relevance.*

Now the ideal types that are continually being constructed in everyday life are subject to constant adjustment and revision on the basis of the observer's experience, whether the latter is direct or indirect. As for direct social experience, the knowledge of the contents of the other person's consciousness acquired in the We-relationship modifies the ideal-typical interpretive schemes whether the latter are positional or neutralizing. All our knowledge of our fellow men is in the last analysis based on personal experience. Ideal-typical knowledge of our contemporaries, on the other hand, is not concerned with the other person in his given concrete immediacy but in what he is, in the characteristics he has in common with others. To interpret the behavior of a contemporary as typical means to explain it as the behavior of a "man like that one," of "one of them." Orientation toward the world of contemporaries is necessarily and always "They-orientation."

4. Degrees of Anonymity in the World of Contemporaries. The Concreteness of the Ideal Type

The They-orientation is the pure form[17] of understanding the contemporary in a predicative fashion, that is, in terms of his typical characteristics. Acts of They-orientation are, therefore, intentionally directed toward another person imagined as existing at the same time as oneself but conceived in terms of an ideal type. And just as in the cases of the Thou-orientation and the We-relationship, so also with the They-orientation can we speak of different *stages of concretization* and *actualization*.

In order to distinguish from one another the various stages of concretization of the We-relationship, we established as our criterion the degree of closeness to direct experience. We cannot use this criterion within the They-orientation. The reason is that the latter possesses by definition a high degree of remoteness from direct experience, and the other self which is its object possesses a correspondingly higher degree of anonymity.

It is precisely this degree of anonymity which we now offer as the criterion for distinguishing between the different levels of concretization and actualization that occur in the They-orientation. The more anonymous the personal ideal type applied in the They-orientation, the greater is the use made of objective meaning-contexts instead of subjective ones, and likewise, we shall find, the more are lower-level personal ideal types and objective meaning-contexts pregiven. (The latter have in turn been derived from other stages of concretization of the They-orientation.)

Let us get clear as to just what we mean by the anonymity of the ideal type in the world of contemporaries. The pure Thou-orientation consists of mere awareness of the existence of the other person, leaving aside all questions concerning the characteristics of that person. On the other hand, the pure They-orientation is based on the presupposition of such characteristics in the form of a type. Since these characteristics are genuinely typical, they can in principle be presupposed again and again. Of course, whenever I posit such typical characteristics, I assume that they now exist or did once exist. However, this does not mean that I am thinking of them as existing in a particular person in a particular time and place. The contemporary alter ego is therefore anonymous in the sense that its existence is only the individuation of a type, an individuation which is merely supposable or possible. Now since the very existence of my contemporary is always less than certain, any attempt on my part to reach out to him or influence him may fall short of its mark, and, of course, I am aware of this fact.

The concept which we have been analyzing is the concept of the anonymity of the partner in the world of contemporaries. It is crucial to the understanding of the nature of the indirect social relationship. We shall presently be discussing the important consequences of this concept for our over-all problem. But first we must deal with certain other meanings of anonymity.

Anonymity may mean the generality of the typifying scheme. If the scheme is derived from the characteristics of a particular person, then we speak of it as relatively concrete and rich in specific content. But if the scheme is derived from the characteristics of a previously constructed personal type, then we speak of it as relatively more anonymous. We can say, then, that the concreteness of the ideal type is inversely proportional to the level of generality of the past experiences out of which it is constructed. The deeper basis for this is the fact that, as the interpreter falls back on lower- and lower-level ideal types, he must take more and more for granted. He can hardly examine all these more general ideal types in detail but must take them in at a glance, being content with a vague picture. The more dependent he is on such ready-made types in the construction of his own ideal type, the vaguer will be his account of the latter. This becomes immediately obvious when we try to analyze such culture objects as the state, economy, law, art, and so on.

The degree of concreteness of an ideal type also varies directly with the convertibility of its corresponding They-relationship into a We-relationship. To the extent that I conceive the conscious states of my ideal type as belonging to one or more real persons with whom I could have a We-relationship, to that extent is my ideal type more concrete and less anonymous. It is the case, of course, that the conscious states of my contemporary are in principle mere objects of thought for me, not objects of lived experience. Nevertheless, the concreteness of my ideal type of him will be the greater depending on the ease with which I can convert the corresponding indirect orientation into a direct one, the ease with which I can shift from a merely conceptual and predicative understanding to an immediate grasp of the person himself. The personal ideal type is therefore less anonymous the closer it is to the world of directly experienced social reality. The following two examples should illustrate this point.

I think about *N*, my absent friend, assuming toward him the usual They-orientation. Knowing that he is at the moment facing a difficult decision, I construct from my past direct experiences of him the personal ideal type "my friend *N*" or a course-of-action type "how *N* acts in the face of difficult decisions." This ideal type is essentially They-oriented: "People *like N* act in such and such a way when facing difficult decisions." Nevertheless, the ideal type "my friend *N*" is still extremely concrete, and my indirect relationship to him can, technical difficulties aside, at any moment be changed into a direct one. The very validity of the ideal type, as well as its verifiability, is based on this possibility.

Our second example: My friend *A* tells me about *X*, a person he has recently met but whom I do not know myself. He "gives me a picture" of *X*, drawing upon his own direct experience to fashion an ideal type for me. Now of course the picture he sketches will be determined by the way in which he looks back on his meeting with *X*, and this in turn will depend on his interests and the modifications of his attention. But now I will take the ideal type *A* has constructed for me and make my own ideal type out of it on the basis of my own past experience. But since my interests and my modifications of attention will be radically different, so will my ideal type. Moreover, my friend *A* has made the judgment resulting in his ideal type in full and explicit clarity, whereas I necessarily have made mine only in a confused way.[18] I may even question *A*'s judgment. Knowing that he is emotional, I may not accept his characterization of *X*, thinking, "That's the way *A* always sees people."

These two examples should be enough to indicate how complicated are the problems of indirect social understanding. Both involve relatively concrete typifications based on my direct experience of my fellow men. The direct experience involved is either my own or that of an intermediary.

But in both cases the objective meaning-contexts which I use to understand N and X will show the effects of the original subjective meaning-contexts in the minds of those two real individuals.

Let us call an ideal type of this kind a "characterological" type. It should be distinguished from a "habitual" type, which defines a contemporary solely in terms of his function. The concept of a postal clerk, for instance, is a habitual type. The postal clerk is by definition "he who forwards the mail," or, in the example we used, *my* mail. A habitual type is therefore less concrete than a characterological type. It is based on a course-of-action type which it presupposes and refers to. The characterological type, on the other hand, presupposes and refers to a real person whom I could meet face to face. Furthermore, the habitual type is more anonymous. As a matter of fact, when I drop the letter in the box, I don't even need to have in mind the personal type "postal clerk" in the sense of thinking of an individual who has certain specific subjective meaning-contexts in mind as he goes about his work, such as thinking of receiving payment. The only thing relevant for me in this situation is the *process* of forwarding, and I merely "hang" this on the abstract type "postal clerk." And I don't even have to think of a postal clerk as such as I mail the letter. It is enough for me to know that somehow it will reach its destination.[19]

Under the heading of habitual types come those types which deal with the "behaving" or the "habit."[20] The fixation in conceptual form of external modes of behavior or sequences of action,[21] derived from either direct or indirect observation, leads to a catalogue of material course-of-action types, to which corresponding personal types are then adjoined. But these course-of-action types can be of different degrees of generality: they can be more or less "standardized," that is, they can be derived from behavior of greater or lesser statistical frequency. The ideality of the personal ideal type based on such frequency types (in other words, the irreducibility of the kinds of behavior to the conscious experiences of real other people) is, however, in principle independent of the degree of generality of the behavior itself.[22] On the other hand, the "standardization" of typified behavior can in turn refer back to a previously constructed personal ideal type. Let us take as an example Weber's "traditional behavior," "the great bulk of all everyday action to which people have become habitually accustomed,"[23] which is already based on the previously constructed personal ideal type of the man who acts according to custom; and, as an additional example, let us take all behavior oriented to the validity of an order. This latter means, in terms of the constitution of ideal types of contemporaries, that the valid order functions as an interpretive scheme for them. It establishes as required conduct definite patterns of action and definite personal ideal types, to the extent that the person accepting such standard types and orienting himself to them can be assured that his behavior will be adequately interpreted by contemporaries oriented to the same order. However, every such interpretation by contemporaries

must take account of a fundamentally important fact. These concepts of collective entities, which are found both in common sense and in juristic and other technical forms of thought, have a meaning in the minds of individual persons . . . as something with normative authority. This is true not only of judges and officials, but of ordinary private individuals as well . . . ; such ideas have a powerful, often a decisive, influence on the course of action of real individuals.[24]

This cursory observation, however, is by no means an exhaustive account of the situation which involves a valid order; for example, the coercive apparatus that goes along with every regulative order is of the greatest relevance from the point of view of sociology.[25] The point of importance for us here is that even behavior that is oriented to the validity of an order is, in our sense of the term, habitual behavior. Our concept of the habitual is, therefore, broader than that found in ordinary usage.

There are other ideal types that are characterized by a still greater degree of anonymity than the habitual ideal types. The first group of these consists of the so-called "social collectives," all of which are constructs referring to the world of contemporaries.[26]

This large class contains ideal types of quite different degrees of anonymity. The board of directors of a given corporation or the United States Senate are relatively concrete ideal types, and the number of other ideal types which they presuppose is quite limited. But we frequently use sentences in which ideal types like "the state," "the press," "the economy," "the nation," "the people," or perhaps "the working class"[27] appear as grammatical subjects. In doing this, we naturally tend to personify these abstractions, treating them as if they were real persons known in indirect social experience. But we are here indulging in an anthropomorphism. Actually these ideal types are absolutely anonymous. Any attribution of behavior we make to the type permits no inference whatever as to a corresponding subjective meaning-context in the mind of a contemporary actor. "For the subjective interpretation[28] of action in sociological work," says Max Weber,

> these collectivities must be treated as solely the resultants and modes of organization of the particular acts of individual persons, since these alone can be treated as agents in a course of subjectively understandable action. . . . For sociological purposes . . . there is no such thing as a collective personality which "acts." When reference is made in a sociological context to a "state," a "nation," a "corpora-

tion," a "family" or an "army corps," or to similar collectivities, what is meant is, on the contrary, *only* a certain kind of development of actual or possible social actions of the individual persons.[29]

In fact, every "action" of the state can be reduced to the actions of its functionaries, whom we can apprehend by means of personal ideal types and toward whom we can assume a They-orientation, regarding them as our contemporaries. From the sociological point of view, therefore, the term "state" is merely an abbreviation for a highly complex network of interdependent personal ideal types. When we speak of any collectivity as "acting," we take this complex structural arrangement for granted.[30] We then proceed to attribute the objective meaning-contexts, in terms of which we understand the anonymous acts of the functionaries, to the personal ideal type of the social collective. We do this in a manner that parallels our interpretation of individual actions by means of typical conscious experiences in the minds of typical actors. But when we proceed in this way, we forget that, whereas the conscious experiences of typical individuals are quite conceivable, the conscious experiences of a collective are not. What is lacking, therefore, in the concept of the "action" of a collective is precisely this subjective meaning-context as something that is even conceivable. That people should ever have been led to take such a metaphor literally can only be explained psychologically, that is, attributed to the fact that certain value systems have been at work here.

Needless to say, our reduction of statements about social collectives to personal ideal typifications does not foreclose a sociological analysis of these constructs. On the contrary, such an analysis is one of the most important tasks of sociology. Only a sociological theory of construct formation can bring to completion our previously postulated theory of the forms of the social world. Such a theory will have as its primary task the description of the stratification of social collec-

tivities in terms of their relative anonymity or concreteness.
Here it will be crucial to determine whether a social collectivity is essentially based on a direct or an indirect social
relationship, or possibly on a relationship of both kinds, existing between the component individuals. It will also be necessary to study the exact sense, if any, in which a subjective
meaning-context can be ascribed to a social collectivity. This
will involve determining whether, by the subjective meaning-contexts of a collectivity, we do not really mean those of
its functionaries. This is the problem of the responsibility of
officials, a question of major importance in the fields of constitutional and international law.[31] Another question deserving
investigation is whether and to what extent the concept of
social collectivity can serve as a scheme of interpretation for
the actions of contemporaries, since it is itself a function of
certain objective standards common to a certain group. Such
standards may be matters of habitual conduct, of traditional
attitude, of belief in the validity of some order or norm, and
they may be not only taken for granted but obeyed. Here,
indeed, is one legitimate sense in which one can speak of the
subjective meaning of a social collectivity. Even so, there are
so many complexities in this way of speaking that we are in
danger of confusing one problem with another and one type
with another. This in turn may lead us once again into the
illusion that we have discovered a type-transcending behavior and revive the discredited notion of a "free" type.[32]

What we have said about social collectivities holds true for
languages as well. Here, too, a correlation can be set up
between the product and that which produces it; we can
hypostatize, for instance, an ideal anonymous "German
speaker" corresponding to the German language. But here,
as in the case we just discussed, we must beware of treating
this typical speaker as a real individual with his own subjective contexts of meaning. It is quite illegitimate, for instance,
to speak of an "objective language spirit,"[33] at least in the
social sciences.[34] Whether such concepts are permissible in

other disciplines is not for us to say here.

These observations apply as well to all culture objects. To the ideal objectivity of a culture construct there corresponds no subjective meaning-context in the mind of a real individual whom we could meet face to face. Rather, corresponding to the objective meaning-context of the culture object we always find an abstract and anonymous personal ideal type of its producer toward which we characteristically assume a They-orientation.

Finally, this applies also to all artifacts such as tools and utensils. But to understand a tool, we need not only the ideal type of its producer but the ideal type of its user, and both will be absolutely anonymous. Whoever uses the tool will bring about typical results. A tool is a thing-in-order-to; it serves a purpose, and for the sake of this purpose it was produced. Tools are, therefore, results of past human acts and means toward the future realization of aims. One can, then, conceive the "meaning" of the tool in terms of the means-end relation. But from this objective meaning-context, that is, from the means-end relation in terms of which the tool is understood, one can deduce the ideal type of user or producer without thinking of them as real individual people. In my opinion it is erroneous to speak, as Sander does, of the meaning of a tool in the same sense that one speaks of the meaning of an action.[35]

The artifact is the final member of the series of progressive anonymizations marking the typifying construction of the social world. We started out with the immediate grasp of another person which we have in the Thou-relationship, the experience upon which every ideal type is ultimately based. We then studied the characterological and habitual ideal types, the social collectivity, and, finally, the tool. Although these examples do not exhaust all the members of the series, they do illustrate their progressive anonymization and corresponding gradual loss of concreteness.

5. Social Relationships between Contemporaries and Indirect Social Observation

As social relationships in the face-to-face situation are based on the pure Thou-orientation, so social relationships between contemporaries are based on the pure They-orientation. But the situation has now changed. In the face-to-face situation the partners look into each other and are mutually sensitive to each other's responses. This is not the case in relationships between contemporaries. Here each partner has to be content with the probability that the other, to whom he is oriented by means of an anonymous type, will respond with the same kind of orientation. And so an element of doubt enters into every such relationship.

When I board a train, for instance, I orient myself to the fact that the engineer in charge can be trusted to get me to my destination. My relationship to him is a They-relationship at this time, merely because my ideal type "railroad engineer" means by definition "one who gets passengers like myself to their destination." It is therefore characteristic of my social relationships with my contemporaries that the orientation by means of ideal types is mutual. Corresponding to my ideal type "engineer" there is the engineer's ideal type "passenger." Taking up mutual They-orientations, we think of each other as "one of them."[36]

I am not therefore apprehended by my partner in the They-relationship as a real living person. From this it follows that I can expect from him only a typical understanding of my behavior.

A social relationship between contemporaries, therefore, consists in this: Each of the partners apprehends the other by means of an ideal type; each of the partners is aware of this mutual apprehension; and each expects that the other's interpretive scheme will be congruent with his own. The They-relationship here stands in sharp contrast to the face-to-face situation. In the face-to-face situation my partner and I are sensitively aware of the nuances of each other's subjective experiences. But in the They-relationship this is replaced by the assumption of a shared interpretive scheme. Now, even though I, on my side, make this assumption, I cannot verify it. I do, however, have more reason to expect an adequate response from my partner, the more standardized is the scheme which I impute to him. This is the case with schemes derived from law, state, tradition, and systems of order of all kinds, and especially with schemes based on the means-end relation, in short, with what Weber calls "rational" interpretive schemes.[37]

These properties of social relationships between contemporaries have important consequences.

First of all, because of the element of chance that is always present, I cannot even be sure that the relationship exists until it has already been tried out, so to speak. Only retrospectively can I know whether my ideal type of my partner was adequate to him, either in the sense of meaning-adequacy or causal adequacy. This again differs from the face-to-face situation, where I can constantly correct my own responses to my partner. Another consequence is that the only in-order-to and because-motives of my partner that I can take into account in making my own plans of action are the motives I have already postulated for him in constructing my ideal type of him. To be sure, in the They-orientation, as in the face-to-face situation, I set up my project of action in such a way that my partner's because-motives are included in my own in-order-to motives; and I proceed in the expectation that his interpretive scheme of me as ideal type is adequate to mine of him as ideal type. If the partner in question is a postal clerk, for instance, the mere fact that my stamped letter lies before him will ordinarily become a genuine because-motive for his proceeding to forward it. Yet I cannot be sure of this. It may happen that there is a slip-up and that he will misdirect the letter before him, thereby causing it to be lost; to this extent he will fall short, of course, of my personal ideal type of a postal clerk. And this, in turn, of course, may have happened because he misinterpreted the address I put on the letter. All this results from the fact that we are not in direct touch with each other, as in the face-to-face situation.

In the face-to-face situation the partners are constantly revising and enlarging their knowledge of each other. This is not true in the same sense of the They-relationship. Certainly it is true that my knowledge of the world of my contemporaries is constantly being enlarged and replenished through every new experience from whatever part of the social world the latter may come. Furthermore, my ideal-typical schemes will always be changing in accordance with every shift in my situation. But all such modifications will be within a very narrow range so long as the original situation and my interest in it remain fairly even.

In the We-relationship I assume that your environment is identical with my own in all its variations. If I have any doubt about it, I can check on my assumption simply by pointing and asking you if that is what you mean. Such an identification is out of the question in the They-relationship. Nevertheless I assume, if you are my contemporary, that your environment can be understood by means of principles of comprehension drawn from my own. But even here the assumption is much less probable than it would be if we were face to face.

However, my environment[38] also includes sign systems, and in the They-relationship also I use these as both expressive and interpretive schemes. Here again the degree of anonymity is of major importance. The more anonymous my partner is, the more "objectively" must I use the signs. I cannot assume, for instance, that my partner in a They-relationship will necessarily grasp the particular significance I am attaching to my words, or the broader context of what I am saying, unless I explicitly clue him in. As a result, I do not know, during the process of choosing my words, whether I am being understood or not. This explains why I cannot immediately be questioned as to what I mean and possibly correct any misunderstandings. In indirect social experience there is only one way to "question a partner as to what he means," and that is to use a dictionary—unless, of course, I decide to go to see him or call him up; but in this case I have left the They-relationship behind and have initiated a face-to-face situation. As a matter of fact, any They-relationship characterized by a relatively low degree of anonymity can be transformed into a face-to-face situation by means of passing through various intermediate stages.[39]

In the world of direct social experience there is a radical difference between *participation* and *observation*. This difference disappears when we get into the world of contemporaries. The reason is that in the latter we never encounter real living people at all. In that world, whether we are participants or observers, we are dealing only with ideal types. Our whole experience is in the mode of the "They." Nevertheless, the ideal type of an observer in the world of contemporaries necessarily differs from the ideal type of a participant in that same world. For, as we have noted, the ideal type varies with the interests of the person who constructs it. The latter's aim is always to visualize a certain objective meaning-context, which he already grasps, as someone else's subjective context of meaning. Now, the total context of experience with which the observer approaches the other person differs from that of the participant. Likewise his interests are radically different. His ideal type can be more or less detailed, more concrete or more formalized, of a greater or lesser degree of anonymity. Whatever the case, it will always be different.

Now, it may be that what is above all interesting to the observer of a social relationship among contemporaries is the conscious experiences of the two participants. Or it may be the course of the relationship. If the former is the case, the observer will either construct or draw from his past experience an ideal type equipped with those conscious experiences which anyone in such a relationship would necessarily observe in himself. The observer then "identifies" himself with this ideal type; he lives it out, imagining himself involved in just this situation. He can then imagine himself having all those experiences which are by definition proper to the ideal type in question. He can also make definite statements about the nature of the relationship he is observing and about the interrelations between the corresponding ideal types that are involved. He can do this quite easily because, as a human being, he is more than just an observer since he himself has in the past been involved in innumerable social relationships, direct and indirect. He may indeed have had such relationships with the very persons he is now observing. Indeed, he may even now be involved in a direct Thou-orientation with one of these persons. Such cases as the last are especially frequent.

Observation of the social behavior of another involves the very real danger that the observer will naïvely substitute his own ideal types for those in the minds of his subject. The danger becomes acute when the observer, instead of being directly attentive to the person observed, thinks of the latter as a "case history" of such and such an abstractly defined type of conduct. Here not only may the observer be using the wrong ideal type to understand his subject's behavior, but he may never discover his error because he never confronts his subject as a real person. Social observation thus tends to develop into second-order ideal-typical construction: the observed actor is himself an ideal type of the first order, and the presumed ideal type in terms of which the actor understands his partner is an ideal type of the second order. Both of these are logical constructions of the observer and are determined by his point of view.

This situation is very significant from the standpoint of every empirical social science involving indirect observation. Its ideal-typical concept formation underlies the principles of meaning-adequacy and causal adequacy which we have yet to discuss. Interpretive sociology, however, must go beyond this. It must construct personal ideal types for social actors that are compatible with those constructed by the latter's partners. This aim may be regarded as a postulate for interpretive sociology. Upon closer scrutiny, it reduces to a more basic principle—the postulate of meaning-adequacy. This postulate states that, given a social relationship between contemporaries, the personal ideal types of the partners and their typical conscious experiences must be congruent with one another and compatible with the ideal-typical relationship itself.

A good example of the type of clarification that is required lies in the field of legal sociology. This discipline encounters great difficulties when it seeks to formulate descriptions of legal relationships between various partners, e.g., legislator and interpreter of the law, executor and subject of the law. Legal sociology seeks to interpret these relationships in terms of the subjective meanings of the persons in question. But, in doing this, it confuses the ideal types in terms of which each of the persons imagines his real partner with the sociologist's own ideal types of the partner. There are only two possible ways to remedy this situation and make possible a genuine descriptive concept of the kind desired by legal sociologists. The first would be to fix from the beginning the standpoint from which the type is to be constructed. This would mean that the legal sociologist would identify himself with one of the actors, postulating as invariant not only the latter's acts but also his interpretive schemes of his partners. The sociologist would then have to regard the ideal-typical concepts so constructed as binding upon himself. If this were the procedure adopted, the kind of sociological concept used would be directly derived from the field of law itself: legislator, judge, lawyer, partner, verdict, execution, etc. The alternative would be to come up with a principle according to which these more general ideal types can be transformed into the individual ideal types which the partners have of each other in concrete situations.

NOTES

1. In his still too little appreciated *Allgemeine Gesellschaftslehre* (Jena, 1930).

2. Weber, *Wirtschaft und Gesellschaft*, p. 14, point 4 [E.T., p. 119].

3. [There is an unfortunate linguistic ambiguity here. A friendship, it is true, is (happily) not a continu*ous* series of contacts in the Cantorian sense that between any two contacts there is another. It is a series of continu*al* or recurring contacts. But, although it is not a continu*ous series*, it can be spoken of as a continu*ous relationship* unless every *au revoir* is a temporary "breaking-off" of the friendship.]

4. The different forms of orientation relationships and social interaction in the world of contemporaries remain to be described exactly.

5. ["Aufeinanderbezogen . . . aufeinander eingestellt."]

6. We are here using "immediacy" in such a way as to include what Husserl calls "experience in a secondary originality" (*Logik*, p. 206); cf. above [i.e., *The Phenomenology of the Social World*—Ed.], sec. 33, p. 164.

7. On this point, as well as on the problem of the anonymity of the ideal type, see the sketchy but important contribution of Felix Kaufmann, "Soziale Kollektiva," *Zeitschrift für Nationalökonomie*, 1:294–308.

8. [*Ihreinstellung* in the original. We are adopting Luckmann's rendering "They-orientation" as the best English expression of the "distancing" that Schutz wished to emphasize here.]

9. On this point see below [i.e., *The Phenomenology of the Social World* —Ed.], sec. 39, p. 194.

10. Nevertheless, I can simultaneously experience someone as a mere contemporary and endow him with an enduring self having his own subjective contexts of meaning which are open to my inspection. See below [i.e., *The Phenomenology of the Social World*—Ed.], p. 186.

11. The example is taken from Felix Kaufmann, "Soziale Kollektiva," p. 299.

12. Weber, "R. Stammlers Überwindung der materialistischen Geschichtsauffassung," *Gesammelte Aufsätze zur Wissenschaftslehre*, p. 325.

13. Even the cheater is oriented to the rules; otherwise he could not really cheat.

14. [*Idealtypus fremden menschlichen Verhaltens:* literally, "ideal type of the human behavior of another person."]

15. [Schutz also called this the "action-pattern type."]

16. For the sake of convenience we are dealing here only with acts, but

our remarks can be applied *pari passu* to products of all kinds and to their generation.

17. [*Die Leerform*, literally, "the empty form."]

18. This point is made by Husserl in his *Formal and Transcendental Logic*, pp. 51 and 52, where he discusses the "understanding-after" which characterizes our grasp of other people's judgments: "Accordingly, we must distinguish between another's non-explicit judgment indicated by an explicitly stated linguistic proposition on the one hand, and a corresponding explicit judgment or clarification of what was meant on the other hand. . . ." "If it is a matter of another person's judgment, and I do not share his belief, then what I have before me is a mere representation of that belief as 'the belief that such and such is the case.' "

19. Just as I can use the telephone without knowing *how* it works. See above [i.e., *The Phenomenology of the Social World*—Ed.], sec. 17, p. 88.

20. [Schutz has these words in English as "the 'behave' " and "the 'habit.' "]

21. For a critique of behaviorism as a sociological method see Mises, "Begreifen und Verstehen," *Schmollers Jahrbuch*, 54:139ff.

22. We shall discuss this problem in greater detail when we take up the relation between causal adequacy and meaning-adequacy in Chap. 5 [in *The Phenomenology of the Social World*—Ed.]. Cf. sec. 46, p. 234.

23. *Wirtschaft und Gesellschaft*, p. 12 [E.T., p. 116].

24. *Ibid.*, p. 7 [E.T., p. 102]. But cf. Kelsen's critique of this position in his work, *Der soziologische und juristische Staatsbegriff* (Tübingen, 1922), pp. 156ff.

25. On this point see Voegelin's excellent study, "Die Einheit des Rechtes und das soziale Sinngebilde Staat," *Internationale Zeitschrift für die Theorie des Rechts*, 4 (1930): 58–89, esp. 71 ff.

26. The fact that, in the notion of the social collective, concepts of a metaphysical, axiological, and epistemological nature are presupposed is something lying outside the scope of this study. On this point we can only refer the reader to Felix Kaufmann's "Soziale Kollektiva," in *Zeitschrift für Nationalökonomie*, which we have already quoted repeatedly.

27. For an analysis of such concepts we recommend Mises' critique of the concept of class (*Die Gemeinwirtschaft* [Jena, 1922], pp. 316 f.). [The English reader is referred to Mises' *Socialism* (New Haven, 1951), pp. 328–51, which is the translation of this, and to his *Theory and History* (New Haven, 1957), pp. 112 ff. and 142 ff.]

28. [*Verstehende Deutung.*]

29. *Wirtschaft und Gesellschaft*, pp. 6 f. [E.T., p. 101].

30. In connection with this problem see Kelsen's critique of Weber's views in his *Allgemeine Staatslehre* (Berlin, 1925), pp. 19 ff., pp. 66–79; and, for the concept of functionary, see pp. 262–70.

31. Cf. Kelsen, *op. cit.*, pp. 48 ff., 65 ff., 310 f.

32. In his essay on stammering, Max Weber demonstrated that in the concept "United States of America" there is a sixfold overlaying and confu-

sion of types (*Gesammelte Aufsätze zur Wissenschaftslehre*, pp. 348 f.).

33. Cf. Vossler, *Geist und Kultur in der Sprache* (Heidelberg, 1925), pp. 153 f. [E.T., Oscar Oeser, *The Spirit of Language in Civilization* (London, 1932), p. 138.]

34. Felix Kaufmann, *Strafrechtsschuld*, p. 39.

35. "Gegenstand der reinen Gesellschaftslehre," *Archiv für Sozialwissenschaften*, 54:370: "By 'artifacts' we mean all physical things which owe their origin to human acts, which, in other words, are signs of a 'meaning' which they designate."

36. In situations like this, the gradual transition from the world of direct social experience to the world of contemporaries is very visible. As a theatergoer, I am important to the actor only as a member of the public. The author who is publishing a book thinks of his reader only as the typical reader, choosing his expressive schemes according to what he imagines are the reader's preconceived ideas and interpretive habits. It would be the task of a theory of the forms of the social world to describe and elucidate all these situations with respect to their content, that is, the proportions of direct and indirect social experience to be found in them. The true precursor of such a theory was no doubt Wiese's theory of relationship.

37. On this concept see below [i.e., *The Phenomenology of the Social World*—Ed.], Chap. 5, sec. 48.

38. In our sense of the word. See above [i.e., *The Phenomenology of the Social World*—Ed.], sec. 34, p. 170.

39. One example of such an intermediate stage is correspondence, which Simmel has so masterfully contrasted with speech: "One may say that, whereas speech reveals the secret of the speaker by means of all that surrounds it—which is visible but not audible, and which also includes the imponderables of the speaker himself—the letter conceals this secret. For this reason, the letter is clearer than speech where the secret of the other is *not* the issue; but where it *is* the issue, the letter is more ambiguous. By the 'secret of the other' I understand his moods and qualities of being, which cannot be expressed logically, but on which we nevertheless fall back innumerable times, even if only in order to understand the actual significance of quite concrete utterances" (*Soziologie*, 2d ed. [Munich, 1922], p. 286) [E.T., Kurt H. Wolff, *The Sociology of Georg Simmel* (Glencoe, Ill., 1950)].

III

Freedom, Responsibility, and Human Dignity

9

Freedom

MAURICE MERLEAU-PONTY

Again, it is clear that no causal relationship is conceivable between the subject and his body, his world or his
society. Only at the cost of losing the basis of all my certainties can I question what is conveyed to me by my presence
to myself. Now the moment I turn to myself in order to
describe myself, I have a glimpse of an anonymous flux,[1] a
comprehensive project in which there are so far no 'states of
consciousness', nor, *a fortiori*, qualifications of any sort. For
myself I am neither 'jealous', nor 'inquisitive', nor 'hunchbacked', nor 'a civil servant'. It is often a matter of surprise
that the cripple or the invalid can put up with himself. The
reason is that such people are not for themselves deformed
or at death's door. Until the final coma, the dying man is
inhabited by a consciousness, he is all that he sees, and enjoys
this much of an outlet. Consciousness can never objectify

Reprinted from *Phenomenology of Perception*, trans. Colin Smith (1962),
pp. 434–56, by permission of Humanities Press Inc., New York.

itself into invalid-consciousness or cripple-consciousness, and even if the old man complains of his age or the cripple of his deformity, they can do so only by comparing themselves with others, or seeing themselves through the eyes of others, that is, by taking a statistical and objective view of themselves, so that such complaints are never absolutely genuine: when he is back in the heart of his own consciousness, each one of us feels beyond his limitations and thereupon resigns himself to them. They are the price which we automatically pay for being in the world, a formality which we take for granted. Hence we may speak disparagingly of our looks and still not want to change our face for another. No idiosyncrasy can, seemingly, be attached to the insuperable generality of consciousness, nor can any limit be set to this immeasurable power of escape. In order to be determined (in the two senses of that word) by an external factor, it is necessary that I should be a thing. Neither my freedom nor my universality can admit of any eclipse. It is inconceivable that I should be free in certain of my actions and determined in others: how should we understand a dormant freedom that gave full scope to determinism? And if it is assumed that it is snuffed out when it is not in action, how could it be rekindled? If *per impossible* I had once succeeded in *making myself into* a thing, how should I subsequently reconvert myself to consciousness? Once I am free, I am not to be counted among things, and I must then be uninterruptedly free. Once my actions cease to be mine, I shall never recover them, and if I lose my hold on the world, it will never be restored to me. It is equally inconceivable that my liberty should be attenuated; one cannot be to some extent free, and if, as is often said, motives incline me in a certain direction, one of two things happens: either they are strong enough to force me to act, in which case there is no freedom, or else they are not strong enough, and then freedom is complete, and as great in the worst torments as in the peace of one's home. We ought, therefore, to reject not only the idea of causality, but also that of motivation.[2] The alleged motive does not burden my decision; on the contrary my decision lends the motive its force. Everything that I 'am' in virtue of nature or history —hunchbacked, handsome or Jewish—I never am completely for myself, as we have just explained: and I may well be these things for other people, nevertheless I remain free to posit another person as a consciousness whose views strike through to my very being, or on the other hand merely as an object. It is also true that this option is itself a form of constraint: if I am ugly, I have the choice between being an object of disapproval or disapproving of others. I am left free to be a masochist or a sadist, but not free to ignore others. But this dilemma, which is given as part of the human lot, is not one for me as pure consciousness: it is still I who cause the other to be for me, and who cause us both to be as members of mankind. Moreover, even if existence as a human being were imposed upon me, the manner alone being left to my choice, and considering this choice itself and ignoring the small number of forms it might take, it would still be a free choice. If it is said that my temperament inclines me particularly to either sadism or masochism, it is still merely a manner of speaking, for my temperament exists only for the second order knowledge that I gain about myself when I see myself as others see me, and in so far as I recognize it, confer value upon it, and in that sense, choose it. What misleads us on this, is that we often look for freedom in the voluntary deliberation which examines one motive after another and seems to opt for the weightiest or most convincing. In reality the deliberation follows the decision, and it is my secret decision which brings the motives to light, for it would be difficult to conceive what the force of a motive might be in the absence of a decision which it confirms or to which it runs counter. When I have abandoned a project, the motives which I thought held me to it suddenly lose their force and collapse. In order to resuscitate them, an effort is required on my part to reopen time and set me back to the moment preceding the making of the decision. Even while I am deliberating, already I find it an effort to suspend time's flow, and to keep open a situation which I feel is closed by a decision which is already there and which I am holding off. That is why it so often happens that after giving up a plan I experience a feeling of relief: 'After all, I wasn't so very particular'; the debate was purely a matter of form, and the deliberation a mere parody, for I had decided against from the start.

We often see the weakness of the will brought forward as an argument against freedom. And indeed, although I can will myself to adopt a course of conduct and act the part of a warrior or a seducer, it is not within my power to be a warrior or seducer with ease and in a way that 'comes naturally'; really to *be* one, that is. But neither should we seek freedom in the act of will, which is, in its very meaning, something short of an act. We have recourse to an act of will only in order to go against our true decision, and, as it were, for the purpose of proving our powerlessness. If we had really and truly made the conduct of the warrior or the seducer our own, then we should *be* one or the other. Even what are called obstacles to freedom are in reality deployed by it. An unclimbable rock face, a large or small, vertical or slanting rock, are things which have no meaning for anyone who is not intending to surmount them, for a subject whose projects do not carve out such determinate forms from the uniform mass of the *in itself* and cause an orientated world to arise—a significance in things. There is, then, ultimately nothing that can set limits to freedom, except those limits that freedom itself has set in the form of its various initiatives, so that the subject has simply the external world that he gives himself. Since it is the latter who, on coming into being, brings to light significance and value in things, and since no thing can impinge upon it except through acquiring, thanks to it, significance and value, there is no action of things on the subject, but merely a signification (in the active sense), a centrifugal *Sinngebung*. The choice would seem to lie between scientism's conception of causality, which is incompatible with the consciousness which we have of ourselves, and the assertion of an absolute freedom divorced from the outside. It is impossible to decide beyond which point things cease to be ἐφ'ἥμιν. Either they all lie within our power, or none does.

The result, however, of this first reflection on freedom would appear to be to rule it out altogether. If indeed it is the case that our freedom is the same in all our actions, and even in our passions, if it is not to be measured in terms of our conduct, and if the slave displays freedom as much by living in fear as by breaking his chains, then it cannot be held that there is such a thing as *free action*, freedom being anterior to all actions. In any case it will not be possible to declare: 'Here freedom makes its appearance', since free action, in order to be discernible, has to stand out against a background of life from which it is entirely, or almost entirely, absent. We may say in this case that it is everywhere, but equally nowhere. In the name of freedom we reject the idea of acquisition, since freedom has become a primordial acquisition and, as it were, our state of nature. Since we do not have to provide it, it is the gift granted to us of having no gift, it is the nature of consciousness which consists in having no nature, and in no case can it find external expression or a place in our life. The idea of action, therefore, disappears: nothing can pass from us to the world, since we are nothing that can be specified, and since the non-being which constitutes us could not possibly find its way into the world's plenum. There are merely intentions immediately followed by their effects, and we are very near to the Kantian idea of an intention which is tantamount to the act, which Scheler countered with the argument that the cripple who would like to be able to save a drowning man and the good swimmer who actually saves him do not have the same experience of autonomy. The very idea of choice vanishes, for to choose is to choose *something* in which freedom sees, at least for a moment, a symbol of itself. There is free choice only if freedom comes into play in its decision, and posits the situation chosen as a situation of freedom. A freedom which has no need to be exercised because it is already acquired could not commit itself in this way: it knows that the following instant will find it, come what may, just as free and just as indeterminate. The very notion of freedom demands that our decision should plunge into the future, that something should have been *done* by it, that the subsequent instant should benefit from its predecessor and, though not necessitated, should be at least required by it. If freedom is doing, it is necessary that what it does should not be immediately undone by a new freedom. Each instant, therefore, must not be a closed world; one instant must be able to commit its successors and, a decision once taken and action once begun, I must have something acquired at my disposal, I must benefit from my impetus, I must be inclined to carry on, and there must be a bent or propensity of the mind. It was Descartes who held that conservation demands a power as great as does creation; a view which implies a realistic notion of the instant. It is true that the instant is not a philosopher's fiction. It is the point at which one project is brought to fruition and another begun[3]—the point at which my gaze is transferred from one end to another, it is the *Augen-Blick*. But this break in time cannot occur unless each of the two spans is of a piece. Consciousness, it is said, is, though not atomized into instants, at least haunted by the spectre of the instant which it is obliged continually to exorcise by a free act. We shall soon see that we have indeed always the power to interrupt, but it implies in any case a power to *begin*, for there would be no severance unless freedom had taken up its abode somewhere and were preparing to move it. Unless there are cycles of behaviour, open situations requiring a certain completion and capable of constituting a background to either a confirmatory or transformatory decision, we never experience freedom. The choice of an intelligible character is excluded, not only because there is no time anterior to time, but because choice presupposes a prior commitment and because the idea of an initial choice involves a contradiction. If freedom is to have *room** in which to move, if it is to be describable as freedom, there must be something to hold it away from its objectives, it must have a *field*, which means that there must be for it special possibilities, or realities which tend to cling to being. As J. P. Sartre himself observes, dreaming is incompatible with freedom because, in the realm of imagination, we have no sooner taken a certain significance as our goal than we already believe that we have intuitively brought it into being, in short, because there is no obstacle and nothing *to do*.[4] It is established that freedom is not to be confused with those abstract decisions of will at grips with motives or passions, for the classical conception of deliberation is relevant only to a freedom 'in bad faith' which secretly harbours antagonistic motives without being prepared to act on them, and so itself manufactures the alleged proofs of its impotence. We can see, beneath these noisy debates and these fruitless efforts to 'construct' us, the tacit decisions whereby we have marked out round ourselves the field of possibility, and it is true that nothing is done as long as we cling to these fixed points, and everything is easy as soon as we have weighed anchor. This is why our freedom is not to be sought in spurious discussion on the conflict between a style of life which we have no wish to reappraise and circumstances suggestive of another: the real choice is that between our whole character and our manner of being in the world. But either this total choice is never mentioned, since it is the silent upsurge of our being in the world, in which case it is not clear in what sense it could be said to be ours, since this freedom glides over itself and is the equivalent of a fate—or else our choice of ourselves is a genuine choice, a conversion

---

*'avoir du champ'; in this sentence there is a play on the word 'champ' =field (Translator's note).

involving our whole existence. In this case, however, there is presupposed a previous acquisition which the choice sets out to modify and it founds a new tradition: this leads us to ask whether the perpetual severance in terms of which we initially defined freedom is not simply the negative aspect of our universal commitment to a world, and whether our indifference to each determinate thing does not express merely our involvement in all; whether the ready-made freedom from which we started is not reducible to a power of initiative which cannot be transformed into *doing* without taking up the world as posited in some shape or form, and whether, in short, concrete and actual freedom is not to be found in this exchange. It is true that nothing has *significance* and value for anyone but *me* and through anyone but me, but this proposition remains indeterminate and is still indistinguishable from the Kantian idea of a consciousness which 'finds in things only what it has put into them', and from the idealist refutation of realism, as long as we fail to make clear how we understand significance and the self. By defining ourselves as a universal power of *Sinn-Gebung*, we have reverted to the method of the 'thing without which' and to the analytical reflection of the traditional type, which seeks the conditions of possibility without concerning itself with the conditions of reality. We must therefore resume the analysis of the *Sinngebung*, and show how it can be both centrifugal and centripetal, since it has been established that there is no freedom without a field.

When I say that this rock is unclimbable, it is certain that this attribute, like that of being big or little, straight and oblique, and indeed like all attributes in general, can be conferred upon it only by the project of climbing it, and by a human presence. It is, therefore, freedom which brings into being the obstacles to freedom, so that the latter can be set over against it as its bounds. However, it is clear that, one and the same project being given, one rock will appear as an obstacle, and another, being more negotiable, as a means. My freedom, then, does not so contrive it that this way there is an obstacle, and that way a way through, it arranges for there to be obstacles and ways through in general; it does not draw the particular outline of this world, but merely lays down its general structures. It may be objected that there is no difference; if my freedom conditions the structure of the 'there is', that of the 'here' and the 'there', it is present wherever these structures arise. We cannot distinguish the quality of 'obstacle' from the obstacle itself, and relate one to freedom and the other to the world in itself which, without freedom, would be merely an amorphous and unnameable mass. It is not, therefore, outside myself that I am able to find a limit to my freedom. But should I not find it in myself? We must indeed distinguish between my express intentions, for example the plan I now make to climb those mountains, and general intentions which evaluate the potentialities of my environment. Whether or not I have decided to climb them, these mountains appear high to me, because they exceed my body's power to take them in its stride, and, even if I have just read *Micromégas*, I cannot so contrive it that they are small for me. Underlying myself as a thinking subject, who am able to take my place at will on Sirius or on the earth's surface, there is, therefore, as it were a natural self which does not budge from its terrestrial situation and which constantly adumbrates absolute valuations. What is more, my projects as a thinking being are clearly modelled on the latter; if I elect to see things from the point of view of Sirius, it is still to my terrestrial experience that I must have recourse in order to do so; I may say, for example, that the Alps are *molehills*. In so far as I have hands, feet, a body, I sustain around me intentions which are not dependent upon my decisions and which affect my surroundings in a way which I do not choose. These intentions are general in a double sense: firstly in the sense that they constitute a system in which all possible objects are simultaneously included; if the mountain appears high and upright, the tree appears small and sloping; and furthermore in the sense that they are not of my own making, they originate from outside me, and I am not surprised to find them in all psycho-physical subjects organized as I am. Hence, as Gestalt psychology has shown, there are for me certain shapes which are particularly favoured, as they are for other men, and which are capable of giving rise to a psychological science and rigorous laws. The grouping of dots

•• •• •• •• •• ••

is always perceived as six pairs of dots with two millimetres between each pair, while one figure is always perceived as a cube, and another as a plane mosaic.[5] It is as if, on the hither side of our judgement and our freedom, someone were assigning such and such a significance to such and such a given grouping. It is indeed true that perceptual structures do not always force themselves upon the observer; there are some which are ambiguous. But these reveal even more effectively the presence within us of spontaneous evaluation: for they are elusive shapes which suggest constantly changing meanings to us. Now a pure consciousness is capable of anything except being ignorant of its intentions, and an absolute freedom cannot choose itself as hesitant, since that amounts to allowing itself to be drawn in several directions, and since, the possibilities being *ex hypothesi* indebted to freedom for all the strength they have, the weight that freedom gives to one is thereby withdrawn from the rest. We *can* break up a shape by looking at it awry, but this too is because freedom uses the gaze along with its spontaneous evaluations. Without the latter, we would not have a world, that is, a collection of things which emerge from a background of formlessness by presenting themselves to our body as 'to be touched', 'to be taken', 'to be climbed over'. We should never be aware of adjusting ourselves to things and reaching them where they are, beyond us, but would be conscious only of restricting our thoughts to the immanent objects of our intentions, and we should not be in the world, ourselves implicated in the spectacle and, so to speak, intermingled with things, we should simply enjoy the spectacle of a universe. It is, therefore, true that there are no obstacles in themselves, but the self which qualifies them as such is not some acosmic subject; it runs ahead of itself in relation to things in order to confer upon them the form of things. There is an autochthonous significance of the world which is constituted in the dealings which our incarnate existence has with it, and which provides the ground of every deliberate *Sinngebung.*

This is true not only of an impersonal and, generally speaking, abstract function such as 'external perception'. There is something comparable present in all evaluations. It has been perceptively remarked that pain and fatigue can never be regarded as causes which 'act' upon my liberty, and that, in so far as I may experience either at any given moment, they do not have their origin outside me, but always have a significance and express my attitude towards the world. Pain makes me give way and say what I ought to have kept to myself, fatigue makes me break my journey. We all know the moment at which we decide no longer to endure pain or fatigue, and when, simultaneously, they become intolerable in fact. Tiredness does not halt my companion because he likes the clamminess of his body, the heat of the road and the sun, in short, because he likes to feel himself in the midst of things, to feel their rays converging upon him, to be the cynosure of all this light, and an object of touch for the earth's crust. My own fatigue brings me to a halt because I dislike it, because I have chosen differently my manner of being in the world, because, for instance, I endeavour, not to be in nature, but rather to win the recognition of others. I am free in relation to fatigue to precisely the extent that I am free in relation to my being in the world, free to make my way by transforming it.[6] But here once more we must recognize a sort of sedimentation of our life: an attitude towards the world, when it has received frequent confirmation, acquires a favoured status for us. Yet since freedom does not tolerate any motive in its path, my habitual being in the world is at each moment equally precarious, and the complexes which I have allowed to develop over the years always remain equally soothing, and the free act can with no difficulty blow them sky-high. However, having built our life upon an inferiority complex which has been operative for twenty years, it is not *probable* that we shall change. It is clear what a summary rationalism might say in reply to such a hybrid notion: there are no degrees of possibility; either the free act is no longer possible, or it is still possible, in which case freedom is complete. In short, 'probable' is meaningless. It is a notion belonging to statistical thought, which is not thought at all, since it does not concern any particular thing actually existing, any moment of time, any concrete event. 'It is improbable that Paul will give up writing bad books' means nothing, since Paul may well decide to write no more such books. The probable is everywhere and nowhere, a reified fiction, with only a psychological existence; it is not an ingredient of the world. And yet we have already met it a little while ago in the perceived *world*. The mountain is great or small to the extent that, as a perceived thing, it is to be found in the field of my possible actions, and in relation to a level which is not only that of my individual life, but that of 'any man'. Generality and probability are not fictions, but phenomena; we must therefore find a phenomenological basis for statistical thought. It belongs necessarily to a being which is fixed, situated and surrounded by things in the world. 'It is improbable' that I should at this moment destroy an inferiority complex in which I have been content to live for twenty years. That means that I have committed myself to inferiority, that I have made it my abode, that this past, though not a fate, has at least a specific weight and is not a set of events over there, at a distance from me, but the atmosphere of my present. The rationalist's dilemma: either the free act is possible, or it is not—either the event originates in me or is imposed on me from outside, does not apply to our relations with the world and with our past. Our freedom does not destroy our situation, but gears itself to it: as long as we are alive, our situation is open, which implies both that it calls up specially favoured modes of resolution, and also that it is powerless to bring one into being by itself.

We shall arrive at the same result by considering our relations with history. Taking myself in my absolute concreteness, as I am presented to myself in reflection, I find that I am an anonymous and pre-human flux, as yet unqualified as, for instance, 'a working man' or 'middle class'. If I subsequently think of myself as a man among men, a bourgeois among bourgeois, this can be, it would seem, no more than a second order view of myself; I am never in my heart of hearts a worker or a bourgeois, but a consciousness which freely evaluates itself as a middle class or proletarian consciousness. And indeed, it is never the case that my objective position in the production process is sufficient to awaken class-consciousness. There was exploitation long before there were revolutionaries. Nor is it always in periods of economic difficulty that the working class movement makes headway. Revolt is, then, not the outcome of objective conditions, but it is rather the decision taken by the worker to will revolution that makes a proletarian of him. The evaluation of the present operates through one's free project for the future. From which we might conclude that history by itself has no significance, but only that conferred upon it by our will. Yet here again we are slipping into the method of 'the indispensable condition failing which . . .': in opposition to objective thought, which includes the subject in its deterministic system; we are setting idealist reflection which makes determinism dependent upon the constituting activity of the subject. Now, we have already seen that objective thought and analytical reflection are two aspects of the same mistake, two ways of overlooking the phenomena. Objective thought derives class consciousness from the objective condition of the proletariat. Idealist reflection reduces the proletarian condition to the awareness of it, which the proletarian arrives at. The former traces class-consciousness to the class defined in terms of objective characteristics, the latter on the other hand reduces 'being a workman' to the consciousness of being one. In each case we are in the realm of abstraction, because we remain torn between the *in itself* and the *for itself*. If we approach the question afresh with the idea of discovering, not the causes of the act of becoming aware, for there is no cause which can act from outside upon a consciousness—nor the conditions of its possibility, for we need to know the conditions which actually produce it—but class-consciousness itself, if, in short, we apply a genuinely existential method, what do we find? I am not conscious of being working class or middle class simply because, as a matter of fact, I sell my labour or, equally as a matter of fact, because my interests are bound up with capitalism, nor do I become one or the other on the day on which I elect to view history in the light of the class struggle: what happens is that 'I exist as working class' or 'I exist as middle class' in the first place, and it is this mode of dealing with the world and society which provides both the motives for my revolutionary or conservative projects and my explicit judgements of the type: 'I am working class' or 'I am middle class', without its being possible to deduce the former from the latter, or *vice versa*. What makes me a proletarian is not the economic system or society considered as systems of impersonal forces, but these institutions as I carry them within me and experience them; nor is it an intellectual operation devoid of motive, but my way of being in the world within this institutional framework.

Let us suppose that I have a certain style of living, being at the mercy of booms and slumps, not being free to do as I like, receiving a weekly wage, having no control over either the conditions or the products of my work, and consequently feeling a stranger in my factory, my nation and my life. I have acquired the habit of reckoning with a *fatum,* or appointed order, which I do not respect, but which I have to humour. Or suppose that I work as a day-labourer, having no farm of my own, no tools, going from one farm to another hiring myself out at harvest time; in that case I have the feeling that there is some anonymous power hovering over me and making a nomad of me, even though I want to settle into a regular job. Or finally suppose I am the tenant of a farm to which the owner has had no electricity laid on, though the mains are less than two hundred yards away. I have, for my family and myself, only one habitable room, although it would be easy to make other rooms available in the house. My fellow workers in factory or field, or other farmers, do the same work as I do in comparable conditions; we co-exist in the same situation and feel alike, not in virtue of some comparison, as if each one of us lived primarily within himself, but on the basis of our tasks and gestures. These situations do not imply any express evaluation, and if there is a tacit evaluation, it represents the thrust of a freedom devoid of any project against unknown obstacles; one cannot in any case talk about a choice, for in all three cases it is enough that I should be born into the world and that I exist in order to experience my life as full of difficulties and constraints—I do not choose so to experience it. But this state of affairs can persist without my becoming class-conscious, understanding that I am of the proletariat and becoming a revolutionary. How then am I to make this change? The worker learns that other workers in a different trade have, after striking, obtained a wage-increase, and notices that subsequently wages have gone up in his own factory. The appointed order with which he was at grips is beginning to take on a clearer shape. The day-labourer who has not often seen workers in regular employment, who is not like them and has little love for them, sees the price of manufactured goods and the cost of living going up, and becomes aware that he can no longer earn a livelihood. He may at this point blame town workers, in which case class-consciousness will not make its appearance. If it does, it is not because the day-labourer has decided to become a revolutionary and consequently confers a value upon his actual condition; it is because he has perceived, in a concrete way, that his life is synchronized with the life of the town labourers and that all share a common lot. The small farmer who does not associate himself with the day-labourers, still less with the town labourers, being separated from them by a whole world of customs and value judgements, nevertheless feels that he is on the same side as the journeyman when he pays them an inadequate wage, and he even feels that he has something in common with the town workers when he learns that the farm owner is chairman of the board of directors of several industrial concerns. Social space begins to acquire a magnetic field, and a region of the exploited is seen to appear. At every pressure felt from any quarter of the social horizon, the process of regrouping becomes clearly discernible beyond ideologies and various occupations. Class is coming into being, and we say that a situation is revolutionary when the connection objectively existing between the sections of the proletariat (the connection, that is, which an absolute observer would recognize as so existing) is finally experienced in perception as a common obstacle to the existence of each and every one. It is not at all necessary that at any single moment a *representation* of revolution should arise. For example, it is doubtful whether the Russian peasants of 1917 expressly envisaged revolution and the transfer of property. Revolution arises day by day from the concatenation of less remote and more remote ends. It is not necessary that each member of the proletariat should think of himself as such, in the sense that a Marxist theoretician gives to the word. It is sufficient that the journeyman or the farmer should feel that he is on the march towards a certain crossroads, to which the road trodden by the town labourers also leads. Both find their journey's end in revolution, which would perhaps have terrified them had it been described and represented to them in advance. One might say at the most that revolution is at the end of the road they have taken and in their projects in the form of 'things must change', which each one experiences concretely in his distinctive difficulties and in the depths of his particular prejudices. Neither the appointed order, nor the free act which destroys it, is represented; they are lived through in ambiguity. This does not mean that workers and peasants bring about revolution without being aware of it, and that we have here blind, 'elementary forces' cleverly exploited by a few shrewd agitators. It is possibly in this light that the prefect of police will view history. But such ways of seeing things do not help him when faced with a genuine revolutionary situation, in which the slogans of the alleged agitators are immediately understood, as if by some pre-established harmony, and meet with concurrence on all sides, because they crystallize what is latent in the life of all productive workers. The revolutionary movement, like the work of the artist, is an intention which itself creates its instruments and its means of expression. The revolutionary project is not the result of a deliberate judgement, or the explicit positing of an end. It is these things in the case of the propagandist, because the propagandist has been trained by the intellectual, or, in the case of the intellectual, because he regulates his life on the basis of his thoughts. But it does not cease to be the abstract decision of a thinker and become a historical reality until it is worked out in the dealings men have with each other, and in the relations of the man to his job. It is, therefore, true that I recognize myself as a worker or a bourgeois on the day I take my stand in relation to a possible revolution, and that this taking of a stand is not the outcome, through some mechanical causality, of my status as workman or bourgeois (which is why all classes have their traitors), but neither is it an unwarranted evaluation, instantaneous and unmotivated; it is prepared by some molecular process, it matures in co-existence before bursting forth into words and being related to objective ends. One is justified in drawing attention to the fact that it is not the greatest poverty which produces the most clear-sighted revolutionaries, but one forgets to ask why a return of prosperity frequently brings with it a more radical mood among the masses. It is because the easing of living conditions makes a fresh structure of social space possible: the horizon is not restricted to the most immediate concerns, there is economic play and room for a new project in relation to living. This phenomenon does not, then, go to prove that the worker makes himself into worker and revolutionary *ex nihilo,* but on the contrary that he does so on a certain basis of co-existence. The mistake inherent in the conception under discussion is, in general, that of disregarding all but intellectual projects, instead of considering the existential project, which is the polarization of a life towards a goal which is both determinate and indeterminate, which, to the person concerned, is entirely unrepresented, and which is recognized only on being attained. Intentionality is brought down to the particular cases of the objectifying acts, the proletarian condition is made an object of thought, and no difficulty is experienced in showing, in accordance with idealism's permanent method, that, like every other object of thought, it subsists only before and through the consciousness which constitutes it as an object. Idealism (like objective thought) passes by the side of true intentionality, of which it is true to say that it *belongs to* its object rather than that it posits it. Idealism overlooks the interrogative, the subjunctive, the aspiration, the expectation, the positive indeterminacy of these modes of consciousness, for it is acquainted only with consciousness in the present or future indicative, which is why it fails to account for class. For class is a matter neither for observation nor decree; like the appointed order of the capitalistic system, like revolution, before being thought it is lived through as an obsessive presence, as possibility, enigma and myth. To make class-consciousness the outcome of a decision and a choice is to say that problems are solved on the day they are posed, that every question already contains the reply that it awaits; it is, in short, to revert to immanence and abandon the attempt to understand history. In reality, the intellectual project and the positing of ends are merely the bringing to completion of an existential project. It is I who give a direction, significance and future to my life, but that does not mean that these are concepts; they spring from my present and past and in particular from my mode of present and past co-existence. Even in the case of the intellectual who turns revolutionary, his decision does not arise *ex nihilo;* it may follow upon a prolonged period of solitude: the intellectual is in search of a doctrine which shall make great demands on him and cure him of his subjectivity; or he may yield to the clear light thrown by a Marxist interpretation of history, in which case he has given knowledge pride of place in his life, and that in itself is understandable only in virtue of his past and his childhood. Even the decision to become a revolutionary without motive, and by an act of pure freedom would express a certain way of being in the natural and social world, which is typically that of the intellectual. He 'throws in his lot with the working class' from the starting point of his situation as an intellectual and from nowhere else (and this is why even fideism, in his case, remains rightly suspect). Now with the worker it is *a fortiori* the case that his decision is elaborated in the course of his life. This time it is through no misunderstanding that the horizon of a particular life and revolutionary aims coincide: for the worker revolution is a more immediate possibility, and one closer to his own interests than for the intellectual, since he is at grips with the economic system in his very life. For this reason there are, statistically, more workers than middle class people in a revolutionary party. Motivation, of course, does not do away with freedom. Working class parties of the most unmistakable kind have had many intellectuals among their leaders, and it is likely that a man such as Lenin identified himself with revolution and eventually transcended the distinction between intellectual and worker. But these are the virtues proper to action and commitment; at the outset, I am not an individual beyond class, I am situated in a social environment, and my freedom, though it may have the power to commit me elsewhere, has not the power to transform me instantaneously into what I decide to be. Thus to be a bourgeois or a worker is not only to be aware of being one or the other, it is to identify oneself as worker or bourgeois through an implicit or existential project which merges into our way of patterning the world and co-existing with other people. My decision draws together a spontaneous meaning of my life which it may confirm or repudiate, but not annul. Both idealism and objective thinking fail to pin down the coming into being of class-consciousness, the former because it deduces actual existence from consciousness, the latter because it derives consciousness from *de facto* existence, and both because they overlook the relationship of motivation.

It will perhaps be objected, from the idealist side, that I am not, for myself, a particular project, but a pure consciousness, and that the attributes of bourgeois or worker belong to me only to the extent that I place myself among others, and see myself through their eyes, from the ·outside, as 'another'. Here we should have categories of For Others and not For Oneself. But if there were two sorts of categories, how could I have the experience of another, that is, of an *alter ego?* This experience presupposes that already my view of myself is half-way to having the quality of a possible 'other', and that in my view of another person is implied his quality as *ego*. It will be replied that the other person is given to me as a fact, and not as a possibility of my own being. What is meant by this? Is it that I should not have the experience of other men if there were none on the earth's surface? The proposition is self-evidently true, but does not solve our problem since, as Kant has already said, we cannot pass from 'All knowledge begins with experience' to 'All knowledge derives from experience'. If the other people who empirically exist are to be, for me, other people, I must have a means of recognizing them, and the structures of the For Another must, therefore, already be the dimensions of the For Oneself. Moreover, it is impossible to derive from the For Another all the specifications of which we are speaking. Another person is not necessarily, is not even ever quite an object for me. And, in sympathy for example, I can perceive another person as bare existence and freedom as much or as little as myself. The-other-person-as-object is nothing but an insincere modality of others, just as absolute subjectivity is nothing but an abstract notion of myself. I must, therefore, in the most radical reflection, apprehend around my absolute individuality a kind of halo of generality or a kind of atmosphere of 'sociality'. This is necessary if subsequently the words 'a bourgeois' and 'a man' are to be able to assume meaning for me. I must apprehend myself immediately as centred in a way outside myself, and my individual existence must diffuse round itself, so to speak, an existence in quality. The For-Themselves—me for myself and the other for himself—must stand out against a background of For Others—I for the other and the other for me. My life must have a significance which I do not constitute; there must strictly speaking be an intersubjectivity; each one of us must be both anonymous in the sense of absolutely individual, and anonymous in the sense of absolutely general. Our being in the world, is the concrete bearer of this double anonymity.

Provided that this is so, there can be situations, a direction* of history, and a historical truth: three ways of saying the same thing. If indeed I made myself into a worker or a bourgeois by an absolute initiative, and if in general terms nothing ever courted our freedom, history would display no structure, no event would be seen to take shape in it, and anything might emerge from anything else. There would be no British

*'sens' (Translator's note).

Empire as a relatively stable historical form to which a name can be given, and in which certain probable properties are recognizable. There would not be, in the history of social progress, revolutionary situations or periods of set-back. A social revolution would be equally possible at any moment, and one might reasonably expect a despot to undergo conversion to anarchism. History would never move in any direction, nor would it be possible to say that even over a short period of time events were conspiring to produce any definite outcome. The statesman would always be an adventurer, that is to say, he would take advantage of events by conferring upon them a meaning which they *did not have*. Now if it is true that history is powerless to complete anything independently of consciousnesses which assume it and thereby decide its course, and if consequently it can never be detached from us to play the part of an alien force using us for its own ends, then *precisely because it is always history lived through* we cannot withhold from it at least a fragmentary meaning. Something is being prepared which will perhaps come to nothing but which may, for the moment, conform to the adumbrations of the present. Nothing can so order it that, in the France of 1799, a military power 'above classes' should not appear as a natural product of the ebb of revolution, and that the rôle of military dictator should not here be 'a part that has to be played'. It is Bonaparte's project, known to us through its realization, which causes us to pass such a judgement. But before Bonaparte, Dumouriez, Custine and others had envisaged it, and this common tendency has to be accounted for. What is known as the significance of events is not an idea which produces them, or the fortuitous result of their occurring together. It is the concrete project of a future which is elaborated within social co-existence and in the One* before any personal decision is made. At the point of revolutionary history to which class dynamics had carried it

*In the sense of *Das Man*, the impersonal pronoun (Translator's note).

by 1799, when neither the Revolution could be carried forward nor the clock put back, the situation was such that, all due reservations as to individual freedom having been made, each individual, through the functional and generalized existence which makes a historical subject of him, tended to fall back upon what had been acquired. It would have been a historical mistake at that stage to suggest to them either a resumption of the methods of revolutionary government or a reversion to the social conditions of 1789, not because there is a truth of history independent of our projects and evaluations, which are always free, but because there is an average and statistical significance of these projects. Which means that we confer upon history its significance, but not without its putting that significance forward itself. The *Sinngebung* is not merely centrifugal, which is why the subject of history is not the individual. There is an exchange between generalized and individual existence, each receiving and giving something. There is a moment at which the significance which was foreshadowed in the One, and which was merely a precarious possibility threatened by the contingency of history, is taken up by an individual. It may well happen that now, having taken command of history, he leads it, for a time at least, far beyond what seemed to comprise its significance, and involves it in a fresh dialectic, as when Bonaparte, from being Consul, made himself Emperor and conqueror. We are not asserting that history from end to end has only one meaning, any more than has an individual life. We mean simply that in any case freedom modifies it only by taking up the meaning which history *was offering* at the moment in question, and by a kind of unobtrusive assimilation. On the strength of this proposal made by the present, the adventurer can be distinguished from the statesman, historical imposture from the truth of an epoch, with the result that our assessment of the past, though never arriving at absolute objectivity, is at the same time never entitled to be arbitrary.

We therefore recognize, around our initiatives and around

that strictly individual project which is oneself, a zone of generalized existence and of projects already formed, significances which trail between ourselves and things and which confer upon us the quality of man, bourgeois or worker. Already generality intervenes, already our presence to ourselves is mediated by it and we cease to be pure consciousness, as soon as the natural or social constellation ceases to be an unformulated *this* and crystallizes into a situation, as soon as it has a meaning—in short, as soon as we exist. Every thing appears to us through a medium to which it lends its own fundamental quality; this piece of wood is neither a collection of colours and tactile data, not even their total *Gestalt*, but something from which there emanates a woody essence; these 'sense-data' modulate a certain theme or illustrate a certain style which is the wood itself, and which creates, round this piece of wood and the perception I have of it, a horizon of significance. The natural world, as we have seen, is nothing other than the place of all possible themes and styles. It is indissolubly an unmatched individual and a significance. Correspondingly, the generality and the individuality of the subject, subjectivity qualified and pure, the anonymity of the One and the anonymity of consciousness are not two conceptions of the subject between which philosophy has to choose, but two stages of a unique structure which is the concrete subject. Let us consider, for example, sense experience. I lose myself in this red which is before me, without in any way qualifying it, and it seems that this experience brings me into contact with a pre-human subject. Who perceives this red? It is nobody who can be named and placed among other perceiving subjects. For, between this experience of red which I have, and that about which other people speak to me, no direct comparison will ever be possible. I am here in my own point of view, and since all experience, in so far as it derives from impression, is in the same way strictly my own, it seems that a unique and unduplicated subject enfolds them all. Suppose I formulate a thought, the God of Spinoza, for example; this thought as it is in my living experience is a certain landscape to which no one will ever have access, even if, moreover, I manage to enter into a discussion with a friend on the subject of Spinoza's God. However, the very individuality of these experiences is not quite unadulterated. For the thickness of this red, its thisness, the power it has of reaching me and saturating me, are attributable to the fact that it requires and obtains from my gaze a certain vibration, and imply that I am familiar with a world of colours of which this one is a particular variation. The concrete colour red, therefore, stands out against a background of generality, and this is why, even without transferring myself to another's point of view, I grasp myself in perception as *a* perceiving subject, and not as unclassifiable consciousness. I feel, all round my perception of red, all the regions of my being unaffected by it, and that region set aside for colours, 'vision', through which the perception finds its way into me. Similarly my thought about the God of Spinoza is only apparently a strictly unique experience, for it is the concretion of a certain cultural world, the Spinozist philosophy, or of a certain philosophic style in which I immediately recognize a 'Spinozist' idea. There is therefore no occasion to ask ourselves why the thinking subject or consciousness perceives itself as a man, or an incarnate or historical subject, nor must we treat this apperception as a second order operation which it somehow performs starting from its absolute existence: the absolute flow takes shape beneath its own gaze as '*a* consciousness', or a man, or an incarnate subject, because it is a field of presence—to itself, to others and to the world—and because this presence throws it into the natural and cultural world from which it arrives at an understanding of itself. We must not envisage this flux as absolute contact with oneself, as an absolute density with no internal fault, but on the contrary as a being which is in pursuit of itself outside. If the subject made a constant and at all times peculiar choice of himself, one might wonder why his experience always ties up with itself and presents him with objects and definite historical phases, why we have a general notion of time valid through all times, and why finally the experience of each one of us links up with that of others. But it is the question itself which must be questioned: for what is given, is not one fragment of time followed by another, one individual flux, then another; it is the taking up of each subjectivity by itself, and of subjectivities by each other in the generality of a single nature, the cohesion of an intersubjective life and a world. The present mediates between the For Oneself and the For Others, between individuality and generality. True reflection presents me to myself not as idle and inaccessible subjectivity, but as identical with my presence in the world and to others, as I am now realizing it: I am all that I see, I am an intersubjective field, not despite my body and historical situation, but, on the contrary, by being this body and this situation, and through them, all the rest.

What, then, becomes of the freedom we spoke about at the outset, if this point of view is taken? I can no longer pretend to be a cipher, and to choose myself continually from the starting point of nothing at all. If it is through subjectivity that nothingness appears in the world, it can equally be said that it is through the world that nothingness comes into being. I am a general refusal to be anything, accompanied surreptitiously by a continual acceptance of such and such a qualified form of being. *For even this general refusal is still one manner of being, and has its place in the world.* It is true that I can at any moment interrupt my projects. But what *is* this power? It is the power to begin something else, for we never remain suspended in nothingness. We are always in a plenum, in being, just as a face, even in repose, even in death, is always doomed to express something (there are people whose faces, in death, bear expressions of surprise, or peace, or discretion), and just as silence is still a modality of the world of sound. I may defy all accepted form, and spurn everything, for there is no case in which I am utterly committed: but in this case I do not withdraw into my freedom, I

commit myself elsewhere. Instead of thinking about my be-
reavement, I look at my nails, or have lunch, or engage in
politics. Far from its being the case that my freedom is always
unattended, it is never without an accomplice, and its power
of perpetually tearing itself away finds its fulcrum in my
universal commitment in the world. My actual freedom is
not on the hither side of my being, but before me, in things.
We must not say that I continually choose myself, on the
excuse that I *might* continually refuse what I am. Not to
refuse is not the same thing as to choose. We could identify
drift and action only by depriving the implicit of all phe-
nomenal value, and at every instant arraying the world
before us in perfect transparency, that is, by destroying the
world's 'worldliness'. Consciousness holds itself responsible
for everything, and takes everything upon itself, but it has
nothing of its own and makes its life in the world. We are led
to conceive freedom as a choice continually remade as long
as we do not bring in the notion of a generalized or natural
time. We have seen that there is no natural time, if we understand thereby a time of things without subjectivity. There is,
however, at least a generalized time, and this is what the
common notion of time envisages. It is the perpetual reiteration of the sequence of past, present and future. It is, as it
were, a constant disappointment and failure. This is what is
expressed by saying that it is continuous: the present which
it brings to us is never a present for good, since it is already
over when it appears, and the future has, in it, only the
appearance of a goal towards which we make our way, since
it quickly comes into the present, whereupon we turn towards a fresh future. This time is the time of our bodily
functions, which like it, are cyclic, and it is also that of nature
with which we co-exist. It offers us only the adumbration and
the abstract form of a commitment, since it continually
erodes itself and undoes that which it has just done. As long
as we place in opposition, with no mediator, the For Itself
and the In Itself, and fail to perceive, between ourselves and
the world, this natural foreshadowing of a subjectivity, this

prepersonal time which rests upon itself, acts are needed to sustain the upsurge of time, and everything becomes equally a matter of choice, the respiratory reflex no less than the moral decision, conservation no less than creation. As far as we are concerned, consciousness attributes this power of universal constitution to itself only if it ignores the event which upholds it and is the occasion of its birth. A consciousness for which the world 'can be taken for granted', which finds it 'already constituted' and present even in consciousness itself, does not *absolutely* choose either its being or its manner of being.

What then is freedom? To be born is both to be born of the world and to be born into the world. The world is already constituted, but also never completely constituted; in the first case we are acted upon, in the second we are open to an infinite number of possibilities. But this analysis is still abstract, for we exist in both ways *at once*. There is, therefore, never determinism and never absolute choice, I am never a thing and never bare consciousness. In fact, even our own pieces of initiative, even the situations which we have chosen, bear us on, once they have been entered upon by virtue of a state rather than an act. The generality of the 'rôle' and of the situation comes to the aid of decision, and in this exchange between the situation and the person who takes it up, it is impossible to determine precisely the 'share contributed by the situation' and the 'share contributed by freedom'. Let us suppose that a man is tortured to make him talk. If he refuses to give the names and addresses which it is desired to extract from him, this does not arise from a solitary and unsupported decision; the man still feels himself to be with his comrades, and, being still involved in the common struggle, he is as it were incapable of talking. Or else, for months or years, he has, in his mind, faced this test and staked his whole life upon it. Or finally, he wants to prove, by coming through it, what he has always thought and said about freedom. These motives do not cancel out freedom, but at least ensure that it does not go unbuttressed in

being. What withstands pain is not, in short, a bare consciousness, but the prisoner with his comrades or with those he
loves and under whose gaze he lives; or else the awareness
of his proudly willed solitude, which again is a certain mode
of the *Mit-Sein*. And probably the individual in his prison
daily reawakens these phantoms, which give back to him the
strength he gave to them. But conversely, in so far as he has
committed himself to this action, formed a bond with his
comrades or adopted this morality, it is because the historical
situation, the comrades, the world around him seemed to
him to expect that conduct from him. The analysis could be
pursued endlessly in this way. We choose our world and the
world chooses us. What is certain, in any case, is that we can
at no time set aside within ourselves a redoubt to which
being does not find its way through, without seeing this freedom, immediately and by the very fact of being a living
experience, take on the appearance of being and become a
motive and a buttress. Taken concretely, freedom is always
a meeting of the inner and the outer—even the prehuman
and prehistoric freedom with which we began—and it
shrinks without ever disappearing altogether in direct proportion to the lessening of the *tolerance* allowed by the
bodily and institutional data of our lives. There is, as Husserl
says, on the one hand a 'field of freedom' and on the other
a 'conditioned freedom';[7] not that freedom is absolute within
the limits of this field and non-existent outside it (like the
perceptual field, this one has no traceable boundaries), but
because I enjoy immediate and remote possibilities. Our
commitments sustain our power and there is no freedom
without some power. Our freedom, it is said, is either total
or non-existent. This dilemma belongs to objective thought
and its stable-companion, analytical reflection. If indeed we
place ourselves within being, it must necessarily be the case
that our actions must have their origin outside us, and if we
revert to constituting consciousness, they must originate
within. But we have learnt precisely to recognize the order
of phenomena. We are involved in the world and with others

in an inextricable tangle. The idea of situation rules out absolute freedom at the source of our commitments, and equally,
indeed, at their terminus. No commitment, not even commitment in the Hegelian State, can make me leave behind
all differences and free me for anything. This universality
itself, from the mere fact of its being experienced, would
stand out as a particularity against the world's background,
for existence both generalizes and particularizes everything
at which it aims, and cannot ever be finally complete.

The synthesis of *in itself* and *for itself* which brings
Hegelian freedom into being has, however, its truth. In a
sense, it is the very definition of existence, since it is effected
at every moment before our eyes in the phenomenon of
presence, only to be quickly re-enacted, since it does not
conjure away our finitude. By taking up a present, I draw
together and transform my past, altering its significance,
freeing and detaching myself from it. But I do so only by
committing myself somewhere else. Psychoanalytical treatment does not bring about its cure by producing direct
awareness of the past, but in the first place by binding the
subject to his doctor through new existential relationships. It
is not a matter of giving scientific assent to the psychoanalytical interpretation, and discovering a notional significance for
the past; it is a matter of reliving this or that as significant,
and this the patient succeeds in doing only by seeing his past
in the perspective of his co-existence with the doctor. The
complex is not dissolved by a non-instrumental freedom, but
rather displaced by a new pulsation of time with its own
supports and motives. The same applies in all cases of coming
to awareness: they are real only if they are sustained by a new
commitment. Now this commitment too is entered into in
the sphere of the implicit, and is therefore valid only for a
certain temporal cycle. The choice which we make of our life
is always based on a certain givenness. My freedom can draw
life away from its spontaneous course, but only by a series of
unobtrusive deflections which necessitate first of all following its course—not by any absolute creation. All explanations
of my conduct in terms of my past, my temperament and my

environment are therefore true, provided that they be regarded not as separable contributions, but as moments of my total being, the significance of which I am entitled to make explicit in various ways, without its ever being possible to say whether I confer their meaning upon them or receive it from them. I am a psychological and historical structure, and have received, with existence, a manner of existing, a style. All my actions and thoughts stand in a relationship to this structure, and even a philosopher's thought is merely a way of making explicit his hold on the world, and what he is. The fact remains that I am free, not in spite of, or on the hither side of, these motivations, but by means of them. For this significant life, this certain significance of nature and history which I am, does not limit my access to the world, but on the contrary is my means of entering into communication with it. It is by being unrestrictedly and unreservedly what I am at present that I have a chance of moving forward; it is by living my time that I am able to understand other times, by plunging into the present and the world, by taking on deliberately what I am fortuitously, by willing what I will and doing what I do, that I can go further. I can pass freedom by, only if I try to get over my natural and social situation by refusing, in the first place, to take it up, instead of using it as a way into the natural and human world. Nothing determines me from outside, not because nothing acts upon me, but, on the contrary, because I am from the start outside myself and open to the world. We are *true* through and through, and have with us, by the mere fact of belonging to the world, and not merely being in the world in the way that things are, all that we need to transcend ourselves. We need have no fear that our choices or actions restrict our liberty, since choice and action alone cut us loose from our anchorage. Just as reflection borrows its wish for absolute sufficiency from the perception which causes a thing to appear, and as in this way idealism tacitly uses that 'primary opinion' which it would like to destroy as opinion, so freedom flounders in the contra-

dictions of commitment, and fails to realize that, without the
roots which it thrusts into the world, it would not be freedom
at all. Shall I make this promise? Shall I risk my life for so
little? Shall I give up my liberty in order to save liberty?
There is no theoretical reply to these questions. But there are
these *things* which stand, irrefutable, there is before you this
person whom you love, there are these men whose existence
around you is that of slaves, and *your* freedom cannot be
willed without leaving behind its singular relevance, and
without willing freedom *for all*. Whether it is a question of
things or of historical situations, philosophy has no function
other than to teach us once more to see them clearly, and it
is true to say that it comes into being by destroying itself as
separate philosophy. But what is here required is silence, for
only the hero lives out his relation to men and the world.
'Your son is caught in the fire; you are the one who will save
him. . . . If there is an obstacle, you would be ready to give
your shoulder provided only that you can charge down that
obstacle. Your abode is your act itself. Your act is you. . . . You
give yourself in exchange. . . . Your significance shows itself,
effulgent. It is your duty, your hatred, your love, your steadfastness, your ingenuity. . . . Man is but a network of relationships, and these alone matter to him.'[8]

NOTES

1. In the sense in which, with Husserl, we have taken this word.
2. See J. P. Sartre, *L'Être et le Néant*, pp. 508 ff.
3. J. P. Sartre, *L'Être et le Néant*, p. 544.
4. J. P. Sartre, *L'Être et le Néant*, p. 562.
5. See above, p. 263. This note refers to *Phenomenology of Perception*
[Editor's note].
6. J. P. Sartre, *L'Être et le Néant*, pp. 531 ff.
7. Fink, *Vergegenwärtigung und Bild*, p. 285.
8. A. de Saint-Exupéry, *Pilote de Guerre*, pp. 171 and 174.

10

Responsibility and Existence

GEORGE A. SCHRADER

John Dewey has stated that liability is the beginning of responsibility. Dewey's statement is surely correct, though it might have been put more strongly. Liability is not merely the "beginning" of responsibility but responsibility itself. The English term "responsibility" means, when taken literally, the liability for making a response. We cannot rely too heavily upon the received meaning of the term for an understanding of the concept expressed. But the etymology of the term offers a beginning point, at least, for an understanding of its philosophical meaning. If, for example, responsibility is a generic term which refers to those situations in which a person is required to make a response to someone or something, we might obtain a suitable understanding of the concept by considering the human condition. In what respects,

Reprinted from *Responsibility*, Nomos III, ed. Carl J. Friedrich (New York: The Liberal Arts Press, 1960), pp. 43–70, by permission of the American Society for Political and Legal Philosophy.

for example, is man liable for making a response, to whom, and for what? Is this liability dependent upon his choices, or is it in part or in whole due to factors over which he has no control? If we can answer these questions we may succeed in achieving a fuller understanding of the nature of human responsibility.

In certain philosophical circles, particularly English and American, the appeal is made to language for answering questions about the meaning of ethical concepts. Thus, it is maintained, if we wish to know what such a term as "responsibility" means, we must look to linguistic usage. It is possible to understand the meaning of an ethical term, we are told, only when we know how it is used. The analysis of ethical language has led to the discovery that ethical terms have unique meaning in that they serve to commend and to recommend. This result should not have been particularly surprising to anyone acquainted with the passion of moralists of all times. And it need not be disturbing unless the claim is made, either tacitly or explicitly, that it is the only sort of meaning that ethical terms have or can have. Surely it is possible for linguistic expressions to convey more than one type of meaning. The barest factual statement may be designed to evoke an aesthetic response or an immoral action. Only a mad man would bother to utter true statements about the world with no regard for the interests of his hearers. Kierkegaard relates the doubtless apocryphal story of the man who sought to demonstrate his sanity by the repeated proclamation that "the world is round." It is extremely doubtful if pure theoretical interest is anything more than a limiting case. But factual statements apart, we cannot rule out the possibility a priori that ethical utterances perform more than one linguistic function. The fact that they *commend* or *recommend* does not in itself entail that they do only that. It is completely arbitrary to conclude that ethical statements have no cognitive meaning from the mere fact that they perform non-cognitive functions.

It is quite likely that some proponents of the non-cognitivist theory of ethical language are reinforced in their view by the conviction that there is no cognitive function for ethical language to perform. There are, in other words, no ethical facts to be expressed by language; hence, language cannot function cognitively. It is evident, I believe, that this issue cannot be settled by appeal to language alone. To understand a language we must have some grasp of what the language is attempting to express. Unless we take the most extreme idealist interpretation of language which holds that language constitutes the reality to which it refers, the extra-linguistic situation must be taken into account. To understand the language of love, for example, we must know something of the facts and experience of love. We may then find the language of love meaningful, and be in a position to determine its adequacy. We need not argue that language and the concepts it expresses add nothing to experience in order to insist that experience is essential. To understand the language of ethics we must have some experiential grasp of the ethical predicament of man. Comprehending this situation, we may then assess the function of ethical language and determine to what degree, if at all, it is descriptive. Ethical language is necessarily limited to an emotive function only if there are no ethical facts to express. And this is surely not a question of language but of metaphysics. The term "responsibility" suggests a *descriptive* meaning of the concept. I propose to inquire if any basis for the hypothesis that it has a descriptive meaning can be found in human experience.

If to be responsible is to be liable for responding to someone, to state that man is a responsible being might be simply to state a *fact*—albeit a metaphysical fact. Moreover, to indicate the ways in which man is liable by specifying to whom he is liable and for what, might be only to describe further the general features of the human situation. It is important, then, to inquire whether there are in fact certain liabilities attached to the human situation as such and, further, whether responsibility in its various forms can be accounted for in terms of these liabilities.

To begin with the most basic factor in human experience, namely existence itself, we can easily see that *to exist is to be liable.* Man is, as Heidegger describes it, "projected into the world" and responsible for his existence. The resultant "care" which derives from the original fact of his "being-in-the-world" permeates every aspect of his existence. He is, Heidegger argues, responsible for himself and to himself. And this is an ontological fact! The voice of conscience is nothing more than the call issuing from his being for the individual to acknowledge responsibility for his existence. Moral responsibility, instead of being original and ultimate, as some moralists have thought, is rooted in and derived from man's *ontological responsibility.* Man's original liability is not simply that he exists, but that he "has to be." He confronts his existence from the first moment of his awareness as a problem and an object of concern. Man does not exist in the way that a stick or a stone exists but, as Heidegger expresses it, he "ex-sists," that is, he transcends himself in a reflexive relationship.

Self-consciousness is generally conceded by philosophers to be a reflexive relationship, involving a relation of the human subject to itself. But too often self-consciousness is treated as if it were an epi-phenomenal affair. If, as Sartre argues, "the being of self-consciousness is the self-consciousness of being" and, conversely, "the self-consciousness of being is the being of self-consciousness," self-consciousness is constitutive of human existence. The point is not novel with Sartre, since both Hegel and Kierkegaard before him had insisted upon the constitutive character of self-consciousness. As Kierkegaard puts it, "the more consciousness of self, the more self."

To be a self is, in other words, to be a *subject,* and to be a subject is to be self-related and, further, conscious of the relatedness. This reflexivity of the self constitutes its uniquely human character, distinguishing it from the mode of existence of other organic entities. To state this is not to argue that only man is self-related, but rather that only man is conscious of his self-relatedness. When a being is conscious of being related to itself, the reflexivity takes on a new meaning and is constituted as subjectivity. Consciousness of one's relatedness to oneself is a necessary condition for the existence of a subject. Thus it is not a matter simply of the human subject's being conscious of a relatedness which is altogether independent of his consciousness, but that in being self-conscious a unique mode of reflexivity is constituted. If self-consciousness were epi-phenomenal, the difference between man and other organic beings would be relatively insignificant. They would not differ in their basic mode of existence, but only in their mode of awareness. The unique self-awareness enjoyed by man conditions his reflexivity in all of its aspects and, thus, endows his existence with special ontological characteristics. To be a man is to be a self, and to be a self is to be a subject. The peculiar reflexivity exhibited by subjectivity is the ultimate point of reference for all aspects of human existence.

In thinking of self-consciousness it is important not to identify it, as is too often done, with the passivity of intuition. Very frequently we conceive of consciousness on the model of seeing, as if it were an evanescent quantity. On this view, consciousness is dissociated from active processes and regarded as if it were contentless. We need to remind ourselves that feeling, thought, volition, and even physical action are, for the human subject, phenomena of consciousness. We are most intensely conscious of our world when we are most actively engaged with it, and most acutely self-conscious in those moments when we are most involved with ourselves. Neither consciousness nor self-consciousness is a passive and contentless mode of intuition. Intuition is at most one factor in consciousness and always a derivative factor. Anxiety, for example, is a phenomenon of self-consciousness though it is not and has not generally been regarded as a mode of intuition. Even Immanuel Kant, who placed so much stress upon the role of intuition in knowledge, insisted that intuition is possible only through what he termed "self-affection." Philosophers have too often been misled by their own abstractions and nowhere more than in the case of consciousness. Because it is possible to distinguish a content or a process from the awareness of the content, they have sometimes concluded that the awareness is separable from its content. Actually consciousness is never a mere awareness of a content. A necessary condition for my awareness of an object is the multiple determination of myself in relation to the object. Similarly, my self-consciousness requires and is constituted by the various ways in which I determine myself. Each new level of self-awareness involves a new type of self-determination, the complexity of self-consciousness is no less and no greater than the complexity of the self.

The point I have tried to make is that it is not only self-consciousness that is reflexive but the self as a being. We must not lose sight of the double truth that self-consciousness constitutes the reflexivity of the self even as it is constituted by it. To affirm only the one or the other of these propositions is to bifurcate self and self-consciousness and to misunderstand the nature of conscious awareness by identifying it with the passivity of intuition. The relation of the reflexivity of the self to the reflexivity of self-consciousness is reciprocal and necessary. To allow the reflexivity of self-consciousness is necessarily to acknowledge the fundamental reflexivity of the self.

If to be a man is to be a subject and to be a subject is to be reflexively related to oneself, we have found an ultimate ontological basis for human responsibility. Man is responsible, in the first instance, because he is burdened with the ontological necessity responding to himself in the sense of having to answer to himself for what he is and does. The first as well as the last problem man encounters is his own existence. To be is not simply to be liable; it is the original human liability. It is not so much death or even freedom that we dread and seek to escape, but our responsibility to ourselves. We must answer to ourselves not only for what we do but for what we are. Whatever may have been the ultimate origin of our existence, we find that it is now in our own "care" *(Sorge)*. It is something to be cared for and to be cared about. This "care," which Heidegger regards as the most basic feature of human existence, is not psychological or moral but ontological. No man can escape it, since the only way to avoid it would be to make oneself not to be—a power which man as a finite being does not possess. As Kierkegaard pointed out, instead of providing an escape from responsibility, suicide requires a man to take supreme responsibility for himself. Even if it were the final end of his being, which remains problematic, suicide would remain an expression of man's ultimate concern about himself. Only highly intensified concern about oneself could drive a man to attempt his own destruction.

To be a man, then, is to be responsible to oneself for oneself. To state this is in no wise to recommend what a man *ought* to be in some ideal sense, but simply to state what he *is* and *must be*. This reflexive relation founds an ought, a moral ought, but does not in itself constitute a normative ought. The original necessity involved in man's ontological responsibility is more accurately expressed by a *must* than by an *ought*. To be concerned about oneself is not a matter of choice but of fate. It is not a resultant of choice but a condition of choice. In its original ontological mode, responsibility is the *necessity of caring for oneself*, of *answering to oneself for what one is and does*. All other modes of responsibility reflect and express this basic ontological accountability of the self to itself.

It may seem that to make this claim is either to state an altogether trivial point with no significant consequences, or else to smuggle concepts into the analysis which are pregnant with normative meaning. I admit straightaway that the point is obvious enough if one only looks at the human situation, and not only obvious but undeniable. I cannot imagine how anyone could deny it or even consider it without exhibiting responsibility for himself. If, however, the point is obvious, the claim must be innocent of concealed normative implications. In stating that a man *must* care for his existence in the sense of presiding over his own destiny, we are not claiming or even suggesting that he *should* be concerned about himself. At this stage of the analysis there are no explicit or implicit norms involved. To ask whether or not man ought to be responsible for his existence is to ask whether or not he should have been created as he is. I do not propose to ask this kind of normative ontological question, for I see no way of answering it.

If, then, man's ontological concern for his existence does not in itself constitute moral responsibility, how does it found such responsibility? To answer this question it is necessary to consider the problematic features of man's reflexivity. Human existence is, as we have noted above, problematic. Although there are certain factual conditions of his existence which the individual is fated to live with, he must determine what he is to do with and about them. There is no single aspect of man's empirical nature which is not problematic. No matter what his endowments may be, a man may respond to them in a variety of possible ways. And these possibilities can never be finally catalogued until the last human subject has ceased to exist. The individual determines himself as a self in the way that he responds to his own facticity. The fact that he has physical appetites does not in itself determine what sort of person he is to be, for he must decide whether they are to be expressed and if so, how. The most significant fact about man is not that he has sexual appetites, for example, but what he does with them. He must respond to his factual nature, do something with and about it. The fact that he can and must respond to himself in this fashion constitutes his original freedom. *A self is what it chooses to be.* It can be a self only by freely taking over responsibility for itself.

Choices, once made, become part of the individual's facticity and, hence, further materials for decision and response.

Insofar as it is reflexive and problematic to itself it is evident that the self exhibits a fundamental negativity. Sartre has expressed this negativity in a deliberately paradoxical way by stating that "the self *(pour-soi)* is what it is not, and is not what it is." In stating it this way Sartre plays on the ambiguity of the "is" involved in the two parts of the assertion. It is clear from the context of his discussion that even for Sartre the self is and must be identical with itself and, hence, must include both terms of the negation. I am the self that I am not, for only in being it can I not be it. If this seems paradoxical, it is only because the negation is of a *particular mode* of my existence and not of myself as a *totality.* What Sartre wishes to express is that I am not simply identical with myself in the way that a stone is self-identical. My body is mine and constitutive of my existence; yet, I transcend my body in being related to it at all. It is perfectly proper for me to say that I *have* a body while denying that I *am* a body. To affirm the latter would be falsely to reduce myself to a body.

But, we may ask, what does this negativity have to do with responsibility? The negation, we have seen, requires a positive relation of the self to itself and, thus, expresses one feature of the basic ambiguity of human existence. I am and I am not myself at one and the same time in clearly definable ways. Again, this is a condition of volition rather than a result of it. At any time when I choose or make a decision it is on the basis of this fundamental ambiguity. I must respond to myself in the mode of my facticity and the way in which I respond determines what I am to be. But this is a free response which allows wide choice. Through my volition the ambiguity of my situation is made determinate, but it is my volition and action alone which make the determination necessary.

To see how an ought may be founded by man's ontological responsibility, we can ask first: how is an imperative possible for man? Suppose, for example, that I regard it as morally necessary to care for my own body in the sense of securing its health and well-being. The "ought" here is of a different order from the original necessity pertaining to existence, for it may express that which I do not do rather than what I do. I may neglect or abuse my body instead of taking care of it. The "ought" then expresses the discrepancy between what I actually do and what I should do. This is, in fact, most generally the case with ought statements. We think of an imperative only when there is either an actual or a possible discrepancy between what we are doing and what we should do. We would never, I think, use an ought statement where a state of affairs followed naturally and necessarily. As the linguistic analysts have claimed, ought statements are always used to recommend either to ourselves or to others. And it makes sense to recommend an action only if there is some question as to whether or not the action will transpire.

To state that I ought to care for my body in the sense of nurturing it leaves the question open as to whether or not I do care for it in this sense. I may take care of it and thus do what I ought to do, but, if so, it is because I choose to care for it and might have chosen otherwise. The "ought" expressed in the statement is, then, a normative ought. But we must be careful not to conclude too hastily that it is a pure normative statement with only a contingent connection with the facts of existence. We have noted earlier that every man does and must care for and about his body in so far as it is an integral part of his existence. For him to be able not to care for his body in this ontological sense it would be necessary for it not to be his body—which is obviously impossible. It cannot both be and not be his body, and since it is his body it constitutes an object of his concern. We have, then, at least two senses of "care" here, namely caring for and about in an ontological sense and caring for and about in a normative sense. If our analysis is correct, the first is unconditionally necessary in allowing no options, whereas the second is ontologically contingent. Moralists would ordinarily distinguish between the two types of necessity as metaphysical/ontological and moral. And they would usually regard it as a mistake to attempt to derive a moral necessity from an ontological necessity, or normative statements from descriptive statements. Since we have admitted that the affirmation of man's original concern about his existence is a pure descriptive statement, how can it provide a foundation for the imperative of moral obligation? In other words, what has man's inescapable *ontological liability* to do with an alleged *moral liability* to care for one's body in a normative sense?

In spite of the striking difference between the two imperatives, if we may call them that, they have certain equally apparent similarities. In the first place, they both represent modes of liability which require a reflexive relationship of the self to itself. Moreover, both express a particular type of liability, namely concern for one's body. If we look more closely at the "ought" statement, we find that it reflects and presupposes the descriptive statement. If I tell myself that I ought to take care of my body I surely presuppose that it is my body and, further, that it is an object of concern to myself. As a matter of fact, every ought statement assumes this. Ought statements do not in themselves *found* a concern but only *determine* it. To state that I should nurture my body is not to establish concern for my body but rather to specify how I should respond to this concern. My care for my body is, in the ontological sense, ambiguous and problematic. The ought statement prescribes the way in which I should determine this problematic relationship. What I do in the ought statement is to acknowledge the claim which my body makes upon me by being my body. If the ought statement is valid, it can do nothing more than this. Either the fact that I have a body in itself establishes a claim upon me such that I should nurture and affirm it as a vehicle for the realization of my existence, or the moral *ought* commanding this is arbitrary. The moral imperative expresses and must express a *de facto* relationship of the self to itself. So far is it from being a pure normative statement prescribing an ideal, that it actually expresses the ontological condition of the self. Implicit in the statement: I ought to care for my body, is the proposition: I do care for my body. The normative statement is possible only because I can both care and not care for my body. I *must* care in the ontological sense, and the imperative expresses this care even when I do not follow it. But I can *not* care in the sense that I may act contrary to the imperative. I may, in short, act irresponsibly, which means that I may act as if my body were not an object of my care.

The morally conscientious man simply *accepts* his responsibility and acts in conformity with it. The normative ought does not constitute his responsibility simply by laying down an ideal, but only expresses his responsibility. It commands him to care for the body which is in fact an inescapable object of his concern. An *irresponsible* man is clearly a man who is responsible but negates his responsibility. To be *irresponsible* is not to be *non-responsible*, and we commonly recognize this fact, even as we recognize that to be irrational is not the same as to be non-rational. Human beings may be irrational but they cannot be non-rational. Similarly they may be irresponsible but they cannot be non-responsible.

Kierkegaard has described despair as a "disrelationship" within a relationship. We might borrow his term and describe irresponsibility as a disrelationship within a relationship. A man who does not care for himself in the way that he ought to is a person who is disrelated to himself. Such a disrelationship is a form of self-alienation. The ought statement expresses either the actuality or the possibility of this alienation and recommends that it be surmounted. It represents the claim of the self upon itself to acknowledge and affirm itself in the fullness of its being. The call of conscience issues from the depths of the self and thus expresses man's original ontological responsibility. A man can be disrelated to himself only because he is related to himself. The original relatedness founds the possibility of the disrelationship and, hence, of the norm. I have a body which is an integral part of my existence, but I may act as if it were not mine, as if it were simply a thing or an object in the world. To act on the latter assumption is to deny that I am what I am and, hence, implicitly to affirm a falsehood. To assume my responsibility for myself and make it the principle of my action is to exist in the "truth"; to refuse it is to exist in "error." Truth may not be, as Kierkegaard claimed, subjectivity, but truth is surely possible in the mode of subjectivity. To take responsibility for oneself is an essential condition of the "truth" of subjective existence. Truth and moral value are not so disparate as philosophers have sometimes believed.

We have discovered thus far that man is liable in two fundamental ways, namely ontologically and normatively, and, further, that the two modes of responsibility are closely related. The first mode of liability posed no serious problems since no claim was made for its normative status. It was seen to be unconditionally necessary but non-normative. The second mode appears to be just the opposite, namely, normative but wholly contingent. We have not yet seen how the one may found the other. Why does the fact that I am ontologically concerned about my body entail that I ought to take care of it? The answer is, I think, that the normative ought expresses the ontological necessity of care for one's body in the light of one's freedom to disregard and abuse it. Although the normative ought is not a mere reiteration of the original concern for one's body, it is based upon and expresses this fundamental concern. Moreover, it depends for its validity entirely upon the ontological liability. This situation need not be puzzling if we take into account the fact that the normative ought only expresses the necessity of responding to one's facticity, only states the claim which this facticity makes upon one's freedom. No matter how I act I am accountable to myself for the way in which I respond to the claims made upon me by the facts of my existence. If I disregard these claims, my action establishes a "disrelationship" or "aliena-tion" in myself which manifests itself in the form of *guilt*. All guilt is based upon a disrelationship and, hence, is provided by the ultimate reflexivity of the self. Guilt is the awareness of a claim which is not acknowledged. The fact that we feel guilt at all is possible only because our existence continues to make claims upon us even when we refuse to acknowledge them.

A normative claim in the form of an obligation may be first in the order of our awareness, so much so that we may won-der if it has anything to do with the facts of our existence. It may seem to us that we are engaged exclusively in attempt-ing to pursue an ideal. The truth is, however, that the ideal appears to us as an ideal only because of our freedom. The normative ought expresses a relationship of the self to itself as the possibility for a disrelationship. Since the relationship is always prior and derives from our existence, it is never abrogated by the disrelationship. The norm has a binding power upon us even when we act irresponsibly, precisely because we never cease to be responsible for and to our-selves. In other words, moral irresponsibility is possible only because of our ontological responsibility. Kant saw this point with admirable clarity in insisting that the imperative of morality is categorical and unconditional. He saw, further, that it is and must be rooted in the very being of the self. He was mistaken in attributing the force of the imperative to our rational nature. But his insight went deeper than this, for in the formulations of the imperative he made it clear that moral responsibility is ultimately the liability of the self to itself as a subject or, in his terms, as a person. Reason discov-ers and promulgates the law of morality, but it does not constitute it. One is always tempted to ask of Kant: why should I be rational? Kant recognized that an argument is required to show that to be responsible is to be rational in one's conduct. The argument can be supplied only if appeal is made to the facts of self-existence. I cannot escape the imperative of morality only because I cannot escape myself. Even if we were to affirm the synthetic proposition that responsibility entails rationality we would still need criteria of rationality. And such criteria can be supplied only by appeal to the conditions of human existence.

The ontological liability of the self founds moral responsibility for the reason that the ontological conditions of our existence are, also, conditions of our freedom. My moral obligation to myself is a constitutive characteristic of my existence and, in a broader sense, ontological in character. The ought of morality expresses a relation of obligation of the self to itself. If the obligation did not obtain as a real liability, the ought would be an illusion. It is either categorical or no moral responsibility at all. The larger and more inclusive concern of the self includes moral concern. Man is as much a responsible being as he is a rational being. The possibility that the moral ought can appear only as an ideal or that it can appear as an ideal at all depends upon the fact that it may not be fully constitutive of my existence. In other words, it may found a disrelationship or alienation within the self. In the latter instance there is a discrepancy between a claim made upon me and the way in which I act. Action and principle do not conform in that I act as if the principle were not binding upon me. But the discrepancy is a discrepancy within the self in two of its modes. The ought continues to express a basic feature of my existence even when I disregard it. In expressing an actual claim of the self upon itself, the ought is constitutive of my existence. In being repudiated, it continues to be constitutive in that the claim continues to be valid and, even more important, to found the resultant disrelationship and guilt. But in the latter case the ought is constitutive in a deficient mode. The ought is then the measure of my disrelationship to myself.

For purposes of simplicity we have limited ourselves thus far to the analysis of self-responsibility, though responsibility is by no means limited to the reflexivity of the self. In fact, the self would not be a self if it did not exist in a world with other selves. Hence our discussion has offered a somewhat artificial representation of the self as an isolated being. We need not, I think, give up anything that has been said, but it is important to consider the situation of man vis-à-vis the world in order to understand adequately even his responsibility to himself.

In the case of self-responsibility I have maintained that the ultimate condition is the reflexivity of self-existence. I have interpreted responsibility in this context as itself a mode of relatedness of the self to itself. If we enlarge the context to include other beings, we might expect the same fundamental conditions to obtain. And this is indeed the case. If to exist at all is to be responsible, to exist before other beings and together with them in a world is to be liable to them. To state that we must reckon with other beings in our world is to state the most obvious fact imaginable and, yet, a fact of the greatest importance for an analysis of responsibility. *To have a world at all is, like existing, a liability.* If we sometimes desire to be rid of ourselves, at other times we desire to be rid of the world. Both of these fundamental human desires manifest themselves in everyday life and in psychoses. Some individuals try to rid themselves of their world by withdrawing from it, depriving it of all meaning, attempting to cancel it out. They live as if they had no world at all. In exaggerated form they express a normal human concern about the world and, above all, the liability which it poses for man. Responsibility for living in the world may become so dreadful that it is too much for an individual to cross the street, to ride in a train, to confront another human being. Surely no argument is required to show that to live in the world is a liability and a responsibility. And, like our original self-responsibility, it is ontological. We are all concerned about our world even though we may express our concern in different ways. The world makes demands upon us by the mere fact of its being there before and around us. I am concerned that the stars should not fall in, the sun cool off, the automobile run me down, in short that the world be orderly and meaningful. I am oriented toward my world both in general and specific ways. My world-orientation is inseparable from the organization of my subjectivity. If I am mad I can have only a mad world and, if my world is mad, I can only reflect this madness in my subjective existence. A self without a world would be no self at all. As Heidegger describes it, the self is a "being-in-the-world."

That the world is something to be reckoned with, no one would deny. Our plans and aspirations are contingent upon the course of the world. The farmer is most aware of this contingency as it pertains to weather and climate, the financier as it pertains to markets and business cycles. Every man in his own way calculates the probable course of events and adjusts his plans accordingly. But insofar as it is merely this sort of reckoning that is involved in our responsibility as a being-in-the-world, we have discovered no claims made upon us by other beings. Or have we? We have, at least, been forced to reckon with the world and this means to take into account the course of world events. To reckon with the world means not merely to make such calculations but, further, to make appropriate adjustments in the light of them. It would be foolish for a New England farmer to plant his crops in mid-January. If he persisted in actions of this type we would have no hesitation whatever in declaring him irresponsible. And he would be correctly judged irresponsible for the simple reason that he had failed to take into account the world in which he lives.

In using the term "appropriate" with respect to the farmer's action, a double reference is involved. There is, on the one hand, the process of nature which determines climate and, on the other hand, the plans of the farmer. For his action to be appropriate it must exhibit a proper response to both factors. He is no less irresponsible if he fails to consider his own needs and desires than if he ignores the weather. A claim is made upon the farmer by natural processes even though it is qualified by his own plans. As such, the claim is only hypothetical: mind the weather if you would harvest your crops! If he were not a farmer but the pilot of a space-ship, he would reckon with the heavens in a different way. Because of his changed objectives, nature would make differ-ent demands upon him. In each case his purposes would determine which natural factors were relevant for his calcu-lations. Human objectives are highly variable and man's orientation toward the world is largely pragmatic. What con-stitutes appropriate and responsible action in the concrete case is a function of these variables. Yet some objectives one must have and, thus, in one way or another one must respond to the surrounding environment. Appropriateness of re-sponse is necessarily a function of the world one confronts. Every man must exist in the world and, thus, contend with it. And he cannot do this entirely on his own terms. He is responsible for acknowledging the other beings in his world, in the first place, and, in the second place, for knowing what they are. Knowledge is essential for responsible action, since it is through knowledge alone that man can hope to relate himself appropriately to the objects in his world.

The will to truth is based upon the the will to acknowledge what is. The possibility of knowledge presupposes both that there is a world to know and that man is related to this world. Being and the relation to being are prior to truth in all of its modes. To be in a state of objective error is to *mis-take* the world, to *mis-appropriate* it. Viewed objectively, error is a type of disrelation to objects in the world. It is for this reason that error and ignorance are of serious import. I am related to the objects in my world and as they are. This relatedness, again, is a constitutive feature of my existence. I am liable both for acknowledging the objects to which I am as a matter of fact related and, further, for recognizing the nature of my relationship to them.

There is, then, a mode of ontological responsibility toward

objects in the world which is constitutive of the human condition. Even as my own existence constitutes a liability, so, too, does the existence of objects in my world. Whatever I do, I cannot evade this basic responsibility. As in the case of self-responsibility, this original relatedness grounds the possibility of an objective irresponsibility. I can act toward objects in ways that either ignore their existence altogether or misrepresent them. If I act deliberately in this fashion, my action is irresponsible in that it is not appropriate to the nature of the objects involved. To treat a dog, for example, as if it were incapable of feeling pain is to regard it as if it were like a stone. We ordinarily recognize that it is irrational and intellectually irresponsible to assert that a dog is a stone, but we do not always recognize that an action which entails such a false proposition can be equally mistaken and irresponsible. In my assertion I am cognitively disrelated to my world; my assertion is false because it misrepresents what is and, hence, puts me in a false relation to it. By the same token my action is in error because it is not consonant with the world of actuality. The action implies that dogs have no capacity for feelings. If, to justify my action and thus render it responsible, I need to represent dogs as other than they are, my action is without warrant and hence morally wrong. It is evident, I think, that cognitive error and moral error are not so unrelated as is often maintained. Both involve misrepresentation of objects and both involve a relation toward objects which is inappropriate. Objects are what they are initially in full independence of our actions and beliefs. We are originally related to them as they are and can never alter this basic ontological relation. It is this original relation that provides a measure for inappropriate and appropriate action toward objects.

Because of its humanism, the Western philosophical tradition in ethics tends to neglect man's responsibility toward natural objects. We assume all too easily that such objects are present in our world only to be used as we see fit. Regarding man as the supreme end of creation, we feel justified in our action so long as the use we make of natural objects affords us pleasure and satisfaction. I do not intend to pursue the very complex question here as to human responsibility toward creatures of the natural world. But it is evident, I think, that if we are to justify our conduct as responsible in the normative sense, we must evaluate it in the light of the objects in our natural world and our original relation to them within nature. Whether we acknowledge it or not we are liable toward the natural world both ontologically and morally.

In the second formulation of the Categorical Imperative, Kant states that we ought to treat others as ends in themselves and not merely as means. Kant means that we should treat others as morally responsible subjects like ourselves. This formulation is intended to express the pure ought of moral obligation. But if I ask: Why should I treat others as ends-in-themselves? the answer must be: Because they are ends-in-themselves. Kant's ethics has and requires a metaphysical foundation, as he well knew. We cannot understand how we should treat either ourselves or other persons until we understand what it means to be a person. The ought expresses, as I have indicated earlier, an ontological reflexivity in the subject and, secondly, an ontological relation to other men. If I ask: How should I treat another man? the answer Kant gives is: As a man. This is only a formula, to be sure, and a highly abstract formula at that. But it affirms the fundamental requirement of morally responsible action toward other human subjects. We might state the matter even more formally in this fashion: so act toward others that your action is appropriate to the existence of the other. Surely this is both an absolutely necessary condition of responsible action toward others and an instructive principle for determining action. Discrimination on the basis of race is immoral and irresponsible for the reason that it misrepresents the members of another race. It is precisely for this reason that racial discrimination is inevitably accompanied by such elaborate rationalization. For the practice of discrimination to be justified the facts need to be different from what they are. No more eloquent testimony of the awareness of human responsibility can be found than in the urge to rationalize one's conduct. Rationalization is, after all, but a deficient mode of justification. If legitimate reasons cannot be given, the best one can do is to offer pseudo-reasons.

As with ourselves, we are liable to others both morally and ontologically, and the former liability is founded by the latter. I could have no moral responsibility to another man if he did not exist and, further, if I were not related to him. I am in fact related to him as father or brother, neighbor or employer, stranger or friend. We are never related to other human beings simply in the abstract. It is always to some individual that we are related and the particularity of his existence is a factual determinant of the situation. The other makes a claim upon me not only by confronting me as a person but as this particular person. There is, in other words, a facticity with respect to other persons, a concrete determinateness, which is as important as my own facticity. I had nothing at all to do with the fact that I was born of human parents or of these particular parents. Yet from the first moment of my existence the parent-child relationship is constitutive of my existence in its social dimension; it establishes a problem for me so long as we both exist.

It is doubtful if even in a culture whole-heartedly devoted to progressive education any single child has managed to remain completely unaware of the liability of child to parent. Parents have a way of asserting their claims upon their children and of making these claims directly felt. The child is quite literally answerable to the parent for its conduct; it must give an account of itself. But this accounting does not consist solely in the child's measuring his action by the parent's yardstick. The child learns very early to justify his aberrant behavior by reasoning with his father. He is quick in detecting *arbitrary* demands made upon him and in countering them with what he regards as appropriate standards. In challenging the parent the child is asking that the parent justify his demands. With what right, he asks, are these claims made? To act responsibly toward a parent does not entail doing everything that is specifically demanded, since unjustifiable claims may be made upon the child. The child appeals in its challenge to the father as a father and quite properly assumes that the father is a responsible agent. In questioning a specific demand, the child is not necessarily questioning the authority of the father or denying that it has a responsibility toward the father as a parent. It may, of course, persuade itself that it is in no way accountable to the father, but, in the latter case, it will not feel required to justify or to discuss its action with its father. The situation is complicated by the fact that, as with all social relations, responsibility is shared. Justice requires that both parent and child recognize and abide by their responsibilities. Freud has said that the death of his father is the most important single event in a man's life. This may overstate the case, but it hardly exaggerates the importance of the role of the parent in the life of an individual. The problem of the father-relation which has become so prominent in psychoanalysis is not merely a psychological problem. It has, also, moral and ontological dimensions. A sense of disrelatedness to the father is often at the core of psychic distress. The psychical disturbance has both moral and ontological roots in that it reflects both an awareness of the constitutive character of the parent-child relationship and the requirements it imposes for appropriate action. The initial task is that of clarification, which may require what is termed "depth-analysis." The individual is required not only to recollect the decisive events of his relation to the parent, but to grasp the significance of the relationship itself. His recollection must recover the meaning of his own being in relation to that of the father so that he can make a new beginning in understanding and interpreting the relationship. The fact that the problem first appears as an inner conflict is in no way surprising, since to be disrelated to another person is inevitably to be disrelated to oneself. Analysis must reveal the true source and scope of the conflict. It is important to note, however, that clarification is not, in itself, enough to eradicate the disturbance. At most clarification can place the individual in a position to determine freely and responsibly what the father-child relationship is to mean to himself. The decision is all the more serious in that it determines in part, also, what the relationship can mean to the father. No one of us can unilaterally determine the meaning of our relationships with others. If we could, life would be far simpler and our responsibility far less demanding.

Other persons make claims upon us and thus make us liable to them by existing in our world. In the most general terms they demand that we acknowledge them and treat them as persons. This is a demand, incidentally, which no man can forfeit by his own volition. No man can, for example, by selling himself as a slave make himself not to be a person. The relationship of master and slave which assumes this to be possible is founded upon a double deception. The slave fools himself no less than he fools the master; both fool themselves as well as each other. A man remains a man no matter what his condition in the world. He may not demand in any verbal way that he be treated as a man; in fact, he may even recommend that his humanity be disregarded. But the fact that he continues to exist as a man entails that his claim upon us as a human subject has not been removed. We are responsible for acting toward him not only in terms of what he says he is but in terms of what he in fact is. I can no more escape my responsibility toward the other because he regards himself as a slave than I can escape my responsibility toward myself by looking upon myself as a slave. A slave is, by definition, a human subject who is *made to be* simply a tool for the service of others. But no man can actually make himself or another to be merely a slave; he can only make him play the role of a slave. It is not difficult to exhibit the deception and bad faith involved in such a relationship. The other must be treated as a man in order to be kept in the position of slavery, and this fact alone reveals the deception.

It is crucially important to take account of the full dimension of human existence in analyzing our responsibility to others. If, for example, we were to accept the cultural situation as exhaustively determinative of human beings, we would be perfectly justified in treating some men merely as slaves. Culturally viewed, such men might be said to be only slaves. Hence, responsible action would require only that I treat any one of them in a way appropriate to his station in life. A slave would be only a slave, a criminal a criminal, and an aristocrat an aristocrat. To live responsibly would be, as some people actually regard it, to treat each man in a way befitting his cultural situation. And this is, in fact, what conventional morality sanctions. It is, on this view, justifiable to abuse criminals, to exploit slaves, and to defer to the gentry. If we take into account only explicit or voiced claims, conventional morality is more or less satisfactory. But if we refuse to identify the *existence* of a man with the *role* he plays and refuse to deny that he is capable of transcending his appearance as a cultural object, we cannot be content with conventional morality. No man can be identical with his appearance in the way that a stone is simply a stone. To transcend oneself is an a priori characteristic of all human subjects. However wicked a man is, he cannot be simply the embodiment of wickedness in concrete form. The reason is that he has always the possibility of repentance. Curiously enough, those who are most ready to make an absolute judgment upon the wicked man are the first to rejoice at his reform.

We are responsible toward others, then, not simply in terms of their empirical nature but, also, their existence. We are related to others in this twofold way and must take both factors into account if we are to act responsibly toward them. We are accountable to them even as we are accountable to ourselves. Initially as well as continuously it is the fact of their existence which constitutes our liability. But it is, also, their response to us. Other people are continuously presenting us with the necessity for responding to their overtures. They invite our friendship or elicit our scorn. All human relationships have a contractual foundation insofar as they are based upon a reciprocity of response. If another person invites my friendship he makes me liable toward him in a special way. Whether or not I accept his invitation, I am obliged to take account of it in my response to him. I may, of course, be insensitive and not perceive the meaning of his gesture. But if I do perceive it, it makes a claim upon me—not to offer my friendship in return, necessarily, but at least to respond to him as one who has exhibited friendliness toward me. If, however, I do accept his invitation, our relationship has been constituted as a friendship. We are now related to each other within the context of this implicit contract. That we have become friends is a factual characteristic of our mutual situation. For either of us to act toward the other as if this were not the case would be to act irresponsibly.

The social contract theory of the state has recognized the contractual nature of human relations but has too often stressed the formal and political side of it. Marriage is a formal contractual relationship between two people in our society, sanctioned by both state and church. But it represents also a moral contract. The recognition of common-law marriage, for example, acknowledges that more basic contractual relationship involved. Contracts may be broken off on grounds which are valid both legally and morally. But it is one thing to sever a contract for cause and another to pretend that none exists. We do not need to appeal to special moral intuitions in order to know that promises ought to be kept. Such an intuitionist theory as that of Sir David Ross treats ethical norms as if they were divorced from factual situations. It is the fact that one has entered into a contractual relationship with another person which makes it mandatory that promises be honored. To understand what a promise is, is to know to what one has obligated oneself. No special moral intuition is required to understand the commitment involved in promise making. Legal contracts are simply more formally and meticulously defined commitments sanctioned by the laws and authority of the state.

The possibility of a political order depends upon the fact that man is a social being. The establishment of an explicit political order simply formalizes and institutionalizes the reciprocal relatedness of members of a community. For the most part, the individual is born into a fairly developed political order. He has probably had no part in constituting it or in determining its laws and institutions. This fact makes it difficult for some men to understand why they are responsible to this order. They fail to understand what Socrates knew full well, namely that to be born into and develop within a civilized society is to participate in the contractual relationship of the political community. One need not be a Hegelian advocate of an organic and monistic state to recognize this point. One need only take note of the fact that the political order is as fundamental for him as the familial and social order. His original political responsibility is based upon his participation in a community of civilized men. He may choose to be exiled and renounce his citizenship but, as Socrates saw with great clarity, to do so is a responsible political action which must be carefully weighed. It was simply a fact for Socrates that he was a citizen of Athens, as much a fact and as important a fact as that he was a teacher. He could not justify his action simply by an appeal to an abstract norm. Could he have done that, his problem would have been easy and his conscience untroubled. In his analysis of the situation Socrates appealed both to the social and political community of which he was a member and to the explicit demands being made upon him by its official representatives. He defended himself in terms of what they ought to expect of him in their capacity as responsible members of the community. He did not take their pronouncements as the last word in specifying his responsibility as a citizen, but appealed to the contractual foundation of the state in rejecting their claims. Socrates regarded himself as a loyal citizen of Athens even in disobeying its orders, and rightly so. But even in his disobedience he did not fully reject the authority of the political order, for he accepted his imprisonment, and, to the distress of his friends, drank the hemlock. It might be argued, of course, that Socrates would have been fully justified in choosing exile. But, whatever may be said on that point, the fact remains that the evaluation of his action would require consideration of his participation in the Athenian state.

It is impossible to assess political responsibility adequately without an understanding of the nature and origin of the state. It is necessary to understand not only the authority of specific laws but the source from which this authority itself is derived. There are both bad laws and unwritten laws, and politically responsible behavior requires that both be taken into account. We see easily enough that the fact that something is prescribed by law does not make it *morally* right but not so easily that it does not necessarily make it *politically* right. Moral norms have a certain priority over political norms in that they are concerned with the responsibility of men as men. But there are, also, political norms which derive their authority not simply from the constitution of particular states but from the nature of the political community as such.

We have seen that in the case of all of our relations with others, be it as individuals or as members of an organized community, explicit demands are made upon us which are frequently accompanied by sanctions. If we do not hand over our purse to the thief we may be shot, and if we do not obey the speed limit we may be deprived of our license. These are concrete demands upon us and constitute recognizable hazards. But they do not constitute the whole or even the most important part of our responsibility. We may seek to outwit the thief and disarm him, but we are liable for the way in which we treat him. We are not justified in shooting him on the spot in retribution, nor in subjecting him to punishment without due process of law. The important fact is, however, that the law itself is but a rough and approximate statement of our responsibility toward the other. Fortunately, the greater part of our conduct does not require explicit legislation but follows of itself, else the task of making and enforcing laws would be an impossible undertaking. The other person has political rights which may or may not be stated in a constitutional document. These rights are nothing more than the claims which he makes upon us simply by participating with us in a political order. *They are a priori and unconditioned in that they would necessarily be asserted in any political order whatever.* Ultimately these rights follow from the humanity of the citizen. To deny them is in effect to deny that the community is a community of men. No change in explicit rules can erase these claims and absolve us from the responsibility to honor them. No man can be deprived of his rights as a human being, though he may be treated as if he made no such claims upon us. *To state the requirements of a just political order is but to affirm those conditions which lie at the foundation of any political order.* The normative ought derives from the contractual relatedness, both original and historically developed, of men. The ought is not here, any more than in the case of personal morality, simply expressive of an ideal, but is definitional of a situation which factually obtains. *It characterizes our liability and, hence, the condition of our political freedom.*

Throughout this exposition I have stressed the ontological and factual basis of responsibility, insisting that responsibility in the normative sense is founded upon responsibility in the ontological sense. Our liability is initially a *condition* rather than a *consequence* of our decisions. Insofar as we respond to our initial situation we constitute for ourselves further determinate contexts which qualify our liabilities in new ways. In our dealings with others the responses take the form of more or less formal contractual relations. As such, they are factual determinants of our social and political existence. It is mistaken, I believe, to divorce moral responsibility from political responsibility or to divorce either, normatively conceived, from factual liabilities. To understand human responsibility in all of its aspects it is necessary to consider man's total involvement with himself and others in the world. We may, for certain purposes, concentrate on some one aspect of his involvement but never without a certain measure of artificiality. The ultimate responsibility is existence itself. To exist means to be in a world, and in a social as well as a natural world. *Man is a responsible being, personally, naturally, socially, politically.* He may live irresponsibly in any or all of these contexts, but he cannot live non-responsibly. To be in a position to assess the explicit claims which are made upon him, he must understand the basic structure on which these demands are predicated. He must, in other words, have an ontological as well as an empirical understanding of himself, of nature, and of the social and political order.

11

Human Dignity

GABRIEL MARCEL

If it is possible for me to take an over-all view of the spiritual journey I have undertaken to describe in this book, I am tempted to think now that the year 1936 marked a decisive turn in my life. In May 1936, a new government was formed, known as the Popular Front. The failure of this coalition cannot be denied by anyone today. One sign of this failure was the fact that Léon Blum and his associates not only were unable to avert the threat of war already existing at that time, but undoubtedly by their illusions and their weakness contributed to making the conflict inevitable. Besides, it should not be forgotten that Léon Blum declared in 1932 that Hitler would never be able to seize power. It can be asserted now that a clear-sighted statesman, aware of the

Note: Reprinted by permission of the publishers from Gabriel Marcel, *The Existential Background of Human Dignity*, pp. 114–35. Cambridge, Mass.: Harvard University Press, Copyright, 1963, by the President and fellows of Harvard College.

danger presented by Hitlerism, could have held the Führer back and perhaps driven him to suicide. It is true that the Rhineland had been remilitarized before Léon Blum came to power. But the same spirit of surrender was to be found in everyone, with the exception of a few Rightists whose influence was almost nil at that time; and that spirit of surrender was concealed only by an anti-Fascist rhetoric in which no clear intelligence could place any trust.

This reference to the political events of that period may be surprising in the present context. Yet it seems indispensable. For, thus confronted by historical circumstances which I think I am in a position to say I felt immediately as exceptionally grave, my prospective thought, as always on the dramatic and not specifically philosophic level, began to experience what it is no exaggeration to describe as a change of focus. By this I mean that the anthropological problem, considered of course in its ethical aspect, became for me at that time increasingly acute.

It could not be said, however, that there was a complete break in my evolution. The dramas of ambiguity which I analyzed in the preceding chapter presuppose and at the same time give evidence of a complete reappraisal of the human being as such. It may even be said that if we compare *Le Chemin de crête* with *Un Homme de Dieu*, the evolution which I am trying to clarify here is already apparent. *Un Homme de Dieu* closed with a prayer, an anguished appeal to Him who alone knows me as I am: in other words, the theocentric reference remained explicit there. This is no longer the case in *Le Chemin de crête*. The heroine, having reached the stage of being absolutely in the dark about her own nature and her own worth, no doubt appeals to invisible powers to come to her assistance, but she has not even a name for them, and perhaps she no longer considers them distinct from the noblest parts of herself. The truth is that Ariane will never escape from the labyrinth. Liberation for her can be effected only through the medium of the written word, diary-writing, an extremely illusory liberation by which not even she herself can be deceived.

In this play, one can already hear, though still rather faintly, disturbing echoes of the events of the outside world, and it is possible to imagine that the uneasiness felt by all the characters without exception, though in no way explained by the increasing confusion on the political scene, is, however, an expression of this confusion and, as it were, a microcosmic projection of it.

But *Le Dard*, written a few months later, during the first weeks of 1936, and therefore slightly before the events which I have just recalled, includes a specific reference both to the Hitler threat, which had been constantly growing in the three previous years, and to the evolution which was becoming more apparent among Leftist intellectuals, the very ones who were to champion the Popular Front. But need I say that this evolution was not to stop after the terrible hiatus of the war and the Occupation? *Le Dard* develops the theme to which, fifteen years later, I was to give articulate expression on the philosophical level in the introduction to *Les Hommes contre l'humain*[1] entitled "L'Universel contre les masses." I wish to point out here that my original intention was to give this title to the whole book. I yielded, however, to the wishes of my publisher, who, of course, thought it lacked commercial appeal. Today, however, I feel that the title under which the book appeared, *Les Hommes contre l'humain*, is much less faithful to my essential purpose.

And so we come, at the end of the singularly tortuous path we have followed, to the central problems I had stated at the beginning of this book and which, under various forms, will, almost without interruption, be our primary consideration to the very end. It is actually on the essence of human dignity that the conflict in *Le Dard* is focused, and this conflict is between Professor Eustache Soreau and the German singer, Werner Schnee.

As is almost always the case, I find it difficult to be very precise about the origin of this work. The few preparatory notes I was able to lay my hands on do not enable me to find out from where, as we say in French, "l'idée est sortie." It should be pointed out that the word "sortir," when applied to a thought, has always a somewhat vague meaning and corresponds to a metaphor which cannot be made explicit: that of a light suddenly issuing from darkness. All I can say with certainty is that in a certain essayist of the Left, who came from a family of very modest means, I thought I had sensed or, at any rate, imagined, the bad conscience which is the distinctive characteristic of my hero. A book recently published by this writer makes me think that in reality he resembled my Eustache Soreau much less than I thought, for it reveals that, unlike the hero of my play, he had a Christian upbringing.

It is of course necessary to keep in mind here my central observation: otherwise, the references to my dramatic works, as I have said repeatedly, lose all their significance. No more here than elsewhere did I start from abstract ideas to be dramatically illustrated afterwards. In other words, I did not have in mind two different or even opposite conceptions of man and of his essential dignity. On the contrary, this opposition took shape in relation to the two central characters and to the concrete situation in which they are involved. It should be further understood that the spectator (or the reader) is urged to go beyond the particular case presented to him in order to find its essential significance. We may add that this significance is in the strongest sense of the word an historical one; that is to say, it cannot be fully perceived without reference to the events which were to follow. Thus, the final scene of the play anticipates the great drama which was to take a more precise form after the end of the second World War, and whose denouement we today are still unable to foresee. I might note in passing that the play, performed for the first time in Paris in 1937, was presented by the students of the University of Brussels in 1949, as I recall, and it seemed so close to present-day issues that many were surprised to learn that it had been written before the war.

Eustache Soreau, as I have said, belonged to a Parisian family of very modest means. An excellent and hard-working student, he has won scholarships, distinguished himself in examinations and *concours,* and is presently teaching in a Paris lycée. He has been the tutor of a wealthy politician's son and has married his pupil's sister, Béatrice Durand Fresnel. His father-in-law, who congratulates himself on having given his daughter to an impecunious young man, has used his political influence to advance Soreau's academic career. So Eustache has been lucky. He acknowledges the fact and even speaks of it repeatedly with a feeling of bitterness verging on exasperation. An acquaintance of his, Gertrude Heuzard, a girl who was a militant worker with him in the ranks of the Socialist party and who lost her teaching position for having carried her revolutionary propaganda into the classroom, never stops showing Eustache, by insinuations and caustic allusions, that she looks upon him as a turncoat, hating him for allowing himself to become a bourgeois. By marrying into a rich family, he has betrayed the class to which he belonged —the working class. Eustache's mother, on the other hand, a good but somewhat vulgar woman, whose mental capacity is that of a concierge or a charwoman, treats her daughter-in-law with almost servile respect, which makes Eustache angry. He is hypersensitive; his bad conscience gnaws at him, as evidenced by his violent outbursts whenever he expresses his anti-Fascist convictions. I was very much interested in showing that success—a certain kind of success—may become a source of resentment. Similarly, a friend of mine, recently returned from countries in Dark Africa formerly belonging to the French Union, told me that the natives there appeared to her deprived of a revolution, frustrated and bitter because they had received as a gift what apparently they would have preferred to snatch, like spoils after a battle.

Sometime before, while a lecturer at the University of Marburg, Eustache had known a young German, Werner Schnee, who had become his friend. The latter is a singer of lieder, an artist capable of interpreting with delicacy and depth the great German Romantic composers. But his accompanist, Rudolf Schonthal, who is a Jew, has received shameful treatment at the hands of the Nazis and has been forced to leave Germany. In a gesture of solidarity, Werner also has left his native country, to the great displeasure of his wife Gisela, who claims she is not interested in politics any more than she is interested in "that ugly Jew with the protruding ears." The Soreaus have opened their home to Werner and his wife. The young singer has just come back from Switzerland where his friend Rudolf is dying, a victim of Nazi cruelty.

But cohabitation will bring out into the open the latent hostility between Eustache and Werner.

Every opinion and every judgment of Eustache Soreau is inspired by his desire to remain in line with a certain class ideology. And indeed his constant desire not to betray the social milieu of his birth may appear a noble thing in principle. But it will soon be discovered that this preoccupation is vitiated, as it were, by his bad conscience. Toward Béatrice whom he loves, however, and who has deep affection for him, his conduct is unjust and almost hateful; he blames her for supporting the cause of the privileged bourgeoisie which he despises. But, though probably not blind to her parents' shortcomings, she has no desire to break her ties with them. Between her family and her husband she tries to be a steadying influence in a rapidly worsening situation. With a clearsightedness not unmixed with deep compassion she follows the progress of the sort of moral disease from which Eustache is suffering: a guilty conscience.

Werner Schnee, by leaving his homeland, has shown his horror of Hitlerism; yet for his part, he wishes to remain independent of all parties, whatever they may be. Eustache

reproaches him for not associating with the other German
political refugees, but it is because he does not wish to develop a refugee mentality, which would be distasteful to him
as a kind of uniform like any other. Eustache accuses him of
being an individualist. But this is only a label, and Werner
dislikes all labels. Above all, he intends to remain a man—a
word which grates on Eustache's nerves. We have here a
fundamental point. Werner despises what he calls ideology.
He sees that if his friend likes Beethoven, it is because he
ascribes to the German composer a democratic ideology very
similar to his own. Now, whatever Beethoven's political opinions may have been, they have nothing to do with his genius,
which is all that matters. For his genius is an integral part of
his humanity—that is to say, his way of touching the hearts
of all men. It is in this respect that he is universal. In the eyes
of Werner, however, the partisan spirit he finds in Eustache
is exactly the opposite of this kind of universality. Werner
accuses him of judging others, not on their intrinsic qualities
but according to the category into which they fall. Needless
to say, Eustache reacts vigorously to the way in which
Werner judges him, and hostility grows between the two
men. What makes it worse is the fact that Eustache vaguely
feels his wife's sympathy for Werner and his jealously is
aroused. Finally Eustache commits a shameful act. Werner
has told him in the strictest confidence that an emissary from
the Hitler government has come to him with a proposal that
he return to Germany where he would be offered an engagement in an opera house on condition that he give his alle-
giance to the political regime. He has refused, of course. He
would have disgraced himself by accepting such an offer. Yet
he has refrained from telling his wife Gisela about it; she
would not have understood. Yielding to some shameful impulse, Eustache discloses to the young women the secret
entrusted to him by Werner. She flies into a rage when she
learns that they could have returned to Germany. They separate, and the wife eventually joins a German baron who has

been courting her for some time and with whom she will be able to return home without any difficulty.

Thus Eustache, always obsessed by the idea of treason, treason to his class—that is, to an entity—betrays a real human being, one he used to call his friend. Werner is generous enough to give his wife the little money he has left; he will soon be reduced to poverty. From every side, to be sure, he receives invitations, because he has the gift of arousing sympathy. But he refuses to make use of this gift to derive material advantage from it. A scruple the nature of which he himself is unable to understand prevents him from drawing any profit from the ability he has of touching men's hearts, as if he, too, had fallen a prey to a *guilty conscience,* to such an extent that he wonders if in a certain mysterious way he has not been tainted by Eustache. However, this guilty conscience prompts him to do something heroic, a thing that some will call the act of a madman. He, too, is going to return to Germany, but without the passport offered by Hitler's henchmen. He knows from now on what his fate will be: he will be arrested, and this is what he wants because he suddenly realizes that this gift, this favor of grace, which has been granted to him, he may find useful in helping the unfortunate political prisoners with whom he will mingle. Here let us understand clearly that there can be no question for him of political affiliation since he will continue to the end to be a nonpolitical man. What counts for him is the fact that those political prisoners are unfortunate, innocent people who are being shamefully treated. He will bring to them at least the benefit of his presence, of the music that lives in him and that can be bestowed as charity. There is also another reason for this decision: Werner has come to realize that Eustache was right in suspecting him and that, in fact, he is in love with Béatrice. And as the latter in turn has serious grievances against Eustache, since out of spite he has finally become the lover of the bitter and resentful Gertrude, Werner feels that if he remained in France, neither she nor even he himself could resist temptation. By his decision to return to Germany under the conditions I mentioned, he sets up before her an insurmountable obstacle. And this is what he explains to Béatrice in the last scene of the play—to Béatrice, who finds it difficult to rise with him to such heights. More than that, his leaving under such circumstances appears to her as a kind of suicide. "Not in the least," Werner objects, "suicide is a crime . . . I am simply putting myself at the disposal . . ." "Of what?" asks Béatrice. "Of the cause? Of the revolution?" "I am not interested in the cause," he says emphatically, "I am interested in men." And as he senses that perhaps Béatrice is going to weaken and abandon to his fate the husband she despises, he appeals to her: "You cannot leave him. You must always remember that you are the wife of a pauper . . . Poverty is not lack of money or lack of success. Eustache has had money, he has had success. He has remained poor and grown poorer still. No doubt he will never be cured of his poverty. This is the greatest evil of our time; it spreads like a plague. No physician has yet been found to treat it. It cannot even be diagnosed. Perhaps the artist will be spared, even if he starves. And also the true believer who can pray . . . All other people are in danger."

> *Béatrice.* You ask me to live with a leper.
> *Werner.* Leper colonies are going to multiply here on earth, I fear. To very few people will grace be granted to live there, knowing they are among lepers and yet not finding them repulsive. Much more than grace, they will need a viaticum to sustain them on their way.
> *Béatrice.* I am not brave enough, Werner, I assure you.
> *Werner.* You will think of me, as I think of Rudolf. Later on I shall be in you a living presence, as Rudolf still is in me. You will remember then what I told you here a few weeks ago. If there were only the living, Béatrice . . .[2]

The words he spoke were these: "If there were only the living, I think life on this earth would be quite impossible."

But all this calls for a commentary which penetrates to the core of what I wish to make clear in the course of this book: what *is* this poverty which is neither lack of money nor lack of success and which, we are told, is going to spread like leprosy? It might be said, I think, that it is the spirit of abstraction which finds in our own day—and we must not hesitate to say so—its most terrifying though not its only incarnation in communism. But this spirit of abstraction cannot be separated from a certain lack of love, and by this I mean the inability to treat a human being as a human being, and for this human being the substituting of a certain idea, a certain abstract designation. The leper colonies which are going to multiply on earth (let me recall that this was written in 1936) are the popular democracies, to the extent that they are committed to the spirit of abstraction in its Marxist form. But we must hasten to add that any technocracy, even if it belongs to the capitalist system, can be guilty of the same fundamental error. When it goes so far as to consider the individual within the framework of society as a mere unit of production and to judge his worth only in terms of productivity, it also tends to create communities of lepers, however attractive their outward aspect may be. When, for example, I see huge buildings being erected on the outskirts of Paris, impersonal, merciless structures, not for human beings to dwell in (for "to dwell" still has a human connotation) but to be "incorporated into," I have the immediate and almost physical feeling of this universal threat which today weighs upon human beings, so that, after passing through these suburbs where everything changes before our eyes at such amazing speed, I have even gone so far as to say that it was already the setting up of a communist society.

Here, the reader may very well raise an objection to the abrupt and arbitrary manner in which his attention has been diverted from the very particular cases which I have treated in my plays to a wholly general situation which refuses to be confined within the limits of such specific cases. He may well question, for example, what possible connection there is between a guilty conscience and technocracy. Undoubtedly, this would appear to be a strong objection; but I shall say only that anyone who raises the objection places himself on a plane which is, as a matter of fact, altogether different from mine, not only with respect to my plays, but also with respect to the existential philosophy which I have tried to develop since I began my independent thinking.

It is of course obvious that if one remains in the realm of notions, it is quite impossible to extract from an idea such as that of technocracy or, for that matter, of any social regime considered in terms of its distinctive characteristics, anything resembling what I have called a guilty conscience. But what matters to me is not technocracy taken in itself, since it is still, after all, an abstraction, but rather what it tends to do to the individuals who will have to live under it. Moreover —and this is of the utmost importance—the world we live in, which is also the world of my plays, is one in which technocracy does not reign supreme. Technocracy is felt as a distant threat, and at the same time as a spirit tending more and more to inform life. A character like Eustache cannot be separated from this context, namely, that of a changing society in which the class struggle as Marx had conceived of it, within the framework of a society moving towards industrialization (such as it appeared to that remarkable observer), the class struggle, let me repeat, tends to be replaced by very different relations, infinitely more subtle and less rigid springing from the fact that a certain section of the bourgeoisie joined the proletariat and that a very large portion of the proletariat formed a bourgeois class. Now if I were asked why I made Werner Schnee a singer—Werner, a man struggling for the universal against the masses—I would answer that my motives for that choice became apparent to me a posteriori,

and always for the same reason, because I did not pass from
the abstract idea to the concrete, but rather the reverse. A
singer like Werner Schnee is, essentially, an unselfish, dedicated person, since the task to which he has devoted his life
consists in making available to others the work of the great
creative artists: Werner is a mediator, as any instrumentalist
would be, but mediation here is more evident and vital than
in any other case, because the voice is part of the human
being, much more so than an instrument such as a violin or
a piano. It could also be said that the spiritual climate of
Werner is admiration. The question for him is to use this
power within him to serve what he admires and, in effect, to
make it admirable to listeners—but, needless to say, not just
any listeners. In this domain there is no room for just *anybody*, since there are people to whom an art will always
remain something alien—because of a *disgrace* whose nature
and significance actually escape us. It is a fact that we simply
have to accept. And the existence of these "outsiders," or,
more exactly, these Boeotians, does not detract from the
universality of the message, for this universality, in terms of
logic, must be conceived not in extension but only in comprehension. In an interpreter like Werner Schnee, the self, it
would seem, tends to be absorbed in the inspired act of serving the beautiful work of art, which does not mean, of course,
that vanity can be excluded from it. Such is the nature of the
human being that this vanity can force its way in anywhere,
as a kind of corrosion. But we can safely say that the conditions leading to a perfect interpretation tend in some way to
preclude this intervention. This is most certainly true in the
case of Werner Schnee, and the sympathetic feeling he inspires in those around him can surely be ascribed to the fact
that he exists as little as possible for himself. In that, by the
way, he may be likened to the believer. We may recall Werner's words to Béatrice quoted earlier: the artist will probably be safe from this disease of poverty as well as the true
believer who can pray. In either case, salvation comes from

transcendence, even if, here and there, it takes on very different aspects; and this transcendency, as we shall see more and more clearly, is closely related to universality.

It may be necessary here to return to what I meant by admiration. It is not enough to say that it has been of tremendous importance in my own life, and that, for me, the inability to admire is the supreme misfortune. I have always felt that admiration was of the same order as creation, that undoubtedly it was even a sort of merciful dispensation by which those who have been denied the gift of creating visible things can nevertheless reach the level on which the creative spirit reveals itself. The idea of a relationship between admiration and creation may be surprising at first, because it would seem that people tend to confuse creation and production. Yet it could be said, generally speaking, that any production depends on a technique and that creation, on the contrary, is of a meta-technical order. This may seem at first a purely verbal distinction. But what I have tried to show is that in reality any creation is a response to a call received, and it is receptivity that we should stress here while pointing out that a serious error is made whenever receptivity and passivity are confused, as it seems to me they are in Kant, for example. This idea, which I discussed for the first time in a study included later in the volume entitled *Du refus à l'invocation,* belongs therefore to approximately the same period as *Le Dard*, and the relationship is as clear as can be between *Le Monde cassé* and *Position et approches concrètes.* I shall quote a passage from this essay which is directly related to the idea of active or creative receptivity:

We already find in the process of acquiring knowledge the paradox which is at the heart of creation proper, but this paradox may perhaps be more easily detected in the artist than in the areas where knowledge is elaborated and where the pragmatic in all its forms comes to cover up the initial mystery of the *naissance-au-réel* (becoming aware of the real) whose depth is essentially unfathomable. The artist appears to himself as sustained by the very thing he tries to incarnate. Thus in him the identification of receiving and giving is finally effected. But this can be achieved only in his own particular sphere corresponding in this register to the *area* such as I described it when I analyzed the *chez soi*. There is every reason to believe that there is no difference of nature but merely a difference of power between the ability to feel and the ability to create; both presuppose not only the existence of a *soi*, but of a world in which the *soi* recognizes itself, exercises and spreads itself; a world in between the closed and the open, between *having* and *being*, and of which my body appears necessarily the symbol or the materialized nucleus. But we are entitled to suppose that we are grossly deceived by appearances in our hypostasis when we treat as independent, circumscribed reality what may be only the emergence of some measureless kingdom whose submerged regions and underwater ramifications can be sighted only accidentally and by sudden illuminations. Might not the very fact of living, in the full sense we give the word when we speak of our own life, of human life, imply for one who would go to the heart of the matter, the existence of a metaphysical Atlantis, unexplorable by definition, but whose presence actually gives our own experience its dimension, its value, and its mysterious quality?[3]

It would be appropriate, of course, in the perspective we have adopted here, to state more explicitly what was treated in this passage in allusive and metaphorical terms. The difficulty is, however, that what we are considering could not in all likelihood be conceptualized without contradiction. For the concepts can be formed only from the sphere which lies, as I have said, between having and being. And it could be said that thought, when it comes to these obscure shores, uses a method of approach entirely different from the one it uses when it applies itself to knowing or even to understanding something. I need hardly say that here we find again, though at a deeper level of experience, what has been said earlier about participation. But what I wish to emphasize is that a careful examination of active receptivity can help us formulate our conception of man and of what we have called human dignity. Indeed, the time has come to deal squarely with this notion of dignity.

We must admit that in current phraseology what is called the dignity of the human being is described in terms of Kantism (here, by the way, reduced to its simplest expression). I refer to the idea according to which the inalienable value of man lies in the fact that he is a rational being, that stress is placed on his faculty of understanding and comprehending the intelligible order of the world, or rather on his faculty of conforming to certain maxims considered as universally valid. To my mind, there can be no question of challenging the legitimate value of such an interpretation. Yet, at the same time, it seems to me difficult to deny that during the last hundred years or so this rationalism, respectable as it may be, has lost much of what can be termed its vitality, as if it had gradually loosened its hold on men's minds. And the development of the philosophy of existence in its various aspects, and also, we might add, of the philosophy of life espoused by Bergson and his followers, could not be understood without this increasing lack of interest in a form of thought threatened by the dangers of formalism.

It is my own profound belief that we cannot succeed in preserving the mysterious principle at the heart of human dignity unless we succeed in making explicit the properly sacral quality peculiar to it, a quality which will appear all the more clearly when we consider the human being in his nudity and weakness—the human being as helpless as the child, the old man, or the pauper. Here we should consider a paradox which appears at first glance to be extremely embarrassing.

Do we not run the risk, as a rule, of letting ourselves be deceived by what I would like to call a decorative conception of dignity—and the word "dignity" here is significant—which we more or less confuse with the display of pomp that usually accompanies power? It is considered advisable, for example, to surround the judicial power with appearances and conditions likely to command respect, or, if one prefers, to put a certain distance between men entrusted with high duties and ordinary people. It would be an error, certainly—perhaps even an aberration—to deny the necessity of enhancing, even by artificial means, the value of certain institutions when these assume, in any degree whatever, the character of a sacerdotal function. But at the same time there is always the fear that, *humanly speaking*, this pomp may conceal only emptiness and deceit—and if so, it can be truthfully said it turns against itself, as it were, and finally in the eyes of the critical observer deals a crushing blow to its own authority. This remains true even if we leave aside such things as uniforms or pompous display to consider only the attitudes, the solemn tone of voice, the gestures: these, as often as not, may arouse in the one who remains "outside" a questioning attitude which can easily turn into challenge and revolt.

It is in this line of existential thought that rationalism, it seems to me, shows its weakness, a weakness that the men of the present day can hardly fail to notice. It is as if we had become more and more aware of the fact that reason may become sham and parody. But considerations of another kind point in the same direction: it can be said that our times will have witnessed what I might readily term a gradual secularization of reason, a functional treatment tending more and more to reduce reason to a series of technical operations depending on a descriptive science. Around it there is hardly anything left of the aura which still accompanied the word *Vernunft*, for example, for Kant and his followers. I do not claim, however, that this process of reduction can ever become exhaustive enough to leave nothing deserving attention or even respect; I am in my own mind deeply convinced of the contrary. But I doubt that the language of the traditional rationalist philosophy, as it was in the past, is capable of conveying to the mind of modern man this reality which one might be tempted to call residual, and which undoubtedly must be described as both immediate and secret. These two words seem to contradict each other, but the contradiction, if we pause to reflect, appears inherent in what we call the sacred.

The phenomenologist, Emmanuel Lévinas, in a recent treatise entitled *Totalité et infini*,[4] showed, I think, great insight in this, by stressing the irreducible originality of what he calls the "face to face," that is to say, how the other person's face appears to me. He thinks—and I am strongly tempted to go along with him in this—that the otherness we speak of here can in no way be reduced to the one which a dialectic of the Hegelian type can, through conflict, finally reduce to identity. Here, otherness presents a consistency which is wholly lacking in the world of objects or objectifiable data. I shall not examine here the way in which Emmanuel Lévinas tries to avoid the pluralism such a position may seem to imply. It is rather surprising that in designating a person who is "other" but who, at the same time, presents himself to me to be not only confronted but greeted, he does not use the term which seems to me the only adequate one—"neighbor." We should note that this word takes its full meaning only when preceded by the possessive adjective, the possessive in this case no longer being used to claim ownership.

It goes without saying that here again we find—doubtless at a deeper level of experience—what has been said earlier of the vocative "thou." It is in a philosophy centered on the second person that the words "my neighbor" come to have meaning.

It is apparent, on the other hand, that from the experience implicit in the words "my neighbor" we are drawn almost imperceptibly to the affirmation of a fraternity. But here we come to an important point which we have no right to overlook. In principle I can call "my brothers" only those born of the same father as I. Brotherhood, or fraternity, implies a common sonship. And everything leads one to think that the first French revolutionists, when they laid at the very foundation of the Declaration of the Rights of Man, liberty, equality and fraternity—in their eyes an indivisible unit—were actuated by an underlying deism which was later to be questioned. It may seem paradoxical that the inscription "Liberty, Equality, Fraternity" appears on all public buildings in an officially "laique" country where, for a long time, the belief in a God who is Father of all men has been purely a matter of choice. Under these conditions, fraternity has become nothing more than an "as if": men must behave toward one another *as if* they were brothers. What we see here is only a vague aspiration or perhaps a dim nostalgic feeling for a past era when fraternity was an article of faith. The situation respecting equality is quite different, since this word expresses an exigency which tends to be more and more institutionalized, considerably more attention being given, incidentally, to rights than to duties and obligations. But a very important question can be raised here, one which has been in my mind since the end of the second World War and which has also been approached, though in an indirect manner, by an Austrian who has been residing in the United States since the last war and has taught in American universities. I refer to Count Kühnelt-Leddihn and to his book, *Liberty or Equality*.[5] It is, of course, on the conjunction *or* that the stress is placed. As for me, without knowing anything at that time of the writings of Count Kühnelt-Leddihn, I had, for the first time in Lisbon in 1949, attempted to show that, contrary to the belief of the men of 1789 and their innumerable followers, there would appear to exist between equality and fraternity a secret opposition connected with the fact that these two exigencies stem from two different sources. As

I have already noted, equality is essentially the claiming of something; it is, in the fullest sense of the word, ego-centric. I am your equal, his equal, or their equal. Probing further, we would not have any difficulty in finding, after Nietzsche and Scheler, the presence of resentment at the heart of equality. It must, of course, be added that this presence, which is not, and in a sense cannot, be ascertained, remains hidden under a rational or pseudo-rational camouflage. There is no reason why I should not be your equal; it would be even irrational to admit that I am not.

One would have to show further by what processes one passes from evident equality in certain rights to equality that is much less evident in all rights, to the supposed equality of the subjects themselves, this equality of all men—supposing the word has a meaning, which is exceedingly doubtful—justifying the equality of rights.

But with fraternity, it seems to me, the case is very different. Unlike equality, fraternity is essentially hetero-centric: you are my brother, I recognize you as such, I greet you as my brother. It is certainly evident that the reverse is possible here. It may happen, if I am wronged by you, that I have to remind you reproachfully that, after all, I am your brother. But this is only a derived case. And, further, it is very likely that in such an event I would address these words of blame to you in the name of my rights trampled upon by *you*—that is, in the name of equality much more than of fraternity. But if we focus our attention on the act of expansive recognition forming the basis of fraternity, it will be seen as a spontaneous movement exactly the reverse of the claim implied in equality: you are my brother and, because you are my brother, I rejoice not only in anything good which may happen to you but also in acknowledging the ways in which you are superior to me. Why should I feel the need of being your equal? We are brothers through all our dissimilarities, and why should these dissimilarities not imply inequalities in your favor—surely I shall not say to my detriment—for, since we are brothers, it is exactly as if the radiance emanating from your gifts, acts, and works were reflected on me. This I shall express perhaps if I say very simply: "I am proud of you," which indeed would be meaningless, even impossible, if I were intent on being or on showing myself your equal.

But here I should close what may well be regarded as a long parenthesis: everything we have said leads us to think that if human dignity can today be fully recognized without our necessarily falling into the old groove of abstract rationalism, it is on condition that we place ourselves in the perspective of fraternity and not of equalitarianism. Here I must return to a thought I may have conveyed earlier in this discussion. I think it would be wrong, or at any rate unwise, to claim that human dignity is the concern only of those, whatever their form of worship may be, who explicitly recognize God as Father of all men, this dignity appearing as the very mark of the *imago dei*. Or, more exactly, I feel that such a position could not be accepted purely and simply, although there cannot be any question of explicitly rejecting it. To accept it would be to make light of the fact that an unbeliever—I do not say an atheist, since the term does not fit in this context—may, in fact, have a keen and exacting sense of human dignity and give in his actions the most irrefutable proof of it. I do not have in mind particularly those who are against injustice and oppression in speech only, for such a verbal protest is of doubtful value, except when it involves risks for the one who formulates it. What I am thinking of, rather, is an active interest in the oppressed, whoever they may be. And in practice this interest does imply the consciousness of a fraternal relationship with those very people who are to be defended. Shall we say that those unbelievers entertain, in spite of everything, a belief in God as a father, a belief which remains concealed under their opinions as free-thinkers? In this connection, I myself have dwelt on the important fact that each of us can be mistaken about what he thinks he believes and what he actually believes. And, if this is so, then belief is really a mode of being and can by no means be likened to an opinion, that is, to something one possesses.

I feel, however, that one should not go so far as to interpret this in an apologetic sense. As for the unbeliever, I should prefer to say this: insofar as he truly possesses the militant character I have just described, he has an active and even poignant experience of the mystery inherent in the human condition and in everything in it which is hazardous, precarious, and, at the same time, tragic. And what we discover in this line of thought is compassion, in the strongest sense of the word, and consequently to the degree that it implies in the person who feels it nothing at all resembling a feeling of superiority. This would amount to saying, then, that dignity must be sought at the antipodes of pretension and rather on the side of weakness. Here again, as I have done so often, I shall quote the words of one of my characters, Arnaud, at the end of *Les Coeurs avides*. His father is a man who seems to be always speaking "to the gallery," in a dogmatic and somewhat solemn manner and, as a result, he himself is the only one deceived by this verbal pomposity intended to impress his audience. In this final scene, he yields to weariness and dozes off. His son, Arnaud, a devout Christian, in whom the spirit of a child still lives, meditates before the sleeping old man: "It won't be long now," he says to himself, "before all these sentences he has been delighting in will be lost in silence. This affectation he takes so seriously will fall from him. He will remain here alone, weak and defenseless, like a child overcome by sleep and still clasping his toy to his breast. When in the presence of the living man who rants and raves, if only we could imagine him lying cold in death tomorrow."

Here we have a contrast which I find especially illuminating for the thought I have tried to bring out in this chapter —the contrast between an affected dignity which, because of its affectation, becomes the very antithesis of dignity, and the inalienable dignity inherent in the condemnation which is the fate of every man from the very fact of his birth. And here lies a paradox whose meaning deserves to be clarified.

At first sight, one might be tempted to say that the fact of man's mortality makes not only his acts but also his being appear ridiculously insignificant. And we must admit that contemporary man is only too prone to follow this line of thought. Now the moment the insignificance of the individual is declared, the way is paved for all forms of tyranny and especially for those which operate today behind a screen of democratic phraseology. But the remarkable thing is that this way is not the only one, and even more remarkable is the fact that within us something builds up to resist this disintegration and downward course. We shall have to determine more clearly and precisely the significance and nature of this resistance, but even now it should be sufficiently clear that this resistance is founded, not on the affirmation of the self and the pretensions it exudes, but on a stronger consciousness of the living tie which unites all men.

NOTES

1. See *Man against Humanity* in Author's Works Cited.
2. *Le Dard*, Act III, scene viii.
3. *Du refus à l'invocation*, pp. 123–24.
4. The Hague: Martinus Nijhoff, 1961.
5. Erik Maria von Kühnelt-Leddihn, *Liberty or Equality: The Challenge of Our Time*, ed. John P. Hughes (London: Hollis & Carter, 1952).

IV

The Existential Conditions
of Politics

12

A Note on Machiavelli[1]

Maurice Merleau-Ponty

How could he have been understood? He writes against good feelings in politics, but he is also against violence. Since he has the nerve to speak of *virtue* at the very moment he is sorely wounding ordinary morality, he disconcerts the believers in Law as he does those who believe that the State is the Law. For he describes that knot of collective life in which pure morality can be cruel and pure politics requires something like a morality. We would put up with a cynic who denies values or an innocent who sacrifices action. We do not like this difficult thinker without idols.

He was certainly tempted by cynicism: he had, he says, "much difficulty in shielding himself" from the opinion of those who believe the world is "ruled by chance."[2] Now if humanity is an accident, it is not immediately evident what would uphold collective life if it were not the sheer coercion

Reprinted from *Signs*, trans. Richard C. McCleary (1964), pp. 211–23, by permission of Northwestern University Press, Evanston, Ill.

of political power. Thus the entire role of a government is to hold its subjects in check.[3] The whole art of governing is reduced to the art of war,[4] and "good troops make good laws."[5] Between those in power and their subjects, between the self and the other person, there is no area where rivalry ceases. We must either undergo or exercise coercion. At each instant Machiavelli speaks of oppression and aggression. Collective life is hell.

But what is original about Machiavelli is that, having laid down the source of struggle, he goes beyond it without ever forgetting it. He finds something other than antagonism in struggle itself. "While men are trying not to be afraid, they begin to make themselves feared by others; and they transfer to others the aggression that they push back from themselves, as if it were absolutely necessary to offend or be offended." It is in the same moment that I am about to be afraid that I make others afraid; it is the same aggression that I repel and send back upon others; it is the same terror which threatens me that I spread abroad—I live my fear in the fear I inspire. But by a counter-shock, the suffering that I cause rends me along with my victim; and so cruelty is no solution but must always be begun again. There is a circuit between the self and others, a Communion of.Black Saints. The evil that I do I do to myself, and in struggling against others I struggle equally against myself. After all, a face is only shadows, lights, and colors; yet suddenly the executioner, because this face has grimaced in a certain way, mysteriously experiences a slackening—*another anguish* has relayed his own. A sentence is never anything but a statement, a collection of significations which as a matter of principle could not possibly be equivalent to the unique savor that each person has for himself. And yet when the victim admits defeat, the cruel man perceives another life beating through those words; he finds himself before *another himself*. We are far from the relationships of sheer force that hold between objects. To use Machiavelli's words, we have gone from "beasts" to "man."[6]

More exactly, we have gone from one way of fighting to another, from "fighting with force" to "fighting with laws."[7] Human combat is different from animal combat, but it is a fight. Power is not naked force, but neither is it the honest delegation of individual wills, as if the latter were able to set aside their differences. Whether new or hereditary, power is always described in *The Prince* as questionable and threatened. One of the duties of the prince is to settle questions before they have *become insoluble* as a result of the subjects' emotion.[8] It would seem to be a matter of keeping the citizens from becoming aroused. There is no power which has an absolute basis. There is only a crystallization of opinion, which tolerates power, accepting it as acquired. The problem is to avoid the dissolution of this consensus, which can occur in no time at all, no matter what the means of coercion, once a certain point of crisis has been passed. Power is of the order of the tacit. Men let themselves live within the horizon of the State and the Law as long as injustice does not make them conscious of what is unjustifiable in the two. The power which is called legitimate is that which succeeds in avoiding *contempt* and *hatred*.[9] "The prince must make himself feared in such a way that, if he is not loved, he is at least not hated."[10] It makes little difference that those in power are blamed in a particular instance; they are established in the interval which separates criticism from repudiation, discussion from disrepute. Relationships between the subject and those in power, like those between the self and others, are cemented at a level deeper than judgment. As long as it is not a matter of contempt's radical challenge, they survive challenge.

Neither pure fact nor absolute right, power does not coerce or persuade; it thwarts—and we are better able to thwart by appealing to freedom than by terrorizing. Machiavelli formulates with precision that alternation of tension and relaxation, of repression and legality, whose secret is held by authoritarian régimes, but which in a sugar-coated form constitutes the essence of all diplomacy. We sometimes *prize* more highly those to whom we give credit: "A new prince has never disarmed his subjects; far from it, he hastens to arm them if he finds them without arms; and nothing is shrewder, for henceforth the arms are his. . . . But a prince who disarms his subjects offends them by leading them to believe that he mistrusts them, and nothing is more likely to arouse their hatred."[11] "A city accustomed to freedom is more easily preserved by being governed through its own citizens."[12] In a society in which each man mysteriously resembles every other, mistrusting if he is mistrustful and trusting if he is trustful, there is no pure coercion. Despotism calls forth scorn; oppression would call forth rebellion. The best upholders of authority are not even those who created it; they believe they have a right to it, or at least feel secure in their power. A new power will make an appeal to its adversaries, provided that they rally around it.[13] If they are not retrievable, then authority will lose half its force: "Men must either be won over or gotten rid of; they can avenge themselves for slight offenses, but not for serious ones."[14] Thus the conqueror may hesitate between seducing and annihilating the vanquished, and sometimes Machiavelli is cruel: "the only way to preserve is to lay waste. Whoever becomes master of a town which has begun to enjoy freedom and does not destroy it should expect to be destroyed by it."[15] Yet pure violence can only be episodic. It could not possibly procure the deep-seated agreement which constitutes power, and it does not replace it. "If [the prince] finds it necessary to punish by death, he should make his motives clear."[16] This comes down to saying that there is no absolute authority.

Thus he was the first to form the theory of "collaboration" and rallying the opposition (as he was the first, moreover, to form that of the "fifth column"), which are to political terror what the Cold War is to war. But where, it will be asked, is the profit for humanism? It lies first of all in the fact that

Machiavelli introduces us to the milieu proper to politics and allows us to estimate the task we are faced with if we want to bring some truth to it. It also lies in the fact that we are shown a beginning of a human community emerging from collective life as if those in power were unaware of it, and by the sole fact that they seek to seduce consciousnesses. The trap of collective life springs in both directions: liberal régimes are always a little less so than is believed; others are a little more so. So Machiavelli's pessimism is not *closed*. He has even indicated the conditions for a politics which is not unjust: it will be the one which satisfies the people. Not that the people know everything, but because if anyone is innocent they are. "The people can be satisfied without injustice, not the mighty: these seek to practice tyranny; the people seek only to avoid it. . . . The people ask nothing except not to be oppressed."[17]

In *The Prince*, Machiavelli says no more than this about the relationships between those in power and the people. But we know that in the *Discourses on Titus Livy* he is a republican. So perhaps we may extend to the relationships between those in power and the people what he says about the relationships between the prince and his advisors. He describes, then, under the name of *virtue,* a means of living with others. The prince should not decide according to others; he would be despised. Nor should he govern in isolation, for isolation is not authority. But there is a possible way of behaving which lies between these two failures. "The priest Luke said of the emperor Maxmilian, his master, who was reigning at the time, that he took counsel from no one and yet never acted according to his own opinions. In this respect he follows a course diametrically opposed to the one I have just sketched out. For since this prince does not reveal his projects to any of his ministers, observations come at the very moment these projects must be carried out, so that, pressed for time and overcome by conflicts which he had not foreseen, he gives way to the *opinions* others give him."[18] There is a way of

affirming oneself which aims to suppress the other person—
and which makes him a slave. And there is a relationship of
consultation and exchange with others which is not the death
but the very act of the self. The fundamental and original
struggle always threatens to reappear: it must be the prince
who asks the questions; and he must not, under pain of being
despised, grant anyone a permanent authorization to speak
frankly. But at least during the moments when he is deliberating, he communicates with others; and others can rally
around the decision he makes, because it is in some respects
their decision.

The ferocity of origins is dissipated when the bond of common works and destiny is established between the prince and
his ministers. Then the individual grows through the very
gifts he makes to those in power; there is exchange between
them. When the enemy ravages their territory, and the subjects, sheltered with the prince inside the town, see their
possessions lost and pillaged, it is then that they devote themselves unreservedly to him: "for who does not know that men
are attached as much by the good they do as by that which
they receive?"[19] What difference does it make, it will be said,
if it is still only a matter of deception, if the chief ruse of those
in power is to persuade men that they are winning when
they lose? But Machiavelli nowhere says that the subjects are
being deceived. He describes the birth of a common life
which does not know the barriers of self-love. Speaking to the
Medici, he proves to them that power cannot be maintained
without an appeal to freedom. In this reversal, it is perhaps
the prince who is deceived. Machiavelli was a republican
because he had found a principle of communion. By putting
conflict and struggle at the origins of social power, he did not
mean to say that agreement was impossible; he meant to
underline the condition for a power which does not mystify,
that is, participation in a common situation.

Machiavelli's "immoralism" thereby takes on its true
meaning. We are always quoting maxims from him which

restrict honesty to private life and make the interest of those in power the only rule in politics. But let us see his reason for withdrawing politics from purely moral judgment; he gives two of them. The first is that "a man who wants to be perfectly honest among dishonest people can not fail to perish sooner or later."[20] A weak argument, since it could be applied equally well to private life, where Machiavelli nevertheless remains "moral." The second reason goes much further: it is that in historical action, goodness is sometimes catastrophic and cruelty less cruel than the easygoing mood. "Cesare Borgia was considered cruel; but it was to his cruelty he owed the advantage of reuniting Romagna and its States, and reestablishing in this province the peace and tranquillity it had so long been deprived of. And all things considered, it will be admitted that this prince was more humane than the people of Florence who, to avoid seeming cruel, let Pistoia be destroyed.[21] When it is a question of holding one's subjects to their duty, one should never be worried about being reproached for cruelty, especially since in the end the Prince will be found to have been more humane in making a small number of necessary examples than those who, through too much indulgence, encourage disorders and finally provoke murder and brigandage. For these tumults overturn the State, whereas the punishments inflicted by the Prince bear on only a few private individuals."[22]

What sometimes transforms softness into cruelty and harshness into value, and overturns the precepts of private life, is that acts of authority intervene in a certain state of opinion which changes their meaning. They awake an echo which is at times immeasurable. They open or close hidden fissures in the block of general consent, and trigger a molecular process which may modify the whole course of events. Or as mirrors set around in a circle transform a slender flame into a fairyland, acts of authority reflected in the constellation of consciousnesses are transfigured, and the reflections of these reflections create an appearance which is the proper place—the truth, in short—of historical action. Power bears a halo about it, and its curse (like that of the people, by the way, who have no better understanding of themselves) is to fail to see the image of itself it shows to others.[23] So it is a fundamental condition of politics to unfold in the realm of appearance: "Men in general judge more by their eyes than their hands. Every man can see, but very few know how to touch. Each man easily sees what he seems to be, but almost no one identifies what he is; and this small number of perceptive spirits does not dare contradict the multitude, which has the majesty of the State to shield it. Now when it is a matter of judging the inner nature of men, above all of princes, since we cannot have recourse to courts we must stick only to consequences. The main thing is to keep oneself in power; the means, whatever they may be, will always seem honorable, and will be praised by everyone."[24]

This does not mean that it is necessary or even preferable to deceive. It means that at the distance and the degree of generality at which political relations are established, a legendary character composed of a few words and gestures is sketched out; and that men honor or detest blindly. The prince is not an impostor. Machiavelli writes expressly: "A prince should try to fashion for himself a reputation for goodness, clemency, piety, loyalty, and justice; *furthermore, he should have all these good qualities. . . .*"[25] What he means is that even if the leader's qualities are true ones, they are always prey to legend, because they are not *touched* but *seen* —because they are not known in the movement of the life which bears them, but frozen into historical attitudes. So the prince must have a feeling for these echoes that his words and deeds arouse. He must keep in touch with these witnesses from whom all his power is derived. He must not govern as a visionary. He must remain free even in respect to his virtues. Machiavelli says the prince should have the qualities he seems to have but, he concludes, "remain sufficiently master of himself to show their contraries when it is expedient to do so.''[26] A political precept, but one which could well be the rule for a true morality as well. For public judgment in terms of appearances, which converts the prince's goodness into weakness, is perhaps not so false. What is a goodness incapable of harshness? What is a goodness which wants to be goodness? A meek way of ignoring others and ultimately despising them.

Machiavelli does not ask that one govern through vices—lies, terror, trickery; he tries to define a political *virtue*, which for the prince is to speak to these mute spectators gathered around him and caught up in the dizziness of communal life. This is real spiritual strength, since it is a question of steering a way between the will to please and defiance, between self-satisfied goodness and cruelty, and conceiving of an historical undertaking all may adhere to. This virture is not exposed to the reversals known to moralizing politics, because from the start it establishes a relationship to others which is unknown to the latter. It is this virtue and not success which Machiavelli takes as a sign of political worth, since he holds up Cesare Borgia (who did not succeed but had *virtù*) as an example and ranks Francesco Sforza (who succeeded, but by good fortune) far behind him.[27] As sometimes happens, tough politics loves men and freedom more truly than the professed humanist: it is Machiavelli who praises Brutus, and Dante who damns him. Through mastery of his relationships with others, the man in power clears away obstacles between man and man and puts a little daylight in our relationships—as if men could be close to one another only at a sort of distance.

The reason why Machiavelli is not understood is that he combines the most acute feeling for the contingency or irrationality in the world with a taste for the consciousness or freedom in man. Considering this history in which there are so many disorders, so many oppressions, so many unexpected things and turnings-back, he sees nothing which predestines it for a final harmony. He evokes the idea of a fundamental element of chance in history, an adversity which hides it from the grasp of the strongest and the most intelligent of men. And if he finally exorcises this evil spirit, it is through no transcendent principle but simply through recourse to the givens of our condition. With the same gesture he brushes aside hope and despair. If there is an adversity, it is nameless, unintentional. Nowhere can we find an obstacle we have not helped create through our errors or our faults. Nowhere can we set a limit to our power. No matter what surprises the event may bring, we can no more rid ourselves of expectations and of consciousness than we can of our body. "As we have a free will, it seems to me that we must recognize that chance rules half, or a little more than half, our actions, and that we govern the rest."[28] Even if we come to assume a hostile element in things, it is as nothing for us since we do not know its plans: "men ought never give way to despair; since they do not know their end and it comes through indirect and unknown ways, they always have reason to hope, and hoping, ought never give way to despair, no matter what bad luck and danger they are in."[29] Chance takes shape only when we give up understanding and willing. Fortune "exercises her power when no barriers are erected against her; she brings her efforts to bear upon the ill-defended points."[30] If there seems to be an inflexible course of events, it is only in past events. If fortune seems now favorable, now unfavorable, it is because man sometimes understands and sometimes misunderstands his age; and according to the case, his success or ruin is created by the same qualities—but not by chance.[31]

Machiavelli defines a virtue in our relationships with fortune which (like the virtue in our relationships with others) is equally remote from solitude and docility. He points out as our sole recourse that presence to others and our times which makes us find others at the moment we give up oppressing them—that is, find success at the moment we give up chance, escape destiny at the moment we understand our times.

Even adversity takes on a human form for us: fortune is a woman. "I think it is better to be too bold than too circumspect, because fortune is a woman; she gives in only to violence and boldness; experience shows she gives herself to fierce men rather than to cold ones."[32] For a man it matters absolutely not who is wholly against humanity, for humanity is alone in its order. The idea of a fortuitous humanity which has no cause already won is what gives absolute value to our *virtue*. When we have understood what is humanly valuable within the possibilities of the moment, signs and portents never lack. "Must heaven speak? It has already manifested its will by striking signs. Men have seen the sea half open up its depths, a cloud mark out the path to follow, water spring forth from the rock, and manna fall from heaven. It is up to us to do the rest; since God, by doing everything without us, would strip us of the action of our free will, and at the same time of that portion of choice reserved for us."[33]

What humanism is more radical than this one? Machiavelli was not unaware of values. He saw them living, humming like a shipyard, bound to certain historical actions—barbarians to be booted out, an Italy to create. For the man who carries out such undertakings, his terrestrial religion finds the words of that other religion: *"Esurientes implevit bonis, et divites dimisit inanes."*[34] As Renaudet puts it: "This student of Rome's prudent boldness never intended to deny the role played in universal history by inspiration, genius, and that action of some unknown daemon which Plato and Goethe discerned. . . . But in order for passion, aided by force, to have the property of renewing a world, it must be nourished just as much by dialectical certainty as by feeling. If Machiavelli does not set poetry and intuition apart from the practical realm, it is because this poetry is truth, this intuition is made of theory and calculation."[35]

What he is reproached for is the idea that history is a struggle and politics a relationship to men rather than principles. Yet is anything more certain? Has not history shown even more clearly after Machiavelli than before him that principles commit us to nothing, and that they may be adapted to any end? Let us leave contemporary history aside. The progressive abolition of slavery had been proposed by Abbé Gregory in 1789. It is passed by the Convention in 1794, at the moment when, in the words of a colonist, "domestic servants, peasants, workers, and day-laborers are manifesting against the appointive aristocracy,"[36] and the provincial bourgeoisie, which drew its revenues from San Domingo, is no longer in power. Liberals know the art of holding up principles on the slope of inopportune consequences.

Furthermore, principles applied in a suitable situation are instruments of oppression. Pitt discovers that fifty per cent of the slaves brought into the British Islands are being resold to French colonies. English Negroes are creating San Domingo's prosperity and giving France the European market. So he takes a stand against slavery. "He asked Wilberforce," James writes, "to join the campaign. Wilberforce represented the influential Yorkshire region. He was a man of great reputation. Expressions such as humanity, justice, national shame, etc. pealed from his mouth. . . . Clarkson came to Paris to stir the torpid energies [of the *Société des Amis des Noirs*], to subsidize them, and to inundate France with British propaganda."[37] There can be no illusions about the fate this propaganda had in store for the slaves of San Domingo. At war with France a few years later, Pitt signs an agreement with four French colonists which places the colony under English protection until peacetime, and re-establishes slavery and discrimination against mulattoes. Clearly, it is important to know not only *what principles* we are choosing but also what forces, which men, are going to apply them.

There is something still more clear: The same principles can be used by two adversaries. When Bonaparte sent troops against San Domingo who were to perish there, "many officers and all the men believed they were fighting for the Revolution; they saw in Toussaint a traitor sold to the priests, the émigrés, and the English . . . the men still thought they belonged to a revolutionary army. Yet certain nights they heard the Blacks within the fortress sing *La Marseillaise*, the *Ça ira*, and other revolutionary songs. Lacroix tells how the deluded soldiers, hearing these songs, raised up and looked at their officers as if to say: 'Could justice be on the side of our barbaric enemies? Are we no longer soldiers of republican France? Could it be that we have become vulgar political tools?' "[38] But how could this be? France was the fatherland of the Revolution. Bonaparte, who had consecrated a few of its acquisitions, was marching against Toussaint-L'Ouverture. So it was evident that Toussaint was a counter-revolutionary in the service of the enemy.

Here, as is often the case, everyone is fighting in the name of the same values—freedom and justice. What distinguishes them is the kind of men for whom liberty or justice is demanded, and with whom society is to be made—slaves or masters. Machiavelli was right: values are necessary but not sufficient; and it is even dangerous to stop with values, for as long as we have not chosen those whose mission it is to uphold these values in the historical struggle, we have done nothing. Now it is not just in the past we see republics refuse citizenship to their colonies, kill in the name of freedom, and take the offensive in the name of law. Of course Machiavelli's toughminded wisdom will not reproach them for it. History is a struggle, and if republics did not struggle they would disappear. We should at least realize that the means remain bloody, merciless, and sordid. The supreme deception of the Crusades is not to admit it. The circle should be broken.

It is evidently on these grounds that a criticism of Machiavelli is possible and necessary. He was not wrong to insist upon the problem of power. But he was satisfied with briefly evoking a power which would not be unjust; he did not seek very energetically to define it. What discourages him from doing so is that he believes men are immutable, and that régimes follow one another in cycles.[39] There will always be two kinds of men, those who live through history and those who make it. There are the miller, the baker, and the inn-keeper with whom the exiled Machiavelli spends his day, chatters, and plays backgammon. ("Then," he says, "dis-putes, vexatious words, insults arise; they argue at the drop of a hat and utter cries that carry all the way to San Casciano. Closed up in this lousy hole, I drain the cup of my malignant destiny down to the lees.") And there are the great men whom he reads history with and questions in the evening, clothed in court dress, and who always *answer him.* ("And during four long hours," he says, "I no longer feel any bore-dom; I forget all misery; I no longer fear poverty; death no longer terrifies me. I pass completely into them.")[40] No doubt he never resigned himself to parting company with spon-taneous men. He would not spend days contemplating them if they were not like a mystery for him. Is it true that these men *could* love and understand the same things he under-stands and loves? Seeing so much blindness on one side, and such a natural art of commanding on the other, he is tempted to think that there is not one mankind, but historic men and enduring men—and to range himself on the side of the for-mer. It is then that, no longer having any reason to prefer one "armed prophet" to another, he no longer acts except at random. He bases rash hopes upon Lorenzo di Medici's son; and the Medici, following their own rules, compromise him without employing him. A republican, he repudiates in the preface to the *History of Florence* the judgment the republi-cans had brought against the Medici; and the republicans, who do not forgive him for it, will not employ him either. Machiavelli's conduct accentuates what was lacking in his politics: a guideline allowing him to recognize among differ-ent powers the one from which something good could be hoped for, and to elevate *virtue* above opportunism in a decisive way.

To be just we must also add that the task was a difficult one. For Machiavelli's contemporaries the political problem was first of all one of knowing if Italians would long be prevented from farming and living by French and Spanish incursions, when they were not those of the Papacy. What could he reasonably hope for, if not for an Italian nation and soldiers to create it? It was necessary to begin by creating this bit of human life in order to create the human community. Where in the discordancy of a Europe unaware of itself, of a world which had not taken stock of itself and in which the eyes of scattered lands and men had not yet met, was the universal people which could be made the accomplice of an Italian city-state? How could the peoples of all lands have recognized, acted in concert with, and rejoined each other? There is no serious humanism except the one which looks for man's effective recognition by his fellow man throughout the world. Consequently, it could not possibly precede the moment when humanity gives itself its means of communication and communion.

Today these means exist, and the problem of a real humanism that Machiavelli set was taken up again by Marx a hundred years ago. Can we say the problem is solved? What Marx intended to do to create a human community was precisely to find a different base than the always equivocal one of principles. In the situation and vital movement of the most exploited, oppressed, and powerless of men he sought the basis for a revolutionary power, that is, a power capable of suppressing exploitation and oppression. But it became apparent that the whole problem was to constitute a power of the powerless. For those in power either had to follow the fluctuations of mass consciousness in order to remain a proletarian power, and then they would be brought down swiftly; or, if they wanted to avoid this consequence, they had to make themselves the judge of proletarian interests, and then they were setting themselves up in power in the traditional sense—they were the outline of a new ruling class.

The solution could be found only in an absolutely new relationship between those in power and those subject to it. It was necessary to invent political forms capable of holding power in check without annulling it. It was necessary to have leaders capable of explaining the reasons for their politics to those subject to power, and to obtain from themselves, if necessary, the sacrifices power ordinarily imposes upon subjects.

These political forms were roughed out and these leaders appeared in the revolution of 1917; but from the time of the Commune of Kronstadt on, the revolutionary power lost contact with a fraction of the proletariat (which was nevertheless tried and true), and in order to conceal the conflict, it begins to lie. It proclaims that the insurgents' headquarters is in the hands of the White Guards, as Bonaparte's troops treat Toussaint-L'Ouverture as a foreign agent. Already difference of opinion is faked up as sabotage, opposition as espionage. We see reappearing within the revolution the very struggles it was supposed to move beyond. And as if to prove Machiavelli right, while the revolutionary government resorts to the classic tricks of power, the opposition does not even lack sympathizers among the enemies of the Revolution. Does all power tend to "autonomize" itself, and is this tendency an inevitable destiny in all human society? Or is it a matter of a contingent development which was tied to the particular conditions of the Russian Revolution (the clandestine nature of the revolutionary movement prior to 1917, the weakness of the Russian proletariat) and which would not have occurred in a Western revolution? This is clearly the essential problem. In any case, now that the expedient of Kronstadt has become a system and the revolutionary power has definitely been substituted for the proletariat as the ruling class, with the attributes of power of an unchecked élite, we can conclude that, one hundred years after Marx, the problem of a real humanism remains intact—and so we can show indulgence toward Machiavelli, who could only glimpse the problem.

If by humanism we mean a philosophy of the inner man which finds no difficulty in principle in his relationships with others, no opacity whatsoever in the functioning of society, and which replaces political cultivation by moral exhortation, Machiavelli is not a humanist. But if by humanism we mean a philosophy which confronts the relationship of man to man and the constitution of a common situation and a common history between men as a problem, then we have to say that Machiavelli formulated some of the conditions of any serious humanism. And in this perspective the repudiation of Machiavelli which is so common today takes on a disturbing significance: it is the decision not to know the tasks of a true humanism. There is a way of repudiating Machiavelli which is Machiavellian; it is the pious dodge of those who turn their eyes and ours toward the heaven of principles in order to turn them away from what they are doing. And there is a way of praising Machiavelli which is just the opposite of Machiavellianism, since it honors in his works a contribution to political clarity.

NOTES

1. A paper sent to the Umanesimo e scienza politica Congress, Rome–Florence, September, 1949.
2. *The Prince*, Chap. XXV.
3. *Discourses*, II, 23, quoted by A. Renaudet, *Machiavel*, p. 305.
4. *The Prince*, Chap. XIV.
5. Chap. XVII.
6. Chap. XVIII.
7. *Ibid.*
8. Chap. III.
9. Chap. XVI.
10. Chap. XVII.
11. Chap. XIV.
12. Chap. V.
13. Chap. XV.
14. Chap. V.

15. Chap. III.

16. Chap. XVII.

17. Chap. IX. We are not far from the definition of the State in Thomas More's *Utopia*: "quaedam conspiratio divitum de suis commodis reipublicae nomine titulogue tractantium."

18. Chap. XXIII.

19. Chap. V.

20. Chap. XV.

21. By failing to wipe out the families which divided Pistoia into factions.

22. *Ibid.*, Chap. XVII.

23. ". . . I think that one must be a prince to know the people's nature well, and a man of the people to know that of the prince." Dedication to *The Prince*.

24. Chap. XVIII.

25. Chap. XVII. My italics.

26. *Ibid.*

27. Chap. VII.

28. Chap. XXV.

29. *Discourses*, II, 29, quoted by A. Renaudet, *Machiavel*, p. 132.

30. *The Prince*, Chap. XXV.

31. *Ibid.*

32. *Ibid.*

33. Chap. XXVI.

34. *Discourses*, I, 26, quoted by A. Renaudet, *Machiavel*, p. 231.

35. *Ibid.*, p. 301.

36. James, *Les Jacobins noirs*, p. 127.

37. *Ibid.*, p. 49.

38. *Ibid.*, p. 295.

39. *Discourses*, I, quoted by A. Renaudet, *Machiavel*, p. 71.

40. Letter to Francesco Vettori, quoted by A. Renaudet, *Machiavel*, p. 72.

13

The Political Paradox

PAUL RICOEUR

Like every event worthy of this name, the event of
Budapest has an infinite capacity for shocking. It has touched
us and stirred us at several levels of our existence: at the level
of historical compassion, caught by the unexpected; at the
level of ordinary political strategy; at the level of reflection
on the abiding political structures of human existence. We
must always bear in mind these several powers of the event.

Yet we need not feel regret over having first evoked its
power of shock without concern for reconciling tactics. However expected the event was, and there are some who maintain that it was, those few who are never caught unawares,
still, the revolt was a surprise precisely because it took place:
the Flames of Budapest. . . . If we want to be instructed by
events, then we must not be in a hurry to solve them.

And then this event, which was left to speak for itself, must

Reprinted from *History and Truth*, trans. Charles A. Kelbley (1965), pp.
247–70, by permission of Northwestern University Press, Evanston, Ill.

be evaluated, it must be reconstituted in the over-all situation. Moreover, we must bring out the unusual meaning contained in it, relating this to the Algerian war, the treason of the Socialist party, the disappearance of the Republican Front, and the resistance of French communists to de-Stalinization. In short, we must pass from absolute emotion to relative consideration.

For my part, the Budapest event, coupled with the October Revolution in Warsaw, has rekindled, confirmed, inflected, and radicalized a reflection on political power. Yet my reflection does not date from this event, since it had already given rise to several studies of which some were delivered at the *Collège philosophique* and others published in *Esprit* and elsewhere. What surprised me in these events is that they reveal the stability, in the very midst of socio-economic revolutions, of the problematic of power. The surprise is that Power has, as it were, no history, that the history of power repeats itself, marks time. The surprise is that there is no real political surprise. Techniques change, human relationships evolve depending upon things, and yet power unveils the same paradox, that of a twofold progress in rationality and in possibilities for perversion.

Many would maintain that the problem of political power in a socialist economy is not fundamentally different from the same problem in a capitalist economy, that it offers comparable if not added possibilities for tyranny, and that it calls for equally if not more strict democratic controls. Yet this is precisely what is rejected by all those who do not subscribe to the relative autonomy of polity in comparison with the socio-economic history of societies.[1]

This autonomy of polity seems to consist of two contrasting features. On the one hand, polity works out a human relationship which is neither reducible to class conflicts, nor to socio-economic tensions of society in general. The State most noted for a ruling class is a State in that it expresses the fundamental will of the nation in its entirety. Hence it is not radically affected, as State, by changes which are neverthe-less radical in the economic sphere. By means of this first feature, man's political existence displays a specific type of *rationality* which is irreducible to dialectics based upon eco-nomics.

On the other hand, politics fosters specific *evils* which are precisely political evils, evils of political power. These evils are irreducible to others, in particular to economic aliena-tion. Thus, economic exploitation *may* disappear while polit-ical evil persists. Moreover, the means which the State em-ploys in order to put an end to economic exploitation may be the occasion for the abuse of power, new in their expression and in their effects, but fundamentally identical in their pas-sional incentive to those of past States.

Specific rationality, specific evil—such is the double and paradoxical originality of polity. It would seem to me that the task of political philosophy is to explicate this originality and to elucidate the paradox of it. For political evil can only be an outgrowth of the specific rationality of polity.

It is necessary to hold out against the temptation to oppose two styles of political reflection, one which stresses the ra-tionality of polity, drawing upon Aristotle, Rousseau, and Hegel, the other emphasizing the violence and untruth of power, following the Platonic critique of the "tyrant," the Machiavellian apology of the "prince," and the Marxist cri-tique of "political alienation."

This paradox must be retained: that the greatest evil ad-heres to the greatest rationality, that there is political aliena-tion *because* polity is relatively autonomous. Let us therefore now treat of the autonomy of polity.

1. The Autonomy of Polity

What will always remain admirable in the political thought of the Greeks is that no philosopher among them—with the possible exception of Epicurus—ever resigned himself to the exclusion of politics from the domain of rationality. All or almost all knew that if politics were declared evil, foreign, and "other," by comparison to reason and philosophical discourse, if politics were literally given over to the devil, then reason itself has capsized. For in that case, reason would no longer be of reality and in reality, at least not to the extent that human reality is political. If nothing is reasonable in man's political existence, then reason is not real, it is floating in the air, and philosophy becomes banished to the world of the Ideal and Duty. No great philosophy ever resigned itself to this, even (and especially) if it begins with the data of everyday existence and at first turns away from the world. Every great philosophy attempts to understand political reality in order to understand itself.

Now, politics discloses its meaning only if its *aim*—its *telos* —can be linked up with the fundamental intention of philosophy itself, with the Good and with Happiness. The Ancients did not understand how a Politics—a political philosophy— could possibly begin with something other than a *teleology* of the State, of the *"res publica,"* itself situated in relation to the final goal of mankind. Aristotle's *Politics* begins thus: "Every State is a society of some kind, and every society, like all forms of association, is instituted with a view to some good; for mankind always acts for an end which is esteemed good. Now if all societies aim at some good, then the State, which is the highest of all societies, and which encompasses all the rest, aims at the highest and most perfect good." The concept of the "good life" mutually implicates politics and ethics.

Henceforth, to reflect on the autonomy of polity is to find in the teleology of the State its irreducible manner of contributing to the humanity of man. The *specific* nature of polity can only be brought to light by means of this teleology. It has the specific nature of an aim, an intention. Through the political good, men pursue a good which they could not otherwise attain and this good is a part of reason and happiness. This pursuit and this *telos* constitute the "nature" of the

Polis. The nature of the State is its end, just as "the nature of each thing is its end."[2]

From this standpoint, political philosophy is induced to determine how this *meaning*—which is the "end" and "nature" of the State—resides in the State as a *whole*, as an entire body, hence how humanity comes to man by means of the body politic. The fundamental conviction of all political philosophy is that he "who by nature and not by mere accident can exist without a state would be a despicable individual, either above or inferior to man. . . . For whoever has no need of society or is unable to live in society is either a beast or a god. The social instinct is natural to all men."[3] If the destination of man passes through a corporate body, through a whole, through a State defined by its "sufficiency," then it is forbidden to begin with the *opposition* between the State and the citizen. The point of view of philosophy is, on the contrary, that the individual becomes human only within this totality which is the "universality of citizens." The threshold of humanity is the threshold of citizenship, and the citizen is a citizen only through the State. Hence the movement of political philosophy starts with Happiness, which all men pursue, moves to the proper end of the State, then to its nature as a self-sufficient totality, and from there to the citizen. Because the "State is the constant subject of politics and government," the movement of political thought proper proceeds from the State to the citizen and not the inverse: "A citizen is one who, in his own country, has the power to take part in the deliberative or judicial administration of the State." Thus the citizen is characterized by the attribute of power: "For according to our definition, the citizen shares in the government of a state."[4]

In its turn, citizenship fosters the "virtues" peculiar to this participation in public power. These are the "virtues" which govern the relationship of government to free men, virtues of obedience distinct from servility, just as the authority of the State worthy of this name is distinct from despotism.

Hence, political thought proceeds from the State, to citizenship, to civism, and not in the reverse order.

Such is the disciplined thought proposed by the ancient model; such also is the disciplined thought which ought to be indispensable for any individual who wishes to gain the right to speak seriously about political evils. A meditation on politics, which would begin with the opposition of the "philosopher" and the "tyrant" and which would reduce the whole exercise of power to the perversion of the will to power, would thereby forever inclose itself within nihilistic moralism. One of the first actions of political reflection should be to push the figure of the "tyrant" off to the side, allowing it to emerge as the frightening possibility which cannot be coped with because men are evil. Still it should not be the object of political science: "It is proper to mention in last place tyranny as the worst of all depravations and the least worthy of the name constitution. For this reason, we have kept it for the end." (Aristotle)

But the automony of polity is something more than this vague, communal destiny of the human animal, something more than the admission of man to humanity by means of citizenship. More precisely, it is the specific nature of the political bond as opposed to the economic bond. This second moment of reflection is basic to what follows; for political evil will be just as specific as this bond and the remedy for the evil as well.

It seems to me that one cannot undertake the critique of the authenticity of political life without having first demarcated the boundaries of the political sphere and acknowledging the validity of the distinction between polity and economics. Every critique presupposes this distinction and can by no means set it aside.

Now, no reflection is a better preparation for this recognition than that of Rousseau. To discover and reiterate within oneself the most profound motivation of the "social contract" is, at the same time, to discover the meaning of polity as such.

A return to Rousseau, linking up with the return to the Ancients—to Aristotle's *Politics* in particular—should provide the basis and the background for every critique of power which could not begin, in any case, with the individual.

The great, invincible idea of the *Social Contract* is that the body politic is born of a virtual act, of a consent which is not an historical event, but one which only comes out in reflection. This act is a pact: not a pact of one with another, not a pact of abstention in favor of a non-contracting third party, the sovereign, who, by not being part of the contract would be absolute. No—but it is a pact of each individual with all, a pact which constitutes the people as a people by constituting it as a State. This admirable idea, so criticized and so badly understood, is the basic equation of political philosophy: "To find a form of association that will defend and protect with the whole common force the person and goods of each member, and in which each, while uniting himself with all, may still obey himself alone and remain just as free as before."[5] Not the exchange of savage liberty for security, but the passage to civil existence through law which is given the consent of all.

One may well express dissatisfaction with the abstraction, idealism, and hypocrisy of this pact—and this is true in certain respects. But first one must recognize in this pact the founding act of the Nation. This founding act cannot be engendered by any economic dialectics; it is this founding act which constitutes polity as such.

One might object that this pact has not taken place. Precisely. It is of the nature of political consent, which gives rise to the unity of the human community organized and oriented by the State, to be able to be recovered only in an act which has not taken place, in a contract which has not been contracted, in an implicit and tacit pact which appears only in political awareness, in retrospection, and in reflection.

Hence, untruth can very easily slip into polity; polity is prone to untruth because the political bond has the reality of ideality: this ideality is the equality of each before all others, "for if each individual gives himself absolutely, the condition is equal for all; and, this being the case, then no one should have reason to make it onerous for others."[6] But before being hypocrisy, behind which is hidden the exploitation of man by man, equality before the law, and the ideal equality of each before all, is the *truth* of polity. This is what constitutes the *reality* of the State. Inversely, the reality of the State, irreducible to class conflicts or to the dynamics of economic domination and alienation, is the advent of a legality which will never be completely reducible to the projection of the interests of the ruling class into the sphere of law. As soon as there is a State, a body politic, the organization of an historical community, there exists the reality of this ideality; and herein is contained a point of view of the State which may never completely coincide with the phenomenon of class domination. If the State is reduced to the ideal projection of the interests of the ruling class, then there is no longer a political State but despotic power. But even the most despotic State is still State in that something pertaining to the common good of the vast majority of citizens comes about through tyranny and therefore transcends the interests of one particular group or the dominant groups. Besides, only the original autonomy of polity can explain the hypocritical use of legality as a cloak for economic exploitation; for the ruling class would not experience the need to project its interests into juridical fiction if this juridical fiction were not first the condition of the real existence of the State. In order to become the State, a class must make its interests penetrate into the sphere of the universality of law; this law can mask the relation of force only in the measure that the power of the State itself flows from the ideality of the past.

I am aware of the difficulties related to the notion of general will, of sovereignty in Rousseau's writings. In the Geneva manuscript, Rousseau spoke even then of the "abyss of politics in the constitution of the State" (just as, in the constitution of man, the action of the soul on the body is the abyss of philosophy). These difficulties are not the fault of Rousseau; they pertain to polity as such: a pact which is a virtual act and which founds a real community; an ideality of law which legitimizes the reality of force; a ready-made fiction to clothe the hypocrisy of a ruling class, but which, before giving rise to falsehood, founds the freedom of citizens, a freedom which ignores particular cases, the real differences of power, and the real conditions of persons, but which is nevertheless valuable because of its very abstraction—such is the peculiar labyrinth of polity.

Rousseau, at bottom, is Aristotle. The pact which engenders the body politic is, in voluntarist language and on the level of the virtual pact (of the "as if"), the *Telos* of the State referred to by the Greeks. Where Aristotle speaks of "nature" and "end," Rousseau uses "pact" and "general will"; but it is fundamentally the same thing; in both cases, the specific nature of polity is reflected in philosophical consciousness. Rousseau recognized the artificial *act* of an ideal subjectivity, of a "public person," whereas Aristotle discerned an objective *nature*. But Rousseau's general will is objective and Aristotle's objective nature is that of man aiming toward happiness. The fundamental accord of these formulae comes out in their very reciprocity. In the two cases, with the *Telos* of the State and the generating *pact* of the general will, it is a matter of manifesting the coincidence of an individual and passional will with the objective and political will, in short, of making man's humanity pass through legality and civil restraint.

Rousseau is Aristotle. Perhaps it should be noted that Hegel supports this view. It is important, since Marx, as we shall see, initiated the critique of the bourgeois State and, he thought, of every State, through the instrumentality of Hegel's *Philosophy of Right*. The whole of Western political thought, epitomized in such giants as Aristotle, Rousseau, and Hegel, is supposedly brought together in the Marxist critique.

When Hegel looks upon the State as reason realized in man, he is not thinking about a particular state, nor any state whatever, but rather about the reality which comes into being through empirical States and to which nations obtain access when they pass the threshold of organization as a modern State, along with differentiated organs, a constitution, an administration, etc., and reach the level of historical responsibility within the framework of international relationships. From this standpoint, the State appears as what is desired by individuals so as to realize their freedom: viz., a rational, universal organization of freedom. The most extreme, the most scandalous formulae of Hegel on the State, which Eric Weil recapitulated in his book on *Hegel et l'état*,[7] should be taken as the limiting expression, as the advanced point of a thought determined to situate all its recriminations within the very interior of, and not outside of the fully recognized political reality. It is on the basis of this limiting expression that we must view all that can be said against the State and against the mad *pretension* which lays hold of its rational *intention.*

2. Power and Evil

There is a specific political alienation because polity is autonomous. It is the other side of this paradox which must now be clarified.

The crux of the problem is that the State is Will. One can stress as much as need be the rationality conferred upon history by polity—this is true. But if the State is rational in its intentions, it nevertheless advances through history by means of decisions. It is not possible to exclude from the definition of polity the idea of *decisions of historic import,* that is to say which change in abiding fashion the destiny of the human assemblage organized and directed by the State.

Polity is rational organization, politics involves decisions: probable analysis of situations, probable projection as to the future. Polity necessarily involves politics.

Polity takes on meaning after the fact, in reflection, in "retrospection." Politics is pursued step by step, in "prospection," in projects, that is to say both in an uncertain deciphering of contemporary events, and in the steadfastness of resolutions. Thus, if the political function, if polity, carries on without interruption, one can say in a sense that politics only exists in great moments, in "crises," in the climactic and turning points of history.

But if it is impossible to define polity without including the voluntary moment of decision, neither is it possible to speak of political decisions without reflecting on power.

From polity to politics, we move from advent to events, from sovereignty to the sovereign, from the State to government, from historical Reason to Power.

It is in this fashion that the specific nature of polity becomes manifest within the specific qualities of the means of which it disposes. Considered from the point of view of politics, the State is the authority which holds a monopoly over lawful physical constraint. The adjective "lawful" attests that the definition of the State, in terms of its specific means, refers to the definition of the same State in terms of its end and its form. But should the State ever manage by chance to become identified with its foundation of legitimacy —for example by becoming the authority of the law—this State would still be a monopoly of constraint; it would still be the power of a few over all; it would still cumulate a legitimacy, that is to say a moral power of exacting, *and* a violence without appeal, that is to say a physical power of constraining.

It is in this way that we reach the idea of the entire sweep of politics. Let us say that politics is the sum total of activities which have for their object the exercise of power, therefore also the conquest and preservation of power. Step by step, politics will encompass every activity whose goal or effect will be to influence the division of power.[8]

It is politics—politics defined by reference to power—which poses the problem of political evil. There is a problem of political evil because there is a specific problem of power. Not that power is evil. But power is one of the splendors of man that is eminently prone to evil. Perhaps in history it is the greatest occasion for and the most stupendous display of evil. The reason of course is that power is a very extraordinary phenomenon, since it is the vehicle of the historical rationality of the State. We must never lose sight of this paradox.

This specific evil of power has been recognized by the greatest of political thinkers with a signal unanimity. The prophets of Israel and the Socrates of the *Gorgias* concur unequivocally on this point. Machiavelli's *Prince*, Marx's *Critique of Hegel's Philosophy of Right*, Lenin's *State and Revolution*—and . . . the Khrushchev report, that extraordinary document on the evil in politics—are all in fundamental accord although certainly operating within radically different theoretical and philosophical contexts. This very concurrence attests to the stability of the political problematic throughout history and, thanks to this stability, we *comprehend* these texts as a truth valid for all time.

It is well worth noting that the earliest recorded Biblical prophecy, that of Amos, denounces political crimes and not individual faults.[9] Wherever one might be tempted to recognize a mere survival of the outdated notion of collective sin, previous to the individualization of punishment and fault, one must distinguish the denunciation of political evil as the evil of power. It is man's political existence that confers upon sin its historical dimension, its devastating power and, I would venture to say, its grandeur. The death of Jesus, like that of Socrates, resulted from a political act, a political trial. It was a political authority, the very one which, by its order and tranquility, assured the historical success of *humanitas* and *universalitas*. It was Roman political power that raised the Cross: "He suffered under Pontius Pilate."

Hence sin manifests itself in power, and power unveils the true nature of sin, which is not pleasure but the pride of domination, the evil of possession and holding sway.

The *Gorgias* is certainly in accord with this. One can even say that the Socratic and Platonic philosophy springs in part from a reflection on the "tyrant," that is to say on power without law and without consent on the part of subjects. How is the tyrant—the inverse of the philosopher—possible? This question cuts to the quick of philosophy, for tyranny is not possible without a falsification of the *word,* that is to say of this power, human *par excellence,* of *expressing* things and of communicating with men. The whole of Plato's argument in the *Gorgias* is based upon the conjunction between the perversion of philosophy, represented by sophistry, and the perversion of politics, represented by Tyranny. Tyranny and sophistry form a monstrous pair. Hence Plato ferrets out one aspect of political evil, different from power but intimately linked to it: "flattery," the art of inducing persuasion by means other than the truth. In this way, he brings to light the connection between politics and untruth. The point of his argument is quite important, if it is true that the word is the milieu, the fundamental element of mankind, the *logos* which unifies mankind and founds communication. Thus the lie, flattery, and untruth—political evils *par excellence*—corrupt man's primordial state, which is word, discourse, and reason.

Here, then, we have the elements of a meditation on the pride of power and on untruth, a meditation which shows these two phenomena to be evils linked to the essence of politics. We may rediscover this double meditation within these two great works of political philosophy: Machiavelli's *Prince* and Lenin's *State and Revolution,* both of which attest to the permanence of the problematic of power amid the various forms of governments, amid the evolution of technics and the transformations of social and economic conditionings. The question of power, of its exercise, its conquest, its defense and extension, has an astonishing stability which would make us apt to believe in a certain continuity of human nature.

Much has been said of the evil of "Machiavellism." But should we take the *Prince* seriously, as it must be, then we shall discover that it is by no means easy to evade its problem: how to establish a new power, a new State. The *Prince* evinces the implacable logic of political action: the logic of means, the pure and simple techniques of acquiring and preserving power. The technique is wholly dominated by the essential political relationship between the friend and the enemy: the enemy may be exterior or interior, a nation, nobility, an army, or a counsellor; and every friend may turn into an enemy and vice versa. The technique plays upon a vast keyboard ranging from military power to the sentiments of fear and gratitude, of vengeance and loyalty. The *Prince*, conscious of all the ramifications of power, the immensity, the variety, and the manifold measure of its keyboard, will be equipped with the abilities of the strategist and the psychologist, *lion* and *fox*. And so Machiavelli raised the true problem of political violence, not that of ineffectual violence, of arbitrary or frenetic violence, but that of calculated and limited violence designed to establish a stable state. Of course, one can say that by means of this calculation, inceptive violence places itself under the judgment of established legality; but this established legality, this "republic," is marked from its inception by violence which was successful. All nations, all powers, and all regimes are born in this way. Their violent birth then becomes resorbed in the new legitimacy which they foster and consolidate. But this new legitimacy always retains a note of contingency, something strictly historical which its violent birth never ceases to confer upon it. Machiavelli has therefore elucidated the relationship between politics and violence. Herein lies his probity and his veracity.

Several centuries later, Marx and Lenin returned to a

theme which can be called Platonic, the problem of the "false consciousness." It seems to me that what is most worthy of note in the Marxist critique of politics and the Hegelian State is not its explication of the State by means of the power relations among classes, which would therefore be the reduction of political evil to socio-economic evil, but rather the description of this evil as the specific evil of politics. I believe that the great error which assails the whole of Marxism-Leninism and which weighs upon the regimes engendered by Marxism is this reduction of political evil to economic evil. From this springs the illusion that a society liberated from the contradictions of the bourgeois society would also be freed of political alienation. But the essential point of Marx's critique[10] is that the state is not and cannot be what it claims to be. What does it claim to be? If Hegel is right, the State is conciliation, the conciliation, in a higher sphere, of interests and individuals which are irreconcilable at the level of what Hegel calls civil society, which is what we would call the socio-economic level. The incoherent world of private relationships is arbitrated and rationalized by the higher authority of the State. The State is a mediator and therefore reason. And each of us attains his freedom and rights by means of the authority of the State. I am free in so far as I am political. It is in this sense that Hegel maintains that the State is representative: it exists in *representation* and man is represented in it. The essence of Marx's critique lies in exposing the *illusion* in this pretension. The State is not the true world of man but rather another and unreal world; it resolves real contradictions only in virtue of a fictive law which is, in turn, in contradiction with the real relationships between men.

It is on the basis of this essential *untruth*, of this discordance between the pretension of the State and the true state of affairs, that Marx meets with the problem of violence. For sovereignty, not being the achievement of the people in its concrete reality, but being another, visionary world, is forced to look for support in a real, concrete, empirical sovereign. The idealism of right is maintained throughout the course of history only by means of the caprice of the prince. Thus the political sphere is divided between the *ideal* of sovereignty and the *reality* of power, between sovereignty and the sovereign, between the constitution and the government, or the police. It matters little that Marx was only familiar with constitutional monarchy, for the split between the constitution and the monarch, between law and caprice, is a contradiction *internal* to all political power. This also holds true in the Republic. Notice how last year our right to referendum was usurped by clever politicians who twisted *de facto* power against the sovereignty of the electoral body. This is of the essence of political evil. No State exists without a government, an administration, a police force; consequently, the phenomenon of political alienation traverses all regimes and is found within all constitutional forms. Political society involves this external contradiction between an ideal sphere of legal relations and a real sphere of communal relations—and this internal contradiction between sovereignty and the sovereign, between the constitution and power or, in the extreme, the police. We aspire to attain a State wherein the radical contradiction which exists between the universality pursued by the State and the particularity and caprice which it evinces in reality would be resolved. The evil is that this aspiration is not within our reach.

Unfortunately, Marx did not perceive the absolute character of this contradiction; he viewed it as a mere superstructure, that is to say the transposition onto a superadded plane of the contradictions pertaining to the inferior plane of capitalist society and, in the last analysis, an effect of class opposition. The State, then, is but the instrument of class violence, even though the State may possibly always envisage a scheme or project transcending disparate class interests. Oddly enough, it would seem that the evil peculiar to the State is its very opposition to this grandiose scheme. When the State is thus conceived of as the organized power of the ruling class for oppressing another, then the illusion of the State being universal conciliation is nothing but a particular instance of the vice of bourgeois societies, showing them unable to offset their own deficiency or to resolve their contradictions except by taking flight into the phantom of Right.

I believe it must be maintained, against Marx and Lenin, that political alienation is not reducible to another, but is constitutive of human existence, and, in this sense, that the political mode of existence entails the breach between the citizen's abstract life and the concrete life of the family and of work. I think too that thereby we retain what is best in the Marxist critique, which interrelates with the Machiavellian, Platonic, and Biblical critique of power.

I should like to adduce the Khrushchev report alone as proof. The fundamental fact would seem to be that the criticism of Stalin has meaning only if the alienation of politics is an absolute alienation, irreducible to that of economic society. If it were not, then how is it possible to censure Stalin while continuing to sanction the socialist form of economy and the Soviet regime? The Khrushchev report is inconceivable without a critique of power and the vices of power. But since Marxism does not allow for an autonomous problematic of power, it falls back upon fable and moralizing criticism. Togliatti was somewhat incautious the day he declared that the explanations of the Khrushchev report did not satisfy him, wondering as he did how the phenomenon of Stalin had been possible in a socialist regime. The reply could not be given to him because it can only flow from a critique of socialist power, something which up to now has not been made and which, perhaps, could not be achieved within the compass of Marxism, *at least in so far as Marxism reduces all alienations to economic and social alienation.*

I should like to make it quite clear once and for all that the theme of political evil, which I have just set forth, by no means constitutes a political "pessimism" and does not war-

rant any political "defeatism." Besides, the pessimist and optimist labels are to be banned from philosophical reflection;
pessimism and optimism are but moods and only concern
characterology, which is to say that no use may be made of
them here. Yet it is quite important that we should acquire
a *lucidity* with respect to the evil of power, for this is something which could not be divorced from a thoroughgoing
reflection on polity. This reflection reveals that politics can
be the seat of the greatest evil only because of its prominent
place within human existence. The enormity of political evil
is commensurate with man's political existence. More than
any other, a meditation which would parallel political evil
with radical evil, making of it the closest approximation of
radical evil, ought to remain inseparable from a meditation
on the radical significance of politics. Every condemnation of
politics as corrupt is itself deceitful, malevolent, and infa-
mous, at least if it neglects to situate this description within
the dimension of the political animal. The analysis of polity,
as the progress of man's rationality, is not abolished but constantly presupposed by meditation on political evil. On the
contrary, political evil is serious only because it is the *evil* of
man's rationality, the specific evil of the splendor of man.

In particular, the Marxist critique of the State does not
suppress the analysis of sovereignty, from Rousseau to Hegel,
but rather presupposes the truth of this analysis. If there is
no truth in the general will (Rousseau), if there is no teleology
of history amid "unsocial sociability" and by means of this
"ruse of reason" which is political rationality (Kant), if the
State is not "representative" of man's humanity, then political evil is not grave. It is precisely *because* the State is a
certain expression of the rationality of history, a triumph
over the passions of the individual man, over "civil" interests,
and even over class interests, that it is the most exposed and
most threatened aspect of man's grandeur, the most prone
to evil. Political "evil" is, in the literal sense, the madness of

grandeur, that is to say the madness of what is great—Grandeur and culpability of power!

Henceforth, man cannot evade politics under penalty of evading his humanity. Throughout history, and by means of politics, man is faced with *his* grandeur and *his* culpability.

One could not infer a political "defeatism" on the basis of this lucidity. Such a reflection leads rather to a political *vigilance*. It is here that reflection, ending its long detour, comes back to actuality and moves from critique to praxis.

3. The Problem of Power in Socialist Regimes

If our analysis of the paradox of power is correct, if the State is at once more rational and more passional than the individual, the great problem of democracy concerns the *control* of the State by the people. The problem of the control of the State, like that of its rationality, is equally irreducible to socioeconomic history, as is its evilness irreducible to class contradictions. The problem of the control of the State consists in this: to devise institutional techniques especially designed to render possible the exercise of power and render its abuse impossible. The notion of "control" derives directly from the central paradox of man's political existence; it is the *practical* resolution of this paradox. To be sure, it is, of course, necessary that the State *be* but that it not be too much. It must direct, organize, and make decisions so that the political animal himself might be; but it must not lead to the tyrant.

Only a political philosophy which has perceived the specific nature of polity—the specific nature of its function and the specific nature of its evil—is in a position to pose correctly the problem of political control.

Thus the reduction of political alienation to economic alienation would seem to be the weak point in the political thought of Marxism. This reduction of political alienation has, in effect, led Marxism-Leninism to substitute another problem for the problem of State control, that of the *withering away* of the State. This substitution seems disastrous to me; it grounds the end of the iniquity of the State upon an indefinite future, whereas the true, practical political problem pertains to the limitation of this evil in the present. An eschatology of innocence takes the place of an ethic of limited violence. At one and the same time, the thesis of the withering away of the State, by promising too much for the future, equally tolerates too much in the present. The thesis of the future withering away of the State serves as a cloak and an alibi for the perpetuation of terrorism. By means of a sinister paradox, the thesis of the provisory character of the State turns into the best justification for the endless prolongation of the dictatorship of the proletariat and forms the essence of totalitarianism.

It is quite necessary to realize that the theory of the withering away of the State is a logical consequence of the reduction of political alienation to economic alienation. If the State is merely an organ of *repression,* which springs from class antagonisms and expresses the domination of one class, then the State will disappear along with all the aftereffects of the division of society into classes.

But the question is whether the end of the private appropriation of the means of production can bring about the end of *all* alienations. Perhaps appropriation itself is but one privileged form of the power of man over man; perhaps money itself is but one means of domination among others; perhaps the same spirit of domination is given expression in various forms: in economic exploitation, in bureaucratic tyranny, in intellectual dictatorship, and in clericalism.

Our concern here is not the hidden unity of all alienations. In any case, the reduction of the political form to the economic form is indirectly responsible for the myth of the withering away of the State.

It is true that Marx, Engels, and Lenin have attempted to elaborate this theory on the basis of experience. They interpreted the Paris Commune as the guarantee and the commencement of the experimental verification of the thesis of the withering away of the State; for them it demonstrated that the dictatorship of the proletariat may be something quite different than the mere transfer of the State's power into other hands, but indeed the overthrow of the State machine as the *"special force"* of repression. If the armed populace is substituted for the permanent army, if the police force is subject to dismissal at any moment, if bureaucracy is dismantled as an organized body and reduced to the lowest paid condition, then the general force of the majority of the people replaces the special force of repression found in the bourgeois State, and the beginning of the withering away of the State coincides with the dictatorship of the proletariat. As Lenin says, "it is impossible to pass from capitalism to socialism without a certain return to a primitive form of democracy." The withering away of the State is therefore contemporaneous to the dictatorship of the proletariat, in the measure that the latter is a truly popular revolution which smashes the repressive organs of the bourgeois State. Marx could even say: "The Commune was no longer a State in the literal sense of the word."

In the thought of Marx and Lenin, the thesis of the withering away of the State was therefore not a hypocritical thesis but a sincere one. To be sure, few men have demanded so little of the State as the great Marxists: "So long as the proletariat still has need of a State," reads the *Letter to Bebel*, "it is not in order to secure freedom but to put down its adversaries; and the day when it becomes possible to speak of freedom, the State will cease to exist as such."

But if the withering away of the State is the critical test for the dictatorship of the proletariat, then the crucial question is posed: why has the withering away of the State not *in fact* coincided with the dictatorship of the proletariat? Why, in fact, has the socialist State reinforced the power of the State to the point of confirming the axiom which Marx believed to be applicable only to bourgeois revolutions: "All revolutions have only served to perfect this machine instead of smashing it."[11] The attempt to reply to this question is at the same time to provide the missing link to the Khrushchev report, for it is to explain how the phenomenon of Stalin was possible in the midst of a socialist regime.

My working hypothesis, such as is suggested by the preceding reflection, is that Stalin was possible *because* there was no recognition of the permanence of the problematic of power in the transition from the old to the new society, because it was believed that the end of economic exploitation necessarily implied the end of political repression, because it was believed that the State is provisory, because one had substituted the problem of the withering away of the State for that of its control. In short, my working hypothesis is that the State cannot wither away and that, not being able to wither away, it must be controlled by a special institutional form of government.

Furthermore, it would seem that the socialist State, more than the bourgeois state, requires a vigilant, popular control precisely because its rationality is greater, because it enlarges its sphere of analyses and forecasts so as to encompass sectors of human existence which elsewhere and in former times were given over to chance and improvisation. The rationality of a socialist State, striving as it does to suppress class antagonisms and even aspiring to put an end to the division of society into classes, is certainly greater. But you see at once that its scope of power is also greater as well as the possibilities for tyranny.

It would seem that the task of a critique of socialist power should be to articulate lucidly and faithfully the new possibilities of political alienation, that is to say those which are opened up by the very battle against economic alienation as well as by the reinforcement of State power which this battle entails.

Here are some avenues of approach which might be pursued by an investigation of power in socialist regimes:

1. We should first have to determine in what measure "the administration of things" necessarily involves a "governing of persons" and in what measure the progress in the administration of things gives rise to an augmentation of political power of man over man.

For example: planning implies a choice of an economic character concerning the order of priority in the satisfaction of needs and the employment of means of production; but this choice is from the very outset *more* than a matter of economics. It is the function of a general politics, that is to say of a long-term project concerning the orientation of the human community engaged in the experience of planning. The proportion of the part reinvested and the part consumed, the proportion of cultural and material goods in the general equilibrium of the plan, spring from a "global strategic vision" in which economics is woven into politics. A plan is a technique serving a global project, a civilizing project animated by implicit values, in short, a project which in the last analysis pertains to man's very nature. Hence, insofar as it gives expression to *will* and power, polity is the soul of economics.

Thus the administration of things may not be substituted for the governing of persons, since the rational technique of ordering man's needs and activities on the macroscopic scale of the State cannot extricate itself from all ethico-cultural contexts. Consequently, in the last analysis, political power unites scales of value and technological possibilities, the latent aspirations of the human community, and the means unleashed by knowledge of economic laws. The connection between ethics and technics in the "task" of planning is the fundamental reason why the administration of things *implies* the governing of persons.

2. Next, we should have to determine how the reinforcement of State power, which is intimately linked to the expansion of the jurisdiction of the socialist State in comparison with the bourgeois State, fosters *abuses which are inherent*

to it in virtue of its nature as a socialist State. This would constitute the elucidation of the idea mentioned earlier, that the most rational State possesses the most opportunities for being passional.

Engels pointed out in *Anti-Dühring* that the organization of production will remain authoritarian and repressive, even after the expropriation of expropriators, so long as there is a perpetuation of the old division of work and the other alienations which make working a burden and not a joy. When it is not spontaneous, the division of work still arises from constraint, and this constraint is precisely connected to the passage from hazard to rationality.

The temptation toward forced labor therefore becomes one of the major temptations of the socialist State. But it can easily be seen that the socialist State is the least protected against this temptation, since its method of global planning also endows it with the *economic* monopoly over psychological constraint (culture, the press, and propaganda are encompassed within the plan and are therefore *economically* determined by the State). Hence, the socialist State will have a whole arsenal of means at its disposal, including psychological means ranging from inducements and competition to deportation.

In addition to these opportunities for abuse provided by the organization of the means of production, there is the temptation to overcome irrational resistances by more expeditious means than those of education or discussion. In effect, the rational State encounters resistances of all kinds; some of these result from residual phenomena (described quite well by Chinese Marxists, in particular, and previously by Lenin in the *Infantile Disorder of Communism*). These resistances are typical of the peasantry and the lower middle class, demonstrating that the psychology of workers is not on the same plane as that of technocrats, but remains adapted to long standing situations. Thus we find resistances of a psychological character which do not spring from considerations of the general welfare of the people but from the habituation to outdated economic conditions. Yet all resistances are not subject to this explanation by backward mentalities. The socialist State has a more remote and more vast project than the individual whose interests are more immediate, limited to the horizon of his death or at the very most to that of his children. In the meantime, the State calculates by generations; since the State and the individual are not on the same wave length, the individual develops interests which are not naturally in accord with those of the State. We are familiar with at least two manifestations of this variance between the goal of the State and that of the individual: one concerns the division between investment and immediate consumption, the other the determination of standards and the rate of production. The micro-interests of individuals and the macro-decisions of power are in a state of constant tension, fostering a dialectic of individual demands and State constraint which is an occasion for abuse.

Thus we find tensions and contradictions which are not the remedies for the private appropriation of the means of production. Certain of these tensions and contradictions even derive from the new power of the State.

Lastly, the socialist State is more ideological than the "liberal" State. It may attribute to itself the ancient dreams of unifying the realm of truth within an orthodoxy encompassing all the manifestations of knowledge and all the expressions of the human word. Under the pretext of revolutionary discipline and technocratic efficacity, it can justify an entire militarization of minds; it can do it, that is to say, it has the temptation and the means to do so since it possesses the monopoly of provisions.

All of these reflections converge toward the same conclusion: if the socialist State does not abolish but rather revives the problematic of the State—if it serves to further its rationality while intensifying opportunities for perversion—the problem of the democratic *control* of the State is still more pressing in socialist regimes than in capitalistic regimes, and the myth of the *withering away* of the State stands in the way of a systematic treatment of this problem.

3. The third task of a critique of power in socialist regimes would then consist of coming back to the critique of the liberal state in light of this idea of democratic control. This would enable it to determine which institutional features of the liberal state were independent of the phenomenon of class domination and specifically adapted to the limitation of the abuse of power. No doubt this critique could not be carried out within the specifically critical phase of socialism; the liberal State had to appear almost inevitably as a hypocritical means of perpetuating economic exploitation. Yet today it is indispensable to discern between the instrument of class domination and democratic control in general, at least after the bitter experience of Stalinism. Perhaps it is the case that Marxism in itself embodies the ingredients for this revision when it propounds that a class in its ascending phase pursues a *universal* function. In giving expression to the problem of democratic controls, the "philosophers" of the eighteenth century devised the true *liberalism* which no doubt goes beyond the destiny of the bourgeoisie. It does not follow that just because the bourgeoisie had need of these controls in order to draw limits to monarchic and feudal power and to facilitate its own ascension, that these controls therefore exhaust their abiding significance within their provisory usage. In its profound intention, liberal politics comprised an element of universality, for it was adjusted to the *universal* problematic of the State, beyond the form of the bourgeois state. This explains how a return to liberal politics is possible within a socialist context.

I should like to cite a few examples of this *discernment* applied to the structures of the liberal State, examples of the division between the "universal" aspects and the "bourgeois" aspects of these structures. I shall present them in a problematic manner since we are practically at the end of a critique of socialist power of which the first postulates are scarcely certain:

a) Is not the independence of the "judge" the very first condition of permanent legal remedy against the abuse of power?

It seems to me that the judge is a personage who must be voluntarily placed, by the consent of all, on the fringes of the fundamental conflicts of society.

The independence of the judge, it will be objected, is an abstraction. Quite so. Society requires for its human respiration an "ideal" function, a deliberate, concerted abstraction in which it projects the ideal of legality that legitimates the reality of power. Without this projection, in which the State represents itself as legitimate, the individual is at the mercy of the State and power itself, without protection against its arbitrariness. It stands to reason that the proceedings of Moscow, of Budapest, of Prague, and elsewhere, were possible because the independence of the judge was not technically assured nor ideologically founded in a theory of the judge as a man above class, as an abstraction of human proportions, as the embodiment of law. Stalin was possible because there were always judges to judge in accordance with his decree.

b) The second condition of permanent legal remedy against the abuse of power is the citizen's free access to sources of information, knowledge, and science, independent of those of the State. As we have seen, the modern State determines the way of living since it orients economically all of man's choices by its macro-decisions, its global planning; but this power will become more and more indistinguishable from totalitarian power if the citizens are not able to *form, by themselves, an opinion* concerning the nature and the stakes involved in these macro-decisions.

More than any other, the socialist State requires the counterpart of *public opinion* in the strict sense of the word, that is to say, a public which has opinions and an opinion which is given public expression. It is quite plain what this involves:

a press that belongs to its readers and not to the State, and a press whose freedom of information and of expression is constitutionally and economically guaranteed. Stalin was possible because no public opinion could launch a critique of him. But then again, the post-Stalin State alone has dared to utter that Stalin was evil, *not* the people.

The independent exercise of justice and the independent formation of opinion are the two lungs of a politically sound State. Without these, there is asphyxiation.

These two notions are so important that it was in virtue of them that the overthrow of Stalinism was accomplished; the notions of *justice* and *truth* gave birth to the revolt. This explains the role of intellectuals in the abortive revolution of Hungary and in the successful revolution of Poland. If intellectuals, writers, and artists played a decisive role in these events, it is because the stakes at issue were not economic and social, notwithstanding misery and low wages; the stakes were strictly political, or to be more precise, they were the new political "alienation" infecting socialist power. But the problem of political alienation, as we are well aware of since Plato's *Gorgias,* is the problem of untruth. We have also learned of this through the Marxist critique of the bourgeois State, situated, as it is, entirely upon the terrain of *untruth,* of being and appearance, of mystification, and of falsehood. It is just here that the intellectual as such becomes involved in politics. The intellectual is driven to the fore of a revolution, and not merely within its ranks, as soon as the incentive for this revolution is more political than economic, as soon as it touches upon the relation of power with truth and justice.

c) Next, it would seem to me that the democracy of work requires a certain dialectic between the State and labor councils. As we have seen, the long-term interests of the State, even apart from the consideration of money, do not immediately coincide with those of workers; this stands to reason in a socialist period, in the precise sense of the word, that is to say in a phase of inequality of wages, wherein professional specialization is in opposition to unskilled and skilled laborers, directors, and intellectuals; this also stands to reason in a period of rapid or even forced industrialization. Consequently, only a network of liaisons between the State and associations representing the diverse interests of workers can consolidate the groping quests for a viable equilibrium, that is to say at once economically sound and humanly tolerable. The right to strike, in particular, would seem to be the sole recourse of workers against the State, *even against the State of workers.* The postulate of the immediate coincidence of the will of the socialist State with all interests of all workers seems to me to be a pernicious illusion and a dangerous alibi for the abuse of State power.

d) Lastly, the key problem is that of the control of the State by the people, by the democratically organized foundation. At this point, the reflections and experiences of the Yugoslavian and Polish communists ought to be consulted and analyzed very closely. The question is whether the pluralism of parties, the practice of "free elections," and the parliamentary form of government derive from this "universalism" of the liberal State, or whether they irremediably pertain to the bourgeois period of the liberal State. We must not have any preconceived ideas: neither for nor against; neither for Occidental custom, nor for radical criticism; we need not be in a hurry to answer. It is certain that planning techniques require that the socialist form of production not be given over to the hazard of popular vote; that it be irrevocable, as is the republican form of our government. The execution of the Plan calls for full powers, a government of long continuance, a long-term budget. Yet our parliamentary techniques, our manner of interchanging the majorities in power, would not appear very compatible with the modern rationality of the State. And yet, on the other hand, it is just as certain that *discussion* is a vital necessity for the State; through discussion it is given orientation and impetus; discussion curbs its tendency to abuse power. Democracy is discussion. Thus it is necessary that this discussion be *organized* in one way or another. Here we encounter the question concerning parties or the unique Party. What may argue in favor of the pluralism of parties is that this system has not only reflected tensions between social groups, determined by the division of society into classes, but it has also invested political discussion as such with organization, and it has therefore had a "universal" and not merely a "bourgeois" significance. An analysis of the notion of "party," on the sole basis of the socio-economic criterion, therefore seems to me dangerously inadequate and liable to encourage tyranny. This is why it is necessary to judge the theory of multiple parties and the theory of a single party not only from the standpoint of class dynamics, but equally from the viewpoint of the techniques of controlling the State. Only a critique of power in socialist regimes could further advance this question. Yet this critique has hardly been launched.

I do not know whether the term political "liberalism" can be saved from falling into disrepute. Perhaps its affinity with economic liberalism has compromised it once and for all, although of late, the label "liberal" tends to constitute a misdemeanor in the eyes of social fascists in Algeria and in Paris, and thus recovers its bygone freshness.

If the term could be saved, it would state rather well what ought to be said: that the central problem of politics is *freedom*: whether the State *founds* freedom by means of its rationality, or whether freedom *limits* the passions of power through its resistance.

NOTES

1. Throughout this essay, particularly in the second section, the author contrasts polity (*le* politique) with politics (*la* politique). By polity, the author intends the ideal sphere of political organization and historical rationality; by politics, the empirical and concrete manifestations of this ideal sphere, the sum total of the means employed to implement the ideal sphere of polity.—Trans.

2. Aristotle, *Politics*, I,2 (1252 b 32)—Trans.

3. *Ibid.* (1253 a 2–3, 28–30)—Trans.

4. *Ibid.*, III, 1(1275 a–b)—Trans.

5. J. J. Rousseau, *Contrat social* (Paris: Garnier, 1960), p. 243.—Trans.

6. *Ibid.*, pp. 243–44.—Trans.

7. "If, then, society is the foundation, the by no means formless matter of the State, the conscious reason of self is wholly on the side of the State: outside of it there may be concrete morality, tradition, work, abstract right, sentiment, virtue, but there can be no reason. Only the State thinks, only the State can be totally thought"—*Hegel et l'état* (Paris: Vrin, 1950), p. 68. For the definition of the State, cf. p. 45.

8. Max Weber calls politics "the sum total of efforts with a view to participating in power, or of influencing the division of power either within the State or between States"—*Politik als Beruf* (Munich, 1926).

9. *Amos*, I:3–15: ". . . since they have crushed Galaad . . ., since they have taken a large number of captives and delivered them to Edom . . ., since they have hunted down their own brother at the sword's point without compassion . . ., since they so coveted Galaad's land that they would rip open the womb of pregnant women, I shall not recall the sentence I have pronounced."

10. Cf. J. Y. Calvez, *La Pensée de Karl Marx*, in the chapter on political alienation.

11. Marx, *The Eighteenth Brumaire of Louis Bonaparte*.

14

The Need for a Philosophy of Democracy

JOHN WILD

As a philosopher still impressed by the *historical* importance of political theory, and as a human individual participating, to some extent, in the life of a so-called democratic nation, I have been disappointed and even depressed by recent literature devoted to democracy, and even more by the general attitudes which seem to prevail in public arguments and debates on this topic. In such arguments, the notion of democracy seems very generally to be taken for granted with little sense of the need for distinguishing between what is essential and what is incidental or derived. And in the literature on the subject, which is relatively slight in comparison with that on socialism and communism, less attention is paid to basic philosophical patterns of thought and feeling than to more evident, but perhaps more superficial, matters of formal procedure.

Reprinted from *Contemporary American Philosophy*, ed. John E. Smith (1970), pp. 194–210, by permission of Humanities Press Inc., New York.

The terms *free country* and even *free world* are often used. But it is rare that one finds any serious discussion of the different interpretations to which this term (freedom) is open, of the relation of freedom to responsibility, and of individual to political, or social, freedom. These terms seem to have fallen into the obscurity of the obvious which covers many problems. In this paper I shall try first of all to raise some of these problems, which, in my opinion, are not pseudo-problems of pure theory but real difficulties and confusions which affect actual political policies. In the second place, I shall make a few suggestions as to how some of these difficulties might be corrected.

The Formalist View of Democracy

In more general discussions of the subject, democracy is commonly identified primarily with formal procedures of a certain kind.[1] Three of these are of particular importance: regular elections, majority rule, as I shall call it, and the existence of opposition parties. I shall not argue that these procedures are not needed in large-scale democratic groups. My point will be that they are not essential, that exceptions may be found, and that they do not penetrate to the heart of what those who believe in democracy really mean.

Turning now to regular voting procedures, this is no doubt a need for large democratic groups of millions of individuals. But it is easy to think of large-scale nations, like Russia, where regular elections are held, which we would not call democratic. What is evidently missing here is an opposition party. The formality of voting is insufficient. It makes a difference what one is voting for and what one is voting against. But this is not the only difficulty. When we think of democracy, most of us think primarily of the nation-state and of the procedures by which the ruling officers of such vast corporate structures are chosen. But we know of the importance attached by De Tocqueville and other keen observers to the

role played by smaller groups of different kinds from governmental departments and provinces, down to business corporations, special interest groups, and the family.

There is strong justification for holding that unless the normal individual can play an active democratic role in the
processes of such small subordinate groups, the large-scale
national democracy cannot be sustained. It is in these smaller
groups that the individual may in some cases be on the winning and in others on the losing side, so that permanent
frustration and embitterment may be avoided. It is here also
that he may learn by direct confrontation to tolerate and to
respect those holding attitudes different from his own—an
essential aspect of democracy. But many of these smaller
groups can carry on democratically with only rare, or even
no elections, because a consensus can be achieved. So for this
reason also, it would be a mistake to think of regular elections
as essential to the democratic process. It is needed in gigantic
organizations, but even here exceptions may be found. So it
is secondary and derived.

Let us next turn to the principle of majority rule. There is
to be no discrimination between equal individuals. Each vote
is to count for one. This idea of equality is a fundamental
value of democracy, as we shall see, and it is the first premise
from which the principle of majority rule is derived. When
the group is divided, the opinion of a majority, when freely
expressed, shall prevail. When examined in abstraction, this
certifies itself as a genuinely democratic principle of equality
and justice. But the facts of actual practice point to certain
qualifications which show that this principle is not fundamental but derived. Majority is a relative term. So we must
ask what kind of a majority? A majority of whom? In principle, we are inclined to say a majority of those qualified or
eligible to vote. But we all know that this does not agree with
procedures generally recognized as democratic.

For presidential elections in the United States in recent
years, a turnout of more than 70 per cent of the eligible

voters is unusual. This means that a 'majority' of 36 per cent of those properly qualified can win. When we use the term here we are, therefore, referring to a majority of those not only qualified but with sufficient concern to take the trouble to vote. This factor of concern is even more evident in the procedures of smaller special interest groups, like associations for specific reforms, learned societies, etc. Here it is well known that the common affairs of the society are run by a small number of those with special qualifications and an exceptional interest in these affairs. As long as the more indifferent majority makes no vigorous protest, performs certain minimal functions like the paying of dues, and grows in number, few of us would want to say that it is being governed in a non-democratic manner. But it would be highly dubious to identify this procedure with majority rule, since the important decisions are made by the voting of a very small minority, with the general consent of the rest. This indicates the weakness in any attempt to identify democracy with the principle of majority rule.

This weakness becomes even more evident when we think of those instances, like the well-known case of Germany in 1933, when a majority, or plurality, of the citizens voted to establish the Hitler dictatorship. Surely it is a mistake to identify the essence of democracy with a procedure that can be used to destroy it. This principle of majority rule is not essential. It is secondary or derived.

When we come to the third procedural principle, the right to disagree within limits, and the existence of loyal opposition parties, we are getting closer to something essential, but we have not yet arrived. Opposition groups struggling for a different kind of dictatorship can exist in countries which no one either here nor there would view as democratic. Has China now become a democracy because of the opposition of Liu Shao-chi and his followers? Here again we are dealing with a formal procedure and abstracting from all content. It makes a difference what the opposition party stands for, and what it is that is being opposed. What are the distinctive meanings and values of democracy? The essence lies here, not in formal principles.

If the presence of recognized opposition does not ensure democracy, we need to examine more carefully the widely held assumption that the absence of such opposition ensures non-democracy. In many of the developing countries of Africa, for example, we now find a condition of one-party rule with no recognized opposition parties. Hence it is believed that this is a great setback for democracy. But under the conditions now prevailing, is this necessarily true? With two or more tribal groups, each opposing the rest in free elections and parliamentary conflict, might it not happen that they would cancel out each other so that no decisions could be made? This might conform to certain traditional conceptions of minimum government. But would such a perpetual stalemate be what we now mean by democracy? All the formal procedures might be there. Only nothing would be done. Is it not possible that under one-party rule with a small group of leaders or only one, decisions might be made that would move the country by improved education and industry, for example, in a democratic direction accepted without serious protests by the more passive majority? This may be an imperfect condition. But is it anti- or even non-democratic? We cannot hope to give definite answers to such questions unless we get away from formal procedures, and approach more closely to the essential meaning of democracy. What is its basic aim? What is it moving towards? What is the underlying philosophy of democracy?

Negative Freedom and Government

We come closer to an answer to these questions when we turn to the content of the American Bill of Rights and to the corresponding attitudes embodied in the British and the French traditions. These are concerned with the weak and fragile individual. First, they try to protect him in his weakness against the paralysing influences of uncontrolled group power, against arbitrary arrest, seizure, and torture. Then in an affirmative way they aim at fostering and promoting the free and responsible activities of thinking and choosing which he alone can perform, and which have an essential value for the democratic community. Thus he should have access to reliable information through freedom of publication, of the press, and other public media. It is only on this basis that he can develop sound and responsible beliefs. He should have the right to express these beliefs whatever they may be, and the right to meet in free assemblies where opposing views are defended and criticized.

In the *United Nations Declaration of Human Rights,* a document of major importance for democratic theory, these rights of the individual are further extended. He has a right to domicile in a country where he may be supported by the powers of a full community so that he may live his own life, and pursue his projects without arbitrary deprivation or restraint. He has a right, furthermore, to periods of rest and leisure, and to adequate medical care to protect him, in his weakness, against the constant dangers of physical breakdown and ill health. Finally, since he is born in abysmal ignorance, he has the right, not specifically recognized in the American constitution, to an education, so that he may learn to think and to choose responsibly without avoidable impediments.

From these democratic articles and declarations, we may infer that a primary concern for the peculiar powers and dignity of the fragile and ephemeral human individual belongs essentially to the meaning of democracy. Any violation of these so-called rights, wherever and however it occurs, is undemocratic. Here we are confronted not with a mere formal procedure, but with a principle having actual content, and ruling out certain ways of thought and action of specifiable kinds. Disrespect for the individual person is always undemocratic. This is not a derivative, or instrumental, principle, but one that is true essentially and without exception. This, I believe, is correct. But further questions need to be asked, two of which are especially important.

The first is concerned with individual freedom. Does this freedom have no limits? Does the free individual have a right to do or to think anything he pleases, so long as he does not interfere with the similar rights of others, as J. S. Mill maintained? If this is not true, and if democracy is committed to certain stable values and meanings, how can it be defended against the charge of dogmatism or fanaticism of some kind?

The second question concerns the nature of democratic rule. Does it mean merely the minimum of government, or does it possess distinctive features which mark it off from other forms of rule? The liberal tradition in nineteenth-century political theory, which is still dominant, has given answers to these questions which are oversimple, and which have dulled the image of democracy in the minds of many in the West.

This tradition, throughout its history, has defended a negative conception of freedom as *freedom from* restraint of any kind, including that of self-imposed responsibilities. When conceived in this way, freedom bears no affirmative connotations favouring one mode of thinking or acting over another. This conception has no doubt served an important function in criticizing fixed views of liberty put forth by dogmatists who knew exactly what the free man should do in any circumstances. But it has now led to a negativistic view of democracy as standing for no affirmative aims, but only for endless criticism and dissent. If a society is to maintain itself in time, however, its affairs must be ordered affirmatively in one direction rather than in another, with little interest in arriving at justifiable agreement on affirmative goals, the decisions of actual practice will be dominated by the drift of power. Thus, as the critics of modern democracy have cogently argued, this show of negative freedom is a convenient and self-righteous mask for the rule of force.

Liberal thought has consistently opposed the continental conceptions of a general will over and above the wills of the individual members of a group, and of a group soul or substance with a life and unity of its own in which the individual members participate. There is certainly some truth in this rejection of group mythology, which has enabled traditional liberalism to avoid many pitfalls of totalitarian political theory in the past. But it is also a one-sided view which has dangers of its own. Whether or not there is such a thing as a group substance, it is clear that every child is born into a society which is ordered and structured in certain ways. The child is necessarily assimilated into these structures which tend to drift, and in a certain sense live a life of their own. Otherwise, it is impossible to understand what a democratic Bill of Rights is protecting the individual against. The liberal conception of a democratic society as a set of atomic individuals free to set up a minimal government to pursue their private wishes without external compulsion is a self-destructive myth. This negative freedom is not enough. Affirmative action must be taken, or freedom will be submerged in the drift of social power.

Similar objections may be raised against the liberal answer to the second question concerning democratic action and government. When society is conceived as a mere association of atomic individuals, each entitled to the exercise of a purely negative freedom, it becomes impossible to distinguish sharply between democratic and non-democratic governments. Any common order, or rule, infringes on the individual's negative freedom. The democratic ideal is, therefore, identified with the maximum possible anarchy of the individual units, and the minimum possible government to sustain it without criminal violence and revolution. But this negative ideal of political action has turned out to be mistaken and irrelevant to the mass societies of our time. Social

patterns and institutions are constantly drifting in unforeseen directions to produce unforeseen and often unjust
consequences. Hence in politics, to do nothing is a form of
positive action leading to positive and often evil results. The
idea that these evils of drift may be quickly corrected by the
legislative decrees of popular representatives has been
shown to be fantasy. As critics once more have pointed out,
it has contributed to that notorious self-righteousness which
so often cloaks the drift of American social and political
power.

To many thinkers who understand the force of these objections, it appears that the whole traditional ideal of democracy, which they identify with traditional liberalism, must be
abandoned. We must give up the notion of a negative freedom for the individual, and must recognize the priority of
objective social patterns, which Hegel called *objektiver
Geist*, over individual opinion and desire *(subjektiver Geist)*.
This means that traditional individualism must be abandoned. These notions are taking us closer to Hegel and Marx
than to anything that can properly be called *democracy*,
which is indissolubly bound up with the independence of the
free individual *(subjektiver Geist)* and his control over the
powers of the group *(objektiver Geist)*.

In my opinion these critical statements are oversimple and
open to serious question. Democracy is bound up with the
dignity and social power of individuals. But it is not necessarily committed to traditional individualism. I shall now try
to show this by indicating democratic ways of answering
these two critical questions concerning negative freedom
and negative government without falling into the mistakes of
traditional liberalism.

Affirmative Freedom and Democratic Action

The liberal ideal that democracy means only endless criticism and dissent, and that it stands for nothing affirmative has
weakened it basically and dimmed the image of it in many

contemporary minds. As a result, it is now widely taken for granted as a mere procedure, indifferent to affirmative meanings or values of any kind. In this sense, it may appeal more to intellectuals, professionally engaged in the task of criticism than to living men who are constantly forced to make vital decisions for themselves and others. As a matter of fact, it has recently been ably defended precisely on the ground that it is entirely open, committed to nothing, and radically relativistic in its point of view, no one belief being really sounder than any other.[2] The individual and the group, are therefore, free at any time to doubt any view, to believe anything, and to try out any way of life they may arbitrarily prefer. Hence the dogmatism and fanaticism attaching to other political theories are avoided.

This relativistic position is open to several serious objections of which we shall consider only one. If this view is to guide our thought and practice, does it not commit us to a firm belief in the value of free inquiry, and an open way of life not constrained by arbitrary dogmatism? To this the defenders of relativism may reply that inquiry and openness are not specific values in the sense of something to be done. They are only instruments by which such values may be found. Therefore, they still remain free and uncommitted—seekers only and not finders. But is this isolated seeking not an artificial abstraction? Can we seek without any hope of finding? If it is serious and not a mere game, does this seeking not commit us to a belief in what we may find, and ultimately to action on the basis of this belief? Here we must drop the argument.

But perhaps we have carried it far enough to justify the following statements. The founders of democracy in the West, who acted in the British, French, and American revolutions, believed in free inquiry and the open life as values, superior to those achieved by the suppression of meaning, dictatorial authority, and arbitrary action. Furthermore, they did not hold this belief irresponsibly with no concern for the evidence available in human experience. Perhaps a stronger case can now be made for this belief. If so, there is an alternative to the negative conception we have been discussing.

Democracy cannot be reduced to a mélange of scepticism and relativism. It stands for certain values of which freedom of inquiry is certainly one. Responsible action in the light of what is revealed, imperfect though it be, is another. In spite of the dangers and risks involved, such action is better than the drift of blind power. Since it is the fragile human individual alone who is able to engage in such inquiry, democracy requires respect for any individual, and a concern for protecting him against the constraints of arbitrary power. Hence the democratic bill of rights, which have far-ranging implications for social action with respect to education for all, social welfare, the elimination of discrimination, etc. This view is far from relativism. Let us now consider two objections.

According to the interpretation of democracy we are suggesting, freedom has both a negative aspect, freedom *from*, and an affirmative aspect, freedom *for*—what is seen to be required by the human situation, that is, obligations and responsibilities. It is easy for us to think of these aspects as being essentially incompatible and opposed. Hence two sets of questions can be raised, first by those, like Sartre, who identify freedom with negation, and second by those who identify it with the positive fulfilment of certain obligations. The former will say that by subjecting the free individual to various obligations imposed by facts, by nature, and by other extraneous factors, the democratic theorist is infringing on his negative freedom which transcends any fact, and any obligation supposedly required by nature or by other external factors.

To this we may reply that human freedom is not absolute but limited, and that we do not become free by ignoring these limits. Furthermore, a theory which expects of man that he transcend all facts, including those of his own existence, cannot be distinguished from nihilism, for nothingness also transcends the given facts. We may also point out that the responsible man understands these obligations and imposes them on himself. They are not simply imposed from the outside. They involve a factor of autonomy which is not the same as negation. Finally, it must be emphasized that there is no freely accepted responsibility which is not open to further questioning, revision, correction, and even abandonment by the free minds of men. So the negative element is still present, though the possibility of finding and creating meaningful answers is not ruled out *a priori*. But this brings us to an opposed type of question that will be raised by those who are partial to a rigorous affirmative freedom.

They will say that obligations which are still open are not binding. How can we really believe in principles that we are questioning as we lay them down? This reduces the whole enterprise of democracy, as we are explaining it, to a mere game that calls for no unqualified commitment, and cannot, therefore, be taken seriously. Our answer to this must here take the form of a brief reference to the phenomenology of belief which must play an important role in the philosophy of democracy if this is ever fully formulated.

The opinions that we have *about* various matters are unstable and easily come and go. They may even be forgotten. Hence it is only an exceptional opinion that can survive a period of serious doubt, and here the objection holds good. But what we call belief, or conviction, is a different phenomenon. My belief *in* a friend or a principle is the permanent basis for my acts. I have assimilated it into my being by a long process of criticism and habituation which involves an element of doubt. In fact, it is fair to say that until I have seriously doubted a belief, it has not really become my own. So the notion that doubt is necessarily destructive of belief is simply false. Doubt may destroy ungrounded conviction. So the fanatic is afraid of being questioned. But it will not destroy a grounded belief which is aware of the uncertainties and the evidence against. Here we must remember that belief and life in the concrete world always involve elements of vagueness and risk.

Politics rests on beliefs of this kind. Hence it is perfectly possible to believe very firmly in the many values, obligations, and responsibilities of democracy in spite of a constant doubt that is always open to revision and correction. Such a believer certainly believes in constant negation and criticism. But he also believes firmly and affirmatively in the possibility of finding patterns of meaning which can survive such criticism, in the responsibility of all individuals to realize them, in so far as possible in the concrete, in the widening of this field of responsibility and autonomy, in the dignity of all individuals everywhere, and in the need for protecting them against the arbitrary restraints of group authority and power. This brings us to the second question concerning the traditional liberal theory of negative government. Is there a democratic alternative?

Negative Government and Democracy

Liberal thought was right in attacking the conception of a group soul or substance, which has turned out to be a myth without empirical foundation. But strong doubt may be raised as to whether liberalism has really freed itself from this notion, which, as we shall see, still hovers in the background. There is no group substance. This is correct. The liberal mind then infers that society is composed exclusively of individuals acting with different instruments in various ways for various ends. This is also correct as far as it goes. When society decides to act, it is always an individual who makes the decision in behalf of the group. When the state executes a criminal, there is always an individual executioner who presses the button.

But who, or what, is this individual?

The liberal mind is still apt to think of him as an isolated thing, or substance, enclosed within his body, and to think of society as a group, or collection, of such separated substances. This assumption is based on trends in our intellectual history that go back to ancient Greece. But it is basically one-sided, and when expressed without qualification, is mistaken. This is because it ignores certain relational patterns, like those of family life, in which the 'individual' is involved continuously from the beginning, and which are not collective in character. Thus the family is not a mere collection of individuals. It is a 'collection' acting in accordance with certain formal patterns which we indicate by such relational terms as husband and wife, brother and sister, parent and child. These patterns order and form the individual's life in certain stable and determinate ways.

Thus the family speaks a language, and from infancy on, the child is both taken over by the language of his parents and actively takes it over until he learns to speak it for himself. Now, this language that he learns is not a mere collection. The English language, for example, is not a collection of all the words spoken at different times and places by English-speaking individuals. It is an ordered collection with a unity and wholeness of its own. It has a history, a beginning and an end, and in a very real sense lives a life of its own, not *apart from* the successive generations of individuals speaking it, but *in them* and *through them*. This is true not only of language and the family but of hunting, fishing, industry, exchange, art, government, and every purposeful activity in which the individual is engaged.

It is the failure of the liberal mind to focus these patterns of social life that leads him, and most of us, to think of the social as something out there, over against us as individual substances, which can influence us from the outside and oppress us in various ways. Having made the mistake of regarding individuals as initially separated things or substances, and of society as a mere collection, he is then forced to regard social patterns, so far as he recognizes them too late, as other things outside of him with powers that can compel him to do things that he does not wish to do. This lies at the root of the negative theory of government and social control as an infringement of the rights of isolated individuals. On this liberal view, it is impossible to identify any distinctive features of democratic as against non-democratic forms of social control. Democracy has to be negatively conceived as the maximum absence of government or its minimum necessary degree.

But if there is no such *thing* as a group soul apart from the individual members, a mistake has been made. There are no social patterns or powers which exist apart from the individuals, and which help them or hinder them from the outside. Individuals exist only in and through these power-structures which, in turn, exist only in and through their individual carriers. The control, or lack of control, over such structures, which are always in change, is something to be exerted, or not exerted, by individuals over something not outside but *in* themselves. What is this something? It is an ordered set of habits, attitudes, and modes of understanding in each individual which enables him to perform his allotted tasks and to co-operate with the others. This *is* the club, the labour union, the industry, the army, the nation, or whatever the 'group' may be. When these individual habits and attitudes become confused, the group becomes confused; when they disintegrate, the group disintegrates; when they operate smoothly and coherently the social life is maintained, and radiates the tremendous power that results from organized co-operation. But now we must note two ways in which this social life may be maintained. This will shed some light, I believe, on the distinctive features of what we now mean by democratic government and action.

The first way is the way of drift, as we may call it, which is an ever-present factor in human life. Under this condition, the individual members interiorize the group patterns only to the degree that is required to carry on their separate functions, and no further. In learning to perform their functions well, they must also develop a certain flexibility which enables them to adapt to unexpected situations, but this is not carried very far. They have some understanding of the whole enterprise in which they are engaged, but this is usually dim and confused. They do not raise questions about the common purpose, and are not interested in mutual discussion and debate. They are satisfied with the *status quo,* and this attitude is encouraged by the decision-makers in positions of power.

These leaders, too, are loyal to the institution as it is, rather than to the members. They believe in *it* rather than in *them.* They do not rely exclusively on the force of habit to ensure conformity, but seek to enforce it by the laying down of rules, and by threats and punishments of various kinds. They discourage mutual discussion and the formation of small pressure groups. Aside from the interchange that is required for the efficient performance of their interlocking functions, they are interested in keeping the individuals separate and alone as the lonely members of an effective system.

Power structures of this kind have maintained themselves with great efficiency by drifting in this way for centuries under accidental autocratic control. Many of the gigantic power systems of our time are sustained by such drift. Nevertheless it is against power systems of this kind that the individual must be protected if he is to become responsible. This, I believe, is the reason for the Bill of Rights, inspired by a different ideal of democracy, which points towards another way and in another direction.

Those who are moved by this ideal see that unguided power corrupts. They see the dangers of blind power-structures, the conflict of power, the manipulation of power for its own sake, power politics, and the rule of power. They do not seek the elimination of power-structures, for this would mean the elimination of human life. Existence is power. But they seek for the responsible control of such power by individuals who alone are able to find meaning, and to give a meaningful response. Hence in their weakness they must be protected against the power systems which always surround them and must carry them into a senseless drift unless they are constantly watched and infused with meaning. This is the democratic ideal as it should be understood in the age of power.

But protection is not enough. Individuals are not innately free and responsible. If they are to become free, they must decide for this on their own. They may be helped, however, by the processes of formal and informal education to develop a flexibility which goes beyond the special functions they perform. They may be encouraged to internalize not only these but the whole public world that surrounds them on their fringes—to raise questions where it is obscure and confused, and to criticize its injustices and distortions. They should be encouraged to think for themselves and to form their own beliefs. As adults, they must be given the opportunity to meet together in small and large groups for the discussion of opposed views of common interest, in the hope that patterns of meaning may emerge which may survive criticism and elicit agreement. When this happens, common action may be taken, first of all in the form of protest, which is an essential factor in the ethos of democracy too often unduly subordinated or neglected.

Modern democracy, as a dynamic self-amending process, has always recognized the right to criticize and to form loyal opposition parties which can vote against the government. But in the mass societies of the present time, these voting procedures may ignore vital issues, and may simply conceal blind drifts of power. In recent years, therefore, minority groups in 'democratic' countries, facing the distortions and corruptions resulting from such drifts, have had to devise new techniques of protest, in order to call attention to their grievances and to have them seriously discussed. This democratic development has not been sufficiently studied. But we may note here how strikes, boycotts, sit-ins, and public demonstrations, only fifty years ago in the United States regarded as illegal infractions of the law, have now been recognized as an authentic expression of democratic freedom, and, therefore, as legal. This is indeed right, since democracy rests on the resolution of differences in the light of free and open discussion by the electorate. But people cannot be expected to consider those blind tendencies and their unforeseen effects of which they are unaware. When these inequalities and distortions are clearly focused through the agency of protest they may be widely and seriously discussed and debated. Out of this open debate and criticism, acceptable ways of controlling the drift may be devised. Then democratic action may occur.

But this will be quite different from what the liberal tradition has envisaged. It will not take the form of legislating social patterns into existence *de novo*. This is only a dream. It will always take the form of correcting and controlling social institutions that are already in existence. Such action will never be undertaken by isolated individuals interested only in living their private lives. This is the condition of the lonely crowd, or the lonely technicians, who are precisely in the state of drift.

When the believer in democracy speaks of the individual and his dignity, as he must, he will be referring not to a separated substance, originally complete in itself, nor to a set of such substances. He will be referring rather to many individuals, all individuals, ultimately the whole of mankind, in so far as they are capable *with each other* of controlling the drift of nature and habit into which they have been thrown. They need not be, and probably never will be, a majority in the strict sense of this term, for the majority is usually lethargic and indifferent. But this private lethargy will prevent them from interfering not only with the miseries and abuses which arise from drift, but also with the justices that correct them. So the task is not completely hopeless, for in history we find examples of concerned minorities who have changed the destinies of small groups as well as of larger ones while the majorities have gone along. But such responsible action requires leadership of a special kind.

Traditional liberal theory has failed to focus the distinctive traits of democratic leadership, and has even questioned the notion of a democratic élite as inconsistent with the whole ideal. This is certainly a mistake. If anything like democracy is ever to be worked out, it demands an élite, but an élite of a peculiar kind. Such leaders must care not so much for the technical majority which is content to drift as for the major minorities who really care for the common interest. They will be loyal not so much to the institution as it is, as to its real possibilities in the direction of greater freedom, responsibility, and opportunity for all.

They will pay attention to the concept of mankind, and will recognize it as a democratic ideal based on the worth and dignity of the individual wherever he may be. For when we think of mankind, we do not think of power complexes, nor allied states, nor leagues of nations. These are not mankind. When we use this term we are thinking rather of all individuals everywhere, including the various power patterns by which they live, but using them and controlling them for the sake of a meaningful human existence on this earth. This type of leader will be more interested in positive purposes than in laying down rules and punishments. He will try to stir up free discussion and criticism even when this is directed against policies he supports. He will encourage the formation of special interest groups both small and large, and will listen to their demands.

He will oppose the disintegration that leads individuals into the drift of the lonely masses, and will help them to communicate and to unite. When the drift of power-structures ends in conflict, as it ultimately must, he will try for negotiation, since the unleashing of blind power is the end of responsibility and, if it persists, of the democratic enterprise. He will seek to avoid this at any cost. So when overarching meanings cannot be found, he will seek for a balance of power which at least checks it and holds it in leash. But as a democratic leader he must seek for something more, not subservience to power but control over it for the interests of mankind. This is the aim of democratic action.

The Traditional View as Corrected

If negative freedom is only a moment in such action, and if it is essentially concerned with the fostering of certain existential values like freedom and equality of opportunity for all individuals, we can understand the proper, but subordinate, place which is to be assigned to voting procedures in democratic theory. In large-scale groups, like the nation-state, regular elections for the choice of rulers and the broad outlines of policy by those who are concerned is always advisable. But they are not essential to democracy. For example, in those small-scale groups which play a necessary role in the democratic process and where a consensus can be achieved, they are not required. The principle that each vote should count for one is valid as an ideal, for it is based on the capacity of the individual to interiorize the whole public world and its patterns, if he cares to do so, and to arrive at sound and informed beliefs on basic issues. But procedures are still democratic if such decisions are made by a majority of those who are really concerned, and are accepted by a largely indifferent majority. The protection of minorities and their right to organize opposition parties is sound and democratic so far as it goes, for it is based on the dignity of the individual person and his capacity for responsible thought and action. But under modern conditions, it must be extended to include the right of minority groups to protest against deprivations and injustices to which both the government and loyal opposition are indifferent.

Without these qualifications, the voting procedures of so-called democratic states may be high-sounding disguises for a power drift of selfish interests, as the Marxists have pointed out. And even with these qualifications, such drift is a constant danger, which has been accentuated by individualistic interpretations of democratic theory. On these views, both individual freedom and social action are negatively conceived. The former is identified with the absence of all constraint, including that of self-imposed obligations to authentic values, even those of freedom and democracy. The individual is, therefore, negatively free to do anything, even nothing, if he likes. Social action is also regarded negatively as a necessary evil which is to be checked and reduced to a minimum. But since power is an inescapable fact of life, this must lead to an inadvertent drift produced *in* the individuals not by outside forces but by their very indifference. This drift, I believe, is contrary to the basic aim of democracy—the deliberate control of group power, not subservience to it. This traditional, liberal view is not only internally inconsistent, but inconsistent with the facts.

In this paper I have tried to suggest, in outline, an alternative philosophy of democracy which might free it from these inconsistencies. It cannot be properly understood negatively as a form of scepticism and relativism concerning value. It is a definite point of view basically concerned with the dignity of every human individual, and with certain values which he alone can achieve, including those of free inquiry, the finding of grounded meanings, and, in the light of these, responsible action to control the drift of power. The checking and balancing of power are often necessary, but they are half-way measures which cannot be equated with control. This cannot be achieved by the voting procedures of isolated and indifferent individuals. It can be achieved only by the constant action of concerned individuals who accept a joint responsibility for what is being done.

As over against the drift of power under autocratic rule,

this mode of democratic action has at least four distinctive features. First, it arises from the free discussion and choice of a majority of those who are actually concerned. Second, each individual accepts a real share of responsibility for the decisions of rulers he has helped to select, and keeps a constant watch over what is being done. Third, these rulers remain in touch with the currents of public desire and belief as they emerge from larger and smaller groups in the community—both leading them and being led. Finally, they are responsible not to any fixed power-structure, but to the people and their ideals of equality and freedom in the control of power.

According to democratic philosophy, this mode of democratic action is not only an instrument by means of which other intrinsic values, like peace and social welfare, are to be attained. It has an intrinsic value of its own which takes precedence over other interests, and is to be preserved at any cost. Under any conditions and at all times it is good for individuals to care for their common destiny, and to control the blind drift of power by free and responsible action.

NOTES

1. Cf. David Spitz, *Patterns of Anti-democratic Thought* (New York: Macmillan, 1965), and H. B. Mayo, *An Introduction to Democratic Theory* (New York: Oxford Press, 1960). I am not singling out these works for special criticism. Each of them contains valuable insights and some high-level philosophical argument. But in *this respect*, each is representative of a widespread present tendency with which I am in disagreement.

2. Cf. T. L. Thorson, *The Logic of Democracy* (New York, Holt, Rinehart & Winston, 1962).

15

Voluntary Association: The Basis of an Ideal Model, and the "Democratic" Failure

Wᴉʟʟɪᴀᴍ Lᴇᴏɴ McBʀɪᴅᴇ

Too much of the recent discussion about voluntary associations has been based upon the usually unstated presupposition that their alleged ideality or lack of ideality is measurable against the yardstick of a general sociopolitical system that is assumed to be optimal—namely, "democracy," understood in a vague sense to mean something like the prevailing American system of institutions. Although adequate documentation of this assertion would entail a lengthy essay of a kind very different from what I propose to undertake here, some indication of its truth would be obtainable from a content analysis of recent American works in political science and philosophy. The presupposed normative bias in favor of "democratic" institutions on the contemporary American model would, I think, be found to be quite strong.

Reprinted from *Voluntary Associations*, Nomos XI, ed. J. Roland Pennock and John W. Chapman (1969), pp. 202–32, by permission of the publishers, Atherton Press, Inc. Copyright (c) 1969, Atherton Press, Inc. New York. All rights reserved.

Professor McConnell's paper in this volume* is a specific case in point. It carefully questions some of the alleged values of voluntary associations and in certain cases comes to a negative conclusion concerning them; but it assumes, throughout, that the American system of institutions has been and remains pre-eminently successful, and its critique is premised on that assumption.

One of the strong points of that system, in the eyes of those most concerned to defend it, is the fact that it encourages the existence within itself of a plurality of voluntary associations. Such a defense implies, among other things, that voluntary associations are desirable social forms—contrary to the skepticism with which some important political theorists of the past have treated them. On what basis can the valuableness of voluntary associations be asserted? Though much of the literature is not concerned with this point, it seems to me that the assertion of value in a certain form of social structure must ultimately be based on appraisal of that structure's effects on the individuals who constitute it. Moreover, if it is desirable for subgroups within a society to be organized in accordance with the principle of voluntary association, it seems inconsistent entirely to deny the value of that principle for the organization of a given society as a whole. Thus, what is of most importance in assessing the ideality of voluntary associations is not the issue of balancing powers between, for instance, smaller voluntary associations and the state, but rather the phenomenon of voluntariness itself and its relevance for individual associates. These considerations can be applied to the contemporary American system. What would be the result of reversing the currently conventional perspective, and of measuring the "democratic" system against a standard supplied by analyzing the principle of voluntary association in this way?

What I propose to do in this paper, then, is to re-examine

*"The Public Values of the Private Association," in *Voluntary Associations*, pp. 147–69 (Editor's note).

the reasons why voluntary associations ought generally to be regarded as ideal social forms (while admitting—as everyone, I believe, must—that some *particular* voluntary associations may be extremely undesirable from a point of view external to those associations) and to conclude by indicating why, given the ideality of voluntary associations, one ought to condemn certain important aspects of so-called "democratic" institutions, at least in the forms to which they have now evolved. The reexamination will begin (I) by rejecting several spurious or inadequate reasons for regarding the principle of voluntary association as ideal, and it will fix (II) on the concept of *responsibility* as the best clue to understanding that ideality; it will then consider (III) the complexities and paradoxes involved in any social or political course of action aimed at "maximizing responsibility" through voluntary association. Next, the question will be raised (IV) whether an entire society modeled on the principle of voluntary association is conceivable, and it will be answered affirmatively. Finally, the conclusion will indicate (V), on the basis of these considerations, why certain current "democratic" institutions actually militate *against* the promotion of those values which will have been seen to render voluntary association desirable in the first place.

I

Among the logical alternatives to (1) a society in which individuals would enjoy the maximum opportunity to participate in voluntary associations, a plurality of which would exist within the total society, four other extreme possibilities appear outstanding: (2) a pluralistic society of nonvoluntary associations, as exemplified (if we admit a broad enough definition of "society") by primitive clan arrangements; (3) a totally atomistic, nearly anarchical society in which the single universally accepted rule restricting individual enterprise would be a prohibition against forming voluntary associations; (4) a monolithic totalitarian society whose members would be under the maximum possible amount of compulsion (from a single dictator, from a small group, or even from a combination of nonhuman forces, such as those that could be envisaged by a science-fiction type of imagination) to participate in the activities of the whole; (5) a voluntary but monolithic Rousseauean society, in which private associations would be discouraged because of the dangers to unanimity that they pose. Actual present-day societies, of course, exhibit elements of all five of these rather extreme types.

Each of the last three enumerated types, I would maintain, can be seen as being better able than the others to promote at least one major social value which is not necessarily best promoted by society 1, that of plural voluntary associations. Within the fifth type, the value of unanimity might be maximized, while rationality (of a certain sort) could be better promoted by society 4 and wish-fulfillment by society 3. Historically, however, each one of these values (unanimity, rationality, and wish-fulfillment) has at some time or other been linked instead, incorrectly, with the principle of voluntary association in one or another of its forms. It may therefore be useful to begin by considering the reasons for rejecting each of these values as a basis for justifying the principle of voluntary association, in order subsequently to discover better the value by reference to which that principle *can* be justified.

Unanimity. If unanimity or "consensus" is upheld as the quality which a society ought to strive hardest to exemplify, then it might be thought, along with Rousseau, that a society built upon the principle of voluntary association would be best suited to reach the stars. In this context, voluntary association is usually conceived as the harmonious joint action of the society's total membership. Upon closer analysis, however, a very serious ambiguity is found to be latent in the phrase, the "principle of voluntary association." For it might well be the will of a certain number of members of a given society that they not only associate with all the others as "fellow citizens," but that they also associate at the same time in a special way with a few others as members of one or several more restricted subsocieties, to be called "private associations" by comparison with the larger ("public") society. Would the implementation of this latter wish be a violation of the "principle of voluntary association"? At first glance, the answer seems obvious: no, of course not. But what if it were the will of a certain number—whether of a vast majority, a small majority, or a tiny minority makes no essential difference—of the members of the great society that the creation of smaller subsocieties within it should not be allowed, because the new tendencies to faction would almost certainly result in the decline of over-all unanimity, and because the end result of an unchecked decline in unanimity would be the total dissolution of the association itself? In such a case, if private associations were to be formed just the same, then the "principle of voluntary association" of the whole society would in a certain sense be violated, and the decline of its unanimity would be under way. In fact, many historical examples can be pointed to as vindications of the fear that private associations *can* seriously weaken unanimity within societies and sometimes even destroy them.

From the point of view of a whole society which holds the "principle of voluntary association" very dear, then, it would seem that everything possible should be done to discourage the formation of *private* associations and to encourage civic-minded persons—meaning, hopefully, all the members of a given society—to repress all the particularistic inclinations which would lead them to want to form such subsocieties. But this is, of course, an absurd-sounding conclusion. The ambiguity from which it has resulted is itself based on a failure to analyze sufficiently the fact that an individual's will to associate can refer simultaneously to associations that are on several different levels of generality. "Acts of will' which result from commitment to one such association may or may not clash with those resulting from commitment to another. Individuals are even capable of retaining, within limits, diverse voluntary commitments which, on the basis of a purely logical analysis of the respective associations in question, could be shown to be incompatible. But there is no way of deciding, purely on the basis of the principle of voluntary association, which commitment ought to prevail in the case of a recognized clash; a mere difference in size or degree of generality among the associations in question is certainly no argument in favor of the largest or most general one. Though there may sometimes be practical advantages (e.g., considerations of efficiency) to subordinating the smaller subsocieties to the largest available voluntary association, the advocate of the principle of voluntary association certainly does not have to be, in addition, a proponent of hierarchical subordination; in fact, it is obvious that strong insistence on the latter principle may often thwart implementation of the former. In theory, any two associations with a difference in membership of even a single individual are potentially in conflict; but is this theoretical possibility a sufficient reason for endeavoring to minimize it in advance by conferring on one universal association a position of dominance or even of exclusiveness in a given place and at a given time? Certainly not—unless, in addition to being committed to voluntary association as an ideal, one is also, and perhaps even more strongly, committed to the value of unanimity or consensus.

Considerable textual evidence can be adduced for maintaining that the supremacy of the value of unanimity is more fundamental than is the principle of voluntary association in the thought of Rousseau,[1] though the two usually appear linked together in his writings. I have now indicated why such a linkage must issue, logically, in the Rousseauean society of "voluntary association" in which, paradoxically but understandably, *private* associations are to be suppressed.[2] The monolithic Rousseauean society is not to be mistaken for the monolithic but nonvoluntary totalitarian society, number 4 above, to which its critics have sometimes attempted to assimilate it;[3] but it is a society in which, as Rousseau himself insists most vigorously, a *plurality* of voluntary associations is to be eschewed. Although any discussion of voluntary associations must acknowledge a great historical debt to Rousseau for his posing of some of the fundamental problems, his own effort to combine the value of unanimity with the principle of voluntary association represents a serious, albeit suggestive, confusion.

Our own conclusion here must be that the value of unanimity and the principle of voluntary association are not, and can never be, necessarily realizable simultaneously to their fullest possible extents—if one takes, as I do, the Rousseauean society to be a less than full realization of that principle. Although this would seem self-evident and hardly worth laboring, the two possible ideals are on occasion still treated as if they were, or ought by some *fiat* to be, linked together. This inconsistency is sometimes voiced even by would-be defenders of a society of *plural* voluntary associations. We may recall, for example, that there existed in current American political discussions several years ago a vogue, since past, of speaking in terms of a "consensus" society, which presumably would still have remained as pluralistic as before. Such a state of affairs—pluralism *with* consensus—could conceivably exist in a large measure at a particular time (e.g., rival political parties in a certain society might differ primarily in memberships and generally agree on policy goals), but this coincidence would be *mere* coincidence from a logical point of view. The danger of having too unreflective a belief in the possibility of a pluralistic consensus society is that, when pluralism begins to detract from consensus, the true believer who happens also to be a holder of power in the society may be strongly tempted to *enforce* a "consensus" of his own.

The tendency to link consensus with pluralism appears in other, less obvious forms, as well.[4] For example, Professor

McConnell's paper in this volume especially exalts the role of American private associations in maximizing "order and stability," even though he entertains serious doubts about the effects of these associations on the value of freedom. I take "consensus" and "order" to be decreasingly strong and increasingly vague versions of unanimity. The advocate of order as a social ideal may, at one extreme, be stating a truism (since the very concept of "association" implies some minimum degree of order) or, at the other extreme, be endorsing a repressive form of social organization in which "consensus" is enforced.[5] A certain modicum of "order," conceived as a lesser degree of unanimity, is of course socially desirable; but the mere existence of a plurality of voluntary associations in a society will not necessarily tend to promote order, as we have seen, and it may well have the opposite effect. Only if the society accepts some prior demarcation of spheres within which alone private voluntary associations are permitted to operate freely will there be much likelihood of a harmonious coexistence of the principle of voluntary association with the value of order or of (relative) unanimity. But such a demarcation would represent a partial reversion to the Rousseauean tactic of *restricting* the principle of voluntary association in the name of that principle itself. The need to reject unanimity as the primary basis for justifying the principle of voluntary association, then, has been reconfirmed.

Rationality. Rationality is another social value the promotion of which has sometimes been urged as the ground for favoring the principle of voluntary association. Indeed, Professor Harris' essay in this volume* tends to support such a position, nor is he by any means the first to make the equation of the rational society with one based on that principle. But the dialectic of development, through improved communications, from gradually self-voluntarizing private

---

*"Voluntary Association as a Rational Ideal," in *Voluntary Associations*, pp. 41–62 (Editor's note).

associations to an increasingly noncompulsory political community and from the public agencies of that community back into educative private associations is too neat, the Peircean and idealist optimism too unsupported by logic and evidence, the assumption of good faith on the part of all participants too naive to render this conjunction very plausible. There is, to put it simply, no sufficient reason for assuming that a polity based on "deliberate consent" will automatically move toward a consensus concerning some sort of political "truth" as opposed to, let us say, what may not be true but is generally pleasing; in fact, as I have noted above, there is not even a sufficient reason for assuming that such a polity will necessarily move toward a consensus at all. Have not nations and private associations, great and small, often shown remarkable if temporary unanimity in rejecting all courses of action that later chroniclers have come to regard as the most rational options available to them at the time, in order to embark on their own versions of the Athenian expedition to Syracuse? "Desire" and "reason," as Plato well saw, do not necessarily fix upon the same goals.[6]

Moreover, the difficulty in determining just what constitutes the ideal of "rationality" is well known. "Unanimity" was considerably easier to understand. Perhaps the clearest, because most extreme, model of a unanimous or consensus society is one in which the brains of all members have been somehow conditioned to produce identical responses to any of a wide range of complex stimuli—though this could not, without a complete perversion of language, be called a "voluntary" society; other forms of social structure in which unanimity might be achieved by very different means may be envisioned with or without the aid of this model.

But the ideally "rational" society lends itself to very widely divergent interpretations. There is, for example, the familiar question whether the more rational society is the highly institutionalized one whose members meticulously follow a highly detailed and coherent set of rules or the one whose

members continually place all rules in question;[7] is the criterion of rationality to be strictness of organization or scope of
allowable possibilities? The history of thought is replete with
examples of acquiescence in the temptation to equate what
is rational with what would ideally be agreed upon by truly
voluntary agents with adequate knowledge, but surely it
should by now be realized that such an equation, at least in
the domain of action (as opposed to "pure theory"), is hope-
lessly oversimplified. I have already noted that the attainment of the highest social rationality would not, in any case,
be a necessary concomitant of the maximization of the principle of voluntary association; we are now left to ponder
whether there exists sufficient agreement as to the nature of
"rationality" in order to make it meaningful as a value to be
sought.

But let us for the moment assume, just for the sake of
argument, that what is socially most rational is the sort of
ideal object that can in principle be agreed upon, at least in
its broad outlines, by the most highly rational individuals in
a given society. It seems most likely that the inefficient, ener-
gy-diverting use to which some members would be inclined
to put the principle of voluntary association would soon lead
to the official curtailment of such diversions in the name of
greater rationality. From Plato on, the advocates of this conception of reason as the supreme social ideal have recognized
that the possibility of indiscriminate voluntary association
would pose a threat to the achievement of that ideal, and
they have been correct. Any attempt to define *substantively*
in advance the nature of a desired "rational" society implies
the rejection of whole classes of possible present actions as
harmful or irrelevant (not always because they are *ir*rational,
but because they are at least *non*-rational from the perspective of the desired society); but there is no means of guaran-
teeing, in the present, against the likelihood that some citizens will want to perform these actions. A monolithic society
in which efficient forms of compulsion have supplanted

voluntariness would therefore be best suited to maximizing the ideal of "rationality," if that ideal is taken to mean a specifically definable, fixed set of characteristics within a society. One might, of course, decide to stipulate that the truly "rational" society simply is a society in which the principle of voluntary association is respected; but on the basis of any other, more restrictive interpretation of the concept of rationality, the society of plural voluntary associations cannot optimistically be assumed to be the one in which "reason" will automatically be most fully exhibited.

Wish-Fulfillment. Closer than either unanimity or rationality as a value, the maximization of which could serve as a reason for favoring the principle of voluntary association, is that of wish-fulfillment, the satisfaction of the greatest possible number of individuals' desires. Wish-fulfillment, like both unanimity and rationality, may of course be challenged by claiming that it is not a worthy social idea; and indeed, the greatest political theorists have for the most part been among its severest challengers. What may at first seem especially odd is the fact that some of those in whose political philosophies the concept of volition or will has been most pivotal, such as Rousseau and Hegel, are particularly vigorous critics of the ideal of wish-fulfillment. But it is something other than mere confusion on their parts that has led to this puzzling situation, as I shall now try to show. I shall contend that, although the fulfillment of wishes is indeed a value which bears its own justification, it is not one which a society based on the principle of voluntary association (in either its Rousseauean or its plural form) is necessarily best able to maximize. This is because "association" always implies placing certain prior limitations in principle, however vague they may be, on what may legitimately be willed.

To associate always entails the acceptance, in however passive a fashion, of certain institutional structures, certain rules of the social whole. This insight was the basis of a good deal of social contract theorizing, and it must be remembered that many of the contract theorists, especially Hobbes, found no difficulty in conceiving even of government by forcefully acquired dominion on the model of consent.[8] To speak of *"voluntary* association" connotes, it seems to me, a much more active degree of consent or acceptance than that of an acquiescent conquered people; the concept of "voluntariness," like that of "acceptance,"[9] admits of degrees. We can even think of a kind of ideal, limiting case of voluntary association in which the desires of all the associates would totally coincide with the activities in which the association as a whole was engaging, and in which there would be no residue of particular desires on the part of any associate. This is undoubtedly Rousseau's model,[10] and it is also the model of a contemporary philosopher whose social thought owes much to Rousseau, Jean-Paul Sartre, in his conception of the *"groupe à chaud"* in the moment of its most complete "'totalization.'"[11] According to Sartre's account, a group of this type would be structureless, neither having nor needing rules. But Sartre's analysis also shows some of the reasons why such a moment cannot be sustained over time, and why the model has a purely ideal value and cannot provide an adequate description of any actual situation: if any capacity for genuinely free action remains with the associates (i.e., if the society in question is anything other than a totally conditioned one), then, by virtue of this fact, there continues always to exist a logical gap between the group's joint activity and the activities of the individuals. Moreover, as Sartre goes on to show, the very nature of most group activity (the effort to achieve certain common objectives, followed by the allotment of tasks in order to preserve these objectives) renders understandable, though not wholly inevitable, an association's retreat from the point of total membership participation towards institutionalization and even bureaucratization. This retreat entails the introduction of increasingly complex sets of rules. Now, the very existence of rules of any sort, however flexible and easily changeable, which have been formulated to guide the activities of an association to which one belongs entails a certain restraint on one's future actions —at the very least, a guidance of one's interests and activities along certain lines rather than any other possible ones. This is simply an explication of the meaning of "association" in general, and of "voluntary association" in particular.

The distinctive and paradoxical feature of an association which retains a high degree of "voluntariness" is, of course, the fact that such restraint is self-imposed, freely accepted. In a genuinely voluntary association, there is an underlying presupposition of self-discipline, which may or may not actually be put to the test: one wills the *non*fulfillment of certain of one's possible or even actual wishes and desires in favor of others, and sometimes even in favor of the desires of other members to which one's own desires might at first have been quite opposed. A genuinely voluntary association will, quite naturally, be such that a cessation of membership at any time will be allowable by its rules, but it is a salient fact about voluntary associations that members need not and do not always resign immediately from associations whose activities run counter in certain ways to their own original individual desires. Members' motivations for remaining members under such circumstances may vary greatly—they may calculate as utilitarians, weighing advantages against disadvantages, or they may have an overwhelming loyalty to the association's long-range goals which appears more important to them than a multitude of short-range mistakes, or they may believe, like Rousseau's citizen, that they were in error in not originally sharing in the sentiments which have proved to be those of the general will,[12] etc., but motivations are not our primary concern here. What is important is to acknowledge the complete compatibility between even the most active, wholehearted participation in a voluntary association and the nonfulfillment of one's wishes, some of which might well have been fulfilled if one had not been under the self-restraint of membership.

Wish-fulfillment, I have maintained, is a value; indeed, it is a fundamental value. But I have now shown that the maximization of wish-fulfillment is not a necessary accompaniment of the establishment of a society based on the principle of plural voluntary association (to say nothing of a monolithic voluntary society!), because, in the cases of some or even of many members of such a society, their participations in voluntary associations may result in self-imposed limitations of the severest kind. At the outset of this section, I suggested that the sort of (barely) conceivable society in which the value of wish-fulfillment could best be maximized would probably be "a totally atomistic, nearly anarchical [one] in which the single universally accepted rule restricting individual enterprise would be a prohibition against forming voluntary associations." It is sometimes forgotten that the thoroughgoing anarchist should be anarchistic not only with respect to the State, which is one outstanding kind of voluntary or involuntary association, but with respect to *all* associations: it is rule itself *(arche)* to which he is opposed. I would maintain (unhappily, because the conception has a certain charm) that it is not possible to conceive of the *totally* anarchistic society, just as the visions of mystics or the dreams of drug-users are said not to be formulable in discursive language, but I have suggested for consideration a society in which the rule of anarchy itself would be transgressed by the existence only of a single rule, that against the formation of voluntary associations. The fact that such a society would undoubtedly be so technologically backward as to place whole classes of what are to us the most banal and easily fulfilled wishes beyond the imaginings of members of that society is interesting, but irrelevant. The Anarcheans would at least find no institutional barriers, whether imposed by themselves or by their neighbors, on the fulfillment of those wishes of which they were capable—except, of course, such wishes as they might experience to join in voluntary associations!

It is not only in the imaginary quasi-anarchistic society, however, that the fulfillment of individual wishes may sometimes be maximized better than in a society based on the principle of voluntary association. Any society in which *"laissez faire, laissez aller"* is a popular slogan certainly has the potential for permitting the unrestrained realization of desires on the part of at least a few, and perhaps even of many, members to a degree that might not be possible for them if they were participants in certain types of voluntary associations. For example, there would undoubtedly be more self-restraint exercised over the inclination to unlimited wish-fulfillment in an *entire* society that was modeled on the principle of voluntary association (a possibility to be explored in Section IV of this paper) than there would be in a *"laissez faire"* society. In summary, even though the idea of wish-fulfillment, like those of unanimity and rationality, is one which is *sometimes* promoted through the activity of forming and participating in voluntary associations, it is not always or necessarily maximized by this activity. Some value other than the three thus far considered must therefore be sought as a basis for regarding voluntary association as itself in some sense an ideal.

II

It would be absurd to maintain that all voluntary associations are *eo ipso* ideal social forms. As long as two voluntary associations conflict with each other with respect to objectives, the alleged ideality of each will be denied by the other. Moreover, the observer of such a conflict, who himself may occupy a third perspective external to those of the associations in question, is likely to deny the accolade of ideality to both. Thus, whatever it is that makes it possible to consider the principle of voluntary association "a good thing," worth espousing, it cannot be the presupposition that every organization based upon that principle will be worthwhile. To employ an old but still useful terminology, the formation of voluntary associations should not be regarded as an end, but only as a means. (Though someone might wish, in opposition to this, to contend that the pattern maintenance of any ordered social system at all, and therefore of any voluntary association, is valuable in itself, I do not think that this is either a very interesting or a very defensible thesis.) The ideality that we are seeking must lie somehow in the end(s) for the achievement of which voluntary association is a particularly suitable means.

There are several diverse types of ends toward which a voluntary association may be conceived as being simultaneously directed; among these are (a) the internal structural goals involved in self-perpetuation and self-reform, (b) the external objectives of the association, and (c) the effects of participation on the members. For reasons that I have just indicated, the first two types cannot serve to account for the ideality of voluntary association *in general:* self-perpetuation and achievement of objectives on the part of a desirable voluntary association is desirable, and on the part of an undesirable one undesirable, and no further generalizations are possible in these respects. But perhaps *all* voluntary associations as such will be found to have a certain desirable effect on their members, merely by virtue of the fact that members voluntarily participate in them. This is what I wish now to suggest.

The existence of voluntary associations does not necessarily, as we have noted, result in an augmentation of the members' agreement (among themselves) or rationality (unless "rationality" is defined to mean simply "the exercise of volition"), or in the greater fulfillment of members' wishes. There are no doubt many other social values, too (such as the promotion of affluence, the raising of cultural standards, or the elimination of warfare), with regard to which the mere existence of plural voluntary associations in a society is neutral in its consequences. But the mere existence of such associations does imply the existence of a certain fact, which is at the same time a worthwhile or valuable fact, about their members: as voluntary participants in the activities of their associations, members are *responsible* for those activities, that is, they have enlarged their roles as agents in the social world and have assumed a certain share of the praise or blame of others for the occurrence of at least a few events in that world.[13] Whether the activities of a given voluntary association prove ultimately more praiseworthy or more blameworthy, the very fact that its members, as active participants, have assumed responsibility for those activities is in any case valuable, because they have managed, through their participation to exploit more fully some of the most important of human capacities. They have in short, realized their distinctively human potentialities for social action, for altering situations, and even for *creating* new social phenomena, and, by so doing, for entering into ethical relationships with all the other human beings whom their activities have affected.[14] It is because of the important role of voluntary associations in promoting these qualities in their members that the existence of such associations in a society is to be considered desirable, and it is in this sense that the principle of voluntary association is to be regarded as an ideal.

Two important objections to this formulation occur to me. The first is that voluntary associations are sometimes used by individuals as a means of trying to *elude* responsibility; membership in a group is sometimes thought to excuse harmful actions carried out on the basis of the group's decision, and the "anonymity of a committee" may be employed to deflect criticism from an individual decision-maker. But the point is that such situations as these occur only when "voluntariness," that is, participation by the members in an association's activities, is, to a large degree, lacking, and when we therefore are not confronted with a genuine voluntary association at all. Despite all its heroic exaltation of "will," the Nazi hierarchy was not, at least to the extent to which it spawned Eichmann-type individuals who presumably felt no sense of personal responsibility for the actions that they performed, a voluntary association; and the members of any group, whether a committee or a nation, who allow themselves to be used as rubber-stamps for the decisions of a single man or of a small clique are not truly participants in a voluntary association.

The second objection is that the value of responsibility, which I have seen voluntary associations as promoting, can also be promoted, and sometimes better promoted, by individuals themselves without the intermediary of a voluntary association; this objection (if it can be considered an objection at all, and not simply an additional comment) is not altogether incorrect. However, it suggests a very abstract view of the social world, is often used as a pretext for nonengagement and inactivity, and at best applies only to exceptional cases. Since a society of atomic individuals is purely fanciful, and since many of the most significant conceivable human achievements can only come about through the joint efforts of many persons, it frequently happens that the isolated individual who avoid group commitments in the name of an exalted conception of purely personal responsibility is in fact denying himself the possibility of ever assuming responsibility for any activities of importance in the social world.[15] It is occasionally possible to engage in such activities outside of any association, but the opportunities for exercising responsibility in this way, especially in modern times, are much less numerous than those open to individuals in a society in which voluntary associations flourish.

If this view of voluntary associations as ideal social forms because they ideally promote responsibility in their individual members is legitimate, it appears to be an interesting way of reconciling the collectivist orientation of much of classical political philosophy with the highly individualistic approach of most modern Western moral theory. In the transition between *The Social Contract* and Kant—a transition in which, however, the key formula concerning "obedience to a law that one has prescribed to oneself" remains constant—the gulf between the two perspectives appears with especially striking clarity. Kant's concern for individual autonomy and dignity, to which the value of responsibility is, of course, closely akin, seemed to leave him with a rather truncated political philosophy in which the potential values of positive group action found practically no recognition. Rousseau was keenly aware of the latter values, but the individual autonomy and dignity which were also his starting-points became quite muffled by the conclusion of his analyses. Both Rousseau and Kant saw the difficulty of ensuring that individuals, confronted with the possibility of deciding and acting, would make decisions and perform actions with full moral responsibility. The divergent orientations of their respective major works may be seen, in a way, as testifying to their divergent appraisals of the potential usefulness of voluntary associations. Both, it may be said, regarded the maximization of responsibility as desirable. Although Rousseau's solution erred by introducing an undue amount of coercion which would be likely in the long run to *reduce* the amount of responsibility exercised by individual citizens, the excessive Kantian emphasis on cultivating individual goodness at the expense of social ethics is not necessarily the only alternative. A further exploration of some of the paradoxes involved in the idea of "maximizing responsibility" by implementing the principle of voluntary association may help indicate in what sense a society of plural voluntary associations can be seen as a middle ground for reconciling these two divergent responses to the problem of encouraging the exercise of responsibility on the part of inherently weak-willed human beings.

III

If we analyze more closely the possible ways of carrying out the project of "maximizing responsibility" through voluntary association, we find that it can be guided into two very opposite directions. One of these directions leads quickly to the destruction of moral responsibility and the perversion of the principle of voluntary association, while the other relies heavily on that principle, correctly understood, to create and maintain a society in which individual autonomy and dignity are respected. The former method consists in the attempt by an individual or a small clique to *impose* certain limited, idiosyncratic, substantive goals upon as association or even upon society as a whole, and psychologically to *manipulate* large blocs of members into accepting as their own both these goals and the fixed tasks useful for achieving them that they have been assigned by their leadership. It involves labeling these goals as supremely rational, so that any deviation from orthodoxy can be treated as sheer stupidity and error, and encouraging those who at first did not agree with the consensus goals to regard their lingering desires for other things as aberrant and shameful. An association or a society in which this method is used thus brings together the ideals of unanimity (genuine but thoroughly coerced), rationality (by definitional fiat), and wish-fulfillment (by means of psychological conditioning and inhibiting) that we have previously considered, but it does so only at the expense of the ideal of moral responsibility. In the employment of this method, the principle of voluntary association is often claimed as the basis of group action. But the social scientist who investigates an association of this type will soon be able to identify it by virtue of the fact that its "consensus" has been created, and the members' acceptance of it manipulated, by a single individual or a clique. In the extreme case of such an association, we find millions, in the gigantic association of a modern state, observing the *Führerprinzip* with apparent enthusiasm and approval. This type of association vaunts the concept of "will" and might be thought to aim at the ideal of maximizing responsibility, since the approval of all is actively sought. But it is clear that such a system, while it may at first seem innocently to be directed toward carrying out the will of the people, ends by simply molding it.

There is an opposite direction in which the means of bringing about a maximization of responsibility in individuals through voluntary association may be sought. This alternative method takes account of the fact that the concept of moral responsibility includes, as I noted earlier, an element of *creativity*, since the objectives toward which responsible social action may be directed are not contained *a priori* in the concept of responsibility, but depend at least in large measure on the initiative of the morally responsible agent. While there are many conceivable compromises between the self-destructive method of "maximizing responsibility" sketched above and the present one,[16] it seems useful to portray the contrast at its most striking. The alternative method, then, involves conceiving of an association's and even of a society's goals essentially in terms of a liberation of the potentialities for creative activity latent in its members, rather than in terms of fixed tasks and roles imposed upon them from above and at best accepted by them through a process of psychological conditioning. (In the case of a voluntary association concerned with a limited range of human activities, the liberation in question is of course possible only within this range. In the case of a society as a whole which has assumed some of the characteristics of a voluntary association—the subject of the following section of this essay— there need be no prior limitations on the range of activities that may be affected as a result of membership.) In this model of voluntary association, dissent (from the objectives of the moment) which is directed toward a furthering of the process of opening up new possibilities for the group is encouraged, even though this entails retreating from the sometimes desirable ideal of unanimity; in fact, it is recognized that to emphasize "general will" and consensus often impairs the development of creativity within a group's membership. Here, "rationality," like "human nature," is recognized to be a changing rather than a fixed concept, requiring constant reinterpretation and redefinition as the achievement of certain of the association's objectives reveals the existence of new, previously unimagined possibilities for further objectives for the membership. And "wish-fulfillment," the other value that was considered earlier in this paper, is seen to be a most desirable but never attainable ideal which is best observed by *expanding* the scope of possible human desires, through the development of new possibilities for group and individual activity, rather than by narrowing it and inhibiting them.

This view of the best means of maximizing responsibility through the principle of voluntary association rests upon a recognition of one of the fundamental paradoxes of social and political philosophy, namely, that the development of responsibility *on the part of individuals* is a most desirable ideal (though surely not the only important one) of morality; and yet that, at the same time, the nature of most of the major objectives to which morally responsible men can address themselves necessitates joint, rather than individual, activity. It is this paradox that lies behind the divergence between Kantian and Rousseauean approaches to ethics. The practical resolution of the paradox, we have now seen, consists in establishing and encouraging voluntary associations in which the burden of decision-making and activity falls upon the entire membership, and at the same time in safeguarding the possibility of forming a plurality of such associations and subassociations within a whole society, permitting one group to be subordinated to another or to society as a whole only in extreme cases of utterly unavoidable clash.

But a further paradox lies ahead. Of course, a society of plural voluntary associations patterned after this second model is not an anarchistic society, because it is a society in which order, in the sense of the following of definite rules of behavior, prevails, rather than the anarchic absence of rules. Somewhat more surprising, however, is the fact that it is a society in which a certain amount of *coercion* may have to be exercised, both at the society's outset and sometimes even after it has become well established. To put it bluntly, talk of "maximizing responsibility" sounds, on one reading, suspiciously like the Rousseauean "forcing to be free." Upon this phrase, commentators unfriendly to Rousseau have—to some extent understandably—placed the most dire interpretations. But since almost no one, when pressed, is willing to maintain that coercion in any form and under any circumstances is invariably worse than a refusal to coerce, the question whether analysis may not reveal a morally acceptable meaning even of Rousseau's formulation should be left open. The maximization of responsibility implies, like the proposal of any social or political program, the exertion of a certain amount of coercion over the members of a given society—if in no other form than by verbal persuasion. The Kantian seems willing, for the most part, to leave the matter at the level of verbal persuasion, and to rely on "the common rational knowledge of morality" of the humble but upright ordinary man to assure the existence of a society in which the value of responsibility is upheld. We have seen, however, that the development of responsibility among members of society can be encouraged by certain types of associations and discouraged by others. Since this is so, the Kantian in a position of political power would not be justified if he failed to stimulate the growth of institutions of the desirable sort.[17]

If some institutions *can* contribute to promoting the value of responsibility, then such institutions *ought* to be established, to the extent to which they do not already exist. But the establishment of such institutions in places in which they do not already flourish (a problem so central to the thought of Rousseau and Machiavelli), as well as the encouragement of acceptance of them on the part of persons who have previously acquiesced in the existence of very different institutions, requires the exercise of coercion by the individuals who destroy the old institutions and bring about reform. In addition, one can never discount the possibility that certain

groups within even a previously flourishing voluntary association or a whole society may attempt, for reasons of their
own, to close off the possibilities for increased creativity that
are to be found in some or many of the other members. The
would-be victims of such an attempt may constitute a
minority or a majority of the entire association or society; this
fact makes no essential difference. At the same time, it may
also happen that still other members, lacking enthusiasm for
the sharing in responsibility which their membership ought
under optimal conditions to promote, may acquiesce passively in the attempted suppression of their fellows. Under
these circumstances, certain specially endowed or specially
well-informed individuals may be entitled to exercise coercion over the would-be suppressors, even though, *ex hypothesi,* this exercise of coercion does not enjoy the active support of the whole membership or even of a majority of it.[18]
Is not this attempted alteration of living patterns, in the
direction of channeling the options and thus to some extent
coercing the choices of those in whom responsibility and
choice are theoretically being maximized, a very clear illustration of what it might mean to force others to be free?

To concede that such contingencies are likely to rise, of
course, is to leave open the further possibility, actually realized so often in the course of world history, that those who
seek to establish or restore the principle of voluntary association in the face of active opposition and passive acquiescence
to it may come in the end to be the tyrannical imposers of
a "consensus" on a mass of individuals which has ceased in
any meaningful sense to act responsibly. Oppressive military
juntas, for example, often use the language of "restoring citizens to their sense of responsibility," or something of the sort,
in justification of tactics that are thoroughly destructive of all
moral responsibility. But to acknowledge that sound principles may be wrongly applied on all sides is not to erect the
admittedly corruptive qualities of power into an "iron law."
I have pointed out that the establishment or the restoration

of the principle of plural voluntary association may sometimes require the coercion, the "forcing to be free," even of
some of those who would best be able to exercise their moral
responsibility by means of that principle, and I now conclude
that the only hope for a society in which the principle has
been neglected or abused lies in the real though slightly
dubious possibility that its establishers or restorers will act
somewhat disinterestedly.[19]

Even established and flourishing institutions, including
some clearly voluntary associations in which there is no question of an attempted repression of some member's possibilities for creative activity by others, may sometimes take coercive steps to correct the effects of *apathy* on the part of their
members. Not everyone, in fact, desires to share in responsibility, however valuable it may be; none of us, in all likelihood, is equally enthusiastic about sharing in it at all times.
Clubs sometimes fine their members for nonattendance, and
some countries fine registered voters who absent themselves
from the polls. It is irrelevant to ask here whether or not
these practices are warranted in every case, but it is important to see that, beneath their appearance of paradox, they
are not necessarily inconsistent even with the ideal of voluntary association. For we saw earlier that membership in a
voluntary association, including the acceptance of its rules,
was perfectly compatible with the nonfulfillment of certain
of one's wishes and desires—including the desire to shirk the
exercise of one's responsibility as a member. The principle of
voluntary association can thus serve as a means of bringing
about at least a small society that is highly moral, because it
enables its members to participate *by their own choice* in
socially significant actions, but it can often do so only by
presenting them with situations in which they must place
self-limitations on their range of choices—especially on the
possible choice of avoiding the exercise of responsibility
while still remaining members.

In summary, a voluntary association patterned after the second model that I have proposed would be one in which, when it was functioning correctly, all the members would share in decisions and actions, none of which would be dictated or imposed either from within or from without the association. Creative suggestions from individuals and the creative use of special talents by individuals would be greatly encouraged, since it would be an association premised on the philosophically sound view that the exercise of responsibility implies the development of creativity. A sharp distinction would be drawn, however, between suggestion and imposition, and no person or small clique would have such a monopoly over the association's channels of communication as to turn his or its suggestions into the effective equivalents of *imposed* suggestions. Through this form of voluntary association, as I implied at the end of the previous section, it becomes possible to develop a practical reconciliation between an ethics that places highest priority on individual moral responsibility and a political philosophy that emphasizes the values of joint social action; thus, the Kantian and Rousseauean orientations both find a place in its conception. But the promotion of this form of association is not without its paradoxical aspects, since to promote some form of social institution entails the use of some form of coercion, *at least* of the gentle form of persuasion, and since there is at least some self-coercion involved on the part of the membership even in the most flourishing of voluntary associations. The constant need that we have felt, in the context of considering these paradoxes, to refer beyond small groups to society as a whole reminds us that one very interesting question, central to all political theory, remains to be raised in order to complete our re-examination of the principle of voluntary associations. That question can be stated as follows: Is there any sense in which a political unit encompassing the whole of a given society—a *polis* or a nation or a world-state—

could be conceived and organized after this model of voluntary association? If so, what might be some of its characteristics?

IV

None of the considerations that I have entertained up to this point indicates that it would be impossible to organize an entire society on the model of a genuinely voluntary association. With the modern breakdown in the long-sacred concept of absolute sovereignty has come the realization that there is no absolute or fixed nature to a "state" as such that would give it an unalterable status in the chain of being and thus render it the *necessary* initiator, locus, or court of last appeal for any particular kind of human activity. The question as to which social activities are best entrusted to a group called "the government" and which to other organized structures within society is one to which the answer is to be found, not in the stars, but in a detailed analysis of what is most practicable in a given society at a given time. A city-state *or* a world-state could be any one of the following: clan-centered, atomistic, monolithic and totally coercive, voluntaristic but monolithic, *or* voluntaristic and pluralistic —to recall the categories listed near the beginning of this essay. Earlier, I assimilated the voluntaristic but monolithic type to Rousseau's ideal republic and indicated some of the threats that such an arrangement would ultimately pose to the principle of voluntary association. Rousseau's intention was certainly to limn a whole society of voluntary association, though without private associations, but his end-product was one in which the original intention became at least partially frustrated. Can an entire society aspire to organize itself as a voluntary association without becoming monolithic in the Rousseauean sense of disallowing the establishment of smaller groups within it?

The answer, it seems to me, is affirmative if we take less

seriously than did most of early modern political theory the alleged dichotomy between public and private spheres. (One of the great merits of Professor Harris' paper in this volume is that he shows several ways in which this distinction can be broken down.) It is surely possible, once we have acknowledged the nonexistence of such a boundary "in nature," to conceive of a society—even, at the limit, one composed of all living members of the human race—that formed a single voluntary association for certain purposes and that consisted of a plurality of voluntary associations for other purposes; both the respective purposes (of the largest association and of the others) and the identities and memberships of the subassociations could be conceived of as fluctuating in response to conditions. As long as the society-wide association always left open the *possibility* that smaller associations might also be formed, and as long as the hierarchical subordination of one association to another remained strictly limited to "extreme cases of utterly unavoidable clash" (as I expressed it earlier), then such a society would approximate very closely to the model of the proper type of voluntary association for maximizing individual responsibility that I have outlined. Plurality and diversity of activities both among the smaller associations and among the individual members would be encouraged in such a society, just as creative dissent was said to be encouraged among the individual members in that model. "Rationality" and common objectives, here as there, would be open concepts subject to constant re-evaluation and renewed discovery, rather than being the fixed, pre-defined contents of an imposed "consensus." And, just as in the previously outlined model, manipulation of the whole by an individual or a small clique —which in this case might well mean a smaller ("private") voluntary association or a combination of them acting as a pressure group—would not be permitted to prevail, so that the responsibility connected with the decision-making and creative activity of the whole society could be shared as fully as possible by all its members. These would be some of the characteristics of an entire society that had become organized as a voluntary association.

An actually existing sociopolitical structure need not, of course, imitate a known model in every respect in order for it to be reasonably assimilated to that model rather than to some other one by a social scientist engaged in constitution-classifying. Nor is there any clear point at which deviation has become so great that any such assimilation constitutes an obvious error. Thus, to say, as some might, that certain contemporary societies have much in common with the ideal of voluntary association as I sketched it is to make an interesting and possibly illuminating claim that admits neither of facile acceptance nor of facile rejection. The term "participatory democracy" has often been applied to conceptions of social organization that share many characteristics with this ideal of voluntary association, and actual small groups alleged to be "participatory democracies" might well be measured profitably by its standards. On the other hand, some claim that "participatory democracy" is an impossibility, and, given certain definitions of that concept, they might well be correct. With respect to the model of voluntary association that I have presented here, I claim only that it is worth considering, that it is generally the best means in the social world in which we live for promoting the very fundamental and desirable (though not *uniquely* desirable) ideal of responsibility, and that it is self-consistent; I am not concerned with giving it a polemical label.

On the other hand, I would object to the use of polemical labels by others as a means of discrediting *a priori* any proposed social model, including this one. Such a use has been made, in recent years, of the word "democracy" *tout court*, especially when it has been taken to mean, as the opening paragraph of this essay expresses it, "something like the prevailing American system of institutions." It will be my final contention that, whereas the asserted ideality of the latter is usually left undemonstrated and often seems to stem from a purely or almost purely emotional conviction ("I like living here," "The American ideology is an ideology of freedom and the Albanian ideology is an ideology of slavery," etc.), this system of institutions as it exists today actually appears in a highly unfavorable light when measured against the assumed ideality of voluntary association as discussed in this essay.

V

There is a fairly extensive contemporary theoretical literature on the concept of democracy, and, in the more detailed analyses of the best of these theorists, enough distinctions are made so that the reader may at least *begin* to be able to comprehend why the Democratic Party, the Students for a Democratic Society, and the Democratic Republic of Vietnam, for example, may all have *some* justification for using the same adjective in ways that are at least partly incompatible with one another. But, when such words as "democracy" and "democratic institutions" are bandied about outside the context of such respectable exercises in fine distinction, it usually becomes clear that a privileged status is assumed to have been conferred on one particular set of social institutions to which these terms have been applied. Perhaps it can be shown that American institutions are the "most democratic" in existence at present, though one can be quite sure that they cannot be shown to be the "most democratic" conceivable; unfortunately, however, too few writers take the trouble to try to show this, and many simply assume it instead. In addition, many writers make the further blunder of simply applying to current American institutions an ideal conception of democracy that they themselves have formed or have been taught, falsely supposing the actual and the ideal to coincide, and then unconsciously wavering between the two meanings, as it suits their purposes, in using the word. But Americans (as well as others, needless to say) live today in a world that differs significantly from the visions and even from the nightmares of Locke or Madison or Jefferson or de Tocqueville. A descriptive sketch, like all descriptions necessarily partial, of some of the actual institutions of contemporary American society would be useful at this point in order to redress the balance between dreams and reality.

What are some of the most salient features of current American political and social institutions? Practically all decisions of major importance affecting the society as a whole, including decisions related to the society's very survival, are made either by the government, which is said to be a government of the people, or by one of several huge private associations—corporations and business, labor, and professional organizations. "The government" has come increasingly, in common usage, to mean primarily the bureaucracy controlled by the Executive Branch. The head of this branch, the President, must stand for election every four years. But these elections entail very little genuine (as distinguished from purely emotional) participation by most members of society: at least one-third of those eligible to vote usually do not do so, and the continued dominance of the two-party system, together with the relatively closed character of each party's own organizational structure, leaves even those who do vote with only a minimum of choice. There is no obligation on the executive's part to fulfill even the expectations to which his explicit campaign pledges may have given rise, and, in an era in which sequences of events are generally acknowledged to pass more rapidly than ever before, the executive is able, within a four-year span, to impose whole series of decisions and ideals on the populace without its possessing any possibility of effectively blocking them. The legislators, some of whom are elected more frequently and might thus be expected to be somewhat closer in sentiment to their constituents, often admit to having abdicated their responsibility in many important areas, especially in the crucial area of foreign affairs, in favor of the Executive Branch.[20] The abdication process seems to a large extent to continue regardless of

whether a particular President is relatively popular or un-
popular among the legislators. This long-range trend receives applause from some academic efficiency experts, who
correctly see in the situation of a strong executive imposing
his wishes on an entire society the best possibility for achieving a "rational state"[21]—in cheerful unconcern about all its
potential liabilities. As for the large *private* associations, most
of which are supported by huge memberships (stockholders,
trade unionists, professionals who must belong in order to
maintain their professional status, etc.) but actually governed
by small "elites," their principal role seems to fluctuate between that of pressure groups, trying to manipulate both
governmental favor and public taste in their directions by
means of the disproportionate power which they enjoy,[22]
and that of quasi-governmental agencies. Once again, these
features find their strong academic defenders—on one side,
those who see "true democracy" shining through the interplay of powerful pressure groups, and on the other those who
regard the trend toward state monopoly capitalism as further
evidence of the increasing rationalization of American society.[23] In short, one sees on many sides a growing advocacy
of the principles of elitism and of bureaucracy, together with
growing resignation, willingly abetted by the elites, to this
tendency on the part of large segments of the population. As
for the actual objectives which some of the most prominent
elites wish to impose on the society at large, one may assume
that not all members of these groups have succeeded in clarifying their intentions. Overt behavior should, however, furnish some indication of intended objectives, and in this case
the latter can hardly be said to be of the sort most likely to
stimulate creativity. What one observes is a vast expansion of
the military establishment, especially in such a way as to
make much of industry a part of it, together with an effort
to impose a certain life-style known as "the American way"
on the widest possible range of societies throughout the
world and to encourage the largest possible number of in-

dividuals, through both peaceful and warlike means, to conform to a negativistic ideology that is best labeled "anti-Communism." Meanwhile, entire segments of the American population have demonstrated by their extralegal actions, that they do not now consider it possible for themselves to participate in the activities of their society by means of the institutions sanctioned under the current legal system.

These facts are familiar commonplaces today, but it is valuable to recall them and to state them relatively concisely. They have been catalogued in such a way as probably to evoke a negative emotional reaction on the part of most readers. Other facts might have been recounted—for example, the effects of certain recent American judicial decisions in expanding the guarantees of civil liberties, or the rise of the Janus-faced practice, encouraging at once both greater participation and greater passivity among citizens, of public opinion polling—in partial mitigation of this reaction. However, my intention has been simply to select certain facts that have seemed to me most useful for measuring the reality of American society against the ideal of a society based on the principle of voluntary association. The purpose of the remainder of our reflections, therefore, should be a limited one; we should not be concerned at this point, for example, with trying to judge whether more "good" or more "evil" prevails on balance, or whether "things" are "better" or "worse" than they were in the past, and so on. With the relevant facts before us, we are now in a position to make the desired measurement, bearing in mind the previously sketched models.

In contemporary American society, is coerced unanimity or creative dissent on important matters the more general rule? Is it the more common assumption that the institutional and other behavior patterns constitutive of political and social rationality (e.g., "the democratic process") are already known and unchangeable and need only to be taught to those still ignorant of them, or that such social patterns as fall under the rubric of "the conventional wisdom" require constant reappraisal and redefinition? Are the desires of the population channeled by pressure groups into directions that sustain both those groups' profits and the institutional arrangements which made such channeling possible in the first place, or is the greatest encouragement given to the liberation of potential talents, to creativity, and to the development of new sets of needs which might escape such imposed patterns as that of planned obsolescence? Are large private associations profiting from a generally favorable attitude toward "pluralism" in order to eliminate, by acquiring disproportionate influence for themselves over the processes of social decision-making, the very purposes which genuine pluralism is intended to serve, or do private associations generally foster the one common purpose which justifies the existence of all of them, namely, the promotion of responsibility on the part of individuals? Finally, is this same purpose one which government and the other organizations of society at large tend to disregard and to consider an undesirable hindrance to their own smooth functioning, or is it one which these organizations are dedicated to stimulating? It would be a foolhardy optimist indeed who could confidently claim that the situation of American society was in every case closer to the second than to the first of the options presented by each of the above questions. One may therefore conclude confidently, without further pressing the case as it might be pressed, that American society is very far from meeting the ideal of voluntary association, and very far indeed from promoting the desirable exercise of responsibility on the part of all its citizens. As a final consequence, one must become more skeptical than ever of those writers who attempt to measure other societies by the yardstick of what they call "democracy," when by this they mean actual American institutions; for, in so doing, they impute an ideality to those institutions which is radically belied by the facts.

Why do so many writers continue to regard the American

version of "democracy" as having a quasi-normative status? A brief and somewhat speculative answer to this question may be in order. It is true that some of the older institutions still extant in American society were, when first proposed and put into effect, great advances over earlier political forms. The notion of representative government—which, as we have noted, has suffered a considerable decline in importance and effectiveness in contemporary America—was an especially brilliant step in the direction of more fully implementing the principle of voluntary association. Part of its justification, however, stemmed from its having been introduced in an epoch in which the scarcity of resources and the lack of technological means made it impossible for the great majority of any population directly to devote any considerable part of its time to social action. Writers who continue to think, however erroneously in light of actual practice, of American "democracy" in terms of representative government are no doubt still influenced by historical memories of the past triumphs of that conception. But today, technology has reduced the time required to implement many socially important decisions (to take a morbid example, the decision to decimate an entire nation's population can be implemented in a single day), and the decline of scarcity has increased the amount of free time, some of which could be devoted to socially responsible activity, that is available to average citizens in the world's more affluent societies. It has thus become possible to conceive of better methods than that of representative government (better, at least, than that of representative government *alone*) for augmenting popular participation in social decision-making. Improvements in transportation and communications, for example, have rendered feasible the direct involvement by interested and informed citizens in areas such as regulation of industry, and by citizens who are in the process of becoming interested and informed in areas such as community development projects and poverty relief programs, which have traditionally been controlled by legislative and/or administrative *fiat*. If the realization of this fact and of the potential usefulness of material historical changes for developing new means of increasing popular participation were to become more widespread among the writers about whose motives I have been speculating, then many of them would, I think, be inclined to reassess their standards of social measurement. For many do, it seems certain, concur at least in a general way with the underlying assumption of this essay that the principle of voluntary association is itself eminently worthwhile.

The reason for regarding voluntary association as so worthwhile, I have contended here, depends upon a view of the *individual* as the focal-point of social values. Those who do not share this view may not, of course, regard voluntary associations as an ideal at all, and there are no doubt many such persons in the ranks of writers, politicians, and military men, among others. I have not undertaken the Sisyphean task of attempting to demonstrate the validity of this basic outlook; rather, I have concerned myself with trying to show that voluntary group activity, far from necessarily diminishing the dignity or even the moral autonomy of the individual, is capable of vastly enhancing each member's role in the achievement of social objectives through creative social change. A whole society in which the ideal of voluntary association can be fully, or nearly fully, realized may still be a very distant dream, though historical changes in material conditions make it more seriously conceivable for large masses of people now than it was in the past. Surely the American society is very far from that ideal, and many critics see in this failure convincing evidence that American society has failed in every important respect. Of course, that is not true. In the development of efficient industrial and war machines, in the production of vast quantities of readily available consumer goods, and even in upgrading the cultural level in some areas, for example, American society has registered notable successes. I have shown that the promotion of voluntary association does not necessarily lead to the maximizing even of certain fundamental values—unanimity, rationality, and wish-fulfillment—that have often been linked with it. Nevertheless, such promotion does lead to a maximizing of the value of *individual responsibility;* and a society or a smaller group in which this value is held in highest esteem will be one in which the principle of genuine voluntary association, rather than the self-contradictory practice of imposing a manipulated "consensus" on a membership that is supposed in all other respects to be passive, flourishes.

NOTES

1. *"Plus le concerte règne dans les assemblées, c'est-à-dire plus les avis approchent de l'unanimité, plus aussi la volonté générale est dominante."* Du Contrat Social, IV, 2.

In his chapter on Rousseau, Talmon states bluntly: "It is of great importance to realize that what is to-day considered as an essential concomitant of democracy, namely, diversity of views and interests, was far from being regarded as essential by the eighteenth-century fathers of democracy. Their original postulates were unity and unanimity." J. L. Talmon, *The Rise of Totalitarian Democracy* (New York: Praeger, 1960), p. 44. One need not, as I do not, subscribe to all of Talmon's conclusions in order to admit the truth of this historical observation.

2. *"Il importe donc, pour avoir bien l'énoncé de la volonté générale, qu'il n'y ait pas de société partielle dans l'Etat, et que chaque citoyen n'opine que d'après lui,"* Du Contrat Social, II, 3.

3. For Rousseau, such a society is *"l'autre extrémité du cercle . . . c'est quand les citoyens, tombés dans la servitude, n'ont plus ni liberté ni volonté."* Du Contrat Social, IV, 2.

4. An early instance of this tendency may perhaps be found in the philosophy of Aristotle. It is not very easy, to say the least, to reconcile his criticism of Plato for overemphasizing the factor of unity in the *Republic* (*Politics*, Book II, esp. Chap. 2) with his advocacy elsewhere of unanimity as an end to be striven for (*Nicomachean Ethics*, Book IX, Chap. 6).

5. A. P. d'Entrèves provides a particularly interesting treatment of "order" as a borderline concept between description and evaluation in *La Dottrina dello Stato* (Torina: G. Giappichelli, 1962), pp. 215–26.

6. This fundamental point remains valid, regardless of whatever divergences from the Platonic conception of rationality may be suggested in the following paragraph and endorsed in the discussion of ideal models in Sections III and IV of this paper.

7. These questions are discussed at length in some of the contributions to Carl J. Friedrich (ed.), Nomos VII, *Rational Decision* (New York: Atherton Press, 1964). Abraham Kaplan's "Some Limitations on Rationality" (pp. 55–64) is especially provocative with respect to the question of defining "rationality," and Heinz Eulau's "Logics of Rationality in Unanimous Decision-Making" (pp. 26–54) attempts to defend the possibility of a concurrence of unanimity and rationality. Eulau is concerned with those who see a necessary *in*compatibility between the two—the converse of my own concern above.

8. *Leviathan*, II, 20.

9. Cf. my article, "The Acceptance of a Legal System," *The Monist* 49, 3 (July 1965), esp. pp. 382–83.

10. *"Mieux l'Etat est constitué, plus les affaires publiques l'emportent sur les privées, dans l'esprit des citoyens."* Du Contrat Social, III, 15.

11. Jean-Paul Sartre, *Critique de la raison dialectique*, Tome I (Paris: Gallimard, 1960), esp. pp. 384–410.

12. *"Quand donc l'avis contraire au mien l'emporte, cela ne prouve autre chose sinon que je m'étois trompé, et que ce que j'estimois être la volonté générale ne l'étoit pas."* Du Contrat Social, IV, 2.

13. On the sense in which "responsibility" is both a descriptive and a normative concept, cf. George A. Schrader, "Responsibility and Existence," in Carl J. Friedrich (ed.), Nomos III, *Responsibility* (New York: The Liberal Arts Press, 1960), pp. 43–70. The initial article in the same volume, J. Roland Pennock, "The Problem of Responsibility," pp. 3–27, is also especially valuable in exploring the meanings of the term and its potential significance for political philosophy.

14. Clearly, the concept of responsibility that I am employing here is one that connotes *activity*—choice, the formulation of projects, the achievement of social objectives—rather than just a passive state. I agree with Pennock (*op. cit.*, p. 13): "We must say that it means more than duty or dutifulness and more than accountability, although it includes these meanings. The 'more than' points toward the exercise of discretion by deliberate and thoughtful decision. . . ."

15. The charge of having reached this impasse has frequently been leveled in recent times against existentialist philosophers, who have emphasized so strongly the concepts of individual responsibility and choice. Such a charge was heard particularly frequently during the immediate post-World War II period, especially from Marxist writers. For example, cf. Henri Lefebvre's *L'Existentialisme* (Paris: Editions du Sagittaire, 1946). However, the subsequent great concern about social problems, especially on the part of Sartre, has helped considerably to mitigate this charge.

16. For example, Norton E. Long says that "A highly important role of responsible citizenship . . . is that of supporting the rules of the game." ("Development of Responsible Citizenship," in *Responsibility, op. cit.*, p. 239). This is a compromise view of responsibility, based on the optimistic assumption that the current rules (Long is thinking of "constitutional," "democratic" regimes) are so eminently worth supporting that to challenge

them is to be irresponsible. One must remember that this was written in a different era from the present one, though it was only a few years ago.

17. In fairness to Kant, it must be pointed out that he explicitly acknowledges something like this at one point in his political treatise: "The *Spirit* of that original contract . . . entails the obligation of the constituted authority to make the type of government conform to this Idea and, accordingly, to change the government gradually and continually, if it cannot be done at one time, so that it will effectively agree with the one and only legitimate constitution, namely, that of a pure republic." *The Metaphysical Elements of Justice*, trans. John Ladd (Indianapolis: Bobbs-Merrill, 1965), p. 112. But this thread in Kant's thought is, unfortunately, seldom alluded to.

18. Considerations of this sort seem to have concerned the authors of a remarkable recent *libellum, A Critique of Pure Tolerance* (Boston: Beacon Press, 1965), which contains essays by Robert Paul Wolff, Barrington Moore, Jr., and Herbert Marcuse. To question in any way the practice of tolerance is a dangerous and dubious exercise, and yet there is an obvious sense in which the tolerance of gigantic social and political forces which threaten to eliminate the very conditions of healthy dissent is itself "repressive," as the title of Marcuse's essay puts it. Though much of Wolff's analysis of contemporary American society and of the ways in which certain large voluntary associations have today lost their *raison d'être* and become obstructive is sound, I cannot entirely agree, for reasons indicated in this article, with his conclusion (p. 52) that "There is need for a new philosophy of community, *beyond pluralism* and beyond tolerance" (italics mine).

19. Problems very similar to those that I have just considered are raised in Rousseau's treatment of "The Legislator" (*Du Contrat Social*, II, 7). Rousseau's idealistic resolution, which consists in envisaging a state-founding "legislator" who does not take part in the actual decision-making and who appeals to a mystical (supernatural) authority in support of his proposals for a constitution, is one which does not augur well for the future of that society, once it has begun to question its superstitions.

20. We may, for example, recall the practice among contemporary American legislators of avoiding criticism of important policy decisions on grounds either that they do not have access to the relevant information, or that they do not wish to detract from the image of national unity and consensus concerning the executive's policy, or both.

21. There is more than a hint of this attitude, for example, in the work of Richard Neustadt, though he would probably not wish to endorse my terminology of "imposition" and "rational State."

22. One has only to think of the advertising and mass communications industries in this connection.

23. David Truman is, of course, only one of many contemporary political scientists who see in the interplay of pressure groups one of the most essential features of democracy; as an instance of the justification of the "trend" that I cite, one might recall the stand taken by a number of liberal thinkers and politicians several years ago in support of the proposed Communications Satellite arrangement.

Selected Bibliography

Note: Secondary sources, non-English literature and journal articles are kept to a minimum.

ARENDT, HANNAH. *The Human Condition.* Chicago: The University of Chicago Press, 1958.

———. "Truth and Politics." In *Philosophy, Politics and Society: Third Series,* edited by Peter Laslett and W. G. Runciman, pp. 104–33. New York: Barnes and Noble, 1967.

BACHELARD, GASTON. *La Formation de l'Esprit Scientifique.* Paris: J. Vrin, 1947.

BARNES, HAZEL E. *An Existentialist Ethics.* New York: Alfred A. Knopf, 1967.

BEAUVOIR, SIMONE DE. *The Ethics of Ambiguity.* Translated by BERNARD FRECHTMAN. New York: The Citadel Press, 1962.

———. *L'Existentialisme et la Sagesse des Nations.* Paris: Nagel, 1948.

_____. *Force of Circumstance*. Translated by RICHARD HOWARD. New York: G. P. Putnam's Sons, 1964.

_____. *Memoirs of a Dutiful Daughter*. Translated by JAMES KIRKUP. Cleveland: World Publishing Co., 1959.

_____. *The Prime of Life*. Translated by PETER GREEN. Cleveland: World Publishing Co., 1962.

BERDYAEV, NICOLAS. *Dream and Reality*. Translated by KATHERINE LAMPERT. New York: Macmillan, 1951.

_____. *The Fate of Man in the Modern World*. Translated by DONALD A. LOWRIE. Ann Arbor: The University of Michigan Press, 1935.

_____. *Slavery and Freedom*. Translated by R. M. FRENCH. New York: Charles Scribner's Sons, 1944.

_____. *Solitude and Society*. Translated by GEORGE REAVEY. London: Geoffrey Bles, 1938.

BERGER, PETER L., and THOMAS LUCKMANN. *The Social Construction of Reality*. New York: Doubleday, 1966.

BINSWANGER, LUDWIG. *Being-in-the-World: Selected Papers*. Translated by JACOB NEEDLEMAN. New York: Basic Books, 1963.

BOSS, MEDARD. *Psychoanalysis and Daseinsanalysis*. Translated by LUDWIG B. LEFEBRE. New York: Basic Books, 1963.

BRAND, GERD. *Die Lebenswelt: Eine Philosophie des konkreten Apriori*. Berlin: Walter de Gruyter, 1971.

BUBER, MARTIN. *Between Man and Man*. Translated by RONALD GREGOR SMITH. New York: Macmillan, 1965.

_____. *I and Thou*. Translated by WALTER KAUFMANN. New York: Charles Scribner's Sons, 1970.

_____. *The Knowledge of Man*. Edited by MAURICE FRIEDMAN. New York: Harper and Row, 1965.

_____. *Paths in Utopia*. Translated by R. F. C. HULL. Boston: Beacon Press, 1958.

_____. *Pointing the Way*. Edited and translated by MAURICE FRIEDMAN. New York: Harper & Row, 1963.

BUGBEE, HENRY G., JR. *The Inward Morning*. College Park, Pa.: Bald Eagle Press, 1958.

BURNIER, MICHEL-ANTOINE. *Choice of Action*. Translated by BERNARD MURCHLAND. New York: Random House, 1968.

BUYTENDIJK, F. J. J. *Phénoménologie de la Rencontre*. Paris: Brouwer, 1952.

CAMUS, ALBERT. *The Myth of Sisyphus and Other Essays*. Translated by JUSTIN O'BRIEN. New York: Alfred A. Knopf, 1955.

_____. *The Rebel*. Translated by ANTHONY BOWER. New York: Alfred A. Knopf, 1956.

_____. *Resistance, Rebellion, and Death*. Translated by JUSTIN O'BRIEN. New York: Alfred A. Knopf, 1960.

DALLMAYR, FRED R. "Existential Phenomenology and Social Science: An Overview and Appraisal." A paper delivered at the ninth annual meeting of the Society for Phenomenology and Existential Philosophy in New York, October 30–November 1, 1970.

DESAN, WILFRID. *The Planetary Man*. Vol. 1. Washington: Georgetown University Press, 1961.

DREYFUS, HUBERT L. *Alchemy and Artificial Intelligence*. RAND Paper P-3244. Santa Monica: The RAND Corporation, December, 1965.

_____. "Why Computers Must Have Bodies in Order to be Intelligent." *The Review of Metaphysics* 21 (September 1967): 13–32.

DUFRENNE, MIKEL. "Existentialisme et Sociologie." *Cahiers Internationaux de Sociologie* 1 (1946): 161–70.

_____. *Jalons*. The Hague: Martinus Nijhoff, 1966.

_____. *Language and Philosophy*. Translated by HENRY B. VEATCH. Bloomington: Indiana University Press, 1963.

_____. *The Notion of the A Priori*. Translated by EDWARD S. CASEY. Evanston: Northwestern University Press, 1966.

————. *La Personnalité de Base: Un Concept Sociologique*. Paris: Presses Universitaires de France, 1953.

————. *Pour l'Homme*. Paris: Seuil, 1968.

————. "The Role of Man in the Social Sciences." *Philosophy Today* 4 (Spring, 1960), 36–44.

EARLE, WILLIAM. *Objectivity*. New York: The Noonday Press, 1955.

EDIE, JAMES M., ed. *An Invitation to Phenomenology*. Chicago: Quadrangle Books, 1965.

————, ed. *New Essays in Phenomenology*. Chicago: Quadrangle Books, 1969.

————, ed. *Phenomenology in America*. Chicago: Quadrangle Books, 1967.

EDIE, JAMES M.; FRANCIS H. PARKER; and CALVIN O. SCHRAG, eds. *Patterns of the Life-World: Essays in Honor of John Wild*. Evanston: Northwestern University Press, 1970.

FARBER, MARVIN. *The Foundation of Phenomenology*. Cambridge: Harvard University Press, 1943.

————, ed. *Philosophical Essays in Memory of Edmund Husserl*. Cambridge: Harvard University Press, 1940.

FRANKL, VIKTOR. *Man's Search for Meaning*. New York: Washington Square Press, 1963.

GADAMER, HANS-GEORG. *Wahrheit und Methode*. Tübingen: J. C. B. Mohr, 1960.

GARFINKEL, HAROLD. *Studies in Ethnomethodology*. Englewood Cliffs: Prentice-Hall, 1967.

GENDLIN, EUGENE T. *Experiencing and the Creation of Meaning*. Glencoe: The Free Press, 1962.

GRAY, J. GLENN. *On Understanding Violence Philosophically and Other Essays*. New York: Harper & Row, 1970.

————. *The Warriors*. New York: Harper & Row, 1970.

GURWITSCH, ARON. *The Field of Consciousness*. Pittsburgh: Duquesne University Press, 1964.

_____. *Studies in Phenomenology and Psychology*. Evanston: Northwestern University Press, 1966.

GUSDORF, GEORGES. *Introduction aux Sciences Humaines*. Paris: Centre National de la Recherche Scientifique, 1960.

_____. *Speaking*. Translated by PAUL T. BROCKELMAN. Evanston: Northwestern University Press, 1965.

HABERMAS, JÜRGEN. *Knowledge and Human Interests*. Translated by JEREMY J. SHAPIRO. Boston: Beacon Press, 1971.

_____. *Technik und Wissenschaft als "Ideologie."* Frankfurt am Main: Suhrkamp, 1968.

_____. *Theorie und Praxis*. 3rd ed. Neuwied: Luchterhand, 1969.

_____. *Toward a Rational Society*. Translated by JEREMY J. SHAPIRO. Boston: Beacon Press, 1970.

_____. *Zur Logik der Sozialwissenschaften*. Tübingen: J. C. B. Mohr, 1967.

HEIDEGGER, MARTIN. *Being and Time*. Translated by JOHN MACQUARRIE and EDWARD ROBINSON. New York: Harper & Bros., 1962.

_____. *Discourse on Thinking*. Translated by JOHN M. ANDERSON and E. HANS FREUND. New York: Harper & Row, 1966.

_____. *The Essence of Reasons*. Translated by TERRENCE MALICK. Evanston: Northwestern University Press, 1969.

_____. *An Introduction to Metaphysics*. Translated by RALPH MANHEIM. New Haven: Yale University Press, 1959.

_____. *Kant and the Problem of Metaphysics*. Translated by JAMES S. CHURCHILL. Bloomington: Indiana University Press, 1962.

_____. "Letter on Humanism." Translated by EDGAR LOHNER. In *Philosophy in the Twentieth Century*, ed-

434   SELECTED BIBLIOGRAPHY

ited by WILLIAM BARRETT and HENRY D. AIKEN, 2: 270–302. New York: Random House, 1962.

————. *On the Way to Language.* Translated by PETER D. HERTZ. New York: Harper & Row, 1971.

————. *What Is Called Thinking?* Translated by FRED D. WIECK and J. GLENN GRAY. New York: Harper & Row, 1968.

————. *What Is a Thing?* Translated by W. B. BARTON, JR., and VERA DEUTSCH. Chicago: Henry Regnery, 1967.

HUSSERL, EDMUND. *Cartesian Meditations.* Translated by DORION CAIRNS. The Hague: Martinus Nijhoff, 1960.

————. *The Crisis of European Sciences and Transcendental Phenomenology.* Translated by DAVID CARR. Evanston: Northwestern University Press, 1970.

————. *Erfahrung und Urteil.* Edited by LUDWIG LAND-GREBE. Hamburg: Claassen, 1964.

————. *Formal and Transcendental Logic.* Translated by DORION CAIRNS. The Hague: Martinus Nijhoff, 1969.

————. *Ideas: General Introduction to Pure Phenomenology.* Translated by W. R. BOYCE GIBSON. New York: Macmillan, 1931.

————. *Logical Investigations.* Translated by J. N. FINDLAY. 2 vols. New York: The Humanities Press, 1970.

————. "Phenomenology." Translated by C. V. SOLOMON. In *Realism and the Background of Phenomenology,* edited by RODERICK M. CHISHOLM, pp. 118–28. Glencoe: The Free Press, 1960.

————. "Phenomenology and Anthropology." Translated by RICHARD G. SCHMITT. In *Realism and the Background of Phenomenology,* edited by RODERICK M. CHISHOLM, pp. 129–42. Glencoe: The Free Press, 1960.

————. *Phenomenology and the Crisis of Philosophy.* Translated by QUENTIN LAUER. New York: Harper & Row, 1965.

————. *The Phenomenology of Internal Time-Consciousness.* Edited by MARTIN HEIDEGGER and translated by JAMES

S. CHURCHILL. Bloomington: Indiana University Press, 1964.

INGARDEN, ROMAN. *Time and Modes of Being.* Translated by HELEN R. MICHEJDA. Springfield, Ill.: Charles C. Thomas, 1964.

JAMES, WILLIAM. *Essays in Radical Empiricism.* New York: Longmans, Green, 1912.

_____. *Essays on Faith and Morals.* Cleveland: World Publishing Co., 1962.

_____. *The Principles of Psychology.* 2 vols. New York: Dover Publications, 1950.

JASPERS, KARL. *The Future of Germany.* Edited and translated by E. B. ASHTON. Chicago: The University of Chicago Press, 1967.

_____. *The Future of Mankind.* Translated by E. B. ASHTON. Chicago: The University of Chicago Press, 1960.

_____. *General Psychopathology.* Translated by J. HOENIG and MARIAN W. HAMILTON. Chicago: The University of Chicago Press, 1964.

_____. *Man in the Modern Age.* Translated by EDEN and CEDAR PAUL. New York: Doubleday, 1957.

_____. *The Origin and Goal of History.* Translated by MICHAEL BULLOCK. New Haven: Yale University Press, 1953.

_____. *Philosophy.* Translated by E. B. ASHTON. 3 vols. Chicago: The University of Chicago Press, 1969–71.

_____. *Reason and Existenz.* Translated by WILLIAM EARLE. New York: The Noonday Press, 1955.

JUNG, HWA YOL. "Confucianism and Existentialism: Intersubjectivity as the Way of Man." *Philosophy and Phenomenological Research* 30 (December 1969): 186–202.

_____. *"Jen:* An Existential and Phenomenological Problem of Intersubjectivity." *Philosophy East and West* 16 (July–October 1966): 169–88.

_____. "Leo Strauss's Conception of Political Philosophy: A

Critique." *The Review of Politics* 29 (October 1967): 492–517.

_____. "The Logic of the Personal: John Macmurray and the Ancient Hebrew View of Life." *The Personalist* 47 (Autumn 1966): 532–46.

_____. "A Phenomenological Critique of the Behavioral Persuasion in Politics: A Philosophical View." A paper delivered at the 1971 Annual Meeting of the American Political Science Association, Chicago, September 7–11.

_____. "The Place of Valuation in the Theory of Politics: A Phenomenological Critique of Political Behavioralism." *The Journal of Value Inquiry,* forthcoming.

_____. "The Radical Humanization of Politics: Maurice Merleau-Ponty's Philosophy of Politics," *Archiv für Rechts- und Sozialphilosophie,* 53 (1967): 233–56.

KIERKEGAARD, SÖREN. *Concluding Unscientific Postscript.* Translated by DAVID SWENSON and WALTER LOWRIE. Princeton: Princeton University Press, 1941.

_____. *The Present Age.* Translated by ALEXANDER DRU. New York: Harper & Row, 1962.

KNIGHT, EVERETT. *The Objective Society.* New York: George Braziller, 1960.

KOCKELMANS, JOSEPH J. *Phenomenology and Physical Science.* Pittsburgh: Duquesne University Press, 1966.

KOCKELMANS, JOSPEH J., and THEODORE J. KISIEL. *Phenomenology and the Natural Sciences: Essays and Translations.* Evanston: Northwestern University Press, 1970.

KWANT, REMY C. *Phenomenology of Social Existence.* Pittsburgh: Duquesne University Press, 1965.

_____. *Encounter.* Translated by ROBERT C. ADOLFS. Pittsburgh: Duquesne University Press, 1960.

LAING, R. D. *The Divided Self.* New York: Pantheon, 1969.

_____. *Knots.* New York: Pantheon Books, 1970.

_____. *The Politics of Experience.* New York: Pantheon Books, 1967.

_____. *The Politics of the Family and Other Essays.* New York: Pantheon Books, 1971.

_____. *Self and Others.* 2nd rev. ed. New York: Pantheon Books, 1969.

LAING, R. D., and D. G. COOPER. *Reason and Violence.* New York: Random House, 1971.

LAING, R. D.; H. PHILLIPSON; and A. R. LEE. *Interpersonal Perception.* London: Tavistock Publications, 1966.

LANDGREBE, LUDWIG. *Major Problems of Contemporary European Philosophy.* Translated by KURT RINEHART. New York: Frederick Ungar, 1966.

LAWRENCE, NATHANIEL, and DANIEL O'CONNOR, eds. *Readings in Existential Phenomenology.* Englewood Cliffs: Prentice-Hall, 1967.

LEE, EDWARD N., and MAURICE MANDELBAUM, eds. *Phenomenology and Existentialism.* Baltimore: The Johns Hopkins Press, 1967.

LEFORT, CLAUDE. "La Politique et la Pensée de la Politique." A selection from *Lettres Nouvelles.* 11th year, new ser., no. 32, pp. 19–70.

LEVINAS, EMMANUEL. *Totality and Infinity.* Translated by ALPHONSO LINGIS. Pittsburgh: Duquesne University Press, 1969.

LÖWITH, KARL. *From Hegel to Nietzsche: The Revolution in Nineteenth-Century Thought.* Translated by DAVID E. GREEN. New York: Holt, Rinehart & Winston, 1964.

_____. *Nature, History, and Existentialism.* Edited by ARNOLD LEVISON. Evanston: Northwestern University Press, 1966.

LUIJPEN, WILLIAM A. *Existential Phenomenology.* Pittsburgh: Duquesne University Press, 1962.

MCBRIDE, WILLIAM LEON. *Fundamental Change in Law and Society: Hart and Sartre on Revolution.* The Hague: Mouton, 1970.

MACMURRAY, JOHN. *Interpreting the Universe.* London: Faber & Faber, 1936.

438   SELECTED BIBLIOGRAPHY

————. *Persons in Relation.* London: Faber & Faber, 1961.

————. *The Self as Agent.* London: Faber & Faber, 1957.

MANDELBAUM, MAURICE. *The Phenomenology of Moral Experience.* Glencoe: The Free Press, 1955.

MARCEL, GABRIEL. *Being and Having.* Translated by KATHARINE FARRER. Westminster: Dacre Press, 1949.

————. *The Existential Background of Human Dignity.* Cambridge: Harvard University Press, 1963.

————. *Homo Viator.* Translated by EMMA CRAUFURD. New York: Harper & Bros., 1962.

————. *Metaphysical Journal.* Translated by BERNARD WALL.. London: Rockliff, 1952.

————. *The Mystery of Being.* Translated by G. S. FRASER and RENÉ HAGUE. 2 vols. Chicago: Henry Regnery, 1950–51.

————. *Philosophical Fragments 1909–1914.* Notre Dame: The University of Notre Dame Press, 1965.

————. *The Philosophy of Existentialism.* Translated by MANYA HARARI. New York: The Citadel Press, 1961.

————. *Problematic Man.* Translated by BRIAN THOMPSON. New York: Herder & Herder, 1967.

MARX, WERNER. *Heidegger and the Tradition.* Translated by THEODORE KISIEL and MURRAY ,GREENE. Evanston: Northwestern University Press, 1971.

MAY, ROLLO. *Love and Will.* New York: W. W. Norton, 1969.

————. *Psychology and the Human Dilemma.* Princeton: D. Van Nostrand, 1967.

MAY, ROLLO; ERNEST ANGEL; and HENRI P. ELLENBERGER, eds. *Existence.* New York: Basic Books, 1958.

MERLEAU-PONTY, MAURICE. *Les Aventures de la Dialectique.* Paris: Gallimard, 1955.

————. *Humanism and Terror.* Translated by JOHN O'NEILL. Boston: Beacon Press, 1969.

————. *In Praise of Philosophy.* Translated by JOHN WILD and JAMES M. EDIE. Evanston: Northwestern University Press, 1963.

————. *Phenomenology of Perception.* Translated by COLIN SMITH. New York: The Humanities Press, 1962.

————. *The Primacy of Perception and Other Essays.* Edited by JAMES M. EDIE. Evanston: Northwestern University Press, 1964.

————. *La Prose du Monde.* Edited by CLAUDE LEFORT. Paris: Gallimard, 1969.

————. *Sense and Non-Sense.* Translated by HUBERT L. DREYFUS and PATRICIA ALLEN DREYFUS. Evanston: Northwestern University Press, 1964.

————. *Signs.* Translated by RICHARD C. MCCLEARY. Evanston: Northwestern University Press, 1964.

————. *The Structure of Behavior.* Translated by ALDEN L. FISHER. Boston: Beacon Press, 1963.

————. *Themes from the Lectures at the Collège de France 1952–1960.* Translated by JOHN O'NEILL. Evanston: Northwestern University Press, 1970.

————. *The Visible and the Invisible.* Edited by CLAUDE LEFORT and translated by ALPHONSO LINGIS. Evanston: Northwestern University Press, 1968.

MINKOWSKI, EUGÈNE. *Lived Time.* Translated by NANCY METZEL. Evanston: Northwestern University Press, 1970.

NATANSON, MAURICE, ed. *Essays in Phenomenology.* The Hague: Martinus Nijhoff, 1966.

————. *The Journeying Self.* Reading, Mass.: Addison-Wesley Publishing Co., 1970.

————. *Literature, Philosophy and the Social Sciences.* The Hague: Martinus Nijhoff, 1962.

————, ed. *Phenomenology and Social Reality: Essays in Memory of Alfred Schutz.* The Hague: Martinus Nijhoff, 1970.

————, ed. *Philosophy of the Social Sciences: A Reader.* New York: Random House, 1963.

————. *The Social Dynamics of George H. Mead.* Washington: Public Affairs Press, 1956.

NABERT, JEAN. *Elements for an Ethic.* Translated by WILLIAM J. PETREK. Evanston: Northwestern University Press, 1969.

NOVAK, MICHAEL. *The Experience of Nothingness.* New York: Harper & Row, 1970.

OLAFSON, FREDERICK A. *Principles and Persons.* Baltimore: The Johns Hopkins Press, 1967.

ORTEGA Y GASSET, JOSÉ. *Man and People.* Translated by WILLARD R. TRASK. New York: W. W. Norton, 1957.

———. *The Revolt of the Masses.* New York: W. W. Norton, 1932.

PALMER, RICHARD E. *Hermeneutics.* Evanston: Northwestern University Press, 1969.

PATKA, FREDERICK. *Value and Existence.* New York: Philosophical Library, 1964.

PFÄNDER, ALEXANDER. *Phenomenology of Willing and Motivation.* Translated by HERBERT SPIEGELBERG. Evanston: Northwestern University Press, 1967.

La Philosophie Analytique. Cahiers de Royaumont, Philosophie No. 4. Paris: Minuit, 1962.

PLATTEL, MARTIN G. *Social Philosophy.* Pittsburgh: Duquesne University Press, 1965.

PLESSNER, HELMUTH. *Laughing and Crying.* Translated by JAMES S. CHURCHILL and MARJORIE GRENE. Evanston: Northwestern University Press, 1970.

POLIN, RAYMOND. *La Création des Valeurs.* 2nd ed. Paris: Presses Universitaires de France, 1952.

———. *Éthique et Politique.* Paris: Sirey, 1968.

———. "The Sense of the Human." Translated by EDOUARD MOROT-SIR and BARBARA REID. *Philosophy and Phenomenological Research* 29 (June 1969): 536–61.

RICOEUR, PAUL. *Le Conflit des Interprétations: Essais d'Herméneutique.* Paris: Seuil, 1969.

———. *Fallible Man.* Translated by CHARLES A. KELBLEY. Chicago: Henry Regnery, 1965.

———. *Freedom and Nature: The Voluntary and the In-*

voluntary. Translated by ERAZIM V. KOHÁK. Evanston: Northwestern University Press, 1966.

_____. *Freud and Philosophy.* Translated by DENIS SAVAGE. New Haven: Yale University Press, 1970.

_____. *History and Truth.* Translated by CHARLES A. KELBLEY. Evanston: Northwestern University Press, 1965.

_____. *Husserl: An Analysis of His Phenomenology.* Translated by EDWARD G. BALLARD and LESTER E. EMBREE. Evanston: Northwestern University Press, 1967.

_____. *The Symbolism of Evil.* Translated by EMERSON BUCHANAN. New York: Harper & Row, 1967.

SADLER, JR., WILLIAM A. *Existence and Love.* New York: Charles Scribner's Sons, 1969.

SARTRE, JEAN-PAUL. *Anti-Semite and Jew.* Translated by GEORGE J. BECKER. New York: Schocken Books, 1948.

_____. *Being and Nothingness.* Translated by HAZEL E. BARNES. New York: Philosophical Library, 1956.

_____. *The Communists and Peace.* Translated by MARTHA H. FLETCHER. New York: George Braziller, 1968.

_____. *Critique de la Raison Dialectique.* Vol. I. Paris: Gallimard, 1960.

_____. *The Ghost of Stalin.* Translated by MARTHA H. FLETCHER. New York: George Braziller, 1968.

_____. *Literary and Philosophical Essays.* Translated by ANNETTE MICHELSON. London: Rider, 1955.

_____. *Search for a Method.* Translated by HAZEL E. BARNES. New York: Alfred A. Knopf, 1963.

_____. *Situations.* Translated by BENITA EISLER. New York: George Braziller, 1965.

_____. *The Transcendence of the Ego.* Translated by FORREST WILLIAMS and ROBERT KIRKPATRICK. New York: The Noonday Press, 1957.

SCHELER, MAX. *Man's Place in Nature.* Translated by HANS MEYERHOFF. New York: The Noonday Press, 1961.

_____. *The Nature of Sympathy.* Translated by PETER HEATH. New Haven: Yale University Press, 1954.

SCHRADER, GEORGE A., ed. *The Existential Philosophers: Kierkegaard to Merleau-Ponty.* New York: McGraw-Hill, 1967.

SCHRAG, CALVIN O. *Experience and Being.* Evanston: Northwestern University Press, 1969.

_____. "The Structure of Moral Experience: A Phenomenological and Existential Analysis." *Ethics* 73 (July 1963): 255–65.

SCHUTZ, ALFRED. *Collected Papers I: The Problem of Social Reality.* Edited by MAURICE NATANSON. The Hague: Martinus Nijhoff, 1962.

_____. *Collected Papers II: Studies in Social Theory.* Edited by ARVID BRODERSEN. The Hague: Martinus Nijhoff, 1964.

_____. *Collected Papers III: Studies in Phenomenological Philosophy.* Edited by ILSE SCHUTZ. The Hague: Martinus Nijhoff, 1966.

_____. *The Phenomenology of the Social World.* Translated by GEORGE WALSH and FREDERICK LEHNERT. Evanston: Northwestern University Press, 1967.

_____. *Reflections on the Problem of Relevance.* Edited by RICHARD M. ZANER. New Haven: Yale University Press, 1970.

SILBER, JOHN R. "Being and Doing: A Study of Status Responsibility and Voluntary Responsibility." *The University of Chicago Law Review* 35 (Autumn 1967): 47–91.

SPIEGELBERG, HERBERT. "A Defense of Human Equality." *The Philosophical Review* 53 (March 1944): 101–24.

_____. "Equality in Existentialism." In *Equality,* edited by J. ROLAND PENNOCK and JOHN W. CHAPMAN, pp. 193–213. New York: Atherton Press, 1967.

_____. "French Existentialism: Its Social Philosophies." *The Kenyon Review* 16 (Summer 1954): 446–62.

_____. *The Phenomenological Movement.* 2 vols. 2nd ed. The Hague: Martinus Nijhoff, 1965.

STEIN, EDITH. *On the Problem of Empathy.* Translated by WALTRAUT STEIN. The Hague: Martinus Nijhoff, 1964.

STRASSER, STEPHAN. *Das Gemüt.* Utrecht: Spectrum, 1956.

————. *The Idea of Dialogal Phenomenology.* Pittsburgh: Duquesne University Press, 1969.

————. *Phenomenology and the Human Sciences.* Pittsburgh: Duquesne University Press, 1963.

STRAUS, ERWIN W. *Phenomenological Psychology.* New York: Basic Books, 1966.

————, ed. *Phenomenology: Pure and Applied.* Pittsburgh: Duquesne University Press, 1964.

————. *The Primary World of Senses.* Translated by JACOB NEEDLEMAN. Glencoe: The Free Press, 1963.

STRAUS, ERWIN W., and RICHARD M. GRIFFITH, eds. *Phenomenology of Will and Action.* Pittsburgh: Duquesne University Press, 1967.

STRAUS, ERWIN W.; MAURICE NATANSON; and HENRI EY. *Psychiatry and Philosophy.* New York: Springer, 1969.

TAYLOR, CHARLES. "Interpretation and the Sciences of Man." *The Review of Metaphysics* 25 (September 1971): 3–51.

THÉVENAZ, PIERRE. *La Condition de la Raison Philosophique.* Neuchatel: Baconnière, 1960.

————. *L'Homme et sa Raison.* 2 vols. Neuchatel: Baconnière, 1956.

————. *What Is Phenomenology? And Other Essays.* Edited by JAMES M. EDIE and translated by JAMES M. EDIE, CHARLES COURTNEY, and PAUL BROCKELMAN. Chicago: Quadrangle Books, 1962.

TILLICH, PAUL. *The Courage to Be.* New Haven: Yale University Press, 1952.

————. *Love, Power, and Justice.* New York: Oxford University Press, 1954.

————. *Theology of Culture.* Edited by ROBERT C. KIMBALL. New York: Oxford University Press, 1959.

TIRYAKIAN, EDWARD. "Existential Phenomenology and the

Sociological Tradition." *American Sociological Review* 30 (October 1965): 674–88.

———. *Sociologism and Existentialism*. Englewood Cliffs: Prentice-Hall, 1962.

TOULEMONT, RENÉ. *L'Essence de la Société selon Husserl*. Paris: Presses Universitaires de France, 1962.

TRAN-DUC-THAO. *Phénoménologie et Matérialisme Dialectique*. Paris: Minh-Tan, 1951.

TYMIENIECKA, ANNA-TERESA, ed. *For Roman Ingarden: Nine Essays in Phenomenology*. The Hague: Martinus Nijhoff, 1959.

VAN BREDA, H. L., and J. TAMINIAUX, eds. *Edmund Husserl 1859–1959*. The Hague: Martinus Nijhoff, 1959.

WAELHENS, ALPHONSE DE. *Existence et Signification*. Louväin: Nauwelaerts, 1958.

———. *La Philosophie et les Experiénces Naturelles*. The Hague: Martinus Nijhoff, 1961.

WEIZSÄCKER, C. F. von. *The History of Nature*. Translated by FRED D. WIECK. Chicago: The University of Chicago Press, 1949.

WILD, JOHN. *The Challenge of Existentialism*. Bloomington: Indiana University Press, 1959.

———. *Existence and the World of Freedom*. Englewood Cliffs: Prentice-Hall, 1963.

———. *Human Freedom and Social Order*. Durham: Duke University Press, 1959.

———. *The Radical Empiricism of William James*. New York: Doubleday, 1969.

WINTER, GIBSON. *Elements for a Social Ethic*. New York: Macmillian, 1966.